Privacy in Colonial New England

Privacy in
Colonial New England

David H. Flaherty

University Press of Virginia

Charlottesville

For Kathy

Preface

THE protection of personal privacy is a major concern of modern America. Technological advances in the making of surveillance devices have threatened privacy in many ways. It is now almost impossible for an individual to protect his personal privacy against a determined intruder. In the early 1960's the Association of the Bar of New York City undertook an examination of the impact of technology on privacy through its Special Committee on Science and Law. As this study began, two questions kept recurring. Did privacy have any meaning for past ages? Or was concern for privacy a product of the unique needs of twentieth-century industrialized society? It became apparent that anyone grappling with the problems surrounding the preservation of privacy today would have to cast a backward glance. If the concept of personal privacy had a past, then the historical perspective, the logic of experience, could be brought to bear on discussions of modern problems.

Professor Alan F. Westin, a political scientist at Columbia University and the director of research for the Special Committee on Science and Law, initiated a series of case studies of privacy in early Greece and Rome, in medieval Europe, and in early Stuart England. In September 1964, while I was a doctoral candidate in history at Columbia University, Professor Westin asked me to assist in the early Stuart case study. I soon discovered that the available secondary literature and primary sources were not adequate for the requisite kinds of inquiries. I then decided to undertake an intensive examination of personal privacy in the American colonies in a fashion that would permit me to pursue whatever resources seemed valuable.

This study is thus an investigation of personal privacy in colonial New England. Was there such a concept? What did it mean? In what ways and for what purposes did individuals want privacy? Did attitudes toward privacy or general conditions affecting its availability change in the colonial era? What kind of balance was struck among such competing interests as privacy, the need for society, the physical conditions of daily life, and the practice of surveillance? On the surface the Puritans, who were the driving force behind the establishment of the New England colonies, seem to have held values antithetic to concern for personal privacy. If indeed the Puritans did not care about privacy, it would be desirable to examine this phenomenon.

The apparently ambivalent attitude of the early Puritans toward privacy make them ideal subjects for examination. The time period involved was the crucial early modern period when so many of our contemporary values were taking shape. The American attitude to privacy emerged from a background of English traditions, and the Puritans were among the first to begin the adaptation of English values to the New World. Finally, New England in the colonial period left enough records of its society to make feasible a careful study of privacy and conditions for its enjoyment.

Focusing on the subject of privacy makes it possible to penetrate the surface manifestations of the Puritan movement in America in order to acquire greater comprehension of its actual impact on everyday life. This study seeks to avoid explanations that cast all Puritans into a single mold. It also refrains from interpreting colonial New England totally in terms of Puritanism, the ideology of the Puritan movement, by indicating the major areas of everyday life where its influence was either transient or nonexistent. The existence of privacy in colonial society had as much to do with the ecology of New England as with Puritanism. Yet this effort to avoid a monolithic interpretation of either Puritanism or the Puritan movement does not ignore the importance of their religious, political, and social impact.

A more expansive aspect of this study is the light it sheds on the social history of individualism in New England society of the seventeenth and eighteenth centuries. The emergence of individualism in the early modern world is often treated in an ethereal manner; the breakdown of the medieval life style associated with gregariousness and communal existence is commonly asserted rather than analyzed. Puritanism was a transitional force linking the medieval and modern eras. Despite its documented concern with watchfulness, Puritanism as a religious ideology put a premium on introspection. In this sense developments in colonial society did not destroy Puritan attitudes toward privacy but simply nurtured the triumph of one side of that attitude, introspection, and the decline of the other side, watching your fellow. Since concern for privacy is so patently a manifestation of individualistic impulses, the focus on privacy fortuitously permits the emergence of individualism to be perceived in a direct manner.

Personal privacy is examined in terms of articulated and inarticulated attitudes, of problems surrounding its preservation, and of the ways in which concern for it functioned in early New England life. The need for privacy was rarely a crucial issue in colonial society, not because privacy was unimportant, but because its availability was so often taken for granted. This study of privacy concentrates at first on the typical individual in his home, family, and local community and then on the individual's general relationship with the major public institutions of society, the church, the government, the law enforcement apparatus, and the courts. Such an analytical and topical approach is necessary, since privacy is a complex value. Conditions for its enjoyment were not static, although there were some fairly stable aspects. In most of the areas under consideration, however, changes were so gradual that only a unified treatment makes it possible to convey a satisfactory impression of the kinds of changes that were occurring. As the argument of the book builds upon itself with recurring reference to certain kinds of questions or problems relating to privacy, the intricate interrelationship of stability and change in the spirit of the times and the conditions of existence serves as a continuing theme.

All dates before 1752 in this volume are given in Old Style, except that the new year is begun on January 1 rather than March 25, to correspond to modern usage.

I am particularly grateful for the financial support of the Special Committee on Science and Law of the Association of the Bar of New York City. The Canada Council and Columbia University supported my doctoral research with fellowships. The Princeton University Research Fund provided typing funds. The University of Virginia Research Committee furnished a subsidy for publication.

The Essex Institute and the Massachusetts Historical Society kindly granted me permission to quote from manuscripts in their collections. Professor Richard B. Morris allowed me to quote from a letter in the Jay Papers at Columbia University. The illustration that appears in the text is reprinted with the permission of the Society for the Preservation of New England Antiquities.

The nature of this topic has made me heavily dependent upon others for critical direction and guidance. As cosponsors of the original dissertation, Richard B. Morris and Alan F. Westin of Columbia University contributed significantly to its shaping. At an early stage of writing Gary B. Nash and Lawrence Stone provided me with critiques of several chapters. The following persons kindly read a chapter for me in a field wherein they were especially competent: Norman F. Cantor, Abbott L. Cummings, John Demos, Leonard W. Levy, Donald G. Mathews, and Edmund S. Morgan. W. W. Abbot, Wesley F. Craven, Joseph F. Kett, John W. Shy, and Gerard B. Warden furnished me with penetrating critiques of the entire manuscript. The generous assistance of these individuals should not be construed as their approval of the methods and conclusions of this work. My indebtedness to my wife is acknowledged on the dedication page.

Charlottesville, Virginia
June 1971

Contents

Tables

Figure

Privacy in Colonial New England

Introduction

IN BOTH the past and present American experience, concern for
personal privacy has meant the desire of individuals to choose
freely under what circumstances, and to what extent, they would
expose themselves, their attitudes, and their behavior to others. This
simple definition has a close relationship to the concept of aloneness;
personal privacy is instinctively defined as wanting to be let alone.
The two jurists, Samuel D. Warren and Louis D. Brandeis, who in
1890 first broadly articulated the legal right of privacy posited "the
right to be let alone" at the core of their explication.[1] Yet neither a
focus on aloneness nor a formal definition provides the analytical
categories necessary for a study of privacy in personal lives.

Privacy actually embodies several different states of psychological
and physical relationship between an individual and the persons
around him, which can be categorized as solitude, intimacy, anonymity, and reserve.[2] These four states can be envisioned as varying
facets of the privacy that individuals experience in their daily lives.
They provide a format by which personal privacy can be examined
in any society past and present, even though the desire for privacy
may fluctuate and the conditions for enjoying it may change.

Solitude, which corresponds to aloneness, is the pristine state of
privacy, in which a person consciously withdraws from others in a
manner that is easily recognizable. An individual may value solitude
at specific times and for various reasons. According to the Puritan
minister Cotton Mather, "a Godly man will sometimes Retire, that he
may carry on the Exercises of Godliness." In 1761 some poetry on the
virtues of solitude by the early seventeenth-century divine John
Donne impressed the young John Adams. He considered the lines "a
very proper Prayer for me to make when I'm in Boston. Solitude is a
Personage, in a clean, wholesome Dress, the Nurse and Nourisher of
Sense."[3] Solitude was readily available in colonial America, whether

---

[1] "The Right of Privacy," *Harvard Law Review*, IV (1890), 191–220.

[2] See Alan F. Westin, *Privacy and Freedom* (New York, 1967), pp. 31–32.

[3] Mather, *The Religion of the Closet* (Boston, 1705; 2d ed., Boston, 1706),
p. 6; *Diary and Autobiography of John Adams*, ed. L. H. Butterfield (Cambridge,
Mass., 1961), I, 221.

for recreational or for religious purposes, although a person might sometimes have to leave his home to find it. In fact the expansive New World often allowed too much solitude. To avoid the resulting loneliness, individuals had to seek a more satisfactory balance of their needs for withdrawal and society.

Yet privacy cannot simply be treated in terms of solitude, since humans spend their lives in recurring contact with others. A person seeks a different level of privacy within his family or in his friendships than in his relations with outsiders. The special intimacy that exists among family or friends protects the privacy of an individual as a member of a special unit. Mutual understandings, long friendships, and kinship are normally as protective and restorative for the individual as solitude. Within the intimate circle of their family and chosen friends the colonists fulfilled their desires for society and gregariousness, while alleviating any loneliness that solitude had induced. They recognized the home as a shelter for the family and friends from the outside world.

Individuals not only value periodic withdrawal into conditions of solitude or intimacy; they also desire protection in a more public setting from continuous recognition and physical surveillance. In modern America anonymity often provides this state of privacy in the public sphere, except in the case of well-known figures. Such nonrecognition engenders some relaxation and freedom from the rigors of role playing and conformity with the behavioral demands of society. The strong desire for anonymity is an aspect of privacy that only modern industrial societies have generally emphasized. Conditions of life within the colonial community made anonymity not only harder to find but less relevant than it is today. The population in the early years was still so small that no person could escape the physical surveillance of others without special efforts. Except in the larger towns, the colonists lived in a society where the community members knew a great deal about their fellow men. Whole neighborhoods shared a special intimacy developed over long years of continuing exposure to one another. In its role as almost an extended family, a colonial village or neighborhood sheltered the privacy of its inhabitants from the intrusions of neighboring towns or the rest of the community rather than of one another. Only the rapid expansion of population in the eighteenth century introduced an urban environment wherein anonymity became readily available.

On the other hand, even when residing in a small community or relaxing in his home, an individual still demands control over what he communicates to others. He expects his privacy to be shielded by a sense of reserve founded upon the willing discretion of his close associates. On a reciprocal basis persons agree to certain limitations upon the extent of their intimacy and enter into a tacit contract to respect each other's privacy. The colonists were only too well aware of individuals who breached this barrier of reserve with inquisitive and embarrassing questions. A Bostonian who traveled to Newbury in the 1760's had the relationship between intimacy, anonymity, and reserve clearly brought home to him. "This Journey of mine led me to think and hitch upon a Rule of Conduct in our Concerns with Mankind, with whom we are *unacquainted*, which I believe will stand us in stead almost universally, and this is never to communicate and open ourselves, first, nor indeed hastily, to Strangers with whom we are not like to have any intimacy, and yet shall have time enough with them to discover we are not Mutes."[4] The degree of the colonists' acceptance of a sense of reserve is difficult to analyze. Yet those aspects of the New England Yankee character that are still recognizable today, especially the traits of restraint and impassiveness, surely had some roots in colonial life.

The Value of Privacy

Psychologists and sociologists, popularizers and scholars, and personal experience have made twentieth-century American society aware of the essential contributions of privacy to the human psyche. Alan F. Westin, the author of *Privacy and Freedom*, concluded that privacy satisfies four main needs blending together in the make-up of individual life: personal autonomy, emotional release, self-evaluation, and limited and protected communication.[5] Glimpses of similar needs underlying the desire for privacy can be seen in colonial New England.

The contribution of privacy to personal autonomy involves the protection of the inner core self, the ultimate resource of the individual. A person seeks protection from the manipulation and dominance of others in defense of his uniqueness and dignity as a person. The autonomy of the self depends upon the maintenance of wells of reserve. Under normal conditions the ultimate sanctuary of the personality is never breached. The last resource of the individual is that

[4] "Philander," Newbury, to "Philocles," Boston (probably Joseph Lee writing to his wife), Dec. 27, 1762, Lee Family Papers, box 1, folder 1661–1753, Massachusetts Historical Society.

[5] See Westin, *Privacy and Freedom*, pp. 32–39, for a fuller explication.

no one can force him to bare his personality and expose his naked self to the shame of total understanding.

Personal privacy also contributes to the individual need for emotional release. Westin has been especially perceptive about the need for relief from the constraints of playing social roles. This "may come in solitude; in the intimacy of family, peers, or woman-to-woman and man-to-man relaxation; in the anonymity of park or street; or in a state of reserve while in a group."[6] Privacy insures protection from surveillance for minor deviations from the stated norms of a society, a function which was particularly significant in colonial New England. It is normally sought for the carrying out of bodily and sexual functions or for recuperation from anxiety, loss, and sorrow before the individual again takes up the burdens of daily life. In similar fashion it provides a change of pace from emotional stimulation. Writing in 1759 John Adams specifically recognized this contribution of privacy: "I must converse and deal with Mankind, and move and stir from one scene of Action and Debate and Business, and Pleasure, and Conversation, to another and grow weary of all before I shall feel the strong Desire of retiring to contemplation on Men and Business and Pleasure and Books. After hard Labour at Husbandry, Reading and Reflection in Retirement will be a Relief and a high refined Pleasure."[7]

A third function of privacy, the provision of a period of self-evaluation, appealed particularly to the Puritans, who emphasized the need of it for personal assessment, reflection on experiences and events, and the pursuit of religious perfection. The recognition of its functional importance by the generality of colonial New Englanders will be illustrated many times in subsequent chapters. To quote again from the sensitive and articulate John Adams: "After attending a Town Meeting . . . a Retreat to reflect, compare, distinguish will be highly delightful. So after a Training Day . . . I shall be pleased with my solitude."[8]

A sense of privacy provides an opportunity for limited and protected communication among individuals. A person can exchange confidences with wife, family, friends, or even strangers, in the secure knowledge that his intimacies are safe from public exposure. He knows his friends and associates will not ask him about many personal matters, and he recognizes no obligation to answer in any event. In the same fashion privacy serves to maintain social distance

[6] *Ibid.*, p. 35.
[7] *Diary*, I, 96.
[8] *Ibid.*

in interpersonal relationships. Even in marriages or work situations a definite reserve is maintained. John Adams tackled this issue directly when he weighed the acceptability of limiting communications:

The first Maxim of worldly Wisdom, constant Dissimulation, may be good or evil as it is interpreted. If it means only a constant Concealment from others of such of our Sentiments, Actions, Desires, and Resolutions, as others have not a Right to know, it is not only lawful but commendable—because when these are once divulged, our Enemies may avail themselves of the Knowledge of them, to our Damage, Danger and Confusion. So that some Things which ought to be communicated to some of our Friends, that they may improve them to our Profit or Honour or Pleasure, should be concealed from our Enemies, and from indiscreet friends, least they should be turned to our Loss, Disgrace or Mortification. I am under no moral or other Obligation to publish to the World, how much my Expences or my Incomes amount to yearly. There are Times when and Persons to whom, I am not obliged to tell what are my Principles and Opinions in Politicks or Religion.

This Kind of Dissimulation, which is no more than Concealment, Secrecy, and Reserve, or in other Words, Prudence and Discretion, is a necessary Branch of Wisdom, and so far from being immoral and unlawfull, . . . [it] is a Duty and a Virtue.[9]

A discussion of the functions of privacy arouses a sympathetic response in the modern American. Yet there is some question whether colonial Americans would have understood what we are talking about, even if an articulate gentleman like John Adams recognizably echoed our sentiments. Even among the many cultures flourishing today, there are marked differences concerning the valuation put on personal privacy. It is difficult to examine past ages with the tools and concepts developed in the modern era to further self-understanding and self-analysis. We must be conscious of the danger of applying our own values to these early Americans. Did the colonists really care about or want personal privacy? Or did their perceptions of such matters as the need for life space or anonymity differ markedly from our own? Such queries deserve initial consideration at this point, since there are a variety of general reasons for asserting that early Americans valued personal privacy.

The beginnings of the human valuation of privacy are as shrouded in obscurity as those of such allied conceptions as liberty, private property, and democracy. Indeed the idea may never have been

---

[9] *Ibid.*, I, 363. "Simulation is a Pretence of what is not, and Dissimulation a Concealment of what is," said Richard Steele in *The Tatler* (1710), quoted in the *Oxford English Dictionary*, s.v. "Dissimulation."

formally introduced into the Western cultural tradition. Historical studies suggest that privacy should be viewed as a characteristic concern of human nature from time immemorial. There is substantial support in research studies for the view that man's initial need for privacy is rooted in his animal origins.[10] Privacy is not only a value but a law of ecology and biology pertaining to the proper spacing of the members of a species. Such findings do provide some explanation for the persistent presence of a concern for privacy in human societies. Westin has concluded on the basis of anthropological studies of primitive peoples that there are some needs for privacy and resulting social norms to protect it in virtually all societies.[11] This is particularly noticeable in such areas as the household, interpersonal relations, physical and sexual etiquette, and significant rituals and ceremonies. Since most societies have indicated an awareness of the value of privacy in certain circumstances, the existence of such an attitude in colonial America should not be surprising.

Although there is considerable validity in the view that man as an animal regularly needs some privacy, Western man prefers to speak of his actions in terms of civilized values. This preference for values over arguments based on biological necessity requires that concern for privacy be posited within the essential framework formed by Western traditions. Without attempting to trace this back to the Greeks and Romans, there are grounds for arguing that Western civilization has indeed always incorporated personal privacy into its system of values.[12] Privacy's emergence as a desired goal in association with biological necessity helped make it an ongoing value in Western culture. Many of the values that Americans cherish began to rise to notable historical consciousness between the fourteenth and sixteenth centuries at the so-called dawn of Western humanism. Privacy can surely be identified in a general sense as one of the cultural goals of sixteenth- and seventeenth-century English society. The

[10] See Westin, *Privacy and Freedom*, pp. 8–22; and Edward T. Hall, *The Hidden Dimension* (Garden City, N.Y., 1966), *passim*. A comment by Ruth Benedict is pertinent: "To point out . . . that the biological bases of cultural behavior in mankind are for the most part irrelevant is not to deny that they are present" (*Patterns of Culture* [Boston, 1934], p. 236).

[11] *Privacy and Freedom*, pp. 12–13.

[12] See the following reports prepared for the Special Committee on Science and Law of the Association of the Bar of New York City: Norman F. Cantor, "Privacy in Western Civilization" (1963); Marvin E. Gettleman, "Privacy in the Perspective of United States History" (1964); Alan F. Westin, "Privacy in Western History: From the Age of Pericles to the American Republic" (1965).

men and women who settled America in the seventeenth century were the heirs of the Western cultural tradition as it had particularly manifested itself in England.

The movement of settlers into a New World created conditions favorable to cultural change, but a wise reflection attributed to Horace is pertinent here: "They change their skies but not their minds who sail across the sea." Values such as privacy constitute an essential core of a culture and are usually traditional in the sense of being historically derived and selected. Seymour Lipset has noted that "the value system is perhaps the most enduring part of what we think of as society, or a social system."[13] As a traditional custom the desire for privacy became a shaper of patterns and standards in the colonial community. Despite our limited knowledge of the extent of the valuation placed on privacy in England prior to the settlement of America, there are valid grounds for asserting that the New England colonists as creatures of their culture valued being alone, or being with their family in an intimate setting, or protecting the intimacy of the family from the outside world. Given a more open society and less rigid class distinctions in colonial New England, it is also likely that concern for privacy was more broadly diffused in colonial America than in the mother country.

However ill-understood the motives for such a concern were at the time, colonial Americans were carrying on the traditional attitude to privacy that they had brought from the mother country. They wanted privacy because they valued it, not simply because they needed it. With respect to this and other values, Americans are carrying on similar traditions today. Lipset has argued persuasively that "there is more continuity than change with respect to the main elements in the national value system."[14] It would otherwise be difficult to explain the concern for privacy in modern American society, since there has been no particular moment of decision in the country's history when the populace suddenly declared *de novo* that privacy was a good thing. Such similar values in the national pantheon as success, work, individualism, and freedom have certainly been with us since the foundings.[15] These values normally become operative

---

[13] *The First New Nation: The United States in Historical and Comparative Perspective* (New York, 1963), p. 123. Also see *International Encyclopedia of the Social Sciences,* ed. David L. Sills (New York, 1968), s.v. "Culture."

[14] *First New Nation,* p. 103.

[15] See Robin M. Williams, Jr., *American Society* (2d ed. rev., New York, 1960), chap. 11.

only in concrete situations and are difficult to isolate in philosophical terms. The value placed on privacy by the colonists will be frequently and specifically illustrated in the body of this work.

The difficulties of avoiding the imposition of present-day values on the past raise the issue of the concepts of space and social distance that the colonists held. We are much aware of the need for individual life space in the modern world. We build space around ourselves in our homes and offices and maintain certain distance zones, be they intimate, personal, social, or public, in our relationships with other persons.[16] In our associations with intimate friends, casual acquaintances, and authorities we develop avoidance rules, interaction norms, and means of psychological isolation, such as dreams and reveries. How did the colonists in their general culture and individual lives make use of space? Under what conditions did they feel crowded? Did they use psychological means to withdraw into themselves under such circumstances? The major problem in establishing the existence of such concerns in colonial America is to leave behind some of our modern associations with privacy. It is far too simple, for example, automatically to associate crowding within a home with lack of privacy and to conclude as John Demos has done that "sustained privacy is hard to imagine, in *any* part of the Old Colony setting."[17] In the search for privacy an individual can often circumvent such problems as crowding through the use of either physical or psychological mechanisms. Twentieth-century Americans who want to be alone may enter a room and shut the door, while the English, who rarely have had the luxury of a room to themselves, "never developed the practice of using space as a refuge from others. They have in effect internalized a set of barriers."[18] In modern Arabic society, where there is no word for privacy and no physical privacy in the family, an Arab simply stops talking for a period of time when he wants to be alone. For another situation in which privacy is attained despite the restricted availability of space, consider how residents of France sometimes make use of the outdoors. A crowded French home serves simply as a refuge for the family from outsiders, while space outside the home is for recreation and for socializing.[19]

[16] Hall, *Hidden Dimension,* chap. 10.

[17] *A Little Commonwealth: Family Life in Plymouth Colony* (New York, 1970), p. 152. Michael Zuckerman has similarly commented: "In the little towns of Massachusetts, then, there was no place of privacy, no time of a man's life when he could rest secure from scrutiny" (*Peaceable Kingdoms: New England Towns in the Eighteenth Century* [New York, 1970], p. 116).

[18] Hall, *Hidden Dimension,* p. 131; Westin, *Privacy and Freedom,* p. 12.

[19] Hall, *Hidden Dimension,* pp. 135, 148.

This is the kind of solution that the colonists had recourse to in their utilization of meeting houses, taverns, and open spaces. The colonists shared the traditional views of the value of life space embodied in Western culture but often simply had to find alternative ways of implementing their desires for privacy.

There is also some virtue in entering a somewhat speculative realm in an attempt to discover why the colonists valued privacy. Cultural anthropologists on occasion discuss cultures in terms of a dominating idea or character that permeates it. Colonial New England seems to have demonstrated traits of both a shame culture and a guilt culture; it does not seem relevant for our purposes to emphasize the importance of one over the other.[20] Ruth Benedict has described this society as a guilt culture in the sense that the Puritan inhabitants inculcated absolute standards of morality and relied on man's developing a conscience to maintain conformity.[21] Some criminal offenders in seventeenth-century New England, as well as full church members who erred, had not permitted internalized guilt feelings to prevent their illicit acts. They were then punished or threatened with loss of privacy to encourage remorse. Full church members who did not repent had to make a public confession before their peers, while criminals were sometimes exposed to public ridicule in the stocks. The threat of the loss of privacy served as an additional means of social control over religiously inclined New Englanders.

Shame cultures on the other hand rely primarily on external sanctions for good behavior rather than internal mechanisms. Shame results from a loss of honor and self-respect because of the disapproval by other persons of a particular act. Demos has drawn an interesting connection between infant experience and Puritan character structure to argue that considerations of shame and face-saving loom large in a number of areas of New England culture. The indulgence of the first year of life, followed by a strict discipline in the second year and thereafter, crushed the child's assertive and aggressive drives.[22] The avoidance of shame situations, "that sense of having exposed oneself prematurely and foolishly," thus became a major

---

[20] On shame and guilt cultures, see Ruth Benedict, *The Chrysanthemum and the Sword: Patterns of Japanese Culture* (Boston, 1946), esp. pp. 222–27; Erik H. Erikson, *Identity and the Life Cycle* (New York, 1959), pp. 65–74; Helen M. Lynd, *On Shame and the Search for Identity* (New York, 1958), chaps. 1 and 2.

[21] *Chrysanthemum and the Sword*, pp. 222–23.

[22] *A Little Commonwealth*, p. 138.

preoccupation in later life. The colonists were extremely concerned with how they appeared to one another. The use of shame may have been more characteristic of non-Puritans and then become more important to the whole society as the impact of Puritanism and the Puritan movement on its adherents weakened. Privacy prevented the loss of honor and self-respect. It shielded the individual from shame situations, particularly involving intimate matters. Many of the provisions for the protection of privacy gradually introduced in the admissions and disciplinary procedures of the Congregational churches made possible the avoidance of shame and enabled persons to save face.[23] In the final analysis privacy provided supportive help and escape from both guilt and shame situations for the individual colonist.

Additional evidence of the value placed on privacy by the colonists emerges from an examination of the use of the concept in their vocabularies. From at least the fifteenth century the term *privacy* has been used in the English language to mean "the state or condition of being withdrawn from the society of others, or from public interest."[24] This usage has approximated the meaning of privacy as a concept. Its utilization in this sense is evident in a letter written by the Reverend John Davenport, Sr., later one of the founders of Connecticut: "It hath bene the will of God (against my naturall desire of privacy, and retiredness) to make my ministry, for the space of this six yeares, in London, publick, and eminent."[25] Many additional illustrations of the use of the word as a concept appear in this study. The term was also used in a variety of related ways, usually to indicate a state of withdrawal from the public sphere. John Winthrop, Jr., son of the first governor of Massachusetts, was warned to "keepe sufficient privacy" to avoid interference from the authorities. The Watertown church ordained a minister "in their privacy." Pious women met "with all possible Privacy and Modesty" to carry on devotions.[26] This imposition of privacy as a requirement was often

[23] See *infra*, chap. 5.

[24] *O.E.D.*, s.v. "Privacy."

[25] Isabel M. Calder, ed., *Letters of John Davenport* (New Haven, 1937), p. 13. In Rhode Island in 1699 an argument took place among some leading citizens over a specific issue of privacy involving persons qualified to participate in a meeting (see *Records of the Colony of Rhode Island and Providence Plantations in New England,* ed. John R. Bartlett [Providence, 1856–65], III, 389 [hereafter cited as *R.I. Rec.*]).

[26] Joshua Hoyle to John Winthrop, Jr., Dec. 1634, *Winthrop Papers,* ed. Allyn B. Forbes, *et al.* (Boston, 1929–), III, 180; John Winthrop, *Winthrop's Journal:*

associated with an obligation to preserve secrecy. The various General Courts, for example, insisted that their proceedings be kept private,[27] while grand juries similarly sought to protect their privacy.[28]

The colonists associated privacy with a strong sense of what was or should be private rather than public. Access into the private sphere could be denied or the privilege of admission accorded only by a specific invitation. William Burkitt, a late seventeenth-century English divine, characterized daily prayer as "publick in the Congregation," "private in the Family," or "secret in the Closet." The equation of private and family was important. Burkitt further advised: "Be sure that thou art private in thy private Duties, let it be true

---

"*History of New England,*" *1630–1649,* ed. James K. Hosmer (New York, 1908), II, 17; Cotton Mather, *Ratio Disciplinae Fratrum Nov-Anglorum* (Boston, 1726), p. 193.

27 Winthrop, *Journal,* I, 171–72; *Records of the Governor and Company of the Massachusetts Bay in New England,* ed. Nathaniel B. Shurtleff (Boston, 1853–54), I, 189, 350–51, III, 7, IV, pt. 1, p. 16, pt. 2, p. 4 (hereafter cited as *Mass. Rec.*); *R.I. Rec.,* I, 420; *The Public Records of the Colony of Connecticut,* ed. J. Hammond Trumbull and Charles J. Hoadly (Hartford, 1850–90), I, 39, 520, IV, 428 (hereafter cited as *Conn. Rec.*); *The Book of the General Laws for the People within the Jurisdiction of Connecticut* (Cambridge, Mass., 1673; rpt. Hartford, 1865), p. 18 (hereafter cited as *Laws Conn., 1673*); *Acts and Laws of His Majesties Colony of Connecticut in New-England* (Boston, 1702; rpt. Hartford, 1901), p. 23 (hereafter cited as *Laws Conn., 1702*); *Acts and Laws of His Majesty's English Colony of Connecticut in New England* (New London, 1750), p. 29 (hereafter cited as *Laws Conn., 1750*); *Acts and Laws of the State of Connecticut* (New London, 1784), p. 28 (hereafter cited as *Laws Conn., 1784*); *Records of the Colony of New Plymouth in New England,* ed. Nathaniel B. Shurtleff and David Pulsifer (Boston, 1855–61), III, 16–17, XI, 159 (hereafter cited as *Plymouth Col. Rec.*).

28 See, for example, the oaths of grand jurors in *Conn. Rec.,* I, 57; *Laws Conn., 1673,* pp. 54–55; *ibid., 1702,* p. 88; *ibid., 1750,* p. 178; *ibid., 1784,* p. 184; *The Charter and the Acts and Laws of His Majesties Colony of Rhode-Island and Providence Plantations in America, 1719* (Providence, 1719), ed. Sidney S. Rider (Providence, 1895), p. 16 (hereafter cited as *Laws R.I., 1719*); *Acts and Laws of His Majesty's Colony of Rhode Island, and Providence Plantations in America* (Newport, 1730), p. 196 (hereafter cited as *Laws R.I., 1730*); *Acts and Laws of the English Colony of Rhode Island* (Newport, 1767), p. 58 (hereafter cited as *Laws R.I., 1767*); *Acts and Laws, Passed by the General Court or Assembly of His Majesties Province of New-Hampshire in New England* (Boston, 1726), p. 80 (hereafter cited as *Laws N.H., 1726*); *Acts and Laws . . . of New Hampshire* (Portsmouth, 1771), p. 81 (hereafter cited as *Laws N.H., 1771*); also prosecutions for breaches of this oath in *Plymouth Col. Rec.,* II, 96, IV, 101; *Province and Court Records of Maine,* ed. Charles T. Libby, Robert E. Moody, and Neal W. Allen, Jr. (Portland, 1928–), I, 51 (hereafter cited as *Maine Ct. Rec.*).

Secret Prayer. . . . Enter into thy Closet when thou prayest, and shut
thy Door."[29] To be in secret or private was to enjoy privacy. During
the examination of Anne Hutchinson for heresy in 1637, William
Coddington, one of her supporters, objected because the only incriminating evidence had originally been spoken by her in private
to the elders: "I do not know what rule they had to make the thing
publick, secret things ought to be spoken in secret and publick things
in publick." Governor Winthrop responded that "what was spoken
in the presence of many is not to be made secret." To which Coddington replied: "But that was spoken but to a few and in private."[30]
Many recorded references to "private" conversations, especially in
courtroom testimony, and often by illiterate persons, illustrated this
well-established distinction between public and private.[31] The continued emphasis in the writings of Puritan ministers on the common
need for withdrawal and retirement signified a profound awareness
of the desirability of being in private.

The valuation of personal privacy can readily be illustrated in many
instances when the specific term *privacy* was not employed. In 1637,
for example, an English lord arrived in Boston as a tourist and took
up lodgings at "the common inn." When Governor Winthrop returned from a trip, he offered the young aristocrat lodging, "but he
refused, saying, that he came not to be troublesome to any, and the
house where he was, was so well governed, that he could be as private
there as elsewhere." The Reverend Ebenezer Parkman's narrative of
his experiences at a local church council in 1744 included a definition
of privacy which almost precisely anticipated that of Warren and
Brandeis in 1890. The local church members came in ahead of time
to hear the committee's report. "Upon my mentioning it to the Mod-
erator how unfit [this was] till we had Scann'd and finish'd the Preparation of it–we had the privilege to be alone." A generation later
John Adams replied to a girl's query about his reactions should his

[29] *The Poor Man's Help, and Young Man's Guide* (Boston, 1731; rpt. from the
8th English ed. of 1693), title page and p. 78.

[30] "The Examination of Mrs. Ann Hutchinson at the Court at Newton," Nov.
1637, Charles Francis Adams, ed., *Antinomianism in the Colony of Massachusetts Bay, 1636–1638* (Boston, 1894), p. 281.

[31] See, for example, *Records and Files of the Quarterly Courts of Essex County,
Massachusetts, 1638–1683*, ed. George F. Dow (Salem, 1911–21), III, 439
(1667) (hereafter cited as *Essex Rec.*); Massachusetts Archives, IX "Domestic
Relations, 1643–1774", 403–13 (1757), Mass. State Archives, Boston; divorce
case, Early Files in the Office of the Clerk of the Supreme Judicial Court, no.
129735, p. 43, Suffolk County Court House, Boston (hereafter cited as Court
Files Suffolk).

wife disturb him while he was studying law: "No man, but a crooked Richard, would blame his Wife, for such an accidental Interruption. And No Woman, but a Xantippe, would insist upon her Husbands Company, after he had given her his Reasons for desiring to be alone."[32]

Although the recognition of privacy as a customary right can be observed less in colonial rhetoric than in customs and practices, some colonial writers did specifically acknowledge the value of privacy. William Penn wrote a small essay in the 1690's called *Some Fruits of Solitude*, which went through almost a dozen English and American editions by 1800, including a New England printing at Newport in 1749. He embraced as one of the fruits of solitude:

"Privacy"

325. Remember the Proverb, Bene qui latuit, bene vixit, They are happy that live Retiredly.

326. If this be true, Princes and their Grandees, of all Men, are the Unhappiest: For they live least *alone*: And they that must be enjoy'd by every Body, can never enjoy themselves as they should.

327. It is the *Advantage* little Men have upon them; they can be *private*, and have *leisure* for Family Comforts, which are the greatest Worldly Contents Men can enjoy.

328. But they that place Pleasure in Greatness, seek it there: And we see Rule is as much the Ambition of some Natures, as Privacy is the choice of others.[33]

Penn's emphasis on aloneness and retirement from the world for the enjoyment of private comforts, especially within the family, was similar to twentieth-century notions. When the colonists verbalized their attitudes on the subject, they adhered to such a conception of privacy. Even when the value of privacy within the family was only tacitly acknowledged, this was the meaning attached.

THE HISTORICAL SETTING

The historical setting of an era can significantly affect attitudes toward personal privacy and conditions for its enjoyment. The in-

[32] Winthrop, *Journal*, I, 223–24; "The Diary of Ebenezer Parkman," ed. Francis G. Walett, American Antiquarian Society, *Proceedings*, LXXII (1962), 191; Adams, *Diary*, I, 67.
[33] 8th ed., Newport, 1749, pp. 96–97.

fluence is even more marked in a society undergoing religious, social, and economic transformation. Although such changes are not rapid or always pervasive in a preindustrial society, the colonization of New England did occur at a time when the modern world was emerging at a steady pace. Thus, to suggest a static balance of privacy in colonial New England would be misleading. In addition, the settlement of a New World practically guaranteed a gradual metamorphosis of important elements of the Old World heritage, however much it had been in flux to begin with.

The ideology of Puritanism made positive and negative contributions to the preservation of privacy in early New England. Since the intense religiosity of the Puritans overshadowed many other aspects of their lives, Puritanism was a central influence on the colonists' attitudes toward personal privacy. In some areas of life Puritanism was the most important single variable affecting the valuation of privacy in the seventeenth century, and the institution that had the most intimate connection with the value system. It generated not only a series of positive recognitions of the value of privacy, but also norms that could view a demand for it as a subversive act or a shield for wrongdoing. Over a period of time changes in Puritanism itself gradually lessened the negative aspects of this original attitude.

As ordinary human beings, the New England Puritans shared certain basic needs for privacy. In the face of countervailing forces within their own system of beliefs, the Puritans individually and collectively wanted and provided for personal privacy. Any automatic association of Puritanism with the denial of privacy is a reflection of an outdated monolithic interpretation. Puritanism actually supported the concept of privacy in innumerable ways, starting with the regular need for it to conduct one's religious devotions and culminating in the ways devised to protect it in the course of admission to the churches and the conduct of church discipline. The Puritan emphasis on introspective analysis of personal behavior recognized the conscience or the mind as a haven, where man and his God were alone. A woman on trial for witchcraft at Salem refused to tell her "thoughts" about the afflicted children, because "my thoughts are my own when they are in, but when they are out, they are anothers." The court advised Anne Hutchinson: "Your conscience you may keep to your self." The wife of a minister secured a divorce partly because the husband sometimes threatened "to make the Sun shine thro my Soul."[34] The notion inspired by Calvin of the utter depravity of man,

[34] *Narratives of the Witchcraft Cases, 1648–1706*, ed. George L. Burr (New

which would seem to preclude the right to privacy in the interests of continued strivings toward sanctification, was a purely theological and metaphysical concept.[35] It had little effect on the conduct of daily life, at least in the minds of most of the population. Puritanism also had a substantial positive impact on the protection of personal privacy in the colonial courtroom, since the Puritan heritage included opposition to oaths and torture and support of the right of an individual not to incriminate himself.

It would be misleading to ignore the negative influence of Puritanism and the Puritan movement, particularly in the seventeenth century. The key role of Puritanism was in shaping attitudes that could on occasion make a normal desire for privacy subservient to higher goals. It affected the intensity with which persons sought privacy beyond a minimum level. Puritans were encouraged to subordinate privacy to the more pressing purpose of collaborating in the creation of a City Set upon a Hill for the edification of the rest of humanity. The implements of this communal spirit were a pervasive moralism, the concept of watchfulness, the encouragement of mutual surveillance, and the suppression of self to community goals. A search for privacy could be a threat to the spirit of community, which was so strong in early generations in the New World. Towns should be established and run in a collective, cohesive, and communitarian fashion. Parents should carefully regulate behavior within their families for the suppression of evils and the advancement of Puritan ideals. The Puritan concept of the righteous life should be enacted into statutes, and these laws properly enforced, even if this enforcement required some lessening of personal privacy through the use of surveillance techniques. At the very least Puritanism limited the intensity with which seventeenth-century New Englanders could demand privacy in specific circumstances.

So long as the ideology of Puritanism retained its hold on New England society in the seventeenth century, an important element of the population accepted and shared such attitudes related to privacy. As a result, it occupied an ambivalent position in the Puritan scale of values for much of the seventeenth century. Although few people have ever ignored the most elementary demands of individuals for privacy, the prevailing temper of the Puritan movement significantly

York, 1914), p. 230; John Winthrop, *A Short Story of the Rise, Reign, and Ruine of the Antinomians* (London, 1644), in C. F. Adams, ed., *Antinomianism*, p. 165; Mass. Arch., IX, 206–7 (1730).

[35] See Perry Miller, *The New England Mind: The Seventeenth Century* (New York, 1939), p. 36.

altered the relative status of concern for it in the population's scale of values. Even if the practical impact of Puritan moralism was less substantial than might seem apparent at first, the attitude toward personal privacy implicit in the idea of watchfulness, for example, remained an important influence on the way in which a colonist could claim or seek it.

There are several caveats that must be entered in the course of a discussion of the negative impact of Puritanism and the Puritan movement. In the first place there were practical difficulties involved in the implementation of Puritan ideals that were hostile to privacy. Officials charged with local law enforcement found the problems of maintaining basic law and order substantial enough without trying to implement some of the more exotic regulations of personal behavior enacted by the Puritan leadership. Even if an official or a citizen recognized certain standards of behavior as desirable and accepted the obligation to watch over his brethren, it was another step to work vigorously to impose these standards on others, especially if this required overt and regular invasions of someone else's privacy. This aspect of the Puritan's duty posed too great a threat to the delicate balance of personal relationships in small colonial communities. Thus, Puritanism in actual practice did not usually lessen the availability of personal privacy to any great extent.

Some of the temporary excesses of mid-seventeenth-century New England Puritanism were also notable aberrations from traditional English values. In many ways the negative role of Puritanism was only a temporary challenge to privacy as a customary value in colonial society. Many of the problems encountered by the Puritans in implementing certain of their programs, for example those associated with procedures for admission to full church membership or the enforcement of church discipline, arose because these innovations were so contrary to the usages of the mother country.

The social changes that occurred in colonial New England were clearly reflected in the ultimate impact of Puritanism and the Puritan movement on privacy.[36] The variety of changes that occurred within the Puritan movement in the latter half of the seventeenth century directly affected its ascendancy over New England society. Puritanism and the Puritan movement lost much of their initial vitality

---

[36] For an attempt to make an integrated analysis of the components of social change in seventeenth-century New England, see David H. Flaherty, "Puritanism and Change in New England Society" (paper delivered at the Annual Meeting of the American Historical Association, Washington, D.C., Dec. 29, 1969). This essay is the basis for the following summary paragraphs.

through processes of adaptation to ordinary usage, institutionalization, and transformation into an established church. The gradual dissipation of the intensity of the Puritan religious experience was a
significant factor in this transformation. Succeeding generations had
not undergone the experiences that had shaped the founding fathers.
Certain of the individualized and societal forces that had aided the
initial recruitment of Puritans gradually disappeared; the persecution
and adversity that had helped to spark and unite English Puritanism
were almost wholly lacking in the New World. As individuals became less intensely Puritan, their total response to the demands of
the Puritan movement decreased, with inevitable consequences for
the nature of their society, including an increased acceptance of the
general need for personal privacy.

Another variety of forces of social change in the seventeenth century had little to do with internal aspects of the Puritan movement
but nevertheless caused adjustments in the balance of privacy. Either
directly or through a process of modification, traditional elements in
the English heritage of the colonists that had been rejected by the
Puritans became a dominant influence in daily life. The New World
environment had a general impact on society, undermining to some
extent certain tenets of Puritan ideology. A general acclimatization
to life in America unleashed expansionist tendencies. The impact of
geography and the accidents of settlement generated differences
among towns that diluted the influence of the Puritan movement at
the local level. The unregenerate within the Congregational churches,
newer immigrants, and such competing elites as the emerging merchant class became additional counterbalances to the governing influence of the Puritan political and religious establishment. The
corrosive influence of economic success affected all residents of the
colonies. The ultimate failure of the Puritan Revolution in England
meant that New World Puritans lost an essential stimulus to the
further remodeling of society; they became increasingly isolated and
provincial. This hastened the withdrawal of the Puritan movement
from the central direction of New England society. Finally, Puritan
political control encountered a strong threat from the beginnings of
English attempts to integrate New England within a burgeoning im-
perial system. The struggles with the English government in the
1680's over the charter of Massachusetts Bay represented the last
gasp of the Puritan political establishment. A gradual process of
secularization of society and culture accompanied the increasingly
formalized role of the religious ideology of Puritanism in colonial life.

The Puritan movement played an essential role in the formulation of norms and values for the New World society, but in the late seventeenth century it lost its organizing capacity to sanctify standards of conduct and supply their ultimate justification, with important consequences for privacy. The changes that overtook Puritanism and the Puritan movement in the later seventeenth century created fundamental differences in attitudes toward the acceptability and desirability of seeking and demanding personal privacy. Privacy became a more viable desire. In the areas where Puritanism had had an actual practical influence on the balance of privacy, the gradual changes within Puritanism and the Puritan movement made a positive contribution to the restoration of this balance in society as a whole. Puritanism did not cease to be an influence but became much less of a force than it had been during the founding generation, thereby merely contributing to, stimulating, or not impeding significant changes in society. There was a marked response in the fields of legislation, law enforcement, and popular attitudes to the weakening of the Puritan movement. New England did not cease to be of Puritan inclination in religious belief and world view in the late seventeenth century. But Puritanism adapted itself by becoming the basic creed of a group pursuing ordinary lives. Its dominance over routine activities receded in many cases to that portion of daily life traditionally allotted to worship and prayer. Religion made its strongest resurgence at times of personal crisis or during periods of public threats to the existence of a colony. By the eighteenth century the Puritan movement no longer had a pervasive impact on the general population. This enabled New England to become a New World version of an agricultural and preindustrial society in the eighteenth century.

THE BALANCE OF VALUES

The heart of a study of personal privacy is the discovery of the balance of interests affecting privacy in a society. Since too much or too little privacy produces imbalance, every society has processes at the individual and societal levels for adjusting such competing values as privacy, companionship, compulsory disclosure, and physical surveillance. The well-balanced personality displays all of these factors in equilibrium within the limits of the environmental conditions and social norms of his society. An individual further adapts his claims to a private personality to the distinctions inherent in levels of interaction with intimates, casual acquaintances, or strangers. He also has to cope with the normal tendency of persons to invade the privacy of others; privacy has to compete with curiosity. An individual's particular balance of privacy and disclosure is further affected by his status and station in life. In some instances privacy is not a feasible goal because of both class and environmental factors. The upper classes and the middling sort in the colonies both were in a better position successfully to assert demands for privacy than the poor. Their better-developed cultural interests made privacy seem both more possible and more necessary. Crowded and noisy living conditions and poverty, which subordinate privacy to basic family needs, forced readjustments in the balance of privacy that individual colonists sought. If poverty made certain aspects of its enjoyment inaccessible to the poor, wealth provided a superabundance of privacy. Another environmental condition, the plentifulness of open spaces, began to compensate for crowding within the home. The need of the colonial government to maintain surveillance over the population in the interests of enforcing the norms of society was a final competing value in the equation creating a privacy balance.

Both society and the individual worked toward this balance of privacy in colonial New England. Legislators weighed demands for social control versus the claims of the private personality. Individuals responded to conditions formally hostile to privacy, such as crowded living quarters, by using psychological means to achieve isolation or withdrawal. Westin has concluded that limitations on the availability of privacy force a person "to adjust his psychological balances, to find sufficient privacy *despite* these limiting factors."[37] Individuals seem instinctively to seek to readjust an imbalance of privacy, whether too much or too little. The prevalence of crowded living conditions in colonial America made it all the more likely that there was a universal pattern of psychic response to such situations. Westin has neatly summed up this notion of a balance of privacy: "Each individual must, within the larger context of his culture, his status, and his personal situation, make a continuous adjustment between his needs for solitude and companionship; for intimacy and general social intercourse; for anonymity and responsible participation in society; for reserve and disclosure."[38]

The purpose of this study is thus more than simply to illustrate the existence of concern for privacy and the extent to which it was a demanded and cherished value. Nor is it enough to explain why

[37] *Privacy and Freedom*, p. 41.
[38] *Ibid.*, p. 42.

persons wanted privacy–numan nature is fundamentally the same today as it was in the early days of this nation. Since all societies have demonstrated some level of concern for privacy, the goal here must be to explicate the establishment of a balance of sometimes clashing values in each sphere of human existence.

Individuals and families created their own balance of privacy in response to generalized conditions of existence. At varying stages of his life, or indeed of his day, a person chose isolation or intimacy, society or anonymity. Most persons wanted privacy at particular times and took steps to secure or protect it. When a woman met Increase Mather on the road and wanted to discuss her religious problems with him, she "desired those that rode with me to go forward, for she must needs speake with me." When a friend tried to discuss a letter with him in the street, Samuel Sewall in typical fashion "prevail'd with him to come and dine with me, and after that I and he discours'd alone."[39]

The consciousness of the need for privacy in colonial society was subject to important variables. Many of these will be concretely illustrated, while others can simply be taken for granted. Individual personalities, for example, differed in their attitudes to privacy. Whatever may be the cultural norms of a society, an individual can conform to them to a greater or lesser degree. A few may consider personal privacy of no importance whatsoever, while others overemphasize the search for it. To a significant extent a person enjoys and defends his privacy by his own standards. When a colonist suffered an invasion of privacy, it was his decision to initiate a defense or to tolerate the breach. The individual decided where to build his home, how many internal divisions to have in the house, whether or not to keep lodgers and servants, and whether or not to join a church. Through a process of personal adjustment the individual decided the extent to which privacy was an important value in his life.

Yet in another sense, individual colonists sometimes lacked control over conditions for the enjoyment of privacy. A combination of inferior social status and poverty could prevent the implementation of a desire for privacy, or could even weaken that desire. The poor have never been able to enjoy a great degree of privacy in their families, while the elite groups in most societies can afford as much privacy as they want, particularly in those areas such as home building where

[39] "The Autobiography of Increase Mather," ed. Michael G. Hall, AAS, *Proc.*, LXXI (1961), 292; *The Diary of Samuel Sewall*, Massachusetts Historical Society, *Collections*, 5th ser., V–VII (Boston, 1878–82), VI, 232 (1708), also pp. 43–45, 292.

economic considerations are particularly influential. Because of cultural deprivation and force of habit, the poor, who formed a significant segment of the population in a preindustrial society, became acclimated to the minimal availability of privacy in their households. In specific areas such as family life, where an individual can shape his own conditions rather than merely sharing in the general standards of the society, physical privacy may be beyond the comprehension of the poor; it is too far removed from the realm of possibility for them to be concerned about it. Thus a rising standard of living can benefit the privacy of all segments of society.

Yet privacy is not primarily an upper class urge and characteristic. In many areas of life the wealthy simply possess the means of ordering their lives to the advantage of privacy. They can afford large houses with many rooms. They can live in quiet residential areas or the serenity of country estates. To the extent that privacy can be purchased, the wealthier segment of society enjoys an advantage. But when the individual has to test his claim of privacy against the neighborhood and community, laws and law enforcers, or against churches and courts, social status is of only slight advantage. While wealth can guarantee a private home life, elites lead such relatively active lives that they are more subject to general observation by the populace. The poor, on the other hand, acquire a definite anonymity from their lowly position in the public arena.

The quality of colonial life ultimately imposed definite restrictions on the amount of personal privacy that a person could either demand or enjoy. Such practical limitations as building technology restricted the availability of privacy within the home for a significant part of the population. In the early years colonial society as a whole through its elected representatives legitimized invasions of personal privacy for the prevention of sinful disorders in a covenanted community. For a period of time Puritanism challenged the balance of privacy.

Privacy at the personal and societal level is not an absolute value but one which is constantly forced into accommodation with other important individual or societal values. It is thus essential that a study of privacy in colonial society examine varying spheres of daily existence from the differing perspectives of individuals, families, and society as a whole to discover how a balance of privacy was consciously or unconsciously struck in each area, and what priority personal privacy attained in competition with other values that were similarly prized.

PART ONE
Privacy in Family Life

THIS part concentrates on the balance of interests affecting the personal privacy of the individual colonist and his family in and around the family home. In this setting the pertinent dimensions of privacy were primarily solitude, intimacy, and reserve. How available was solitude in the interior and environs of the colonial home? Could the colonists find intimacy for themselves and their families? What were the competing values affecting the preservation of privacy?

These issues are investigated in three main stages. Chapter one focuses on the physical setting affecting the balance of privacy through the mediums of town planning and architecture. To what extent did a desire for privacy successfully compete with other values in the locating of homes? To what degree did the architecture and interior design of homes encourage or diminish the enjoyment of privacy? How much solitude and intimacy could a family and its individual members enjoy from neighbors, outsiders, and from one another within the home? Chapter two examines life within the family and the factors that competed in the creation of a balance of privacy inside the colonial home. Was relief available from generally crowded conditions? Did the circumstances of individual families differ in this respect? What alternative sources of solitude existed for members of the family? In chapter three attention shifts from internal aspects of family existence to the relationships between occupants of the home and nonhousehold members. The latter ranged from neighbors to visiting townspeople. Could the intimacy of the family be protected? Was the family subject to external surveillance? Could an individual find anonymity at any time?

In these chapters the difficulties of adequately assessing the preservation of privacy should be apparent. It is much easier to isolate factors that may have lessened the available degree of personal privacy than it is to identify the perhaps subtle methods developed by individuals to cope with those conditions that became overbearing. Personal and societal norms and environmental conditions merged in the creation of a balance of privacy. One can simply describe the general situation that existed–including the various changes and improvements in conditions–and indicate the compensating factors available to the individual in the course of his particular search for privacy. The only certainty is that individual ingenuity could fashion relief from intolerable circumstances.

1. The Home

THE location and design of the colonial home affected both the degree of personal privacy it could offer and the shield it could set up against surveillance by neighbors and outsiders. Even before a New England colonist moved into his home a series of material preconditions affecting its physical location, architecture, and interior design already existed. Individual differences deriving from varying economic circumstances and the stage of life of a particular couple or family also were important. Finally, the compromises forced on a colonial family by such competing values as the need for society and the limitations of colonial technology affected the homes in which they lived.

TOWN PLANNING

In seventeenth-century New England the initial pattern of settlement was the nucleated community in the form of a compact or linear town.[1] The choice of a compact or a linear pattern reflected the influences of available planning time, English background, and geography, rather than any profound social feelings. The best town planning occurred when some advance work was done, such as that for Cambridge, rather than when a group of settlers suddenly arrived in an area. Yet the broad results of choosing a linear versus a compact pattern were similar. Cambridge was one of many compact communities with gridiron streets and small home lots clustered around a central village green. Linear towns had a single street as the spine of the community with the home lots strung out rather than clustered.

[1] On the nucleated village, see Anthony N. B. Garvan, *Architecture and Town Planning in Colonial Connecticut* (New Haven, 1951), p. 40; John W. Reps, *The Making of Urban America: A History of City Planning in the United States* (Princeton, N.J., 1965), pp. 124, 126–27, 131–38, especially the maps. The important Connecticut towns were compact villages, as were Boston and Newport. Salem, Providence, Springfield, and Deerfield were linear towns. Compare the Salem and Cambridge maps in Reps, pp. 124, 127; see the maps of Providence in John Hutchins Cady, *The Civic and Architectural Development of Providence, 1636–1950* (Providence, 1957), p. 10.

Although provisions for the privacy of homes were a traditional consideration in colonial town planning, they were not dominant. Especially in the first years privacy had to compete with the needs of defense, political organization, religion, and sociability. Watertown declared it was "our reall intent to sitt down there close togither." In Lancaster lots were "laid out for the most part Equally to Rich and poore Partly to keepe the Towne from Scatering to farr."[2] The early chroniclers of New England echoed this desire to create a nuclear community. The town of Plymouth initially assigned small home lots to individuals: "The reason was that they might keep together, both for more safety and defence, and the better improvement of the general employments."[3] For the early Puritans the settlement of New England was a collective venture. Their heightened sense of community required that the population mass together for protection and mutual encouragement. Privacy took second place to other values in the location of homes until Puritan communitarian ideals gradually disintegrated in the face of New World conditions. After the first generations of settlement in New England, the gradual weakening of Puritan influence over the community, familiarity with life in the New World, and the disappearance of the Indian threat to most towns encouraged flexibility in town planning and the location of homes.

Even in the face of the early seventeenth-century emphasis on cohesiveness, some regulations that were incidentally detrimental to privacy were not implemented. In 1635 the Massachusetts General Court agreed that in the future "noe dwelling howse shalbe builte above halfe a myle from the meeteing howse, in any newe plantation," and a year later it extended the order to all towns in the jurisdiction. In 1639, however, several persons were granted permission to continue living in their homes although they were more than a half mile from the meetinghouse. The difficulties in enforcing this rule, coupled with basic expansionist tendencies in society, resulted in the repeal of the law in 1640.[4]

[2] *Watertown Records Comprising the First and Second Books of Town Proceedings . . .* (Watertown, Mass., 1894), p. 4 (1638) (hereafter cited as *Watertown Rec., Town Proc.*); *The Early Records of Lancaster, Massachusetts, 1643–1725*, ed. Henry S. Nourse (Lancaster, 1884), p. 29 (1653).

[3] Nathaniel Morton, *New England's Memorial* (Cambridge, Mass., 1669), in *Chronicles of the Pilgrim Fathers* (Everyman's Library, London, 1910–11), pp. 85–86 (1627); see similar sentiments in William Bradford, *Of Plymouth Plantation*, ed. Samuel E. Morison (New York, 1952), p. 188.

[4] *Mass. Rec.*, I, 157, 181, 257, 291.

The failure to maintain compact and linear towns as the only patterns of settlement had substantial benefits for individual privacy. Although towns were planned to accommodate a limited population,[5] thus preventing overcrowded conditions and stimulating the surplus population to settle new townships, practice did not always follow this pattern. In seventeenth-century towns fields were often turned into home lots as sons settled around fathers or a burgeoning center sought room for expansion. Freedom to leave a town center and settle in a less established area or to live on one's farm was in some instances an important prerequisite to the achievement of a substantial degree of physical privacy. The continuing movement toward less settled areas constantly refurbished this aspect of personal privacy. John Reps, the historian of town planning, has described "the nucleated farming community" as "a European institution that failed to survive in the American environment of boundless land peopled by resourceful and rootless colonists."[6]

The transition from compact towns to scattered farms introduced a flexibility into settlement patterns that also provided an opportunity for greater privacy. After the first few decades more and more inhabitants began to live on the land they farmed. As early as 1632 Governor William Bradford of the Pilgrim colony recognized the first signs of the breakup of Plymouth as a nuclear town.[7] In 1660 Andover, Massachusetts, made an unsuccessful effort to fine anyone who built a house outside of the home-lot area; by the 1670's one-half of the town lived on farms distributed over an area of nearly sixty square miles.[8] During hostilities with the Indians in the 1670's the Connecticut General Court tried to reinstate the old communal ideal:

Whereas by woefull experience in the late warr, many of the inhabitants of this country liveing in a single and scattering way, remote from townships and neighbourhood, have been destroyed and cutt off by the enemie . . . to the ruine of such famalyes, . . . and that the Providence of God seems to testify against such a way of liveing as contrary to religion, so-

[5] The settlers of Springfield in 1636 agreed that they wanted at least 40 families in the town but no more than 50 (Samuel E. Morison, *Builders of the Bay Colony* [rev. ed., Boston, 1964], p. 344).

[6] *Making of Urban America*, pp. 119, 122.

[7] *Of Plymouth Plantation*, p. 253.

[8] Philip J. Greven, Jr., "Old Patterns in the New World: the Distribution of Land in 17th Century Andover," Essex Institute, *Historical Collections*, CI (1965), 143, 147; and Greven, *Four Generations: Population, Land, and Family in Colonial Andover, Massachusetts* (Ithaca, N.Y., 1970), pp. 55–57, 48.

cietie in neighbourhood for common safety, . . . for the future all plantations or townships . . . shall setle themselves in such neerness together
that they may be a help, defence and succour each to other.[9]

But this declaration proved futile. The Reforming Synod of 1679–80
in Massachusetts reported that even among church members there
had been "an insatiable desire after Land, and worldly Accommodations, yea, so as to forsake Churches and Ordinances, and to live like
Heathen, only that so they might have Elbow-room enough in the
world. Farms and merchandising have been preferred before the
things of God."[10] Privacy and elbowroom went hand in hand. Despite
the laments of legislators and churchmen, this insatiable desire for
land persisted. The ease of access to ownership or possession of land
in the New World furnished a secure base for the enjoyment of
privacy.

In new eighteenth-century towns many of the residents lived away
from the central village, and the matter was no longer of much concern. In 1775 the 140 houses in Needham, a town established in 1711,
were scattered over a five-to-eight square mile area.[11] During the
Revolution a European visitor described his arrival at the boundary
of Lebanon, Connecticut. In order to reach the meetinghouse, "I had
six miles more to go, still traveling in Lebanon. Who would not think
after this, that I am speaking of an immense city? and, in fact, this is
one of the most considerable towns in the country, for it consists of
at least one hundred houses; but it is necessary to add that they are
widely scattered and often more than four or five hundred paces
from each other."[12] With such living conditions a great deal of physical privacy was available. Persons actually living on their farms or on
larger-than-average holdings in town centers resided in relative isolation. For this goodly segment of the population physical privacy
was a characteristic of everyday life.

The relatively large size of individual home lots also had an important influence on the preservation of privacy. The desire for land
was so strong among the first settlers that the Puritan dream of a

[9] *Conn. Rec.,* II, 328 (1677). Richard Lyman Bushman documented the urge
to get away from the compact village and live on one's land in his chapter on the
"Outlivers 1680–1740," in *From Puritan to Yankee: Character and the Social
Order in Connecticut, 1690–1765* (Cambridge, Mass., 1967).

[10] Williston Walker, *Creeds and Platforms of Congregationalism* (New York,
1893), p. 431.

[11] A manuscript map of Needham in 1775 can be consulted in the Mass.
Arch.

[12] Marquis de Chastellux, *Travels in North America in the Years 1780, 1781
and 1782,* tr. and ed. Howard C. Rice, Jr. (Chapel Hill, N.C., 1963), p. 229.

cohesive community had to allow for such expectations from the beginning. In the original nucleated villages the family lot provided room for a house and barn, a yard, and a small garden. Even in the seacoast towns the lots were rarely smaller than one acre. A survey of ten Massachusetts and Connecticut towns during the first thirty years revealed a range in house-lot size from one to four acres.[13] Other towns had even larger average lot sizes. In Andover in the 1640's twelve of twenty-two lots contained from four to six acres, while the others ranged from seven to twenty acres. By 1660 twenty-one of thirty-six lots in Andover were from four to five and one-half acres in size, and the rest were larger than six acres. The town of Rehoboth agreed in 1643 that house lots would be distributed in parcels of six, eight, and twelve acres. When Hadley was founded in western Massachusetts around 1660, each planter received a home lot of eight acres. By 1663 there were forty-seven house lots, with individual frontage of eight rods along a one-mile long, twenty-rod wide main street. Early Providence had fifty-two house lots extending in a row along the river bank. These "varied in width from 100 feet to 135 feet, in length from 1600 to 3000 feet, and in area from 4½ acres to 8½ acres," measurements which provided a minimum of about thirty yards between Providence houses even if they were built all in a row.[14] Information concerning home lots in Northampton, Massachusetts, appears in Table 1. Only eighteen of eighty-two lots were smaller than four acres, the amount to which each settler was entitled. The minimum size was two acres.

An English statute of 1589 directed against overcrowding, squatters, fire hazards, and destitution required that no cottage be erected in agricultural areas unless the lot measured four acres.[15] Definite attempts were made to enforce this law during the Stuart period.[16]

[13] See Anne B. MacLear, *Early New England Towns: A Comparative Study of Their Development* (New York, 1908), pp. 81–82; Garvan, *Architecture and Town Planning*, pp. 41, 62; Sumner Chilton Powell, *Puritan Village: The Formation of a New England Town* (Middletown, Conn., 1963), pp. 6–7 and chap. 6.

[14] Greven, "Distribution of Land," pp. 136–37; Greven, *Four Generations*, pp. 45–47; Richard Le B. Bowen, *Early Rehoboth: Documented Historical Studies of Families and Events in This Plymouth Colony Township* (Concord, N.H., 1945–50), IV, 3; Sylvester Judd, *History of Hadley* (Northampton, Mass., 1863), pp. 31–32, 39–40; Cady, *Providence*, pp. 7, 10.

[15] 31 Elizabeth, cap. 7; Maurice W. Barley, *The English Farmhouse and Cottage* (London, 1961), p. 59; William B. Willcox, *Gloucestershire, 1590–1640: A Study in Local Government* (New Haven, 1940), p. 230.

[16] William Lambarde, *Eirenarcha; or, Of the Office of the Justices of Peace* (London, 1581; rev. ed., London, 1614), pp. 475–76; Margaret Davies, *The*

Table 1. Home lots in Northhampton, Massachusetts

Period	Number of new land owners[*]	Average home-lot acreage	Range of home-lot acreage
1653–1658	43	3.5	2 to 4
1659–1660	16	6.1	2 to 12
1661–1662	9	4.0	4 to 5
1662–1663	1	8.0	8
1663–1664	7	3.7	3 to 6
1666–1669	3	4.5	4 to 6
1670–1674	3	4.5	4 to 6

SOURCE: James Russell Trumbull, *History of Northampton, Massachusetts from Its Settlement in 1654* (Northampton, 1898), I, 20, 36, 145–47.
[*] These figures include only those whose home-lot size is known.

The early New England settlers were thus imbued with at least some notion that four acres of land was the minimum requisite for an adequate existence. They expected similar accommodations in New England, especially after tensions concerning survival had subsided. Perhaps as a consequence of this experience, the average size of home lots generally increased with the settlement of each new township, especially as towns failed to adopt or abandoned the open-field system. In Londonderry, New Hampshire, in 1720 colonists provided themselves with frontage of 165 yards along a brook with lots extending inland for sixty acres.[17] Since colonial homes stood on large lots of land in the overwhelming number of communities, physical privacy was hardly a problem, in terms of persons being forced to live in overbearing contiguity.[18] The ordinary colonial family could enjoy intimacy, as well as an almost automatic degree of solitude.

Enforcement of English Apprenticeship: A Study in Applied Mercantilism, 1563–1642 (Cambridge, Mass., 1956), pp. 197–98, 231, 233; *Complaint and Reform in England, 1436–1714*, ed. William H. Dunham, Jr., and Stanley Pargellis (New York, 1938), p. 821. Peter Laslett has warned that although the government had decreed the house plot of a laborer should be four acres in size, "this cannot have been anything like a general rule" (*The World We Have Lost* [New York, 1965], p. 15).

[17] Ralph H. Brown, *Historical Geography of the United States* (New York, 1948), pp. 55, 56.

[18] Kenneth A. Lockridge has presented evidence of a significant decrease in the average size of landholdings from the 17th to the 18th century, somewhat restricting economic opportunity ("Land, Population and the Evolution of New England Society, 1630–1790," *Past and Present*, no. 39 [April 1968], pp. 62–80).

The largest towns became slight exceptions to this usual rule of well-designed towns and spacious house lots. Boston grew from about 7,000 in 1700 to as many as 16,0000 inhabitants in 1775. Newport had slightly more than 2,500 residents in 1700 and around 10,000 at the beginning of the Revolution. About a dozen other places, including New Haven and New London, reached populations of 3,000 to 8,000 around the same time. In Boston and Newport, and to a lesser extent in the other large towns, overcrowding of the occupied area served as an impediment to the availability of physical privacy. Yet the relatively large populations of these places provided the protective anonymity that could less readily be found in small towns.

The market place, wharves, and streets of Boston teemed with people and activity, in contrast to the quiet of other New England towns. Travelers noticed that the houses were close together, as they were in London.[19] An early town law discouraged the division of house lots into more than one plot and declared that "not above one dwelling house shallbe built upon any one lott without the consent of the Townes overseers."[20] The threat of fire helped somewhat to keep houses apart. Despite some evidence of the appearance of multiple-occupancy dwellings and other indications of a degree of crowding, conditions of life within the town of Boston never became intolerable. Its population grew steadily but slowly, and as Walter Muir Whitehill, the historian of Boston's growth, has commented, "there was little likelihood of the town bursting its seams." Whitehill quotes contemporary writers to support his assertion that a "sense of spaciousness" existed in Boston, primarily because of the gardens around the homes.[21] The first map of Boston, the Bonner map of 1722, and its successive editions confirm the continued existence of open spaces within the occupied area. In 1759 the Reverend Andrew

---

The resultant "crowding" that he discusses did not have much influence on personal privacy, since it is the size of house lots that is pertinent to this issue. Farms could have hardly become small enough to diminish substantially the physical privacy available around the home.

[19] John Josselyn, *An Account of Two Voyages to New England Made during the Years 1638, 1663* (London, 1675; rpt. Boston, 1865), p. 125 (1663); Edward Ward, *Boston in 1682 and 1699: A Trip to New England by Edward Ward* . . . (London, 1699), ed. George P. Winship (Providence, 1905), p. 38 (hereafter cited as *Trip to New England*).

[20] *Records Relating to the Early History of Boston*, ed. William H. Whitmore, et al. (Boston, 1876–1909), II, 14 (hereafter cited as *Boston Town Rec.*). See also Darrett B. Rutman, *Winthrop's Boston: Portrait of a Puritan Town, 1630–1649* (Chapel Hill, N.C., 1965), p. 192.

[21] *Boston: A Topographical History* (Cambridge, Mass., 1959), pp. 38, 47.

Burnaby of Scotland found that in Boston "the streets are open and spacious, and well paved; and the whole has much the air of some of our best county towns in England. The country round about it is exceedingly delightful."[22]

In the New England countryside the tranquility of agricultural communities promoted the enjoyment of solitude and intimacy. *The New England Almanack* for 1702 observed: "How happy's then the Country life, That's free from brawls, deceit and strife," where one could "quietly sleep all the night." In 1768 a female resident of Cambridge reflected: "Can there be a happier Seene, than nature display'd in Rural life, free from all the noise and dust of a city, surrounded with your Little ones, Tasting the sweets of domestick peace."[23] Since almost the entire population of New England lived in a peaceful rural setting, they could bask in the ready availability of physical privacy. These particular writers, however, may have been reacting to the contrasting hubbub of the larger towns. On occasion Boston officials took steps against disturbing noises. In 1656 the town permitted two men to set up posts "to stop carts from passing through the paved lane by their houses." In 1742 a town meeting considered remedies "to prevent the great Disturbance Occasioned by Horses and Chaise in great Numbers Crouding into Town and also out of Town till Nine, Ten and sometimes Eleven aClock at Night."[24] A few years later, when the General Court found that traffic in Boston's adjacent streets was giving "great interruption to the debates and proceedings," coaches, carts, and other carriages were forbidden to pass by during sessions. Two years later the legislators erected a chain across the road to stop traffic completely.[25] In 1775 the constable and town watch were ordered to put an end to such disorders as "the driving of Slays thro' the Town, with the beat of Drums and other noises, at unseasonable Times of the Night." After a petition from the inhabitants in 1741, the town passed a law against pigeon-shooting from rooftops.[26]

[22] *Travels through the Middle Settlements in North America, in the Years 1759 and 1760; with Observations upon the State of the Colonies* (3d ed. rev., London, 1798), p. 102.

[23] Samuel Clough, *The New England Almanack* (Boston, 1702); Mrs. Hannah Winthrop to Mrs. Jonathan Belcher, Sept. 8, 1768, Winthrop Papers, Ib, 68, MHS; see also Penn, *Some Fruits of Solitude*, pp. 73–74.

[24] *Boston Town Rec.*, II, 129, XII, 285.

[25] *The Acts and Resolves, Public and Private, of the Province of the Massachusetts Bay*, ed. A. C. Goodell (Boston, 1869–1922), III, 360, 467 (hereafter cited as *Mass. Acts and Res.*).

[26] *Boston Town Rec.*, XXIII, 240, XII, 266, 268–69.

Within any town physical privacy could be protected in several ways, including a move to a quieter locale. The Boston merchant John Hull located his home away from other houses: "My habitation is greatly disadvantageous for trade; yet because I always desired a quiet life, and not too much business, it was always best for me."[27] Wealthier inhabitants eventually satisfied their desire for greater privacy by building country seats in the suburbs or a few miles from the largest towns. In 1743 Governor Thomas Hutchinson built a hill-top home in Milton, seven or eight miles out of Boston, where he spent weekends and summers. A year later Dr. Alexander Hamilton "passed severall pritty country boxes at three or 4 miles' distance from Boston belonging to gentlemen in the town."[28] Individual privacy was not the only reason for this exodus; in 1753 Boston complained to the governor that high taxes were "driving our Wealthy and most able Habitants out of this Town, to Dwell and be Rated in the Countrey." But the town added that "it must be a strong temptation, to be able to Sleep quietly a few Miles out of Boston" and to save on taxes at the same time. "Numbers are gone already, more are going, others are preparing to go."[29]

Well-planned communities and large home lots made positive contributions to privacy throughout the colonial period. The plentifulness of land guaranteed the physical privacy of the family home. Fields, orchards, and trees created a sense of solitude. A man could take individual precautions further to ensure his privacy. The colonists wanted to live close enough together to be protected from isolation and yet continue to enjoy a private situation. It was only in the largest towns where only a small percentage of the total population lived that the privacy of the home was subjected to serious external pressures. In these places the availability of anonymity somewhat offset this disadvantage.

ARCHITECTURE

The settlers of early America had experienced in the mother country a revolution in housing that had started in the late sixteenth century

---

[27] See the footnote in Sewall, *Diary*, MHS, *Coll.*, 5th ser., V, 59 (1674).

[28] Malcolm Freiberg, "Prelude to Purgatory: Thomas Hutchinson in Provincial Massachusetts Politics, 1760–1770" (Ph.D. diss., Brown University, 1950), pp. 31–32; Hamilton, *Gentleman's Progress: The Itinerarium of Dr. Alexander Hamilton, 1744*, ed. Carl Bridenbaugh (Chapel Hill, N.C., 1948), p. 106.

[29] *Boston Town Rec.*, XIV, 240.

and affected every level of English society.[30] Architectural historians refer to the period of English history from 1570 to 1640 as the era of the rebuilding of rural England. During the Middle Ages the idea of communal living had shaped the layout of homes. Persons ate, slept, reproduced, and carried on their daily activities in crowded quarters, often a one-room house. As late as 1550, "most English people were still living in the rather dark, squalid, and cramped dwellings of their medieval forefathers. These were generally two-roomed houses— a hall and bower. . . . The two rooms were not ceiled over, but were open to the rafters and the thatch of the roof."[31] In the last half of the sixteenth century more individual rooms and a second story became characteristic of many homes. In terms of personal privacy the increase in partitioning, in particular a division of the living and sleeping areas, was a significant feature of this housing revolution. The change was gradual; yet W. G. Hoskins has generalized that "by the mid-seventeenth century the typical farmer's house had three to six rooms, rising to eight to ten among the bigger yeomen." According to Maurice Barley, "only poor husbandmen did not aspire to a house of two storeys throughout."[32] By 1640 even the cottages that housed the laboring classes rarely had less than two rooms, and "four labourers in five (of those who left inventories) lived in cottages with at least three rooms."[33]

Privacy was thus increasingly available within most English homes in the early seventeenth century, particularly in East Anglia and the southeastern counties, where many of the immigrants to New England originated. In the home counties evidence of one-room cottages in the eighty years before 1640 is almost nonexistent. As early as the 1560's, the "larger houses might have from six to twelve rooms, and smaller ones from three to five. In this respect Kent and other southeastern counties were far in advance of the rest of England."[34] In

[30] On changes in English architecture, consult M. W. Barley, "Rural Housing in England," in *The Agrarian History of England and Wales*, vol. IV, 1500–1640, ed. Joan Thirsk (Cambridge, 1967), pp. 696–766; Barley, *English Farmhouse and Cottage*; W. G. Hoskins, "The Rebuilding of Rural England, 1570–1640," *Past and Present*, no. 4 (Nov. 1953), pp. 44–59 (reprinted in Hoskins, *Provincial England* [London, 1963]).

[31] W. G. Hoskins, *The Making of the English Landscape* (London, 1955), p. 120; see also Barley, *English Farmhouse and Cottage*, pp. 19–20.

[32] Hoskins, "Rebuilding of Rural England," p. 55; Barley, "Rural Housing in England," pp. 745, 762.

[33] Alan Everitt, "Farm Labourers," in *Agrarian History of England and Wales*, IV, 442.

[34] C. W. Chalklin, *Seventeenth-Century Kent: A Social and Economic History* (London, 1965), pp. 3, 239, 243.

1618 Robert Reyce remarked on the change of values in the building of homes in Suffolk County. In earlier times persons "used in the scituation of their houses to regard proffitt more than pleasure, and safety more than wholsomnes of the aire. . . . These houses were alwayes built low[,] nott with many rooms or above one or two storyes."[35]

A variety of influences stimulated this revolution in housing standards. Rapidly rising farm prices for persons with relatively fixed expenses increased available wealth. Population growth spurred on new building at every level of society. But as Hoskins has written:

We must look for the cause of the Great Rebuilding in the filtering down to the mass of the population, after some two centuries, of a sense of privacy that had formerly been enjoyed only by the upper classes. Privacy demands more rooms, devoted to specialised uses: so we get in the Elizabethan yeoman's house the kitchen, the buttery, the best parlour, two or three separate bedrooms, the servants' chamber, besides the truncated medieval hall now shorn of many of its functions; and to achieve all this in a house of moderate size we have two floors instead of one.[36]

The settlers of New England had shared the experience of a great period of improvement in housing. Many were from those regions of England where the rebuilding had been most marked. Most of the settlers belonged to the social classes that had participated fully in the change of values–the lesser gentry, yeomen, and husbandmen. Such a background guaranteed that concern for the privacy of the family remained an important consideration when it came time to build permanent homes in the New World. A house with several separate rooms had become a minimum necessity of life.

The representative home in seventeenth-century New England had one and one-half to two stories with a central chimney.[37] The main floor contained the hall or living room and sometime kitchen, the

[35] *Suffolk in the Seventeenth Century: the Breviary of Suffolk, by Robert Reyce, 1618* (London, 1902), pp. 49–51.

[36] "Rebuilding of Rural England," p. 54. Barley has criticized Hoskins for overemphasis on the desire for privacy and is more specific in excluding the laboring classes from the housing revolution (*English Farmhouse and Cottage*, pp. 60–61, 124–25). Hoskins would argue that few homes escaped improvement during this period, even the cottages. Obviously the extent to which concern for privacy was predominant is not a subject for statistical verification.

[37] The number of different architectural styles in colonial New England was small. Variations tended to be the result of accident or of change gradually recommended by the new environment in America. Anthony Garvan has found that the house models developed before 1680 dominated domestic architecture for two centuries, while "floor plans and elevations remained almost static" (*Architecture and Town Planning*, p. 5).

parlor or best bedroom, and several small service rooms in the lean-to
that was frequently added to the rear of the house as an individual
family grew in size (see fig. 1). The second floor or upper story
sometimes had two chambers and a garret for storage or sleeping.
Such a house had dimensions of thirty-five to forty feet by fifteen to
twenty feet. It was the usual home of most farmers, craftsmen, and
laborers–in other words, of the large middling class. This basic design still predominated during the eighteenth century, although a
more spacious and partitioned floor plan graced many new homes.

With perhaps four rooms in the average house and the large average size of the colonial family, home life was communal in nature.
This coincided with the Puritan emphasis on the family as a cohesive unit. Yet the practice of partitioning into more specialized
rooms grew in popularity. In any particular home a more precise
differentiation between the living and sleeping areas became one of
the most elementary distinctions. This gradual increase in the use
of partitioning within the home secured increased possibilities of
solitude for family members and alleviated the inevitability of overbearing intimacy. Partitioning sometimes took the form of subdi-
viding large rooms either with full-scale walls or with temporary
dividers such as blankets, which could be hung from beams or
rafters.[38] Many partitions have long been removed from colonial
homes that are extant today, permitting oversimplified generaliza-
tions about the size and layout of early houses. Attaching various
rooms to the shell of the house was another favorite method of providing more room, especially as a young couple's family gradually
expanded. The lean-to was only the most usual such addition.

Early colonial thinking on the matter of partitioning can be examined in the following episode. In 1638 John Winthrop, Jr., received
a letter from an English gentleman, who later became the deputy
governor of the Massachusetts Bay Colony, containing instructions
about a home to be built for him in Ipswich.[39] Samuel Symonds was
a man of considerable wealth who brought five of his ten children
with him when he came to New England in the late 1630's. The house
was to be thirty to thirty-five feet long and sixteen to eighteen feet
wide. Despite this large size, "it makes noe great matter though
there be noe particion upon the first flore; if there be, make one biger
then the other." Communal living was still expected, although a

---

[38] For the continued use of blankets to set off rooms in early 19th-century
New England, see "Notes on Furnishing a Small New England Farmhouse,"
Old Time New England, XLVIII (1958), 80.

[39] *Winthrop Papers*, IV, 11–12.

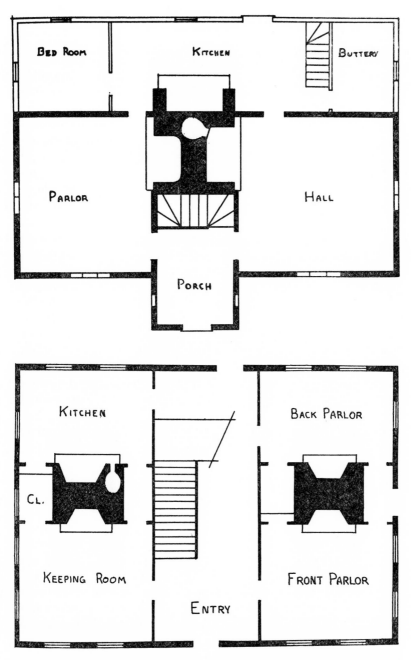

Fig. 1. Characteristic floor plans of seventeenth-century central chimney house with added lean-to (above), and eighteenth-century central passage house with four rooms and keeping-room closet. From Abbott L. Cummings, ed., *Rural Household Inventories* (Boston: Society for the Preservation of New England Antiquities, 1964)

house of this type normally was subdivided on the main floor because of the central chimney. The deputy governor also wanted as few windows as possible, and the necessary ones not to be too large. His directions for the second floor were even more instructive: "In this story over the first, I would have a particion, whether in the middest or over the particion under I leave it." The main sleeping quarters were to be divided, but not the garret, since only some children and servants slept there. These instructions provided some indications of a nascent concern for privacy. The house was built on a five-hundred-acre farm, which of course guaranteed substantial privacy for the family from outsiders.

Household inventories furnish evidence that the number of separate rooms in colonial homes gradually increased between 1630 and 1775.[40] Although much more research can be done, the trends are unmistakable. There are forty readily available room-by-room inventories for Essex County, Massachusetts between 1638 and 1664.[41] Sixty-five per cent of these houses had three or more rooms, 45 per cent had four or more rooms, and 22 per cent five or more rooms. There was an average of 3.3 rooms per house. This sample supports the general view that homes were of moderate size during the first generation. The smaller houses of the first settlers may have satisfied a need for security and community amid an unknown wilderness. An examination of inventories for rural Suffolk County between 1675 and 1775 furnishes substantial evidence of growth in the number of rooms. It is evident from Table 2 that at least after the first generation colonial homes were increasingly partitioned. These statistics show that a living room, kitchen, and two bedrooms (using their modern names) were practically minimum family requirements. As individual families increased in size, more rooms were added on the main floor and then additional bedrooms upstairs. These Suffolk County homes primarily housed farmers, who were fairly reluctant to build new homes. Most of the largest houses belonged to wealthier persons, but there was no absolute correlation between the size of

[40] Inventories filed in probate proceedings often listed the items room by room, making it possible to obtain some statistical evidence for the increase in home size. The whim of the executors, not the relative wealth of the estate, seems to have determined whether or not a room-by-room inventory was carried out. One cannot assume that an estate which is not listed room by room involved a one-room house. The method here employed is derived from M. W. Barley, "Farmhouses and Cottages, 1550–1725," *Economic History Review*, 2d ser., VII (1955), 291–301.

[41] *The Probate Records of Essex County, Massachusetts, 1635–1681* (Salem, 1916–20), I.

Table 2. Household inventories of rural Suffolk County, Massachusetts

	Number of inventories	Five or more rooms	Four or more rooms	Average number of rooms per house
1675–1699	41	45%	68%	4.3
1700–1749	31	65%	80%	5.7
1750–1775	39	87%	95%	6.0

SOURCE: Abbott L. Cummings, ed., *Rural Household Inventories, 1675–1775* (Boston, 1964). This volume includes all the complete room-by-room inventories recorded for rural towns in Suffolk County.

homes and economic status. Various cultural values, including a desire for greater privacy, obviously influenced the size of homes persons wanted. The sense of spaciousness impressed on the populace by the physical characteristics of the New England landscape may even have stimulated an urge to build larger homes. In general more and more physical privacy was available within colonial homes with the passage of time.

The poorest colonists and the new settlers without permanent homes were always likely to have inadequate housing from the viewpoint of physical privacy.[42] Such houses had a large room perhaps twenty feet square downstairs with a chamber or garret overhead. A house commonly built in Providence before 1676 had a story and a half with a hall fifteen feet by sixteen feet and a chamber in the garret.[43] Many of these houses were modified later in the century by adding another room with a fireplace on the other side of the chimney and building a lean-to in the rear. These two-room houses resembled the cottages of the poorest segment of the English laboring classes. If the first settlers chose to move into larger houses, their small cottages and other temporary dwellings were sometimes occupied by newly arrived settlers and poor families. One-room houses were unusual in colonial America, although not nonexistent. As late as 1767 John Adams visited a poor family in Braintree in which the husband, wife, and five children occupied "one Chamber, which

[42] See Harold R. Shurtleff, *The Log Cabin Myth: A Study of the Early Dwellings of the English Colonists in North America* (Cambridge, Mass., 1939), pp. 20–35, for a survey of the several types of temporary dwellings, including the cottage, then used. For a description of the primitive conditions in which some of the first settlers lived, see Edward Johnson, *A History of New England: The Wonder-Working Providence of Sions Saviour in New England* (London, 1654), ed. J. Franklin Jameson (New York, 1910), pp. 113–14, 210–11.

[43] Cady, *Providence*, pp. 8–9, 11.

serves them for Kitchen, Cellar, dining Room, Parlour, and Bed-
chamber. . . . These are the Conveniences and ornaments of a Life of
Poverty. These the Comforts of the Poor. This is Want. This is
Poverty!"[44]

In the early eighteenth century a new architectural style appeared
in the Georgian mansions of the colonial elite. These houses were a
product both of the revival of classical ideals in architecture and of
the fortunes some of the colonists had accumulated. Large homes
had always existed but were conspicuously few in number. A report
to the Colonial Office in the 1670's stated that "no house in New
England hath above 20 Rooms; Not 20 in Boston, which have above
10 Rooms each."[45] Eighteenth-century mansions had at least four
spacious rooms on the main floor with a hallway dividing the house.
The style spread from the mansions to lesser houses. The rapid growth
of population in the eighteenth century stimulated the building of
new homes, which often incorporated some of these innovations. The
sumptuous and spacious accommodations of the colonial mansion obviously provided substantial privacy for the inhabitants. These homes
had many rooms, were located on large tracts of land, and occasionally housed servants in separate outbuildings. The intimacy of the
family setting could be delicately balanced, while at the same time
a degree of withdrawal from the family was possible within the home.
These mansions represented the ultimate physical privacy in the
colonial era.

The introduction of the hallway in larger eighteenth-century homes
was a significant event in the history of privacy in America. Despite
obvious improvements over the simple cottage, the absence of hallways had remained a basic flaw in the floor plan of the central-
chimney house. Movement from one part of the house to another
required passage through adjacent rooms. For this reason, three servant girls in their early twenties had the following experience in the
Salem home of Nicholas Manning in 1680, while his wife was away.
They went downstairs early one morning and, while going through
their master's bedroom to reach the kitchen, found him in bed with
his sister. From the kitchen they were able to watch the brother and
sister through the open bedroom door and see the pair's lack of
clothing when they arose.[46]

[44] *Diary*, I, 332–33.
[45] Quoted in Richard S. Dunn, *Puritans and Yankees: The Winthrop Dynasty
of New England, 1630–1717* (Princeton, N.J., 1962), p. 173.
[46] Mass. Arch., VIII ("Depositions, 1662–1766"), 8–9. Manning ended up in
court on incest charges.

The prevailing architectural styles in the New England colonies adequately preserved the privacy of the family to the extent that the gaze of outsiders could not easily penetrate the solid façade of colonial houses. The only breaches in the walls were for heavy wooden doors and small windows. At least one window in each room was essential for lighting purposes, and corner rooms had one in each wall. Samuel Sewall of Boston had a window installed in his bedchamber "a little to enlighten the darkness of it."[47] Personal privacy benefited from the prevailing prejudice against large windows as ostentatious and extravagant luxuries. In the spring and summer of 1751 the Reverend Ebenezer Parkman of Westborough had a new home built. He ordered 13 windows installed with "24 Squares in Each Window 7 by 9 Dimensions of Glass." Soon after its completion Parkman recorded the reaction of his close friend, one of the socially prominent men in the town. "N. B. Lieutenant Tainter was very Sharp upon me about the pride of Ministers, when he saw the Window Frames. . . . I endeavour'd to let him know that I was myself griev'd that the windows were so large and I have often said it that I wish'd they were less."[48]

Most windows were not curtained. Probate records for Boston and Salem in the first half of the eighteenth century list window curtains in less than 10 per cent of the household inventories, although far more minute items are included. Those using curtains were spread evenly through the various strata of society: "Even at mid-century only one in five of the household inventories of wealthy Boston citizens mentions any window curtains at all." These records indicate that "window curtains were not widely used in colonial Boston and Salem in the first half of the eighteenth century, and when used they occurred most often in only one room, usually the best bedroom."[49] The lack of curtains on windows did not reflect an absence of concern for privacy. Curtains were hung only as decorations in the finest room in the house, for the cost of the material and the need for natural lighting discouraged their use throughout the home. More importantly, colonial window glass was not very transparent, and its opaqueness protected those inside from the gaze of outsiders. Many houses were on farms or set well back on large home lots, rendering curtains on the upstairs windows less necessary and making it more difficult to peer unnoticed through a main floor window. In addition,

---

[47] *Diary*, MHS, *Coll.*, 5th ser., VII, 18, also 12–13.
[48] "Diary," AAS, *Proc.*, LXXV (1965), 63, 84.
[49] Anna Brightman, "Window Curtains in Colonial Boston and Salem," *Antiques*, LXXXVI (1964), 184–87.

since most of the window glass used in New England was imported
until well into the eighteenth century, some homeowners could not
afford glass in all or any of their windows and substituted such items
as oiled cloth or paper, which were barely translucent.

An incident involving Samuel Sewall in 1708 suggests that colonial homeowners were sensitive about neighbors' windows. This
kind of problem was probably only encountered in large towns. On
September 6 Sewall discovered "that Mr. La Bloom has set up another
Window on the partition-wall behind him and me, that stands half on
my Ground." The next day Sewall viewed the window and advised
about it: "All say tis unjust." On September 8 Sewall ordered "Mr.
Hirst to speak to Mr. Labloom to take away his Window." Sewall
took matters into his own hands on September 9: "I meet the Work-
man by Mr. Pemberton's Gate, and forewarn him from making of it;
and warn him off the Ground, and threaten to take away his scaffold-
ing if he proceed."[50] Presumably Sewall was successful in removing
this threat to his privacy.

When necessary, window shutters could afford a considerable
measure of privacy. In 1743 when Ann Leonard of Boston accused
her husband of beating her and entertaining lewd women, their
neighbors, John and Rebecca Milliken, were interrogated:

Q. Do you know any thing of said Henry's beating or striking his Wife.
A. [John M.] The said Henry had made Shutters to his Windows, but I
   have often heard a Quarrelling and after that have heard a noise
   which I apprehended to be a Striking a person against a Wall. . . .
Q. What do you know of his frequently having Bad Women at his house.
A. [Rebecca M.] I have seen with said Henry Severall Women of bad
   Characters . . . and this at late Hours of the night—but said Henry
   made Window Shutters and Stopt up all Cracks least he should be
   seen or over heard as I verrilly believe.[51]

Several characteristics of colonial construction could create problems when the household attempted to secure solitude within the
home. This was particularly true of the poor quality of floor, wall,
and ceiling construction. Since most houses were built entirely of
wood, it was sometimes easy to see and hear through the floors and
walls.[52] Upstairs floors and the partition walls of rooms were often

[50] *Diary*, MHS, *Coll.*, 5th ser., VI, 235–36.

[51] Mass. Arch., IX, 278–80, divorce, Ann Leonard v. Henry Leonard.

[52] Boston authorities had some success in stopping the building of timber
houses. Yet in 1722 Captain John Bonner, the mapmaker, estimated that only
1,000 of the town's 3,000 houses were of brick construction ([*Map of*] *The
Town of Boston in New England* [Boston, 1722]).

only single-boarded. Knotholes and cracks served as peepholes for the curious. Many individuals gave testimony in court of what they had seen through a crack or hole. When Elisha Engerson was alone with Dorothy Satarly in a room in a Maine home in the 1690's, "Elizabeth Cresy loockt into a Crak and She See dot [Dorothy] upon hir Back and hir coats up and She saw hir thighs and His Breeches down and Laying upon hir and hir hands about his nek and forder seth not."[53] There was a similar occurrence in Windham County, as Elizabeth Reed testified in a divorce case: "Some time in the Month of April 1732 I being at the House of Peter Cross of Mansfield I there Saw Nicholas Blancher. I was then Desired by the Wife of Peter Cross to goe to the Brook to Fetch Water to make Some Punch, on which request I went to fetch Water and on my Return Back to the house the Door being Shut I look'd in at a hole in the End of the house, there I saw the said Blancher and the said Cros's Wife on the bed in the act of Adultery."[54]

The absence of ceilings over upstairs chambers in some homes occasionally decreased solitude, since a person could look into every room from the roof beams. In New Haven in 1653 Mistress Goodman charged several females with calling her a witch. The young ladies testified that "she came in hott one day and put off some cloathes and lay upon the bed in her chamber. Hanah said she and her sister Elizabeth went up into the garret above her roome, and looked downe and said, looke how she lies, she lyes as if some bodey was sucking her."[55] One night in Newbury in the 1760's a widowed lodger "heard a Man and Woman discoursing in the Chamber over the Room where the Deponent lodged and there being no cieling over head . . . the deponent went up Chamber and looked in." She saw the mistress of the house engaged in sexual relations with a male friend.[56] These incidents were hardly typical of the colonial household, but they illustrate a persistent problem.

Many colonial homes lacked satisfactory soundproofing. Conversations in one room were sometimes privy to anyone in the house,

---

[53] *Maine Ct.* Rec., IV, 46; and also see Introduction, p. xxxix.

[54] Windham Superior Court, Sept. 1738, in Connecticut Archives, Crimes and Misdemeanors, IV (1737–55), doc. 342, Connecticut State Library, Hartford.

[55] *Records of the Colony or Jurisdiction of New Haven, from May, 1653, to the Union, Together with the New Haven Code of 1656*, ed. Charles J. Hoadly (Hartford, 1858), p. 34 (hereafter cited as *New Haven Col. Rec., 1653–1665*).

[56] Divorce, Benjamin Ingersoll v. Lydia Ingersoll, 1765, Court Files Suffolk, no. 129741, p. 61; see also the divorce case of Dougherty v. Little, 1768, *Legal Papers of John Adams*, ed. L. Kinvin Wroth and Hiller B. Zobel (Cambridge, Mass., 1965), I, 288n.

creating a delicate situation for a person trying to carry on a private conversation, and arbitrarily exposing even a communication of slight consequence to the attention of others. Noise carried easily through the home to disturb anyone enjoying some degree of retirement. Ruth Cushman of Taunton "lived in the same house with Elijah Cobb and his wife in the year 1766 and as nothing but a single wall parte the Rooms I had frequent opportunity of hearing their Conversation."[57] She was able to tell the court how Elijah treated his wife. Presumably families adjusted to such problems in various ways. Cracks could be blocked up, and important conversations conducted in a low voice. The problem did not exist in families where the husband and wife were the only resident adults. Better homes had walls that were plastered in some fashion, perhaps with clay, thereby reducing the noise level throughout the home.

On the whole the residents of colonial New England built bigger and better homes for themselves as their familiarity with life in the New World increased. A rising standard of living and the accumulation of capital made possible and increased the demand for larger homes. New styles in architecture made larger homes fashionable, especially in the eighteenth century. Changes in the impact of the Puritan movement on society as a whole encouraged the growth of conspicuous consumption, while the attractiveness of forced communal living in a nuclear center declined. The newest houses had more individual rooms and sometimes even hallways. The construction of larger homes and increased partitioning made more and more privacy available in family life. Houses protected colonial families well from external observation. The layout of towns, the plentifulness of land, an agricultural way of life, low population density, and architectural improvements created a hospitable environment for privacy.

[57] Divorce, Katherine Cobb v. Elijah Cobb, 1767, Court Files Suffolk, no. 129748, p. 99; see also *New Haven Town Records, 1649–1684*, ed. Franklin B. Dexter (New Haven, 1917–19), I, 466 (1661); and the experience of Dr. Alexander Hamilton in a Rhode Island inn, 1744, *Gentleman's Progress*, p. 148.

2. *The Family*

WITHIN the confines of the home, the primary place where colonists sought privacy, an adequate privacy balance normally depended upon the existence of intimacy for the family and some degree of solitude for individual members of the household. The family was the normal milieu in which individuals achieved an initial balance among society, intimacy, and isolation. Husbands and wives sought privacy at certain times from other members of the household. Growing children attempted more and more to shield some aspect of their daily lives and inner selves. Apprentices and servants pursued some semblance of a private life. At the same time the mechanics of living imposed definite limitations on the amount of individual privacy available within the family. The size of families obviously influenced the quality of life. The large number of persons in the typical colonial household often created crowded conditions, especially in sleeping accommodations. Lodgers and servants sometimes represented an alien element to be absorbed into the family unit before the balance of intimacy could be restored.

Family members normally spend much of their home life in contact with one another, and yet at the very least are enjoying privacy from the outside world. The colonists could take considerable satisfaction in the protection from outside surveillance afforded by their homes. Individual members of the family could also be alone on a variety of occasions. But the main aim inside the home was for the family to enjoy intimacy when alone together.[1] Intimacy should not become unbearable or inescapable. Evaluating the situation within the colonial home requires an investigation of the circumstances in which the family and other household members conducted their

---

[1] The consequences of a failure to recognize intimacy as an important dimension of privacy in family life are well illustrated in John Demos's comments concerning privacy in Plymouth Colony. He questioned whether privacy was "a meaningful concept at all" in small homes with limited living space housing large families (*A Little Commonwealth*, p. 46). He concluded that "there was little privacy for the residents" within these homes (p. 181). In these instances he is using the concept of privacy mostly in the sense of solitude and withdrawal. Demos noted that "large families in small houses created an inevitable sense of intimacy," as if intimacy was always undesirable (p. 134).

lives. Did the interpersonal relationships of parents, children, servants, and lodgers result in a pleasant intimacy or degenerate into overbearing togetherness? To what extent did parents, children, servants, and lodgers interfere in each other's lives? Could the colonists find solitude within the home? Was family life conducted in an atmosphere that maintained respect for private personalities?

FAMILY AND HOUSEHOLD SIZE

Knowledge of family and household size in colonial New England for the period before 1750 is limited.[2] In his recent study of Dedham, Massachusetts, Kenneth Lockridge has presented some data for the seventeenth century that help to fill this vacuum.[3] His figures for 1648 and 1700, combined with data from the Massachusetts Census of 1764, as shown in Table 3, suggest that the size of families was relatively stable. The data developed by John Demos for family size in Plymouth Colony indicate a basic consistency in the number of children per family living to maturity in the seventeenth century. His analysis of a Rhode Island town led him to conclude that "the mean and median size of Bristol families in terms of blood members changed very little between 1689 and 1774."[4] On the other hand, Philip Greven in his generational study of Andover, Massachusetts,

2 Estimates of colonial family size have been made at various times; many erred by exaggeration. See William B. Weeden, *Economic and Social History of New England, 1620–1789* (Boston, 1894), I, 273; Carl Bridenbaugh's editorial note in Hamilton, *Gentleman's Progress*, p. 238; Charles Francis Adams, *Three Episodes of Massachusetts History* (5th ed., Boston, 1896), II, 689–90. The estimates by such contemporaries as the Rev. Ezra Stiles are so disparate and of such questionable accuracy that they have not been quoted here. See *Extracts from the Itineraries and Other Miscellanies of Ezra Stiles, D.D., LL.D., 1755–1794, with a Selection from His Correspondence,* ed. Franklin B. Dexter (New Haven, 1916), p. 11; Edmund S. Morgan, *The Gentle Puritan: A Life of Ezra Stiles, 1727–1795* (Chapel Hill, N.C., 1962), pp. 11, 117; Francisco de Miranda, *The New Democracy in America: Travels of Francisco de Miranda in the United States, 1783–1784,* tr. Judson P. Wood and ed. John S. Ezell (Norman, Okla., 1963), pp. 107, 125, 170, 175, 184–85, 188–90.

3 See *A New England Town, The First Hundred Years: Dedham, Massachusetts, 1636–1736* (New York, 1970), and "The Population of Dedham, Massachusetts, 1636–1736," *Economic History Review,* 2d ser., XIX (1966), 325ff. See also John Demos, "Notes on Life in Plymouth Colony," *William and Mary Quarterly,* 3d ser., XXII (1965), 270; in this particular instance Demos's figures are exaggerated because his sample was too small.

4 "Families in Colonial Bristol, Rhode Island," *WMQ,* 3d ser., XXV (1968), 53; and *A Little Commonwealth,* p. 192.

Table 3. Families and Households in Dedham, Massachusetts

	1648	1700	1764
Total population*	410	750	1,919
Persons per family	6.1	6.75	6.2
Persons per house	5.3	over 6.0	8.0
Percentage of families in dual-occupancy homes	40%†	40%†	45.4%

SOURCES: The figures for 1648 and 1700 are from Kenneth A. Lockridge, "The Population of Dedham, Massachusetts, 1636–1736," *Economic History Review,* 2d ser., XIX (1966), 326, 343n. The 1764 figures are from the Massachusetts Census of that year.
* These figures include both whites and blacks.
† These figures are derived from Lockridge's statement "that no less than 80 per cent of adult, married men had their own houses" (p. 343n). The remaining 20 per cent of the families had to live in the same houses as the more fortunate 80 per cent.

has presented a persuasive case for substantial change in family size, especially between the seventeenth and eighteenth centuries, or between the first two generations and the third and fourth. Although all commentators have agreed on the relatively large size of colonial families, Greven has shown that families in the third generation in Andover were smaller than they had ever been in the seventeenth century, the result of decreasing rates of fertility, higher ages of marriage for women, and rising mortality rates.[5] Among completed families in seventeenth-century Andover only 40.7 per cent had less than seven children living to age twenty-one, whereas this figure rose to two-thirds of the completed families in the third generation. This evidence suggests that there was a significant decrease in the average size of the family in the eighteenth century, lessening the threat of crowding within the home. Tables 4 and 5 present information on family size in the late colonial period based on actual censuses. The data suggest that average family size continued to decline in the latter half of the eighteenth century: on the average the total number of persons in these families in 1764 was less than six.

Nevertheless, colonial families were almost double the average size of families two hundred years later. It was the high average number of children produced by each marriage that made the colonial families so large. The colonial family could encompass grandparents, unmarried relatives, and servants and lodgers, but few

[5] *Four Generations,* pp. 30–31, 111–12, and 200–204.

Table 4. Families in Massachusetts Bay Colony, 1764

Counties	White persons per family		Total population per family	
	Average	Median	Average	Median
Suffolk	6.3	5.7	6.6	5.9
Essex	5.3	5.4	5.5	5.6
Middlesex	5.7	5.8	5.8	5.9
Plymouth	5.8	5.9	6.1	6.0
Bristol	5.7	5.7	5.9	5.9
Worcester	5.9	6.0	6.0	6.0
Hampshire	5.9	5.9	6.0	6.0
Berkshire	6.0	5.9	6.6	6.1
Barnstable	5.6	5.7	5.9	5.9
Dukes	6.5	6.2	7.5	7.5
Nantucket	5.5	5.5	5.9	5.9
York	6.0	6.1	6.2	6.3
Cumberland	6.3	6.4	6.4	6.5
Lincoln	6.2	6.4	6.3	6.5
Total	5.8	5.9	6.0	6.0

SOURCE: Massachusetts Census of 1764.

Table 5. Families in Rhode Island, 1774

Counties	White persons per family		Total population per family	
	Average	Median	Average	Median
Newport	5.4	6.0	6.1	6.9
Bristol	5.6	5.5	6.1	6.1
Providence	5.9	5.8	6.1	6.1
Washington (King's)	5.8	6.0	6.7	6.7
Kent	6.2	5.9	6.5	6.3
Total	5.8	6.0	6.3	6.4

SOURCE: Rhode Island Census of 1774, in U.S. Bureau of the Census, *A Century of Population Growth* (Washington, D.C., 1909), pp. 162–63.

homes contained persons in all of these categories.[6] These families existed independently as small nuclear families, most often in separate households. The six persons in the average New England family around 1765 were living in a four-to-six-room house. In about half

[6] In 1635 the Boston home of William and Anne Hutchinson sheltered a total of 18 persons, including 11 children, 3 in-laws, and 2 servants (Emery Battis,

of the families there were more than six persons, making the achievement of physical privacy more difficult. For the other half of the
families, privacy was more readily available.

Some important limitations inherent in the data based on the
census of 1764 modify the initial picture of relatively crowded conditions. The static figures ignore the varying experiences of individuals
at different stages of their lives.[7] The degree of privacy a person
sought or could enjoy, the circumstances in which he lived, and the
degree to which he challenged the privacy of others changed from
infancy through childhood, adolescence, maturity, and old age. In
the particular context of mean family size, individual experiences
varied considerably. In small families, such as those of young married
couples with no children or a few children in infancy or early childhood, privacy was readily available within the home. The raw figures
for numbers of persons living within such homes, which suggest
crowding, are misleading. A couple married in their mid-twenties
might often have a six-person household after a decade of marriage,
but all of their four children would be under the age of ten and thus
relatively minor factors in the privacy balance. In addition, some
children died in infancy or before reaching maturity. Similarly, in
the homes of elderly couples, most of whose children had already
grown up, married, and begun their own separate families, conditions
for the enjoyment of privacy were almost ideal.

The high average size of families primarily reflects the situation in
the homes of middle-aged couples between the ages of 35 and 50.
The childbearing years of these couples were coming to an end; yet
there were still adolescents of advanced age living with them, as well
as younger children.[8] Children were normally spaced two or more
years apart over as long as a twenty-year period, resulting, by any
calculations, in large families.[9] Children in their teens or early twenties affected the privacy balance within the home much more than
their younger brothers and sisters. Parents no doubt kept this in
mind when arranging such matters as sleeping quarters. Perhaps
parents were more inclined to place their children approaching ad-

*Saints and Sectaries: Anne Hutchinson and the Antinomian Controversy in the
Massachusetts Bay Colony* [Chapel Hill, N.C., 1962], pp. 73–74).

[7] In his critique of an earlier draft of this chapter presented to a Conference on
Social History at the State University of New York, Stonybrook, Oct. 24, 1969,
John Demos pointed out the importance of a developmental approach that em-
phasizes variations in complete individual life cycles in a general approach to
social behavior.

[8] See Demos, "Families in Colonial Bristol," pp. 45–46.

[9] See Demos, *A Little Commonwealth*, pp. 69, 67–68.

olescence outside the home as servants. Yet these older siblings normally left the home to set up their own families before the younger children matured, keeping the conditions of daily existence in large households from becoming intolerable. Thus parents could raise a fairly large number of children while maintaining humane circumstances within the family. The maturity of children normally coincided to some extent with the most prosperous years of a man's career; so he could also afford a bigger home or an enlarged one at this appropriate point. Persons had radically different experiences at various stages in their lives with respect to the availability of personal privacy within their families.

The relatively large size of families was only part of the situation affecting privacy. Since there were more families than houses in Massachusetts Bay Colony in 1764, it is more significant to know the average number of persons living in each house, as well as the percentage of families that were sharing homes. The size of the population in the single dwelling unit was a primary influence on individual privacy; the mingling of families in one household threatened not only the privacy of the individual but the collective intimacy of the family. The figures in Tables 6 and 7 are far more graphic than those

Table 6. Persons living in occupied dwellings in Massachusetts Bay Colony, 1764

Counties	White persons per house		Total population per house	
	Average	Median	Average	Median
Suffolk	7.6	6.7	7.9	7.0
Essex	7.4	6.8	7.6	7.1
Middlesex	6.8	6.6	7.0	6.9
Plymouth	7.0	6.8	7.3	7.2
Bristol	6.8	6.8	6.9	6.9
Worcester	6.6	6.6	6.7	6.6
Hampshire	6.6	6.5	6.7	6.6
Berkshire	7.3	6.4	8.1	7.5
Barnstable	6.6	6.9	7.1	7.2
Dukes	7.2	7.2	8.3	8.3
Nantucket	8.0	8.0	8.5	8.5
York	8.2	8.1	8.4	8.2
Cumberland	11.5	6.9	11.6	7.0
Lincoln	6.4	6.3	6.4	6.3
Total	7.1	6.9	7.3	7.2

SOURCE: Massachusetts Census of 1764.

Table 7. Families in dual-occupancy homes in Massachusetts Bay
Colony, 1764

Counties	% of total population of colony	Average % of All Families	Median % of All Families
Suffolk	14.5%	34.4%	24.4%
Essex	17.5	55.6	38.4
Middlesex	13.5	32.8	28.2
Plymouth	9.0	33.6	33.2
Bristol	8.5	31.0	28.0
Worcester	12.5	20.0	17.6
Hampshire	7.0	19.2	12.6
Berkshire	1.3	35.8	11.8
Barnstable	5.0	33.4	35.2
Dukes	1.1	19.8	29.4
Nantucket	1.4	62.8	62.8
York	4.3	52.6	50.0
Cumberland	3.0	90.0	36.2
Lincoln	1.4	4.8	1.6
Total	100.0	37.0	29.2

SOURCE: Massachusetts Census of 1764.
NOTE: The computer included six towns that had more houses than families as negative percentages; however, the surplus houses totaled only 17, out of almost 32,000.

for family size in depicting conditions in some colonial homes. An average of more than one-third of the families in Massachusetts in 1764 lived with another family. In the largest county in New England more than one-half of the families shared homes. All the seaboard counties had one-third of their families in dual-occupied houses. In rural agricultural areas the percentage of persons living in dual-occupancy homes dropped somewhat, although in frontier Berkshire County the average rate climbed again to more than one out of three.

Since the census takers did not record their definitions of a family or a house, these figures on dual occupancy must be interpreted with some care. It is impossible to know for certain how often two complete or unrelated families were living under the same roof. One senses that this was not a common situation. The families of sailors and fishermen sharing homes in part explained the high rates in maritime counties and towns; here the husbands were absent at sea for lengthy periods. The sharing of homes often involved a married couple living with an aged parent or perhaps a widowed relative. This was the most practical way to take care of such persons. A young couple in colonial America normally set up a separate household at the time of marriage, but one of the married children often moved back to the homestead with his family as parents began to grow old or when the father died.[10] Presumably either economic pressures or the practical need to care for older persons led families to live together under normal circumstances. Otherwise there was no apparent tradition behind such a practice. No doubt some families could not afford separate homes. In fact, these figures for dual occupancy are probably excellent indicators of the size of the lower classes in this era. They reemphasize the fact that the poorest families have the most difficulty in achieving the privacy of a house to themselves.[11]

Certain conditions mitigated the harmful effects on privacy of dual occupancy of homes. There is definite evidence of internal divisions of homes in which several families lived.[12] Sometimes there were only one or two interior doorways or openings between the two ends of the house, making it really two homes joined together. If two families lived together, there were probably at least two hearths available for cooking and heating. Certain architectural styles prevalent in the colonies provided for large fireplaces at either end of the house, so that families living together in such homes did not have to share the place around which a great deal of daily life revolved. In fact the proliferation of fireplaces was a major characteristic of colonial architecture as the general standard of living continued to improve in the eighteenth century.

On occasion, two families living in the same house may have been able to separate their daily activities completely, a situation which census descriptions did not take into account. In a four-room house with a central chimney and a lean-to, each family could take one side.

[10] Greven's study of Andover confirms that most married children set up separate households, even if often close to their parents. Occasionally several generations shared the same home when one son inherited the paternal homestead and agreed to take care of his aging parents or his widowed mother, to whom specific parts of the home were assigned in written agreements. Greven does suggest that the general practice of sharing households became more common in the mid-18th century (see *Four Generations,* pp. 75, 98, 137–38, 220).

[11] See John Porter, *The Vertical Mosaic: An Analysis of Social Class and Power in Canada* (Toronto, 1965), p. 5.

[12] I am indebted for information on this point to Abbott L. Cummings of the Society for the Preservation of New England Antiquities.

In many wills, a widow was granted one end of her husband's house during her lifetime, which suggests that it was common to divide up houses into parts. If homes were divided up between an aged mother and her own family, the practice surely extended to relatives or strangers. When the families of two mariners lived together "under the same Roof" in Boston in 1754 and 1755, one portion of the house was known as "the said McCartys end of the house."[13] The French traveler the Marquis de Chastellux visited the Boston home of Thomas Cushing in 1782. After dinner Cushing conducted him "into the apartment of his son [Thomas Cushing, Jr.] and his daughter-in-law, with whom we were invited to drink tea. For although they inhabited the same house with their father, they had a separate household, according to the custom in America, where it is very rare for young people to live with their parents, when they are once settled in the world. In a nation which is in a perpetual state of growth, everything favors this general tendency; everything divides and multiplies."[14] The census figures, of course, do not show such clearly separated existences when they list two families living in one house.

The figures for the multiple occupancy of homes are not consistent from town to town within any particular county. A few towns had no house-sharing, while in others the percentages were high. The practice was probably most common in the larger towns with their numerous craftsmen and laborers, and in the long established towns of the seaboard counties with more older persons in the population. The figures given in Table 7 are the maximums for multiple occupancy, since for purposes of computation it was assumed that no more than two families ever lived together. This assumption is not totally accurate. In the colonial equivalent of a tenement it was probably not unusual for more than two poor families to crowd themselves into one unit, with one or several rooms per family. In other instances the second family sharing a home consisted of a widow or widower and their children, who were counted as an additional family by the census takers. Such special conditions helped create the high average dual-occupancy figures.

Multiple occupancy of homes was probably a much more common phenomenon in mid-eighteenth-century America than in earlier times, primarily a result of the great population boom that was occurring. Although the percentage of population increase was sub-

[13] Divorce, Daniel McCarthy v. Mary McCarthy, 1757, Court Files Suffolk, no. 129734, p. 33.
[14] *Travels*, p. 506.

stantial even in the seventeenth century, there were only 100,000 persons at most in New England in 1700. By the eve of the Revolution this figure was well over half a million. It was no longer so easy to have one's own home. Rising costs and pressures on available land and building materials in the settled areas made it expensive to build a new house. There may also have been more people living in poverty. One solution was for families to share existing houses, to which additions could easily be made. This situation did not coincide with the abandonment of concern for privacy by individual families, however.

Certain predictable effects on privacy created by dual occupancy of homes suggest the limited popularity the custom must have had. Opportunities for being alone could vanish. In New Haven in 1665 Patrick Morran went to the house where Ruth Moore lived with her mother, Goody Pinion, and asked her to accompany him to the ironworks so that they could talk. The mother thought this unnecessary, since "there was a roome in the house they might have been private in." The couple considered this unlikely, since two families lived in the house. Such families could intrude into each other's private activities, as happened when two sea captains and their wives lived together in Boston in 1754. Mrs. James noticed that while Captain McCarthy was at sea his wife was entertaining many male visitors, particularly one William Stone: "Some time after in the night time going into the said Mrs. McCarthys Lodging room to light a Candle as she had one there burning I saw the said Stone in Bed with the said Mrs. McCarty."[15] Couples living together might even have to pass through their respective bedrooms to reach the main part of the home. In Windsor, Connecticut, in the 1670's Thomas Barber, a man in his early thirties, testified in a court case involving Nicholas Sention: "Hee and his wife lodging in the midle room betwene Goodman Sension and his wife and the outward roome. The said Goodman Sension early in the morning used to come out of his bed Chamber with his Shooee on and so passed through the deponente roome and after hee was gone out of that room hee the said deponent saith he heard a noyse of creeking a bed in the chamber."[16] Sention was upstairs in bed with another fellow.

The perils of dual occupancy were such that in the village of Salem in 1680 the Reverend George Burroughs took steps to protect his privacy when forced to live with another family. The Putnams "made

[15] *New Haven Town Rec.*, II, 120; divorce, Daniel McCarthy v. Mary McCarthy, 1757, Court Files Suffolk, no. 129734, p. 33.

[16] Conn. Arch., Crimes and Misdemeanors, I (1663–1706), pt. 1, p. 99.

the most of the new minister's presence in their household to inquire minutely into his manners and to publish their findings to the village."[17] Since the whole village was a hornet's nest of controversy over the last minister, Burroughs was determined to avoid trouble. Aware of the inquisitiveness of the Putnams and fearful of the information they might obtain from his wife, the minister "did require his wife to give him a written covenant, under her hand and seal, that she would never reveal his secrets."[18] This was strong testimony to the curiosity of colonial New Englanders and to the problems inherent in dual occupancy.

The sizes of families and households in colonial New England created a mixed setting for the enjoyment of solitude and intimacy in family life. Certainly such values as privacy had to compete with other necessities of life. The satisfaction of elementary needs for survival was a more basic consideration than privacy, for example. In part colonial families subordinated the achievement of substantial levels of privacy at certain stages in their collective lives to more urgent necessities, including the requirements of a farm.[19] Growing children were desirable in the operation; laborers were expensive and often difficult to hire. Children were also a form of parental insurance against the perils of old age. Nevertheless, the statistics mask a more humane situation than might at first be assumed. Such factors as the varying size of a household during the average family's lifetime and the close relationship of residents in dual-occupancy households mitigated the crowding. Increased wealth, which ordinarily became available in mid-career when the need was greatest, enabled a family to provide more internal privacy for its members. The poor lived in physically cramped quarters, but this is perhaps as common today as it was then.

PARENTS AND CHILDREN

In any colonial family the nature of the relationship between parents and children influenced the preservation of individual privacy. In

[17] Marion Starkey, *The Devil in Massachusetts* (New York, 1950), p. 119. This is the same Burroughs who became a victim of Salem's witchcraft trials in 1692.

[18] Quoted in full in Charles W. Upham, *Salem Witchcraft* (Boston, 1867), I, 267.

[19] For an illustration of this principle in operation in another society, see the study of St. Denis parish in the province of Quebec in the 1930's by Horace Miner, *St. Denis: A French Canadian Parish* (Chicago, 1939), pp. 63–65.

seventeenth-century New England parents were expected to supervise the behavior of family members. The prevailing theory of family
government, while beneficial for the maintenance of good order in a
Puritan society, was inimical to personal privacy. It charged the head
of the household with the duty of surveillance over the behavior of
everyone, of ruling the home with an iron hand and all-seeing eye. A
similar form of patriarchal family government had characterized
Western society since its beginnings.[20] Puritan attachment to the
Mosaic law simply meant that family government was even more
deeply rooted in New England ways. Puritan parents were expected
to maintain a wholesome surveillance over their children as a religious obligation.[21] The Puritan father was meant to be the embodi-
ment of the patriarch of the Old Testament.

The family was the immediate agent of social control in
seventeenth-century New England. Cotton Mather wrote that "families are the Nurseries of all Societies; and the First Combinations of
mankind. Well-ordered Families naturally produce Good Order in
other Societies." As late as his 1703 Massachusetts election sermon,
Solomon Stoddard, the leading minister in the Connecticut Valley,
declared that the inhabitants could best help their rulers "by Governing their own families well; if Family Government be neglected
a people will grow wicked."[22] Maintenance of law and order was
nurtured at the family level. New Haven Colony, and later Connecticut, required families to obtain a copy of the recently printed law
codes "to keep for their use."[23]

The conditions of life and labor in early New England supported
the strict form of family government that one associates with both
patriarchalism and the Puritan movement. Agricultural activity re-

[20] See Lawrence Stone, *The Crisis of the Aristocracy, 1558–1641* (Oxford,
1965), p. 591. For confirmation of the similarity of the New England and English conceptions of the family in the 17th century, see Charles H. and Katherine
George, *The Protestant Mind of the English Reformation, 1570–1640* (Princeton, N.J., 1961), pp. 275–76; R. B. Schlatter, *Social Ideas of Religious Leaders,
1660–1688* (Oxford, 1940), pt. 1, "The Family."

[21] See Arthur W. Calhoun, *A Social History of the American Family* (Cleveland, 1917–19), I, 47; see also *The Colonial Laws of Massachusetts Reprinted
from the Edition of 1660, with the Supplements to 1672, Containing Also, The
Body of Liberties of 1641,* ed. William H. Whitmore (Boston, 1889), p. 9
(hereafter cited as *Laws Mass., 1660*); *Maine Ct. Rec.,* V, 186 (1716).

[22] Mather, *A Family Well-Ordered* (Boston, 1699), pp. 3–4; Stoddard, *Way
for a People* (Boston, 1703), p. 21; see also Benjamin Wadsworth, *The Well-
Ordered Family* (Boston, 1712), preface and p. 84; and Christopher Hill, *Society and Puritanism in Pre-Revolutionary England* (London, 1964), pp. 443–81.

[23] *New Haven Town Rec.,* I, 280 (1656); *Conn. Rec.,* II, 190 (1673).

quired prodigious labor and over-all supervision. Wives, children, and servants recognized that the father ran the farm. Both the scriptures and the state directed them to submit to his rule. In addition, as Christopher Hill has pointed out, "so long as the family farm and the small family business predominated, the patriarchal attitude corresponded to economic realities."[24] In this context even the declining impact of the Puritan movement did not diminish the patriarchal authority implicit in fatherhood in seventeenth-century New England. A son's dependence on his father for the provision of land, or money to purchase land, before he could marry continually reinforced parental authority. A few fathers retained legal control during their lifetimes over land that they permitted their sons to utilize.[25]

Parents watched their children primarily to see that they avoided excessive forms of misbehavior. During the course of a normal day children benefited in terms of privacy by often being ignored by busy parents. Living conditions were such that children did not require constant attention; older siblings frequently undertook essential supervisory functions. The young often led carefree, unregimented lives outside the home in the open spaces of uncongested living. At the same time children interfered minimally in the private lives of their parents. A child's basic infringement on the adult world was during sicknesses.

A Puritan father could make life difficult for his family by consistent surveillance, and although perhaps not so aggressively patriarchal as his ancestors, he did maintain a firm hand on the family. Yet a practical view of family life suggested that other family members should not be tyrannized, especially in terms of surveillance. While colonial parents held some economic leverage over their children, thus prolonging dependence, their control over the behavior of unmarried older sons could hardly have been very repressive in practice. The incessant Puritan demand for repression left an increasing majority of the adult population unmoved as the seventeenth century progressed. The gradual dissipation of the corporate Puritan identity in the latter half of the seventeenth century sapped parental authority of the moral intensity that was the only spur to extraordinary surveillance. Thereafter the relationship of parents and children developed in a more individualistic fashion without the

[24] *Society and Puritanism*, p. 453.
[25] See Greven, "Family Structure in Andover," *WMQ*, 3d ser., XXIII (1966), 244–50; and *Four Generations*, chap. 4. Demos found no evidence for such a general custom in Plymouth (*A Little Commonwealth*, pp. 169–70).

inspiration of an attitude which in some respects rendered concern for personal privacy a decidedly subordinate consideration. In the eighteenth century the relationship of parents and children in terms of mutual respect for privacy perhaps varied as much as it does in more modern times. Indeed in Andover the patriarchal character of seventeenth-century families based on land dependence gradually changed during the maturation of the third and fourth generations in the eighteenth century, as older sons of colonial families began to behave in a more independent fashion and gained their economic and personal autonomy earlier.[26] The degree of economic dependence on parents lessened, and there was a parallel weakening of general parental authority to regulate the lives of older children. After much of the pervasive influence of the Puritan movement on society had disappeared, even the role of patriarchalism was changing.

However much the Puritan conception of the family and its patriarchal structure may have legitimized parental interference and surveillance, the conduct of family discipline demonstrated a strong sense of privacy. Offenses committed within the family that had remained private were punished privately. Children presented in court were released if the father testified that he had corrected them in the intimacy of the family, or else the court sentenced the delinquents, "being under family government," to punishment from their parents.[27] In 1647 the governor of New Haven Colony informed the court that his Negro servant had obtained some strong water and got drunk: "Because it was openly knowne, he thought it necessarie the matter should bee heard in the courte, whereas, had it bine kept within the compase of his own family, he might have given him family correction for it."[28]

In the early years outside authorities did attempt to interfere in the relationships of husbands and wives. There was a series of presentments of husbands and wives for abusing or beating one another,[29]

[26] On the general interrelationship between the economic dependence of sons and the patriarchalism of family structure, see Greven, *Four Generations*, pp. 72–99, 126–33, 148, 154, 222–23, 241–50, 267–69, 272–73, 280–82.

[27] *Records of the Suffolk County Court, 1671–1680*, ed. Samuel E. Morison, Colonial Society of Massachusetts, *Collections*, vols. XXIX–XXX (Boston, 1933), p. 255 (1673) (hereafter cited as *Suffolk Rec.*); *Essex Rec.*, V, 306 (1674).

[28] *Records of the Colony and Plantation of New Haven, from 1638 to 1649*, ed. Charles J. Hoadly (Hartford, 1857), p. 335 (hereafter cited as *New Haven Col. Rec., 1638–1649*).

[29] Court of Assistants, Cambridge, 1638, *Mass. Rec.*, I, 233; Middlesex County Court Records, 1649–63, pp. 31 (1652), 135 (1657), 262 (1662), Court House, Cambridge; *Essex Rec.*, VII, 187 (1679).

which may have exposed marital problems to public scrutiny to an unnecessary extent. Marital discord further came under the purview of the courts between 1659 and 1673 in Hartford, Plymouth, York, and Suffolk counties. In Plymouth the court told a couple "to apply themselves to such waies as might make for the recovering of peace and love betwixt them," and to "that end . . . [we] request Isacke Bucke to bee officious therin."[30] Some couples resented this interference by the Puritan courts in their private lives and at least gave the impression that they could handle their own affairs. When John Barrett was called before a justice of the peace for abusing his wife, he exclaimed: "What hath any man to do with it, have not I power to Correct my owne wife."[31] A Salem woman explained to the court that she had long concealed her husband's mistreatment because she "was rather willing to groane under it then to make a publique discovery of his wicked, and brutish carriage to me."[32] Such examples of concern for the privacy of family affairs should be evaluated in association with the recurrent signs that the New England conscience in the late seventeenth century was gradually becoming secularized. The secular authorities ceased trying to regulate intimate behavior within the family. As such cases as those cited above disappeared from the court records, the privacy of the family was sure to benefit. A statement written during the Massachusetts Excise Bill controversy in 1754 may well represent the ideal standards of the colonists concerning the relationship of officials to private lives within the family. The writer referred to "the exclusive Right that every Man has to the innocent Secrets of his Family. For if an Account of any Part of his innocent Conduct is extorted from him, every other Part may . . . be required, and a Political Inquisition severe as that in Catholick Countries may inspect and controul every Step of his Private Conduct."[33]

SERVANTS

The presence of servants living in some colonial homes as domestics, farm laborers, or apprentices complicated the preservation of privacy. Not every family had servants. The majority of homes either did not require the assistance of outsiders, could not afford the luxury

[30] *Plymouth Col. Rec.*, IV, 93 (1665).
[31] *Maine Ct. Rec.*, I, 264–65 (York Co., 1666). Barrett was forced to submit to the court.
[32] *Essex Rec.*, VI, 297–98.
[33] Samuel Cooper, *The Crisis* (Boston, 1754), p. 5; see also *The Relapse* (Boston, 1755), p. 2.

of servants, or only hired local laborers who lived in their own homes. In seventeenth-century England only a small minority of yeomen and a handful of husbandmen had servants who lived with them.[34] Peter Laslett has estimated that perhaps a quarter or a third of all English families contained servants in Stuart times.[35] Although one might assume that servants would have been even less common in New England than in England, twenty-two (31.5 per cent) of the seventy families in the town of Bristol, Rhode Island, in 1689 had one or more servants, while forty-eight families had no servants.[36] Servants living in homes were probably uncommon in the seventeenth century but somewhat more usual by the eighteenth century as the population grew considerably.[37] In 1728 a Bostonian attempting to calculate the annual "necessary Expences in a Family of but middling Figure, and no more than Eight Persons" included "but One Maid's Wages."[38] Young single persons employed around the home and farm or as apprentices by craftsmen were the most typical servants. Yet it remained unusual for farm workers to live in and be hired on a permanent basis; a farmer and his sons handled most of the regular labor on the typical farm. At the time of the Revolution a commentator on New England reported that "the best and most cultivated parts of the Country to this Day have afforded no Spare Labourers. The Farmers and their Families have mutually assisted each other to reap their Harvests."[39] It seems safe to estimate that perhaps only one-third of the homes in New England in the century before the Revolution housed servants for some period of time as domestics, apprentices, indentured servants, or slaves.[40] On the other hand, a large majority of persons had at some point the

[34] Barley, "Rural Housing in England," pp. 737, 741, and Everitt, "Farm Labourers," p. 400.

[35] *World We Have Lost*, pp. 12–13.

[36] Demos, "Families in Colonial Bristol," p. 46.

[37] On the place of servants in the family, see Edmund S. Morgan, *The Puritan Family: Essays on Religion and Domestic Relations in Seventeenth-Century New England* (rev. paperback ed., New York, 1966), pp. 109–32; also Richard B. Morris, *Government and Labor in Early America* (New York, 1946), pp. 310ff.

[38] *New England Weekly Journal*, Boston, Nov. 25, 1728.

[39] "General Reflections and Remarks," Gay Transcripts, Miscellaneous Papers, III, 36, MHS.

[40] Few indentured servants came to New England after 1645, however, while Negroes, who were only a handful in the 17th century and comprised less than 2.5% of the population in 1764, were concentrated in the homes of the wealthy (Abbot E. Smith, *Colonists in Bondage: White Servitude and Convict Labor in America, 1607–1776* [Chapel Hill, N.C., 1947], appendix, p. 337, and *passim*).

experience of living in households that contained servants, either as members of the family hiring the servants or as servants themselves.

When living in their masters' households, servants were theoretically subject to family government and discipline.[41] The commands of their masters were law. Cotton Mather, the champion of Puritan orthodoxy, tried to indoctrinate both parties on their reciprocal duties: "Masters, When any Servant comes to Live with you, the God of Heaven does betrust you with another Precious and Immortal Soul; a Soul to be Instructed, a Soul to be Governed, a Soul to be brought home unto the Lord." Masters should "enquire critically into their spiritual Estate before God. Be Prudently Inquisitive into their Experiences, into their Temptations, into their Behaviours." (Notice the mitigating "prudently.") Mather further informed servants that they were always under scrutiny: "Servants, your Tongues, your Hands, your Feet, are your Masters, and they should move according to the Will of your Masters. If you are those Eye-servants, who will obey your Masters no longer than their Eye is upon you, know it, the Eye of the All seeing, and Almighty God, is upon you."[42] When servants committed offenses that family discipline could not punish adequately, they were presented to the local courts. Until at least the Revolution servants were sometimes brought to court for stubbornness and running away, testimony to the masters' inability to dominate the servants' lives totally.

Work days were long and inferiors in the family were supposed to have little time for a private life. Masters and mistresses attempted to keep their servants under surveillance during working hours and even circumscribed spare-time activities. An apprentice signed a contract that he would "faithfully serve his said master and dame, and not absent himselfe from their service by night or day, without theire consent."[43] According to the nightwalking statutes, servants

---

Only one-eighth of the Massachusetts families owned slaves in 1764 (Lorenzo J. Greene, *The Negro in Colonial New England, 1620–1776* [New York, 1942], pp. 316–20).

[41] See Morris, *Government and Labor*, pp. 376, 461–500. The English servant was supposed to be similarly subordinate to his master (see George, *Protestant Mind of the English Reformation*, pp. 295–305; Schlatter, *Social Ideas of Religious Leaders*, pt. 1, chap. 3). On the relationship of master and servant in 18th-century England, see J. Jean Hecht, *The Domestic Servant Class in Eighteenth Century England* (London, 1956), chap. 3, esp. pp. 74–75.

[42] *A Good Master Well Served* (Boston, 1696), pp. 17–18, 38.

[43] *Plymouth Col. Rec.*, VI, 25 (1679); see also Morris, *Government and Labor*, p. 366; and a similar contract in England in 1705, quoted in Laslett, *World We Have Lost*, p. 2.

were not allowed out of their masters' homes after dark. Such laws existed and were enforced in some fashion against all servants in the seventeenth century.[44]

Colonial servants could indulge their personal desires by a variety of methods. They could always remain awake after the family had retired.[45] Servants went to visit their friends in homes, taverns, streets, and fields. One master complained about his servant that "we Cann hardly keep her within doores after we are gonn to bed, except we Carry the key of the door to bed with us."[46] The illicit sexual activities in the home of John Davenport, Sr., while he was pastor of the church in New Haven in the 1660's, further illustrate the opportunities for servants to secure privacy. One might expect the strictest discipline to reign in his household. But while father and son and their wives were asleep, a young man visited their maid and spent one and one-half hours in her chamber. He also took her riding after dark. On another occasion the maid had five persons visiting her in the house. Nor did the Davenports learn by this experience. In 1668 one of their servant girls confessed to committing fornication with two separate individuals "when all in the house were in bed."[47]

Thus seventeenth-century servants had several methods of ensuring some semblance of private life. As a group they were not notably susceptible to religious sanctions, and only the fear of punishment might make them obey all the restrictions placed on them. Servants knew that the state limited punishment by masters and severely brought to task those who mistreated their servants.[48] They could also retaliate against masters who treated them harshly, or watched them too closely. The threat of firing the master's house was a power-

---

[44] See, for example, *The Colonial Laws of Massachusetts, Reprinted from the Edition of 1672 with the Supplements through 1686*, ed. William H. Whitmore (Boston, 1887), p. 236 (hereafter cited as *Laws Mass., 1672*); *Laws Conn., 1673*, p. 53; see also New Haven County Court Records, I (1666–98), 164 (1687), 208 (1693), II (1699–1713), 107 (1702), 164 (1704), Connecticut State Library, Hartford; Suffolk County Court Records, 1680–92, p. 40 (1680), p. 207 (1684), photostats in Suffolk County Court House (SCCH), Boston.

[45] See *New Haven Town Rec.*, I, 497–98 (1661); also Morgan, *Puritan Family*, pp. 128–29.

[46] Quoted in Morris, *Government and Labor*, p. 463.

[47] *New Haven Town Rec.*, II, 65–71, 228.

[48] See, for example, *Plymouth Col. Rec.*, III, 71–73, 82 (1655); *Essex Rec.*, VIII, 295–96, 302–3 (1682); see also Morris, *Government and Labor*, pp. 470–77; and Richard Dana, JP, "Pleas before Richard Dana, Esq., Beginning April 19th, 1760, Ending Dec. 5, 1767," for Boston, Suffolk Co., case 108 (1761) and case 65 (1764), in Dana Family Papers, box 3, MHS (hereafter cited as "Minute Book, 1760–1767").

ful weapon. A hired servant could quit; finding a replacement was usually difficult. Edmund Morgan has concluded that "in spite of every disadvantage some servants did manage to have a 'private life,' illegal though it was."[49]

A servant in eighteenth-century New England, like other residents of the colonies, was in a better position to enjoy a substantial degree of personal privacy. The restrictive legislation of the mid-seventeenth century was no longer enforced against him. The laws were selectively applied, mainly to Negroes and Indians,[50] an indication that it was increasingly difficult to deny servants an outlet. In 1749 the Reverend Mr. Parkman of Westborough, master of a son and three servants, worried about "young people's disorderly night walking: have now Such a Number . . . of young persons in my own Family that it causes me some Perplexity when my own do walk contrary to the advice and Counsel which I am frequently giving them."[51] When cases of nightwalking were prosecuted in the courts, they usually were particularly flagrant offenses, such as "keeping company with a leaude woman" or causing disturbances in celebration of Guy Fawkes Day.[52] One servant in New Haven "would goe out a nights and refuse an account where he was." Even the eighteenth-century laws meant to control Negro servants were not rigorously enforced.[53] Religious leaders now warned that "masters should not be tyrannical to their Servants, nor act as tho' they had an arbitrary unlimited power over them."[54] Steady increases in economic opportunities and

[49] *Puritan Family*, p. 131. Demos also recognized the practical limitations on a master's ability to regulate the lives of his servants (*A Little Commonwealth*, pp. 111–14).

[50] *Mass. Acts and Res.*, I, 535 (1703); Suffolk County, Records of the Court of General Sessions of the Peace, 1702–12, pp. 111–12 (1705), SCCH; *R.I. Rec.*, III, 492–93 (1704); *Laws R.I.*, *1719*, p. 52; *ibid.*, *1730*, p. 50; *ibid.*, *1767*, pp. 151–52; *Laws N.H.*, *1726*, p. 48 (1714); *ibid.*, *1771*, p. 52; Richard Dana, JP, "Records of Judgments and Proceedings before Me in Middlesex from March 1746 to 29th August A.D. 1748," for Cambridge, Middlesex Co., case 5, Nov. 15, 1746, in Dana Family Papers, box 3, MHS; Dana, "Minute Book, 1760–1767," for Boston, Suffolk Co., cases 150–51, 1761–62, *ibid.*

[51] "Diary," AAS, *Proc.*, LXXIV (1964), 68. Ministers in particular often needed servants to operate their farms.

[52] *Records of the Court of Assistants of the Colony of the Massachusetts Bay, 1630–1692*, ed. John Noble and John F. Cronin (Boston, 1901–28), II, 107 (Boston, 1641) (hereafter cited as *Mass. Assistants Rec.*); Middlesex Co. Ct. Rec., 1649–63, p. 274 (Charlestown, 1662); Hartford County Court Records, bk. G, no. 7 (1707–17), p. 167 (Hartford, 1710), CSL.

[53] *New Haven Town Rec.*, I, 476 (1661); Greene, *Negro in Colonial New England*, p. 144.

[54] Wadsworth, *Well-Ordered Family*, p. 106.

new settlements enabled the servants to change and improve their lot. They were among the most geographically mobile members of the society.[55] Servants were often hard to obtain, especially as hired hands on farms, and masters became more tolerant of their after-work activities. The size and partitioning of homes had generally increased, so that both the servant and other family members had more opportunity to be alone. Finally, one should not exaggerate the desires of colonial masters to watch over their servants closely and rule their lives like tyrants. The master who received a solid day's work from his servants was liable to look the other way after the long working hours. He too was busy meeting with his friends, perhaps in the local public house and was unlikely to interrupt the activity to chase after his servants if they were engaged in fairly innocent amusements. The age of the servants was also a factor in legitimizing their search for privacy. The younger the servant, the more likely the master would take his duties of enforcing the righteous life seriously.

The other side of this situation in the colonial home was the challenge of servants to the privacy of the family and their fellow servants. Since servants participated in most family activities, they had many surveillance opportunities. When a servant in his early twenties appeared in court in 1657 to testify concerning his master's estate, he prefaced his testimony with the explanation that "I beinge his servant I am privie to some things."[56] Apprentices were required to take a well-intentioned oath to keep their master's secrets, but it has been described as part of a "stereotyped and largely meaningless phraseology."[57] Commentators took notice of the sensitive problems arising from the intermingling of masters and servants. Sir John Barnard, a London merchant and politician, warned masters in a work reprinted in New England to beware of trusting their servants with secrets. Cotton Mather advised servants to "preserve the Honour of your Masters abroad, as well as at Home; and be not a sort of spies, upon the Houses of your Masters, to carry Tales abroad, where-

[55] In the dynamic and expansionist society of 18th-century England servants became much more independent and unwilling to accept physical correction or total domination by their master (Hecht, *Domestic Servant Class*, pp. 77–79). See also Hecht's comments on the leisure-time activities of servants (*ibid.*, pp. 125–40).

[56] *Essex Rec.*, II, 17; but see *ibid.*, VIII, 225 (1681) for a family in which children and servants ate together after the father and mother.

[57] W. E. Tate, *The Parish Chest: A Study of the Records of Parochial Administration in England* (Cambridge, 1946), p. 224; also Morris, *Government and Labor*, pp. 365–69.

by they may be Defamed." Barnard specifically instructed servants to "be careful of the secrets of the family where you live; from whence hardly the most indifferent circumstances must be divulged." He went so far as to state that "if any such trust is reposed in you, suffer the torture, rather than disclose it; . . . it must argue an extreme levity of mind to leak out to one man what was communicated to you by another."[58] Such admonitions may have supported family privacy.

Nevertheless servants knew what took place in their households, and some were not reluctant to gossip.[59] Offended families could follow the example of the Salem couple who brought their servant into court "to be whipped for spying into the chamber of his master and mistress, and for reporting what he saw." Another family escorted their maidservant before Governor Winthrop in 1640 for a misdemeanor and "charged her further with discovering the secretts of the family" to outsiders.[60] The observance of sensational events naturally stimulated the gossip of servants. More often, the repetitive patterns of existence in the colonial family may have encouraged servants to seek out alternative sources of gossip in the community, which at least protected the privacy of their own family.

Finally servants themselves exposed their private lives to the observation of fellow servants. Barnard, in his handbook for servants, issued this warning: "Your next domestick danger will be from your fellow-Prentices; (less favored will try to disgrace you); Look upon them as spies then; but never let them know you are on your guard."[61] Servants worked together and even slept together. A single servant in a family had an advantage here. Nevertheless servants sympathized with each other and shared an intimacy, as well as common sentiments toward nonservants. In some cases they protected the privacy of their fellows even when wrongdoing was involved.[62]

Servants who lived with their masters represented an inevitable challenge to the privacy of the family. They were admitted as members of the family, yet at least in the beginning of their service were strangers to the nuclear household. They were not only an initial threat to the intimacy of the family but had to find some solitude for

[58] Barnard, *A Present for an Apprentice* (London, 1740; rpt. Boston, 1747), pp. 66, 19–20; Mather, *Good Master Well Served*, p. 37. Hecht, *Domestic Servant Class*, p. 81, noted the propensity of servants to retail their masters' business.

[59] See Winthrop, *Journal*, II, 257–58; also Bradford, *Of Plymouth Plantation*, pp. 191–92 (1627); *New Haven Col. Rec.*, 1638–1649, pp. 242 (1646), 243–59.

[60] *Essex Rec.*, I, 58 (1643); *Winthrop Papers*, IV, 232.

[61] *Present for an Apprentice*, p. 39.

[62] See *New Haven Town Rec.*, II, 65–71, 228 (1663, 1668).

themselves. Many of the families that had servants could afford homes built to shelter all the occupants adequately. A hired servant could be dismissed or leave of his own accord if conditions for his enjoyment of privacy deteriorated. Servants were often young children and could be easily assimilated into the family circle, an even easier process on the many occasions when a servant was a relative of his master or mistress. Whether because of a servant's youth or blood ties or just the experience of living together for a few months, servants usually came to be considered part of the families in which they lived. Demos has concluded that intimacy "characterized all their interactions with the master and his family"[63] and that strong ties of feeling bound the whole relationship together. In addition, there was a traditional view that servants, because of their delicate position, must be especially respectful of family privacy. Most colonial servants perhaps had simply the usual problems of a family member in pursuing a degree of solitude for himself.

LODGERS

The presence of lodgers in some colonial homes added to already crowded household conditions and subjected all concerned to mutual surveillance. They posed another direct threat to the preservation of the intimacy of the family. Lodgers included spinsters, bachelors, widows, and young single persons employed in the vicinity. Evidence about how many families housed such strangers is scanty. A substantial number of families never placed themselves in this situation. No one was forced to keep lodgers, an important consideration when investigating the issue in terms of privacy. Families accepting lodgers did so as a commercial proposition, could be selective, and were presumably aware of the possible invasion of privacy. Keeping lodgers was probably more characteristic of families in the larger towns than those in rural areas. The upper classes did not have to keep boarders and would not do so, if they felt concern for the intimacy of their family. Some lodgers were relatives, which put them in a much different category than paying guests, for they were more readily accepted into the intimacy of the family setting.

In the seventeenth century some lodgers could not claim independent status within the household in order to repulse attempts to supervise their private lives. This was especially the case when boarders were young single persons. The New Haven Code of 1656

---

[63] *A Little Commonwealth*, pp. 116, 107, 120–22, 71.

was extraordinarily explicit about the obligations of single persons living as lodgers: "The Governor of which Family . . . shal as he may conveniently, duly observe the course, carriage, and behaviour, of every such single person, whether he, or she walk diligently in a constant lawful imployment, attending both Family duties, and the publick worship of God, and keeping good order day and night, or otherwise."[64] The united colony of Connecticut continued this surveillance requirement in terms more broadly applied than the New Haven regulation. The General Court declared in 1676 that "all such borders or sojourners as doe live in famalies as such, shall . . . be subject to the domesticall government of the said famaly, and shall be ready to give an account of their actions upon all demands." The law of 1702 repeated the substance of this requirement, but by this time the prospects for rigorous compliance were minimal.[65] Although the number of heads of households who complained to the authorities about their lodgers cannot be determined, Puritan fathers may have taken their tasks seriously in the seventeenth century. Common sense dictated that lodgers could hardly live in a household without conforming to a minimum extent with the established regimen, be it strict or lax. Thus the passage of the New Haven and Connecticut laws in the seventeenth century was not surprising, given the prevailing Puritan belief in the necessity of intense moral regulation. Massachusetts did not even bother with the formal establishment of such laws, perhaps on the assumption in the mid-seventeenth century that such a course of action would be automatically followed.

There were obvious limits beyond which boarders could not be disciplined, especially once the dynamic moralism of the first generations had diminished. The attitude of lodgers toward family prayer and reading of the scripture was representative. In 1684 the General Court in Connecticut complained that its 1676 regulations cited earlier had "not answered that expectation of reformation which this Court aymed at," especially "boarders and inmates neglecting the worship of God in the famalyes where they reside."[66] In Massachusetts in the early eighteenth century one lodger specifically resented the family worship requirement and did something about it. Even more significantly, this episode took place in the home of the redoubtable Samuel Sewall. Two lodgers, Sam Hirst and Ben Swett,

[64] Every family was required to have a copy of this law (*New Haven Col. Rec., 1653–1665,* p. 608).

[65] *Conn. Rec.,* II, 280–83; *Laws Conn., 1702,* p. 59.

[66] *Conn. Rec.,* III, 147–48, II, 280–83; for 1690, see *ibid.,* IV, 28–29, where the same lament was repeated.

went out early one morning "to play at Wicket" on Boston Common. When Hirst was absent from prayer, Sewall was greatly displeased. Two days later Hirst repeated his action. Sewall reacted swiftly: "I told him he could not lodge here practising thus. So he lodg'd elsewhere."[67] Fifty or more years earlier Sewall might have taken Hirst before a magistrate for such a flagrant assertion of independence.

The prospect of mutual observation by lodgers and family members brought the issue of privacy sharply into focus. Homes were of such size that this was to be expected, although homeowners who accepted lodgers presumably had houses that were larger than average, or were willing to live with the consequences. Concrete evidence of this surveillance emerged in court cases where the heads of families reported on the activities of their boarders.[68] A case in New Haven County in 1733 produced much information concerning the privacy of some lodgers.[69] When Elizabeth How accused a married man, Moses Atwater, of being the father of her child, his defense was to brand her a woman of easy virtue. A Wallingford couple reported that Elizabeth had sexual relations with their boarder, Joseph Marks, at an earlier time: "The said Joseph Marks boarding at our house observing of him that he was not as other times as to behaviour my husband asked what ailed him and before my husband and my Self he said . . . he did not Care to tell. Afterwards I went into the other Room and there was the said Marks and then I asked him what was the matter with him, and he made answer that he had been Naught with a Girl at Cheshier." Atwater next unveiled an obviously poor couple with whom Elizabeth How had lived in 1730:

Their came on Ellixander Kane A Tranchant [transient] Person to our House Desiring to Lodg theire and he being Weary he went to Bed in a bed on the floore Right before the fire which was made up for our Brother John Winston and after Kane had been abed Sum Time he asked Elizabeth How to Come and Lye with him She having before moved her Cheair Close to his bed Side at which Request she Lay Down by him[;] after Sum time we asked hur to git up and Attend order in the family but Shee gave no heed to it but seemed to fane hurself Aseleep. Afterwards Wee Would have hur git up that our Brother might Go into his bed but Wee could not prevaile with hur So he was forst to Seek other Loging, and

[67] *Diary,* MHS, *Coll.,* 5th ser., VII, 372 (1726).

[68] See the case of Sarah Cornwell, an unwed mother who lived with the family of Ebenezer Hubbard in Guilford in 1712 (New Haven County Court, File Papers, 1700–1719, N-Z, bundle Rex-S, CSL).

[69] The case of Rex v. Atwater can be followed at length in New Haven Co. Ct. Rec., III (1713–39), 380ff; New Haven Co. Ct. Files, 1730–39, M-R, bundle Rex. In spite of the scurrilous testimony, the court held Atwater responsible.

Afterwards wee went to bed in the same Rume at a Small Distance from said Kanes Bed: and after wee had been a bed Sum Time theire was Sutch actions Between them that we feared thare was unseemly Carriage between them and in the morning when wee got up She was in Kanes bed.

Both Joseph Marks and Elizabeth How had lived in homes where their behavior could be readily observed.

Since they shared in the family's activities, lodgers could also maintain a close surveillance over the members of the family.[70] In the ordinary colonial home the design and poor construction made it difficult to keep any activity from their purview, as in the New Haven home of John Uffoote, whose wife secured a divorce on the grounds of his impotency. Later to everyone's astonishment he impregnated his father's maid. Then witnesses reported Mrs. Uffoote's refusal to have sexual relations with her husband. Thomas Langden, who slept in the chamber over their room, had "heard them discourse together and heard her say, if he would not let her alone, she would goe out of the bed, and lye in the floore." Edward Camp had a similar experience: "When they were in bed he heard say plainely stand away, let me alone; some body laye with him whom he asked the reason of this disturbance, and he said alass that was nothing to what they sometimes have." On occasion relations between husband and wife became so vociferous that "the old man hath bine faine to rise out of his bed and call to them, and wish his daughter to attend advice."[71] The presence of persons other than parents and children in the home made some lack of personal privacy inevitable without conspicuous efforts on anyone's part.[72] Poorer families often had little choice but to subordinate a degree of concern for their intimacy to the necessity of additional income.

The problems of mutual observation by lodgers and family were neither new nor insoluble. The most common remedy was for a household gradually to accept a boarder into the intimacy of the family, trusting in his good judgment to respect their privacy. Presumably in most cases this was successful, with the greatest amount of tension occurring at the beginning of the relationship. If either party was dissatisfied with the results, a parting of the ways could be

[70] Lodgers also intruded on the privacy of one another. See the episode in Topsfield in *Essex Rec.*, VII, 300 (1679).

[71] *New Haven Col. Rec., 1653–1665*, p. 211 (1657); see also *Essex Rec.*, V, 31 (1672), VII, 248–49 (1679).

[72] Note the experience of Joanne Brooker, who was a lodger in the home of George Arthur in 1749 (divorce, Mary Arthur v. George Arthur, 1754, Court Files Suffolk, no. 129733b, p. 32).

arranged. Many families avoided the problem by never allowing boarders to live within their homes. Others may have ceased to keep boarders or secured replacements for similar reasons. In homes that sheltered lodgers mutual respect for the privacy of one another was the only viable compromise. In most such houses the uneventful quality of ordinary lives contributed to the protection of individual privacy.

DAILY LIFE

In a home that enjoys a satisfactory privacy balance, members come together on a voluntary basis rather than as a consequence of inescapable togetherness.[73] Residents should not be forced into an overbearing intimacy with one another. This is a crucial measurement of family privacy. A satisfactory balance should provide individual opportunities within the home for retirement from the group and for periods of limited communication. The centering of daily life around the hall and/or kitchen was one of several considerations that helped to emphasize togetherness within colonial homes. This area often constituted half the main floor of the house, while the parlor was reserved for guests or used as a bedroom for the parents. The preparation and eating of meals and a procession of household chores took place in the kitchen. The large fireplace for both cooking and heating exercised the magnetic attraction always associated with the hearth, especially in cold weather. It permitted females to keep close watch on each other. When Margaret Lord of Salem was suspected of stealing in 1678, her confederates, Goody Hoar and her two daughters, feigned innocence. But the court was not deceived: "Queries for Goody Hoar to answer if she be clear of confederacy with Margret Lord: how could Tabbye and Nancie use so many bushels of Indian malt, wheat and pease in a little house with but one fire, and their mother so much at home and know nothing about it?"[74] The simple process of lighting pipes and candles entailed frequent movement into the house and from one room to another. Anyone with a lighted fire was liable to interruption. By proceeding to the heart of family life one could intrude upon all sorts of private activities.[75]

Living space in the colonial home was reduced in a variety of ways. So simple a matter as storing salted meat and grains for winter con-

[73] Serge Chermayeff and Christopher Alexander, *Community and Privacy: Toward a New Architecture of Humanism* (Garden City, N.Y., 1963), p. 204.

[74] *Essex Rec.*, VII, 55.

[75] See *Boston Town Rec.*, II, 147 (1658), VIII, 9 (1701), and *Essex Rec.*, V, 145 (1673).

sumption took up space. A family servant reported that "his master kept the beef in the parlor and the pork in the kitchen."[76] Miscellaneous household utensils and equipment crowded the rooms. Folding beds and trundle beds that could be put out of the way during the day exemplified a desire to relieve some of the crowding. Some homes were employed for multiple purposes. Artisans, shopkeepers, and retailers sometimes used front rooms of their homes to service customers, thus exposing their families to a continued series of intrusions. Homes served as taverns and inns.[77] At the King's Arms in Ipswich in the 1670's the house was divided into "the new chamber which wee commonly call the Kings armes," and "the lower rooms where the family commonly keepeth," from which the pots of beer were drawn.[78] In 1722 Boston had approximately 135 public houses, at least some of which served as homes.[79] Some residents seem to have realized that the use of a home as a place of business compromised their privacy.[80] The postmaster of Falmouth, Maine, complained that "every person who looks for a letter or a news paper freely enters his house, be it post day or not; he cannot afford to set apart a room in his house as an office; he is continually disturb'd in his family, he therfor begs that some other person may be appointed in his stead, unless an office is allowed him."[81] In many such instances intrusions had to be tolerated in the interests of earning a living.

In many ways the desire for privacy in daily life is a product of the kind of work that a person does and the environment in which it is carried out. An individual who toils all day in a modern factory is more likely to seek relief in the form of solitude during his leisure hours. On the other hand "most rural work is done alone, or with a child 'follering' (looking on). The solitary worker's mind is free to roam, dream, scheme."[82] During working hours in the colonies only an individual engaged in intellectual pursuits was overly concerned

[76] *Essex Rec.*, VI, 254–55 (1677).

[77] For the licensing of dwelling houses as taverns, see New Haven Co. Ct. Rec., II, 499 (1713), 501–3.

[78] *Essex Rec.*, V, 34.

[79] Suffolk Co. Gen. Sess., 1719–25, pp. 146–47.

[80] Note the complaints of the Hartford man who ran a prison house in the 1690's (Connecticut Court of Assistants and Superior Court Records, 1687–1715, p. 30 of 35 pp. reversed at the beginning of the volume, CSL).

[81] *Journal Kept by Hugh Finlay, Surveyor of the Post Roads on the Continent of North America . . . 1773 . . . 1774* (Brooklyn, 1867), p. 16 (hereafter cited as Finlay, *Journal*).

[82] James West (pseud. of Carl Withers), *Plainville, USA* (New York, 1945), p. 100n.

about solitude. Ministers solved this problem by having studies into which they could retire for long hours. Many men and women on farms spent a good part of the day in the absence of adults, and if others were physically present, such as in the fields, it was not really a social situation. A woman was more apt to engage in group work around the house and was always closer to social situations with neighbors, which in part made up for her constant preoccupation with the affairs of the household. The availability of solitude within the home outside of working hours was not a pressing issue for the colonists; their need for individual privacy in this sphere was less than that felt in industrialized societies.

In fact the loneliness of working hours meant that many colonists spent the available leisure time in intimate social relationships to alleviate the boredom of their long workday. Leisure time was set aside for socializing. A man wanted to join the company at the tavern or other informal meeting place for relaxation, rather than retire into the bosom of his family, especially if his own home was somewhat crowded. John Adams described the multiplicity of taverns that allured "the poor Country People, who are tired with Labour and hanker after Company." In 1759 a young lady whom Adams was courting asked him if he would "like to spend your Evenings, at Home in reading and conversing with your Wife, rather than to spend them abroad in Taverns or with other Company?" His diplomatic answer had an enlightening conclusion: "Should prefer the Company of an agreable Wife, to any other Company for the most Part, not always. I should not like to be imprisoned at home."[83] That many colonists regularly preferred social occasions as a relief from the solitude of their working day does not imply the abandonment of a sense of privacy. They gathered with intimate friends, who presumably maintained an acceptable reserve in their communications. Such a pattern was repeated most days of the week with Sundays devoted both to recreation and religion.

The several seasons of the year affected the availability of privacy in early America. In winter homes were more crowded, since the snow and cold restricted ventures away from the warmth of the hearth, although the same conditions contributed to the protection of intimacy by cutting down on the number of daily visitors. The men of the household spent more time within the house as agricultural and commercial life slowed down. The only rooms that could com-

[83] *Diary*, I, 214, 67.

fortably be used during waking hours were those in which a fire was kept burning.[84] In most homes this meant the hall or kitchen. In other rooms, which became virtually unusable except for sleeping, even the wealthy only made fires for a special purpose.[85] When a young man climbed through a window to visit a Chelmsford girl on a wintry night in 1658, church members concluded forthrightly: "At such a season of the yeere . . . thus rationally conceived it hardly can, how it should be tollerable to have sat and abode with her without fire and other helpe of warmth, in a modest way. This to all rational men speakes incivillity and immodesty."[86] For several months of the year the great fireplace was the crowded scene of a family group huddled for warmth against the biting cold. The gradual proliferation of fireplaces thoughout the home during the colonial period made possible more solitude and room for retirement during the winter season.

During the rest of the year the outdoors was a sanctuary for those who wanted to be alone in colonial America, as it has been in most societies where homes are generally crowded. The open space of New England was the safety valve for personal privacy. Any colonist who felt crowded could take a solitary walk in the fields and woods without much effort. In the centers of compact towns the village greens served a similar purpose. If household tensions became overbearing, a colonist had only to walk out the front door to find opportunities for being alone. After one husband became angry with his wife, she "went out of the house and Lay Down under a tree and cried."[87] Harvest season provided an additional excuse for young persons to find privacy by going off into the fields. The anthropologist Horace Miner has described a similar situation in a French Canadian agricultural parish: "The opportunities for sexual relations offered by berry-picking has given blueberry time that particular reputation. Veillées [informal family visits] in distant parishes during warm weather of-

[84] A 19th-century writer described the task of spinning on a New England farm during winter, and how "with the warmer weather Aunt Betsy transferred our work to her chamber, where it escaped the espionage of the curious eyes and gossiping tongues that during the winter had at times been excessively annoying" (Sarah A. Emery, *Reminiscences of a Nonagenarian* [1879], pp. 27–29, quoted in David M. Potter and Thomas G. Manning, *Nationalism and Sectionalism in America, 1775–1877* [New York, 1949], p. 107).

[85] A. L. Cummings, ed., *Rural Household Inventories 1675–1775* (Boston, 1964), p. xiv.

[86] John Fiske, "Notebook of Church Matters, 1637–1675," pp. 321–24, typescript, Essex Institute, Salem, Mass.

[87] *Maine Ct. Rec.*, IV, 378–81 (1710).

fer further opportunity. In winter there is less possibility of privacy."[88]

Darkness has always provided additional opportunities for privacy at all seasons. In New England servants and other young persons disappeared into the night with their fellows, much to the dislike of the authorities. It was easy to move about unobserved in a town after dark, since street lighting was unknown until the eve of the Revolution. Inside the colonial home lighting devices were primitive, costly, and in limited supply, making mutual surveillance by individuals more difficult.[89] When a Salem woman found a strange man in her bed, she had to recognize him by his speech for lack of a light.[90] In an incident at Gloucester around 1760 only the discovery of an old lamp foiled the attempt of a married woman and her lover to use the darkness of a room as a shield for their sexual activities.[91]

Whatever the degree of crowding, it was rarely impossible to secure physical privacy within the home in a specific situation or for a particular need. Samuel Sewall of Boston wanted to thank his dying mother-in-law "for all her Labours of Love to me and mine," so he waited till "finding the room free once." When persons in a group decided to hold a private conversation, they "went aside into a Chamber," or "he . . . took me alone into another room."[92] Two men were at the widow Lake's tavern "about some private business" and eventually fought with three others who "came into the room and insisted upon staying in the room."[93]

Solitude could almost always be achieved when a person wanted it, especially outdoors. John Adams contrasted "such silent scenes, as riding or walking thro the Woods or sitting alone in my Chamber, or lying awake in my Bed," with "the distracting Bustle of the Town, and ceremonious Converse with Mankind."[94] It also seems likely that

[88] *St. Denis*, p. 209. Husking time had a similar reputation in New England; see Edward Ward, *Trip to New England*, p. 55 (1699). Cotton Mather denounced "the Rudeness and Lewdness of our Husking Times" in *A Good Evening for the Best of Days* (Boston, 1708), p. 15; see also Parkman, "Diary," AAS, *Proc.*, LXXII (1962), 399.

[89] A Winthrop in Boston once had to write to New London for candles (Wait to Fitz-John Winthrop, Feb. 18, 1678, Winthrop Papers, VII, 23).

[90] *Essex Rec.*, VIII, 103 (1681). For the difficulty of even reading on dark days, see *ibid.*, V, 14–15 (1672).

[91] Divorce, Luskin v. Luskin, 1761, Court Files Suffolk, no. 129735, p. 48.

[92] Sewall, *Diary*, MHS, *Coll.*, 5th ser., V, 408; the other examples occur in testimony in a Massachusetts divorce case, Luskin v. Luskin, 1761, Court Files Suffolk, no. 129735, p. 44.

[93] *Essex Rec.*, VII, 424 (1680).

[94] *Diary*, I, 85.

the colonists resorted to psychological mechanisms for achieving aloneness, such as dreaming or prolonged silence, when a situation demanded it. Isolation is not an essential prerequisite to a sense of privacy.

When Thomas Dudley, later governor of Massachusetts, wrote to the Countess of Lincoln in 1631, he depicted a scene which was probably not unusual in the first homes of early America. He wanted to describe, "our present condition, and what hath befallen us since our arrival here; which I will do shortly, . . . and must do rudely, having yet no table, nor other room to write in than by the fireside upon my knee, in this sharp winter; to which my family must have leave to resort, though they break good manners and make me many times forget what I would say, and say what I would not."[95] The father sought privacy, but the circumstances of life in a newly settled colony could not always support this desire in the face of more pressing needs. Yet Dudley obviously wanted seclusion and expected it even under such circumstances. The lack of privacy was only a temporary phenomenon, as the infrequency of such complaints in the written records of colonial family life attests. A later colonial work on behavior provided guidelines for younger persons that emphasized the importance of respect for personal privacy. "Speak not at the Table: if thy Superiors be discoursing, meddle not with the Matter; but be silent, except thou art spoken unto." "Come not too near Two that are whispering or speaking in secret, much less may'st thou ask about what they confer."[96]

The situation in the colonial home perhaps offends our sense of essential life space, but the colonists themselves did not complain about being crowded. Most were satisfied with their lot. Our judgments are based on a contemporary situation where the home has to serve as a bastion against all kinds of external challenges to privacy and as the usual locale of social life and relaxation. The colonial home did not have to fulfill such compelling needs; the essential intimacy of the family was secure against outsiders, and its occupants had a number of alternative resources at hand to escape any crowding that existed. Certainly many families had to acclimate themselves to some crowding within the home. Yet if the colonial family hardly functioned as an island of serenity, this has rarely been an achievement

[95] *English Historical Documents: American Colonial Documents to 1776*, ed. Merrill Jensen (New York, 1955), p. 143.
[96] *The School of Good Manners* (New London, Conn., 1715; rpt. Boston, 1772), pp. 10, 18.

or even a goal of human existence. The family has infrequently been the ideal locale for the enjoyment of solitude, the most pristine form of privacy; in early America it was the outdoors that provided solitude as the ultimate release from overbearing intimacy.

SLEEPING ACCOMMODATIONS

Beds were scattered throughout the colonial house from the parlor and upstairs chambers that were primarily for sleeping to the garret that could serve as a dormitory. While parents were in the best bed in the parlor, servants and children sometimes bundled on straw pallets and animal skins before the fire. Sharing beds and bedchambers was the accepted practice. Practical necessity and the human satisfactions of sharing the warmth and protection of a small group shaped this custom. It was perhaps a heritage from earlier times when gathering into groups for periods of sleep was essential for personal safety. People did not like to sleep alone in early America. Most colonists placed other needs ahead of solitude when it came to sleeping accommodations. A woman in her late twenties, traveling across Connecticut with her father in 1770, always seemed disappointed and even frightened when another girl did not sleep with her, whether at an inn or in private homes. At an inn in Waterbury she slept in a great old chamber: "Could not fasten the door; felt afraid. Went to bed very tired. I got to sleep. Dreamed somebody was coming to bed to me. Waked up in a fright. Heard people going about in the house. The ladies had sparks, I found out, so I got to sleep again."[97]

Few recognized any invasion of their personal privacy in this custom of sharing beds, primarily because the persons sleeping together were usually husbands and wives or children in a family. There were instances where three daughters slept together, or three older men, and on several reported occasions a husband and wife with a third woman.[98] Perhaps this willingness of adults to share beds with strangers, relatives, or friends was the main difference between colonial sleeping practices and those of today. The Reverend Mr. Parkman lodged overnight in Lancaster with a fellow minister and casually noted: "Mr. Stephen Frost my Bedfellow." There was no indication

[97] Simeon E. Baldwin, ed., "A Ride across Connecticut before the Revolution," New Haven Colony Historical Society, *Papers*, IX (1918), 163–64, 166.

[98] *New Haven Town Rec.*, I, 251 (1655); *Essex Rec.*, III, 413 (1667); *Maine Ct. Rec.*, II, 92 (1660); Conn. Arch., Crimes and Misdemeanors, I, pt. 1, p. 17a; Morgan, *Puritan Family*, pp. 129–30.

that Frost was anything but a stranger to Parkman. The Reverend John Cotton of Plymouth wrote his cousin Cotton Mather "to thanke you for your late courteous entertainment in your bed."[99] Only an outsider like Francisco de Miranda, who visited the United States in 1783–84, argued with his landlord, "because notwithstanding a formal stipulation he had put another guest in my room; thank God he was not put in my bed, according to the custom of the country."[100] In public accommodations guests often slept together in the same room and sometimes in the same bed. The colonists were more concerned with the specific person one might be forced to sleep with, and the danger of children suffocating by being "accidentally over layed in the bed."[101] The day after sleeping with her mother, a young woman's main complaint was that "shee was much crowded by reason of Baldwin's coming to bed to her mother."[102] A woman who had found herself in bed with an unmarried couple evidently kept a close watch on their conduct because she later testified that: "The Bed was very Narrow on which they three were and thinks it almost if not wholly impossible that they should be guilty of that Crime without her knowledge and She observed no such thing."[103] The latter instance suggests that multiple occupancy of both beds and bedrooms did not benefit privacy but may have helped to uphold morality.

Sometimes the average colonial bedchamber might be just another crowded room, as this incident in the 1750's illustrated: "I Ann James of Boston Testify and declare that living with my brother Phinehas James . . . I frequently used to lodge in the Same Roome where the said Mrs McCarthy lay and two nights William Stone of Boston lay with Mrs McCarty in one Bead and I lay with her two Sisters Abigail and Elizabeth Floyd in another bed in the Same Room."[104] Even husbands and wives sometimes shared their bedrooms with lodgers or other members of the family.[105] Only the upper classes and married couples in colonial New England seemed to demand and enjoy some privacy in their beds and bedchambers. When one of Sewall's

[99] Parkman, "Diary," AAS, *Proc.*, LXXII (1962), 179; Thomas Prince Papers, fol. 54, Jan. 6, 1684, MHS.

[100] *Travels,* p. 126 (New London, 1784).

[101] *Essex Rec.*, VI, 368–69 (1677); *Plymouth Col. Rec.*, VI, 45.

[102] Rex v. Baldwin and Wheeler, 1718, New Haven Co. Ct. Files, 1700–1719, N-Z, bundle Rex-S.

[103] Rex v. Stone and Willard, 1728, *ibid.*, 1720–29, L-Y, bundle R-Rex.

[104] Court Files Suffolk, no. 129734, p. 33.

[105] See the divorce case of Thomas Hammet v. Abigail Hammet, 1767, *ibid.*, no. 129747, pp. 90–91.

children had nightmares, she did not burst into her parent's room but knocked and was duly admitted. Sewall transacted important business in his bedchamber and also married a couple there when they "desired Privacy all that might be."[106] In larger homes private bedchambers were also more readily available.

Married couples normally hung curtains around their bed in order to obtain some privacy even in a well-occupied room. The inventories of estates suggest that at least the best bed in the average house was curtained to provide privacy and warmth and to defend "the breast from noxious night vapours."[107] In many cases the curtains hung from the exposed timbers overhead.[108] Since the parent's bed was usually the only one curtained, a concern over privacy, especially for sexual relations, obviously determined the practice. In their curtained beds parents enjoyed some privacy from children and even other adults sleeping in the same room.

The custom of bundling at least in part embodied a search for privacy by young persons in a crowded home.[109] A courting couple was permitted to share a bed for the night, provided they took such measures as remaining fully clothed or keeping a board between them. The origins and extent of the practice remain shrouded in obscurity.[110] The isolation of country life, the couple's desire for privacy, the infrequency of leisure, the costliness of light and heat, and the scarcity of beds help to explain its existence. There have been suggestions that bundling was almost a universal custom among the lower and middling classes between 1750 and 1780. In the draft of an essay for a newspaper in 1761, John Adams argued that young courting couples should get to know each other and told his prospective audience of young ladies that bundling provided some privacy for this purpose. "You must therefore associate yourselves in some good Degree, and under certain Guards and Restraints, even privately with

---

[106] *Diary,* MHS, *Coll.,* 5th ser., VI, 404, 175, V, 222.

[107] Finlay, *Journal,* p. 5 (1773).

[108] Abbott L. Cummings to the author, March 18, 1968. Most of the inventories in Cummings, ed., *Rural Household Inventories,* list curtains for at least one bed.

[109] The relevant volumes on bundling are Dana Doten, *The Art of Bundling* (New York, 1938), and H. R. Stiles, *Bundling: Its Origin, Progress, and Decline in America* (Albany, 1871).

[110] For comments by contemporaries on bundling, see a letter written from London to New Haven in 1764, "The Ingersoll Letters," New Haven Col. Hist. Soc., *Papers,* IX (1918), 292–93; in the 1780's, see the Reverend Samuel Peters, *General History of Connecticut* (2d ed., London, 1782; rpt. New York, 1877), pp. 224–29, and Chastellux, *Travels,* p. 288.

young fellows. And, tho Discretion must be used, and Caution, yet on considering the whole of the Arguments on each side, I cannot wholly disapprove of Bundling."[111]

The New England colonists did not associate the sharing of sleeping accommodations with lack of privacy. Circumstances made it a normal custom for the majority. Philippe Ariès has noted that in seventeenth-century Europe "a real propaganda campaign was launched to try to eradicate the age-old habit of sleeping several to a bed," prompted by a growing emphasis on modesty.[112] There is no evidence of such a campaign in New England. There are only indications that at least in the eighteenth century many individuals considered both a room and a bed to themselves as highly desirable. In 1774 a gentleman in Falmouth offered John Adams accommodations on his next visit: "I said I was very much obliged to him, but I was very well accommodated where I lodged. I had a clean Bed and a very neat House, a Chamber to myself, and every thing I wanted."[113] Although Adams was a particularly sensitive individual, his evident desire for solitude in sleeping arrangements may have been representative of a growing feeling among the populace. It made sense that such attitudes would first emerge in the context of public accommodations.

SEXUAL PRIVACY

Such physical factors as the crowding of beds and bedchambers and the lack of insulation in the home inevitably challenged the availability of sexual privacy for husband and wife.[114] Sometimes intimate acts did not remain hidden from the notice of others in the household, as when lodgers heard a wife refuse to have sexual relations or a woman knew a wife had misbehaved with an unmarried male because "shee heard the noise of the Shakeing of the bed" in the cham-

[111] *Diary*, I, 196.

[112] *Centuries of Childhood: A Social History of Family Life*, tr. Robert Baldick (New York, 1962), p. 116.

[113] J. Adams to Abigail Adams, July 9, 1774, *Adams Family Correspondence*, ed. L. H. Butterfield *et al.* (Cambridge, Mass., 1963), I, 134; When making plans to go to Congress in the fall of 1783, Jefferson requested Madison to arrange suitable lodgings for him: "A room to myself, if it be but a barrack, is indispensable" (*The Papers of Thomas Jefferson*, ed. Julian P. Boyd *et al.*, [Princeton, N.J., 1950–], VI, 336).

[114] Almost all societies, primitive and modern, have sought privacy for sexual relations (see Westin, *Privacy and Freedom*, pp. 14–15).

ber above her room.[115] Presumably married couples learned to accommodate themselves to these limitations on their privacy and took
preventive measures. They expected privacy for sexual relations and
could achieve it more successfully than unmarried persons. Indeed
a New England court indicted one husband in 1640 for inhumane
treatment of his wife, because "he could not keepe from boyes and
servantes, secrete passages betwixt him and his wife about the mary-
age bedd."[116] Parents could arrange their sex life so that the sleep of
others and darkness provided them with privacy.

Yet the number of reported instances of persons having intercourse
in the presence of others raises some doubts about colonial concern
for privacy in sexual relations, or at least makes plain an attitude
toward sexuality which is at variance with the Victorian outlook on
sex as something to be hidden. A widow admitted having sexual relations with a married neighbor one evening while her children were
in bed in the same room. Two traveling ministers woke one morning
"with the Silent Sight of a Young Fellow in the room getting up from
his Girl in the t'other Bed in the Same Room." A Bostonian visited a
married woman two nights, while three girls slept in another bed.[117]
A fisherman personally undressed his wife and prostituted her to a
fellow mariner. Around 1700 a mother in New London County forced
her daughter to go to bed with her stepfather, and as the girl told the
court, "my mother held me by the hand whilst my father did abuse
me and had his will of me."[118] One Mrs. Ingersoll had sexual relations
with a man while they were in the same room with Mr. and Mrs.
Malegen of Newburyport. In Connecticut a female lodger was sleeping with the woman of that house when an undressed male entered
the bed.[119]

Such diverse evidence introduces an important distinction concerning sexual privacy. Most of these illustrations involved an extramari-

[115] *New Haven Col. Rec.*, 1653–1665, p. 211 (1657); Rex v. Baldwin and
Wheeler, 1718, New Haven Co. Ct. Files, 1700–1719, N-Z, bundle Rex-S.

[116] *Winthrop Papers*, IV, 260.

[117] For the widow's case, see Conn. Arch., Crimes and Misdemeanors, I, pt. 1,
p. 141a (1683); the ministers are in Parkman, "Diary," AAS, *Proc.*, LXXII
(1962), 163; for the Bostonian, see divorce, McCarthy v. McCarthy, 1757,
Court Files Suffolk, no. 129734, p. 33.

[118] Suffolk Co. Gen. Sess., 1754–58, Dec. 3, 1756; Rex v. Furlong and Dunn,
Conn. Arch., Crimes and Misdemeanors, I, pt. 2, p. 325a.

[119] Divorce, B. Ingersoll v. Lydia Ingersoll, 1765, Court Files Suffolk, no.
129741, p. 61; Crane's case, 1772, in *The Superior Court Diary of William
Samuel Johnson, 1772–1773*, ed. John T. Farrell (Washington, D.C., 1942),
p. 17.

tal, premarital, or aberrant, rather than a conjugal, relationship. Such illicit sexual activities often occur with relative lack of privacy, since passion or perversity does not always allow for much planning. In Boston around 1770 a mariner arranged for a thirteen-year-old girl to sleep with his wife while he was away, which did not discourage one Serjeant Hatton, who joined them on four successive nights. The wife bribed the girl to tell nobody what she saw.[120] In a more normal episode the presence of another person did hinder an unmarried couple. A New Haven servant admitted an affair with a fellow servant: "The last time he had the use of her body, was befor Martha the other mayd came to the house, and not since, but withall confessed that about a moneth agoe he went into the chamber . . . but could doe nothing, the other mayd being in Bedd with her."[121]

Unmarried couples sought sexual privacy in the same places the other colonists turned to whenever they wanted to be alone. Many such couples first tried to find privacy within a house. A New Haven court was unable to convict Patrick Morran of fornication but warned him "to be more wary for the future, of being in privacy with such persons as those" in a house. A man and woman left a wedding celebration and went "into a little house that stood alone from the other house, where there was no light."[122] When Obadiah Bridges visited Lidia Browne at the home of her father-in-law, "she went into another room followed by Bridges who shut the door and pulled in the latch." Although the girl claimed they had sexual relations, the court only convicted Bridges of lascivious carriage, because "the room in which they were was not a private one."[123] The authorities obviously believed privacy was essential for sexual relations.

When privacy for sexual activity was unavailable within a home, the next best refuge was a barn. In the 1760's a Plymouth widow was accused of often using Thomas Holland's barn for debauchery. She had even gone there one night while her husband lay at death's door. Two years later a married woman from Marshfield was convicted of lying in a barn with a "Gentleman."[124] Persons also found privacy in the fields and woods. Governor Winthrop told of the young woman,

[120] Divorce, William Chambers v. Sussanna Chambers, 1770, Court Files Suffolk, no. 129753, p. 136.

[121] *New Haven Town Rec.*, I, 497–98.

[122] *New Haven Town Rec.*, II, 204 (1667); *Essex Rec.*, II, 420 (1662).

[123] *Essex Rec.*, III, 398, 448 (1667).

[124] Plymouth County General Sessions of the Peace, 1760–82, p. 59 (1763), p. 149 (1765), Court House, Plymouth; see also, for example, fornication admissions in *Essex Rec.*, II, 372–73 (1714), and New Haven Co. Ct. Rec., III, 38.

married to an older man, who attended a drinking party one night. Late in the evening "Britton and the woman were seen upon the ground together, a little from the house."[125] In 1698 two young Maine servants watched a couple making love "among the mosterd topes and other wedes" and then under a tree.[126] Some unwed women from New Haven in the early eighteenth century admitted being put in the condition of motherhood between the town of Wallingford and the home of Daniel Potter. Even within the largest city, the outdoors seemed to afford privacy; in 1702 two Bostonians were convicted of "unlawful Copulation and fornication . . . in the afternoon . . . at the bottom of the Common or Training field in Boston."[127]

This desire for privacy in sexual matters was allied with attitudes favoring modesty in dress, bathing, and the like. Many colonists had strict standards of modesty both in public and private. When Sewall woke up and found his bedroom full of smoke, he slipped on his clothes, "except Stockings," before checking on the extent of the fire.[128] The shocked reaction of the Puritans to the Quaker women who wandered around naked is well known. The prevailing standards were well illustrated by a Salem court that admonished a married woman for dressing while several men were in the room, as well as sitting by the "pondside when her sons and other men were swimming and washing themselves and some of the men who were more modest than the rest were forced to creep up into the bushes and others put on their shirts in the water, letting them fall down by degrees as they came out."[129] Boston had to deal with the subject of modesty in swimming and washing in 1757, when "great Complaint" was "made of many Persons Washing themselves in Publick and frequented Places to the Great Reproach of Modesty and good Manners." The town meeting "voted and Ordered that no Person whosoever above the Age of Twelve Years, shall in less than an Hour after Sun-set undress themselves and go into Water within ten Rods of any Dwelling House in this Town, at that time Inhabited, nor shall any Person being in the Water, swim to such parts of the Town, as to be plainly within Sight of any Dwelling House."[130] Since Boston re-

---

[125] Winthrop, *Journal*, II, 161–62 (1644). Another couple admitted to fornication "in the wood yard" of a house in 1668 (*New Haven Town Rec.*, II, 228).

[126] *Maine Ct. Rec.*, IV, 111; see also *Mass. Assistants Rec.*, II, 49 (1634); New London County Court Records, III (1670–81), 115, 114 (1678), CSL.

[127] New Haven Co. Ct. Rec., II, 39 (1700), III, 89 (1718); Suffolk Co. Gen. Sess., 1702–12, p. 3.

[128] *Diary*, MHS, *Coll.*, 5th ser., VI, 257–59 (1709).

[129] *Essex Rec.*, V, 254 (1674).

[130] *Boston Town Rec.*, XIV, 318.

flected the mores of an urban population, the rest of New England held at least as strict views about modesty.

In the process of achieving personal privacy within the colonial household, an individual had to circumvent a host of problems, especially those associated with crowding. Life within the family provided at best a mixed setting for the enjoyment of physical solitude on an individual basis. In many areas of internal family life general conditions for the enjoyment of solitude and intimacy changed but little in the seventeenth and eighteenth centuries. Households were consistently large, many homes continued to shelter servants and lodgers, and the characteristics of daily existence in an agricultural society remained stable. The sharing of homes by several families was a serious problem for privacy in some instances.

Concern for personal and family privacy was apparent within the home, although certain determining preconditions for its enjoyment remained a stumbling block. A search for privacy, especially in the form of solitude, may have necessitated leaving the home. Absolute physical privacy was always available outdoors and during periods of darkness. Occasionally the colonists may have had to use psychological, rather than physical, means of withdrawal in order to be alone. There are precedents for this form of escape in other societies, past and present, "where communal life makes solitude or intimacy impossible within the living areas."[131] Privacy is so important at regular intervals that the human psyche can make adjustments to, or find outlets from, the most trying circumstances. At the same time life within the home normally provided an acceptable level of intimacy. It ensured social life to alleviate the burden of loneliness and isolation in colonial society. The individualistic and often solitary nature of many activities during the long working days made the colonists much more eager to seek society than solitude in the evening. Moreover, the colonists were accustomed to the communal climate of their domestic life.

Changes in the impact of the Puritan movement on society affected attitudes toward privacy within the family rather than the physical conditions for its enjoyment. The Puritan concept of the family encouraged mutual surveillance and the imposition of strict discipline in the interests of good behavior. The enactment of public laws on such matters made parents even more aware of these duties. As the impact of Puritan ideology on the general populace waned in the

---

[131] Westin, *Privacy and Freedom*, p. 12.

latter half of the seventeenth century, parents lost this stimulation to duty, and their subordinates became less inclined to accept restrictive tenets. With such a change in attitude, the social climate became much more receptive to demands for, and expectations of, personal privacy.

In many areas of colonial family life, social changes and changes in Puritanism and the Puritan movement had little or no impact. Only industrialization would eventually alter the patterns of life in agricultural and somewhat traditional societies that had endured for many centuries. The normal availability of greater privacy within the family awaited much higher standards of living, the reduction of family size, central heating, labor-saving devices that did away with domestic servants, and many other developments and appurtenances of modernized societies. For anyone alive in late-twentieth-century America, the changes in family life affecting the availability of privacy are readily apparent. Unlike the colonists, our problems with crowding occur in the community, so that we want our homes to be uncrowded havens.

3. The Neighborhood and Community

V ISITORS to the home as well as neighbors and residents of the local community challenged the intimacy of the family and the privacy of its individual members. Did surveillance and lack of anonymity on the local scene diminish the availability of solitude and intimacy for family members? Of first importance here is the conception that the residents of the New England colonies had of their home in relationship to the external world.

"A MAN'S HOUSE IS HIS CASTLE"

The New England colonist considered his home as a haven for solitude and intimacy and as a barrier against intrusion by uninvited outsiders. The proverb "a man's house is his castle"[1] epitomizes the immunity erected around a colonial dwelling by both tradition and the common law. This immunity had its origins not in English jurisprudence but in ancient times, biblical literature, and Roman law. Long before the settlement of America the home had come to be envisioned as a place for shelter and privacy. In a case before the court of King's Bench in 1605 Sir Edward Coke interpreted the meaning of this maxim:

1. That the house of every one is to him as his Castle and Fortress, as well for his Defence against Injury and Violence, as for his Repose. . . .
2. It was resolved, That it is not lawful for the Sheriff . . . to break the Defendant's House, to execute any Process. For thence would follow great Inconven. that Men as well in the Night as in the Day should have their Houses (which are their Castles) broke . . . and so Men would not be in Safety or Quiet in their own Houses.[2]

Coke's reference to the value of a retreat for "Repose" and "Quiet" was central to the expectation of privacy in the home.

The maxim "a man's house is his castle" represented the basic co-

[1] John Clarke, *Paroemiologia anglo-Latina . . . Or Proverbs English and Latin* (London, 1639), p. 101. On the background of the maxim, see Nelson B. Lasson, *The History and Development of the Fourth Amendment to the United States Constitution* (Baltimore, 1937), esp. pp. 13–15, 34–35.

[2] *Reports*, pt. 5, "Semayne's Case."

lonial concept of the status of the home. Government, the law, and religious leaders qualified this view somewhat in the early years; yet the phrase represented the expectations of ordinary inhabitants. Rhode Island explicitly recognized the maxim. Its Code of 1647 forbade "forcible Entry and Detainer," except that an officer of the law could break open a house under stringent conditions, "but not in the execution of a process upon the body or goods of any man at the suitt of any subject; for a man's house is to himselfe, his family and goods, as a castle."[3] At Providence in 1663 a Rhode Island constable encountered this reception: "When I was goeing into the howse ther Stoode three with ther axes in ther hand and told me that I should not come in." The constable informed them that he had a court warrant which "Requiered them in the kinges name to obay. Ther answer was that the king they owned and the Court they owned but they would not come out: but weare Resoulfed to knocke Downe any man that should pry in upon them for ther howse was ther Castle and this was the mine [mind] of one and all."[4] If such sentiments formed part of the ready vocabulary of Rhode Islanders in 1663, it surely represented a common attitude toward the home.

The inhabitants of Massachusetts and Connecticut similarly asserted their right to privacy in the home. In Massachusetts the point was made indirectly in 1659 as part of an argument justifying acts against the Quakers. The Quakers intruding into the colony were compared to persons who "should presume to enter into another mans house and habitation" without authorization. A man who owned his own house "would count it unreasonably injurious that another who had no authoritie thereto should intrude and enter into his house without his, the ounors, consent."[5] He could justly slay another who so acted. In another instance some men allegedly sought to intervene on behalf of an abused wife. The husband told one intruder "that he was a meddling knave and bade him go home and order his own wife"; since he considered himself "Lord Paramount in his owne house hee might doe or say what hee would and none should controule him."[6] When the Massachusetts Excise Bill of 1754 required a homeowner to inform the tax collector how much rum his

---

[3] *R.I. Rec.*, I, 168–69.

[4] *Rhode Island Court Records: Records of the Court of Trials of the Colony of Providence Plantations, 1647–1670* (Providence, 1920–22), II, 15–16, 24. These individuals were never prosecuted for resisting the constable.

[5] *Mass. Rec.*, IV, pt. 1, pp. 388–89.

[6] *Essex Rec.*, VIII, 272–73. See also *ibid.*, VII, 251 (1679), where a Salem woman ordered the tythingmen from her home; and *Maine Ct. Rec.*, V, 156–57 (1714).

household had consumed during the past year, pamphleteers denounced the requirement as a breach of the privacy of the home. "It is essential to the English Constitution, that a Man should be safe in his own House; his House is commonly called his Castle, which the Law will not permit even a Sheriff to enter into, but by his own Consent, unless in criminal cases."[7]

The court cases over writs of assistance in the 1760's provided another forum for assertions of the privileged position of the home. The writs granted customs officials the power to search a home suspected of concealing smuggled materials without obtaining a specific search warrant. As part of his defense against these general search warrants in 1761, James Otis, the able Boston lawyer, made this statement: "Now one of the most essential branches of English liberty, is the freedom of one's house. A man's house is his castle; and while he is quiet, he is as well guarded as a prince in his castle. This writ, if it should be declared legal, would totally annihilate this privilege. Custom house officers may enter our houses when they please."[8] Normally such a guarantee of privacy for the home as a retreat or sanctuary was taken for granted. When customs officers tried to search the home of Daniel Malcom, a Boston merchant, in September 1766, he swore that no one had the right to search it and held out for an entire day until the officials gave up. "I thought it was very extraordinary proceedings to break open private Dwellings, that I always understood a Man's House was his Castle, and that it could not be broke open unless for Murder, Treason, and Theft."[9] In 1772 a Report on the Rights of Colonists by a committee of twenty-one Bostonians protested the granting of such powers to the customs commissioners: "Thus our Houses, and even our Bed-Chambers, are exposed to be ransacked. . . . By this we are cut off from that domestic security which renders the Lives of the most unhappy in some measure agreeable. These Officers may under color of Law and the cloak of a general warrant, break through the sacred Rights of the *Domicil*."[10]

---

[7] *Some Observations on the Bill* (Boston, 1754), p. 2. Many other pamphlets expressed similar sentiments. For the broader story of this controversy, see Paul S. Boyer, "Borrowed Rhetoric: The Massachusetts Excise Controversy of 1754," *WMQ*, 3d. ser., XXI (1964), 328–51.

[8] *Legal Papers of John Adams*, II, 142. For Adams's original notes on the trial, see *ibid.*, II, 125.

[9] MHS, *Proc.*, LVIII (1924–25), 44; also p. 46. Malcom's opinion found support in a contemporary guidebook for officials; see *The County and Town Officer* (Boston, 1768), p. 146.

[10] Josiah Quincy, Jr., *Reports of Cases Argued and Adjudged in the Superior*

In an address to a jury in 1774 on behalf of a Maine merchant whose house had been attacked by a mob in 1766, John Adams emphasized "the Indignity offered to the Plaintiff. The Insult and Affront." He declared:

> An Englishmans dwelling House is his Castle. The Law has erected a Fortification round it . . . every Member of Society has entered into a solemn Covenant with every other that he shall enjoy in his own dwelling House as compleat a security, safety and Peace and Tranquility as if it was surrounded with Walls of Brass, with Ramparts and Palisadoes and defended with a Garrison and Artillery. . . . Every English[man] values himself exceedingly, he takes a Pride and he glories justly in that strong Protection, that sweet Security, that delightful Tranquillity which the Laws have thus secured to him in his own House, especially in the Night.[11]

The equation of such an attack on the home with an affront to human dignity approximated one of the traditional bases on which the desire for privacy has been founded. A New England resident believed he had a right to privacy from the outside world within his home and the privilege of repelling anyone who challenged that right.

VISITORS

Secure in the conception of his home as a castle, the colonist still had to protect his bastion of privacy against certain challengers. Strict colonial laws against breaking and entering houses reflected the notion of the home as an asylum for the enjoyment of privacy.[12] The Rhode Island Code of 1647 warned that burglars would be seriously punished for "taking or doing something or nothing."[13] The act of entering a dwelling house at night was sufficient cause for serious punishment. Whippings, brandings, death, banishment, the stocks, and heavy fines were the lot of individuals who entered colonial homes uninvited. The connection between a strong sense of private property and privacy was apparent.

Indians were a special problem in the early days. Laws stated what days they could come to English houses, and how they were

---

Court of Judicature of the Province of Massachusetts Bay, between 1761 and 1772 (Boston, 1865), p. 467.

[11] *Legal Papers of John Adams*, I, 137–38.

[12] Persons who simply disturbed the peace and quiet around homes could also be prosecuted. See *New Haven Town Rec.*, II, 64–65; *Essex Rec.*, VII, 103 (1678), 181–82 (1679); *Mass. Acts and Res.*, II, 24–25 (1715).

[13] *R.I. Rec.*, I, 166–67.

to behave. The Indians were told to first "knocke att the dore, and after leave given, to come in, (and not otherwise;)."[14] One did not have to teach such elements of respect for the privacy of homes to white persons, whose culture inbred this notion, but the Indian had to be taught this unfamiliar practice.

Eavesdroppers and Peeping Toms also threatened the privacy of a home. Such offenders were not often prosecuted, since the matter could be handled in a more practical and perhaps more satisfying manner by the person who discovered the culprit. Yet a Salem servant was whipped in 1637 "for eavesdropping, a common liar and running away." When Thomas Silver presented Mrs. Mary Roffe for disturbing her Newbury neighbors, a friend of Mary's, who just happened to be the town's representative on the county's grand jury, visited Silver to speak in favor of the woman and "threatened to present deponent as an eavesdropper for reporting such a thing of her." Silver protested that "he reported nothing but what he heard in his own house."[15] In 1698 Connecticut established a system enabling justices of the peace to bond persons who habitually disturbed the quiet of the King's subjects. Individuals who "evesdrop mens houses" were included under the law; the provision was continued in the eighteenth-century legal codes.[16] Peeping Toms were similarly held up to ignominy at law. A New Haven man won a slander and defamation suit against a fellow citizen who had accused him of coming "in the night to peep in at his window."[17] John Severns of Salisbury entered a complaint against two young men in 1680, "for hovering about his house, peeping in at the window." Although their intention was probably to entice his servants out of the house, Severn's ideas about privacy obviously did not include such liberties.[18]

Welcome visitors also affected the privacy of the family. Sociability was an accepted condition of life in colonial New England; Governor John Winthrop spoke of "the rule of hospitality."[19] Visiting was a continual pastime in slow-paced colonial society, and diaries were filled with notes of the exchange of visits. Visitors ranged from neighbors and others in the community to relatives and complete strangers. Since they were admitted to the bosom of the family, visitors might

[14] *Mass. Rec.*, III, 6 (1644).

[15] *Essex Rec.*, I, 7, III, 90 (1663).

[16] *Conn. Rec.*, IV, 236–37; *Laws Conn.*, 1702, p. 91; *ibid.*, 1750, p. 185; *ibid.*, 1784, p. 189. For the Maine attitude, see *Maine Ct. Rec.*, III, 64.

[17] New Haven Co. Ct. Rec., I, 114 (1679).

[18] *Essex Rec.*, VIII, 12, 23.

[19] *Winthrop Papers*, III, 424.

witness some intimate activities. Such persons as Samuel Sewall, the prominent public servant, engaged in a constant round of visitations. In Westborough the minister Parkman complained that "company are here every Day, and not a few which is a great Interruption to me." In Boston John Andrews, a merchant, boasted of his wife's "friends which are not a few, I do assure you, as *Lord North* has scarcely a greater Levee than she, especially in pleasant weather; its quite common for her to have from six to ten visitors of a forenoon."[20]

The social pressures to provide hospitality to strangers were perhaps greater in the seventeenth century, or at least until a newly settled area lost some of its roughness, inns were built, and life became more formalized. The front door was always open in a newly settled region or on scattered farms, because of the absence of other accommodations for the traveler and the residents' passion to see a visitor.

In the eighteenth century, some colonists seem to have begun to limit their hospitality, particularly in the settled parts of the country, primarily by closing their homes to strangers. This was especially true among the upper classes. Their homes had never been so open, in part because a stranger without a letter of introduction would approach a less imposing home. In addition, visiting among the "better sort" was always formalized along lines that did not include sudden incursions on their privacy. John Andrews illustrated this in 1772, when he urged a visiting Englishman "to be sociable and call upon us without ceremony."[21] Andrews pointed out a peculiarity of the family in New Boston who invited fifteen British officers to dinner in 1774, "a family noted for their hospitality and kindness to strangers, in admitting *all* comers to their *b–d and board*."[22] In 1754 Henry Flynt, a Harvard tutor, was traveling to New Hampshire and had intended to dine with Parson Ward Cotton of Old Hampton. He met the parson leaving for a private dinner engagement. Flynt decided to visit a public house, but Cotton insisted Flynt accompany him: "Mr. Flynt agreed to go, provided Parson Cotton would pass on before us, [and] make the necessary explanation to show that we were not *interlopers*."[23] Oliver Noyes of South Carolina wrote to David

[20] Parkman, "Diary," AAS, *Proc.*, LXXVI (1966), 88 (1754); see also p. 177 (1755). Andrews, Boston, to William Barrell, Philadelphia, April 14, 1774, Andrews-Eliot Papers, 1772–1811, p. 30, MHS.

[21] Related in a letter to Barrell, Philadelphia, Aug. 13, 1772, Andrews-Eliot Papers, p. 10.

[22] Andrews, Boston, to Barrell, Philadelphia, Aug. 1, 1774, *ibid.*, p. 35.

[23] "Travel Journal of David Sewall," MHS, *Proc.*, 1st ser., XVI (1878), 7.

Jeffries about a local merchant who was to spend a few days in Boston: "I would have you wait on him and if convenient ask him to your House, I know my Brother so well that I think you will not imagine I amm too intruding."[24]

The many taverns and coffeehouses in operation by the eighteenth century made it less necessary for local residents and travelers, especially men, to visit in homes, which were reserved for entertaining relatives and dinner guests. Andrews made this comment about a highly respected young visitor: "This evening being the last he spends in town, shall pass with him at the coffee house."[25] Ordinary inhabitants may rarely have had visitors in their homes, other than relatives and females who visited the wife during the day. Their social life revolved much more around the public house.

Visitors encountered a variety of situations affecting their own privacy. Sleeping accommodations for overnight guests were limited; only the wealthy could afford guest rooms. Some visitors also had to go to great lengths to have private conversations. When Mrs. Denison visited Sewall to discuss their proposed marriage, "she desired that no body should know of her being here" and would not permit any of Sewall's servants to stay in the room while they spoke.[26]

Doors were often left unlocked, and visitors sometimes entered homes without knocking. Horace Miner observed similar informality in the twentieth-century Quebec agricultural community of St. Denis, where "during the day the doors of all houses remain open, and it is customary to enter even a strange house without knocking."[27] Such customs sometimes led to embarrassing intrusions upon the residents' privacy, unless a drawbolt was thrown from the inside to prevent access. In New England a seventeen-year-old girl deposed "that sometime in the summer last year, as she came near Thomas Woodbery's house, she heard Hana Gray laughing, and going in quick without knocking, the door being open, *she being a neighbor,* saw said Hana and Andrew Davis together," engaged in "lascivious carriages."[28] In Sutton, Massachusetts, in 1760 George Gould went to the home of Edward Holman "and knockt at the door, but no body coming, he pushed the door open," much to the surprise of Mrs.

[24] Noyes, Charlestown, to his step-brother, Jeffries, Boston, Jeffries Family Papers, XIII, 31, MHS.

[25] Andrews to William Barrell, Feb. 18, 1774, Andrews-Eliot Papers, p. 29.

[26] *Diary,* MHS, *Coll.,* 5th ser., VII, 206–7 (1718).

[27] *St. Denis,* p. 41; see also Albert Blumenthal, *Small Town Stuff* (Chicago, 1932), p. 127.

[28] *Essex Rec.,* V, 291 (1674).

Holman and her lover, who were just getting out of bed.[29] The visibility of the bed from the front door provides a vivid depiction of the layout of this husbandman's home.

Other visitors demonstrated a lack of respect for the privacy of their hosts once they were in the house. Sarah Powell and Leonard Miller visited the home of John Crosley, a Boston ropemaker, in 1771. Mrs. Crosley and Miller "went up Chamber and I [Sarah Powell] went up to see what they were about and Plainly saw said Miller and Mrs. Crosley together on the bed In the Act of Adultery. This I saw through a Large Crack in the door, the door being locked."[30] She gave the court a graphic description of the proceedings.

Most visitors, however, presumably were less curious. At any rate, although one senses no hesitation in turning away uninvited persons, most guests were relatives, friends, or neighbors who were warmly welcomed into the intimacy of the family. The joys of visiting balanced off a temporary enlargement of the sphere of family intimacy. The traditional stimulations to best behavior for visitors undoubtedly kept many things private.

NEIGHBORS

In the immediate environs of a colonial home, both the family and its individual members met a direct challenge to their privacy. New Englanders were well aware that a neighborhood had an intimate and independent existence, where many matters became common knowledge that were hidden from the townspeople as a whole.[31] The surveillance powers of neighbors were indisputable. A strange horse could arouse curiosity: "Goody Hardy deposed: I saw mr Pester his hos unfastened betweene 8 and 9 in the morning and he seemed to me as if he had Laine all night ther."[32] A more cautious man came to visit a widow and instructed her son to "put his horse out of sight."[33]

---

[29] Massachusetts Divorces, 1760–86, pp. 17–18, SCCH; see a similar occurrence in *Plymouth Col. Rec.*, V, 83 (1672).

[30] Divorce, John Crosley v. Jane C. Crosley, 1771, Court Files Suffolk, no. 129763, p. 27.

[31] See Parkman, "Diary," AAS, *Proc.*, LXXVI (1966), 126 (1754), LXXIV (1964), 46 (1749).

[32] *Essex Rec.*, I, 34–35; see also *ibid.*, V, 143 (1673).

[33] *Ibid.*, VIII, 262 (1682); for other cases of surveillance by neighbors, see *ibid.*, 345 (1682); Sewall, *Diary*, MHS, *Coll.*, 5th ser., VII, 186 (1718); divorce, Luskin v. Luskin, 1761, Court Files Suffolk, no. 129735, p. 46; Holman v. Holman, 1763, Mass. Divorces, 1760–86, pp. 18–19.

If neighbors could not be seen, they could still be heard. This was especially true in the centers of large towns where the houses were relatively close together. In more rural areas the environment was quiet and sounds traveled unhindered for short distances. One Essex County man accused his wife of "unchristian and inhuman carriage to me when at any Tyme I am in the howse with her; wch christian modesty forbids me to speake of; although it be not hid from my neighbors; who are able to give full evidence for me."[34] Since the courts stepped in when the noise became too great, "disturbance of the neighborhood" was a constant source of presentments.[35] Often the offending individuals were dismissed with only an admonition or a small fine, but a point in favor of privacy, a claim to peace and quiet, had been made.

Some neighbors went beyond the customary relationships and actively interfered in the private affairs of their friends. Only a few did so by invitation; most were motivated by unbridled curiosity, the promptings of religious obligation, or both.[36] In Ipswich around 1750 Francis Burnam returned from sea and received from a fellow townsman this tale of his wife's recent activities:

John Cairns of said Ipswich saw my said Wife in the open fields in a very Indecent manner with a Stranger. . . . Upon which sight he was Suspicious that they Intended to be Naught together he watched them to see what they would do: and seeing them Repair to a Private Place in her fathers field in said Ipswich he Past on towards them to see what they were about and coming near he saw a man coming . . . and Expecting the man he saw a coming would Surprise them He made a stop.[37]

Cairns later accosted this latter individual, who turned out to be a deacon of the Ipswich church. The deacon resisted his inquiry for a few minutes and then admitted that the couple had been engaged in adultery. Cairns was presumably following the dictates of his conscience in trying to prevent sin; how much curiosity also prompted him would be difficult to calculate.

A strong sense of moral duty did play a role in such cases and remained an ingredient of New England society, as a result of the ef-

[34] See *Essex Rec.*, VI, 149 (1676), VII, 381–82 (1680), 418 (1680).

[35] See, for example, *ibid.*, I, 156 (1649), 323 (1653); *Maine Ct. Rec.*, II, 197 (1670); *Suffolk Rec.*, p. 183 (1672), p. 632 (1675), p. 781 (1677); Suffolk Co. Gen. Sess., 1743–49, Feb. 6, 1749, SCCH; *ibid.*, 1764–68, July 29, 1766.

[36] In certain instances husbands and wives called in neighbors to arbitrate their differences. See Fairfield, 1665, Conn. Arch., Crimes and Misdemeanors, I, pt. 1, p. 18a; *Essex Rec.*, IV, 90 (1669).

[37] Divorce, Francis Burnam v. Sarah Burnam, 1752, Mass. Arch., IX, 366, 367–69.

forts of a Puritan minority and despite the gradual diminution of their zealousness. In 1710 Cotton Mather recommended that "if any in the neighbourhood, are taking to bad courses, lovingly and faithfully admonish them." In the mid-eighteenth century the Reverend Andrew Eliot of Boston still admonished his flock to be "faithful Monitors" of their neighbors "when they have done amiss."[39] One can question the reception accorded such appeals in the eighteenth century, although in Massachusetts in 1761 Nathaniel Haskell justified interference in his neighbor's affairs strictly on religious grounds. He had heard William Haskell and Mrs. Tabitha Luskin planned to elope but remained skeptical until he saw Tabitha hide a bundle of clothes in the fields. Haskell took them home but then had to face the wrath of William: "He soon in an Abrupt and Angry Manner began with me, Saith he you Concern Your Self about that which is none of your business, You had better Lett her Alone and not try to Hinder her. I Replyed I ought not to Suffer Sin in My Fellow Creature or Neighbour. He told me I had better go Home about my business and Lett her alone."[39] The confrontation between the two Haskells aptly illustrated the prevailing tension between a nascent secularism and the vestiges of Puritan moralism. A deeply held conviction "not to Suffer Sin in My Fellow Creature or Neighbour" could play havoc with the privacy of anyone living near such an individual. Puritanism and the Puritan movement regularly motivated a few persons to interfere in the private lives of others.

Even when an invasion of privacy was accidental, some zealous colonists reacted not with embarrassment but with a display of vigorous moralism. At an inn in Oxford, Connecticut, in 1732 William Brown entered a chamber suddenly and surprised Nicholas Blancher and Mrs. Dorothy Cross "on the bed in an unseemly manner." Instead of retiring from the room in haste, Brown remained to denounce Blancher. A decade later two ministers awoke in an inn one morning to find a young man leaving a girl's bed in the same room: "Astonishing Boldness and Impudence! nor could we let the Girl go off without a brief Lecture."[40]

[38] Mather, *Bonifacius: An Essay upon the Good* (Boston, 1710), ed. David Levin (Cambridge, Mass., 1966), p. 60. Eliot, *An Evil and Adulterous Generation* (Boston, 1753), p. 19; see also *Maine Ct. Rec.*, II, 42–43 (1655), where a court approved the efforts made by neighbors to prevent sin in Mrs. Mary Clay.

[39] Divorce, Luskin v. Luskin, 1761, Court Files Suffolk, no. 129735, p. 45. There is no evidence in the testimony that William and Nathaniel Haskell were related.

[40] Conn. Arch., Crimes and Misdemeanors, IV, doc. 347; Parkman, "Diary," AAS, *Proc.*, LXXII (1962), 163 (1744).

Religion might prompt occasional interference in the privacy of others, but it could also support an attempt not to reveal confidential information. When two women were called as witnesses in 1664, they assured the Ipswich court:

That they did not desire to testify, but what had brought them forth was the busy prattling of some other, probably the one whom they had taken along with them to advise a young woman, whose simple and foolish carriages and words, having heard of, they desired to advise better. This had come to the ears of Daniel Black, who had them summoned as witnesses. They desired to be excused from testifying because what was told them was a private confession which they had never to that day divulged. And the woman had never offended since that time but had lived gravely and soberly.[41]

This case illustrates the delicate relationship to privacy of an undertaking to advise another person, a relationship recognized in part by the decision of the court to receive a brief version of their testimony in summary form and not to call them formally as witnesses.[42]

On at least one occasion a family formally protested the excessive zeal of some neighbors in protecting collective morality. Some Salem residents presented Elizabeth Woodbery for striking a maid of the Hubbards. But Mr. Hubbard delivered a stinging defense of Mrs. Woodbery before the court:

Wee coulde have wished that the rules of charity had been attended herein Especially seeing our neighbours were not ignorant where we dwelt, and might have truely Understood the right of the business had they pleased to have spoken with us which had doubtlesse prevented trouble to the grand-juror, and sinn in others. . . . I wish our people as forward in present[ing] reall breaches of the law of god, and man, as they are in this, which we feare not with out grounds to be an act of malice to her and us.[43]

Such public protests against interference were uncommon; yet this episode suggests the kinds of relationships neighbors ideally sought. The colonists maintained an evident concern for personal privacy in their relations with the neighborhood.

Individuals usually protested neighborhood surveillance without recourse to the courts, probably beginning with a conversational

[41] *Essex Rec.*, III, 194.
[42] The courts occasionally encouraged those who actively interfered in the affairs of their neighbors, especially if such actions served to uphold the law. See *Essex Rec.*, V, 144 (1673), where two men followed a couple; and Middlesex Co. Ct. Rec., 1649–63, pp. 137–38.
[43] *Essex Rec.*, III, 224–25 (1664).

hint, and ultimately resorting to fisticuffs and gunfire if their privacy continued to be invaded. Such action accorded with the best of English traditions. English folklore expresses the longstanding sanction against excessive interference in the affairs of others. One should mind one's own business: "He that prieth into every cloud may be struck with a thunderbolt." Robert Cleaver, the author of the standard English Puritan text on the family, urged his readers to avoid actions that might justly be misinterpreted: "Whereof the wiseman noteth some: as, meddling in other mens matters: Hee that medleth with a strife, that belongeth not to him, is as hee that taketh a dogge by the eares: that is, casteth himselfe into dangers." The Harvard College laws declared that "none shall pragmatically intrude or intermeddle in other mens affaires."[44]

Living near or next to someone was not a guarantee of further intimacy. The relations of neighbors did not evolve beyond casual levels of mutual observation and contact without a formal initiation of a closer relationship. In a deferential and hierarchical society, social class influenced the kinds of relations one had with neighbors more than did mere propinquity. Although colonial New England was in general a democratic society, especially in comparison with the mother country, the concept of deference, which pervaded all aspects of life, modified any elements of antipathy to privacy implicit in the notion of democracy. This was unlike the situation in late-nineteenth-century America when a popular interpretation of the meaning of democracy sometimes associated a conscious search for privacy with aristocratic tendencies. The colonial sense of deference stimulated a respect for other persons, particularly one's betters, and for their privacy. Even among neighbors who were largely of the middling sort, this sense of deference helped to maintain social distance. In a deferential society persons exercised firm control over their comments and inquiries to others. The existence of a sense of reserve in personal relationships was an expected and pervasive trait. The idea of deference effectively confronted some of the levelling tendencies implicit in the practice of democracy. At the same time a democratic society guaranteed to anyone the right to seek personal privacy if he so desired.

The exposure of aspects of one's private life to neighbors was an inevitable condition of life in colonial society, even if a variety of restraints helped prevent the degree of intimacy in a neighborhood

[44] Clarke, *Proverbs English and Latin*, p. 31; Cleaver, *A Godlie Forme of Household Government* (London, 1598; rpt. London, 1603), p. 84; Samuel E. Morison, *The Founding of Harvard College* (Cambridge, Mass., 1935), p. 335.

from becoming oppressive. The notion of neighborhood itself implied intimacy and mutual interaction, particularly in an interdependent society. Neighbors sought to counterbalance this accessibility by evolving a role as an extended group sharing a special intimacy, on a level which encouraged mutual respect for the privacy of one another. In this sense the neighborhood was an extension of the family and kinship systems, particularly since many contained several networks of related families. One's privacy was in no way subject to total visceration by neighbors. Most home lots were of such size that activity in and around the home could not be observed by anyone. Families living on their farms led solitary lives for the most part. In heavily built-up town centers the closeness of life in a particular neighborhood extended a veil of intimacy over local proceedings. It was unusual and unwise for someone to penetrate his neighbor's privacy in destructive fashion; such actions only generated antagonisms and tensions. In actual fact neighbors knew so much about each other already that it required an extraordinary event to stimulate their curiosity.

Although one had some difficulty being alone or unrecognized with neighbors around, compensating factors existed. Warm personal satisfactions in close relations with friendly neighbors offset any diminution of privacy inherent in the situation. An individual benefited by mutual recognition and friendship. A commentator has suggested that in the modern metropolis proximity breeds a "fear of intimacy,"[45] a trait that was markedly absent in colonial life. For the colonists the intimacy of their neighborhoods was one of the pleasant features of their lives. They did not fear intimacy or view it as an inevitable threat to their privacy; they could always withdraw temporarily for a period of retirement. Neighbors who valued the privacy of their own families and persons learned to respect that of other families. The pressures of community opinion would discreetly discipline and even isolate a neighbor who consistently displayed a disregard for the privacy of others. Perhaps few colonists enjoyed a perfect balance between privacy and society in their relations with neighbors, but such dilemmas are inherent in the balance of interests affecting privacy.

THE COMMUNITY

The colonists encountered differing conditions for the enjoyment of privacy in their local communities or townships. Were they constantly

[45] Charles Kadushin, *Why People Go to Psychiatrists* (New York, 1969), p. 60.

recognized by everyone on the streets? Were they subject to continuous observation or intrusion when they left their homes? Did the achievement of privacy in the community setting necessitate anonymity and opportunity for solitude? The size of a town, the range of personal acquaintanceship, the prevalence of gossip, and the facilities for spreading news were among the factors that affected these kinds of personal privacy.

Nearly everyone in New England lived in a town, whether a village of two hundred or less persons or a town of several thousand. By the eighteenth century many people lived outside the town centers on their farms, but they still were within the bounds of a particular town and shared in its communal life. The size of the community was a major variable affecting the availability of anonymity and solitude. As Tables 8 to 12 indicate, the overwhelming majority of New England inhabitants lived in towns with small populations until at least 1750. At that date even the towns that were slightly larger than average had few more than 1,500 inhabitants, only half of whom at most would be adults. Most of these communities shared the characteristics traditionally associated with small towns, including the acquaintanceship of everyone with everybody else, the dominance of personal relations, and the subjection of the individual to continuous observation by the community–all of which detract from privacy.[46] The small town was so dominant in early New England that the lack of anonymity generally associated with it must be emphasized.

The findings of a sociological study of Mineville, a twentieth-century town of about 1,500 inhabitants, suggest the range of acquaintanceship possible in most colonial towns:

The average resident knows the precise residence of about three-fourths of the families in town and the general part of town of the residences of considerably more . . . . The average Mineville adult lists about one-fourth of the people in town as his speaking acquaintances. By sight, name, or reputation he is aware of the presence of approximately nine-tenths of the adult persons, and seven-tenths of the children and youth . . . some residents know practically everyone while others know relatively few.[47]

A study of *Plainville* around 1940 reported that "nearly every man knows almost every other man in the whole county, though the acquaintanceship of women and children is less wide."[48] There were at least 2,000 men in the county out of a total population of 6,500. Albert

---

[46] This study has benefited greatly from the insights into small-town life afforded by Blumenthal, *Small Town Stuff.*

[47] *Ibid.,* p. 124.

[48] West, *Plainville,* pp. 13, 19.

Table 8. Average population of New England towns, 1650–1770

Colony	1650	1700	1750	1770
Massachusetts Bay (includes Plymouth Colony and Maine)	380	690	1,280	1,100
Connecticut (includes New Haven Colony)	345	720	1,650	2,500
Rhode Island	390	500	1,380	2,000
New Hampshire	325	625	640	500
Total	365	645	1,230	1,160

SOURCES: U.S. Bureau of the Census, *Historical Statistics of the United States, Colonial Times to 1957* (Washington, D.C., 1960), p. 756, and C. O. Paullin, *Atlas of the Historical Geography of the United States* (Washington, D.C., 1932), Table 2, p. 42.
NOTE: The founding of a substantial number of new towns caused a decline in the average population of Massachusetts and New Hampshire towns between 1750 and 1770.

Table 9. Population of towns in Massachusetts Bay Colony, 1764

Counties	Number of towns	% of total population in colony	Average population	Median population
Suffolk	18	14.5%	2,023	1,103
Essex	21	17.5	2,083	1,992
Middlesex	35	13.5	967	790
Plymouth	13	9.0	1,720	1,417
Bristol	11	8.5	1,938	1,739
Worcester	35	12.5	890	743
Hampshire	29	7.0	610	437
Berkshire	6	1.3	542	447
Barnstable	10	5.0	1,246	1,228
Dukes	3	1.1	906	851
Nantucket	1	1.4	3,526	3,526
York	7	4.3	1,534	1,569
Cumberland	5	3.0	1,495	1,079
Lincoln	6	1.4	607	435
Total	200	100.0%	1,252	1,091

SOURCE: The Massachusetts Census of 1764.

Table 10. Population of New Hampshire towns, 1773

Counties	Number of towns	% of total population	Average population	Median population
Rockingham	42	48.9%	850	665
Hillsborough	26	18.5	520	464
Cheshire	28	13.0	339	244
Strafford	17	14.8	637	352
Grafton	23	4.9	155	139
Total	136	100.0%	537	413

SOURCE: New Hampshire Census of 1773, in U.S. Bureau of the Census, *A Century of Population Growth* (Washington, D.C., 1909), pp. 150–51.

Table 11. Population of Rhode Island towns, 1774

Counties	Number of towns	% of total population	Average population	Median population
Newport	7	26.7%	2,275	1,232
Bristol	3	4.7	930	979
Providence	8	32.3	2,404	2,375
Kent	4	13.0	1,947	1,894
Washington (King's)	7	23.3	1,981	1,821
Total	29	100.0%	2,055	1,808

SOURCE: Rhode Island Census of 1774, in *A Century of Population Growth*, pp. 162–63.

Blumenthal concluded that "next to the weather and the exorbitant prices of necessities nothing causes more general dissatisfaction with Mineville than the lack of privacy to which its residents must submit themselves. 'Everybody knows your business in this town' is a statement made with monotonous frequency."[49]

In a colonial population of 1,500 there were fewer families, decreasing the task of identification. Also, more families in a colonial town were related directly or by marriage. Groups of families colonized a new town, or sons settled around the family home. Especially in the eighteenth century, these families formed extensive kinship networks that continued to share a level of intimacy normally associated only with the nuclear family, with the significant qualification

[49] *Small Town Stuff*, p. 48.

Table 12. Population of Connecticut towns, 1756 and 1774

Counties	Number of towns		% of total population		Average population		Median population	
	1756	1774	1756	1774	1756	1774	1756	1774
Fairfield	9	10	15.7%	15.2%	2,284	3,015	2,021	2,651
New Haven	8	8	13.9	13.6	2,273	3,353	1,815	2,529
New London	8	8	18.0	17.0	2,933	4,197	2,743	3,968
Windham	12	12	15.3	14.2	1,668	2,344	1,625	2,274
Hartford	18	20	28.0	26.2	2,032	2,594	1,647	2,072
Litchfield	16	18	9.1	13.8	739	1,516	555	1,065
Total	71	76	100.0%	100.0%	1,839	2,603	1,527	2,173

SOURCES: The Connecticut Censuses of 1756 and 1774, in *A Century of Population Growth*, pp. 164–169.

that these related families usually enjoyed separate households.[50] For example, Southampton in Hampshire County, Massachusetts, had 42 families and less than 250 residents in 1749. Twenty-nine of these 42 families had the same name as at least one other family: there were 8 Pomeroy families, 4 Clarks, and 3 each of Lymans, Searls, and Strongs. Perhaps 20 per cent of the town's inhabitants were related Pomeroys. By 1790 the town had 850 residents. There were 18 Pomeroy families, 11 Clarks, 18 Searls, 6 Strongs, and a new group of 13 Clapp families comprising 85 individuals.[51] The continuity of families in Southampton over such a period of time illustrates another problem influencing the preservation of anonymity in the colonial town. Families tended to remain in a town for generations. Population increase usually came about naturally rather than from immigration, especially in the seventeenth century. By 1680 in Hingham, near Boston, "seven-eighths of the population were members of forty-seven families who had come to Hingham before 1641." In Dedham, another town near Boston, "from 1648 to 1700, decade after decade, the inflexible rule is continuity. . . . After 1660 the arrivals we could call complete strangers averaged less than one a year for at least forty years. One new man a year ventured into Dedham, and of these many moved on eventually. During these same years (1660–1700) about one man a year chose to pick up stakes and move on." This lack of mobility seems to have continued in Hingham until the Revolution.[52] But in the frontier town of Kent (inc. 1738) there was a marked "restlessness of the town's population, a mobility wherein the average Kent resident remained only five years before moving on."[53]

[50] An imaginative and extensive treatment of this important subject of kinship networks is a major aspect of Greven's study of Andover (see especially *Four Generations*, pp. 15–16, 138–41, 175, 214–21).

[51] From the list in James Russell Trumbull, *History of Northampton, Massachusetts, from Its Settlement in 1654* (Northampton, 1898), II, 189–90, and from Wendell H. Bash, "Factors Influencing Family and Community Organization in a New England Town, 1730–1940" (Ph.D. diss., Harvard University, 1941), pp. 188–90.

[52] John Coolidge, "Hingham Builds a Meetinghouse," *New England Quarterly*, XXXIV (1961), 442; Lockridge, "Population of Dedham, Massachusetts," pp. 322–23. In his study of Andover, Greven confirmed that "remarkably few second-generation sons moved away from their families and their community." He added that "the majority of families in seventeenth-century Andover remained closely knit and remarkably immobile" ("Family Structure in Andover," p. 256; see also Greven, *Four Generations*, pp. 39–40 and 40n).

[53] Charles S. Grant, *Democracy in the Connecticut Frontier Town of Kent* (New York, 1961), p. 32.

Geographical mobility increased considerably in eighteenth-century Andover.[54] Nevertheless, in most towns continuity in population clearly provided a further detriment to anonymity.

In addition, the men, women, and children of a New England town made one another's acquaintance almost automatically by being brought together on a regular basis in organized community gatherings. Church services and related activities included all members of a family and were centers of social life. The men met regularly as a group for town meetings and for militia training. Children encountered one another in school and church. Seasonal celebrations, markets, fairs, house-raisings, quilting bees, and births brought women into community life as well in a somewhat organized fashion.

The seemingly inevitable intimacy in a colonial community created by the wide range of acquaintanceship, extensive kinship networks, continuity of families, and regular social gatherings had its compensating satisfactions in the balance of societal values. Although anonymity was not easily achieved, the satisfactions of friendship, society, and mutual support that these community relationships embodied could outweigh most inconveniences engendered by such contacts. In fact, intimacy may have overcome some of the disadvantages of lacking anonymity. Kinship networks in a town, for example, did not necessarily decrease the personal privacy available for those sharing in such a series of relationships. Since relatives are accustomed to a more intimate relationship with one another than with local acquaintances, the level of intimacy within kinship networks was not an impassable barrier to individual privacy.

In addition, anonymity was not impossible to achieve in the colonial community. Town officials, for example, never fully succeeded in keeping track of the shifting population. Persons in a larger town did not always know whether a new face was a stranger or simply a resident with whom they had rarely come into contact. A newcomer could sometimes hide his past successfully, if one may judge by the number of married men who moved to other towns and remarried.[55] Wives discovered some of them and divorce proceedings ensued, but others must have escaped detection. In addition, the rapid founding of new towns and the growth in the size of older towns, especially in the eighteenth century, increased the availability of anonymity. Although only about seven Connecticut towns had one hundred or

[54] Greven, *Four Generations*, pp. 123–24, 156–57, 273–75.
[55] See, for example, Mass. Arch., IX, 394–95 and *passim*.

more families in 1700, there were at least fifty such towns in 1756 and sixty-eight in 1774.[56] A significant number of New England towns had populations larger than 3,000 by the late colonial period.

Gossip is another facet of community life usually detrimental to personal privacy, especially when the nature of life in a society encourages observation of the behavior of others and the circulation of news of their activities. Although gossiping is in many ways a normal characteristic of human society, certain circumstances stimulate the practice. The isolated nature of many colonists' activities, the dependence upon oral communications, and the relative absence of formal methods of dispensing news lent urgency to gossip. Writing his text on Puritan family life in England around 1600, the minister Robert Cleaver stated that the name of a gossip "is become odious." In her relations with her neighbors the good wife was "not full of wordes, powring out all in her mind, and babling of her household matters that were more fitter to be concealed."[57] Puritanism was in this instance a force in support of privacy. Nevertheless, despite these warnings about the evil aspects of gossiping, Cleaver asserted that the custom was required by "the lawe of good neighbourhood."

Gossip was inevitably prevalent in colonial life. When Mrs. Elias Row died in 1681, Sewall knew "she was given to Drink and quarrelling," and also the much more intimate information that "she and her husband seldom lay together."[58] When Dr. Alexander Hamilton of Maryland visited Boston in 1744, he "was glad to find that in most of the politer caballs of ladys in this town the odious theme of scandal and detraction over their tea had become quite unfashionable and unpolite and was banished intirely to the assembles of the meaner sort, where may it dwell for ever, quite disregarded and forgott, retireing to that obscure place Billingsgate where the monster first

[56] Connecticut had about 30 towns in 1700, 71 in 1756, and 76 in 1774 (Robert Middlekauf, *Ancients and Axioms: Secondary Education in Eighteenth-Century New England* [New Haven, 1963], p. 45).

[57] *Godlie Forme of Household Government*, pp. 95–96. The Puritan theologian William Ames specifically warned against revealing a secret that a person explicitly or tacitly agreed to keep close, because to do otherwise without cause would be against justice and charity, as well as a pernicious violation of trust, friendship, and honesty: "the unjust revealing a Secret . . . is not onely in the common esteeme of men, but in the Scripture also reckoned amongst the most odious sinnes" (*Conscience with the Power and Cases Thereof* [tr. of 1630 Latin ed., London, 1643], bk. 5, pp. 290–91).

[58] *Diary*, MHS, *Coll.*, 5th ser., VI, "Miscellaneous Entries," p. 16 (1681). For repeated gossip about a minister in Grafton who beat his wife, see Parkman, "Diary," AAS, *Proc.*, LXXIII (1963), 82, 84, 86 (1747).

took its origine." Hamilton probably had observed only a passing phenomenon. A decade later the Reverend Mr. Eliot of Boston accused the New England population of being "not tender of our Neighbour's Reputation, as we ought to be . . . when they have done amiss; we publish their failings, and propagate every idle story or evil Surmise."[59] "The tale bearer from house to house" appeared early as a defendant in the New England courts, a practice which added some measure of legal control over the circulation of evil reports.[60]

In New England towns there were meeting places, in addition to private homes, where individuals could meet and exchange the latest gossip. While women stayed at home or met at wells and markets, husbands gathered to exchange confidences in the intimacy of their favorite tavern or coffeehouse, either during the day or in the evening. The wealthy Colonel Malbone of Newport made a career of news and gossip in the late 1760's. He "spent most of his Time at the Coffee House, which he always left late in the night or rather after midnight. His constant manner was to walk from his seat to Town in the Morning, take a Turn along the Street, take Snuff and inquire News, and turn into the Coffee House. Perhaps another airing in the Afternoon, when he took his Seat for the Evening. . . . He loved to hear news and chat a little upon Politics and the Church."[61]

It is unfortunate that so little is known about activities within colonial inns, taverns, and coffeehouses, since the male population spent a good part of their leisure time in such daily assembly. These places were much more significant as regular centers of community life than the religious or political meeting houses. Philippe Ariès has argued that the "medieval street . . . was not opposed to the intimacy of private life; it was an extension of that private life, the familiar setting of work and social relations."[62] The colonial tavern functioned as a similar extension of the home and a potential haven for privacy among intimates. The regulars enjoyed a familiarity and a collective sense of group privacy that was symbolized in the contemporary proverb "you must not tell tales out of the tavern."[63] Frequenters of

[59] Hamilton, *Gentleman's Progress*, p. 141; Eliot, *Evil and Adulterous Generation*, p. 19. See the earlier denunciations by the Rev. Mr. Wadsworth, who in addition attacked "busie bodies," in *Well-Ordered Family*, p. 29.

[60] *Maine Ct. Rec.*, I, 333 (1667). See also the antigossip case in New Haven in 1661 (*New Haven Town Rec.*, I, 485–86).

[61] A description by the Rev. Ezra Stiles quoted in Morgan, *Gentle Puritan*, pp. 118–19. But compare the Rev. Benjamin Wadsworth, *An Essay to Do Good: By a Dissuasive from Tavern-haunting and Excessive Drinking* (Boston, 1710).

[62] *Centuries of Childhood*, p. 341, 390.

[63] Clarke, *Proverbs English and Latin*, p. 133. Of course tales were told; see

a neighborhood tavern shared a sense of privacy in the public sphere, away from wives, children, and unwanted companions. They could gather in one of the several small rooms into which the usual tavern was divided. In the colonial experience the tavern was not completely a place of public exposure but often the locale for a special kind of intimacy.

A colonist encountered a further challenge to his anonymity as a consequence of the absence or sparsity of established news media. Lacking a flow of interesting material from public sources, the populace sometimes turned to a discussion of the affairs of neighbors and friends. The advent of newspapers in the eighteenth century did somewhat fill the void. Choice foreign items on wars and intrigues satisfied some yearnings for gossip. A Jesuit's alleged affair with one of his spiritual charges in Toulon was the lead story in five issues of the *Weekly Rehearsal* of Boston in the fall of 1731. Yet the newspapers were not of the modern type, and the local news they dispensed was normally of an official or business nature.

For conversation the New Englanders relied on news that reached them via gossip, rumor, letters, the town crier, strangers, and neighbors. Local information about fellow citizens was avidly consumed when nothing of greater intrinsic interest was available. The historian Herbert Osgood described the isolation of the 1690's, when "the interests of the moment, the interests of the town, the neighborhood, the family, the individual himself, absorbed the largest share of the colonist's attention." In 1723 a young Bostonian returned from a trip and immediately "walked up to Mr. Edwards's Shop to hear the News, and see my Friends."[64] The concentration on local affairs presented a threat to the privacy of any local person whose activities became even remotely worthy of attention. This was one of the negative aspects of community life for which some of its more pleasurable characteristics had to compensate. Yet the strong desire for news from further afield was adequate testimony to the tedium of a continuing emphasis on local community affairs; persons readily ignored their neighbors if there was anything more interesting to talk about.

The letters of members of the famous Winthrop family provide many insights into the colonial passion for news. During the winter months in Hartford, John Winthrop, Jr., was usually isolated from

---

Wait Winthrop, Boston, to Mr. Mayhew, Martha's Vineyard, March 25, 1702: "I was told this day that one of their friends said the last night at the Coffee House that . . . " (Winthrop Papers, VII, 129).

[64] Osgood, *American Colonies in the 17th Century* (New York, 1924), II, 435; Parkman, "Diary," AAS, *Proc.,* LXXI (1961), 102.

any news; at other times of the year his letters to places like New London summarized the news that had reached Hartford recently, especially "from any remote parts," which included Boston and New York.[65] His correspondents reciprocated with news they had heard. In the seventeenth century such letters were a primary means of communication for the upper class, who were both literate and able to arrange transmission more easily; with the advent of a postal system in the eighteenth century, they still had the advantage of being able to afford postage. The happiness of the later Winthrops depended on the regular publication of the newspapers. Family members in Boston included fewer local particulars in their letters, "understanding that W. Campbell every week doth forward his News Papers to your place so have nothing to Say to our home affairs."[66] At other times "Mr Campbell's not printing his news now makes me thus perticuler and tedious." Occasionally the Winthrops borrowed British newspapers from the coffeehouse in Boston and forwarded them to New London.[67] Fitz-John Winthrop went so far as to beg a London acquaintance to forward any newspapers that he planned to throw away.[68] Foreign news remained a feature of the family letters, especially if it was fresh from Europe. The avidity of the Winthrops benefited their respective home towns, since only one person had to receive news from outside for it to spread gradually throughout the town.

This hunger for information in rural colonial society accounted for the inquisitiveness that was a regular challenge to personal privacy and the bane of many travelers. In 1686 John Dunton, a London bookseller, visited a public house in Lynn. The innkeeper "wou'd needs be acquainted with us whether we wou'd or no; he was a bold forward sort of a Man, and wou'd thrust himself into our Company."[69] At the first stop of Madam Sarah Kemble Knight's trip from Boston

[65] John Winthrop, Jr., Hartford, to Fitz-John Winthrop in New London, Feb. 5, 1675, and the same, March 3, 1675, Winthrop Papers, V, 122.

[66] Thomas Lechmere, Boston, to Wait Winthrop in New London, May 28, 1711, *ibid.*, IX, 80; see also Lechmere to John Winthrop, FRS, in New London, Jan. 7, 1715, *ibid.*, p. 90. The implication that local Boston news was adequately covered in the newspapers is an interesting one.

[67] John Winthrop, FRS, to Wait Winthrop in New London, May 18, 1709, *ibid.*, p. 14; John Winthrop, FRS, Boston, to Fitz-John Winthrop in New London, Feb. 10, 1706, and April 9, 1706, *ibid.*, pp. 11–12.

[68] Fitz-John Winthrop, New London, to William Cowper, London, Nov. 12, 1698, *ibid.*, VI, 106.

[69] *Letters Written from New England, A.D. 1686*, ed. William H. Whitmore (Boston, 1867), pp. 169–70.

in 1704, the eldest daughter interrogated her: "I told her shee treated me very Rudely, and I did not think it my duty to answer her unmannerly Questions." Dr. Alexander Hamilton suffered similar impositions in 1744 as he toured New England. On one occasion he was overtaken by "a man who bore me company all the way to Portsmouth. He was very inquisitive about where I was going, whence I came, and who I was."[70] The Scottish minister Andrew Burnaby recounted an anecdote in 1759 that he associated with Benjamin Franklin, who found he could never be served in an inn until he had answered a succession of questions. On subsequent trips he summoned all members of the household to his side and delivered a set narration, finishing with the comment that "this is all I know of myself, and all I can possibly inform you of; I beg therefore that you will have pity upon me and my horse, and give us both some refreshment."[71] In 1771 a Bostonian re-created in poetry his friend's recent encounter with a fellow traveler:

Traveller:	"Pray Sir how far you're bound, and why"
	. . . .
Barrell:	"Why damn you Sir, what's that to you
	None of your business what I do."[72]

This inquisitiveness was inspired much more by loneliness, isolation, and boredom than by a conscious disregard for personal privacy. In fact, inquisitiveness may have been a treatment reserved for traveling strangers and somewhat muted in everyday community life. What wealthy travelers like Hamilton and foreigners such as Dunton considered impertinent invasions of their privacy struck the ordinary New Englander as acceptable behavior, which he was quite capable of parrying in the interests of both privacy and society. In 1770 John Adams made a journey from Massachusetts to Maine: "I have had a very unsentimental Journey. . . . Have been unfortunate eno, to ride alone all the Way, and have met with very few Characters or Adventures." He was in a much better frame of mind a few weeks

---

[70] *The Journal of Madam Knight, 1704*, ed. George P. Winship (Boston, 1920), pp. 5–6; Hamilton, *Gentleman's Progress*, pp. 122, 127, 166, 124; see also Rhode Island, 1660, in "Journal of Felix-Christian Spori in America, 1661–2," *New England Quarterly*, X (1937), 538–39.

[71] *Travels*, pp. 109–10. The 1780's English translator of the travel journal of the Marquis de Chastellux added a footnote about the curiosity of Americans and recounted a similar Franklin anecdote (see Chastellux, *Travels*, ed. Rice, p. 586).

[72] John Andrews to William Barrell, Sept. 30, 1771, Andrews-Eliot Papers, p. 1.

later, when he overtook two men on horseback as he was leaving
Falmouth: "At last one of 'em came up. What is your Name? Why
of what Consequence is it what my Name is? Why says he only as we
are travelling the Road together, I wanted to know where you came
from and what your Name was." Adams remarked in his *Diary* that
"after a good deal more of this harmless Impertinence, he turned off,
and left me."[73]

Gossip and inquisitiveness were combined in an efficient system
of passing news around the local community. Blumenthal's study of
twentieth-century Mineville provides a yardstick for measuring just
how fast stories can circulate. "With such community of interest, and
a general desire to tell the other fellow the latest news, it is not surprising that an exceptionally live bit of news, such as the death of a
prominent citizen, attains almost complete circulation in the community in about two hours."[74] Although the telephone simplified the
circulation of news in Mineville, news spread rapidly even in the
colonial community. John Dunton visited Ipswich in 1686 and later
reported to his sister: "Ipswich, my Sister, is a Country Town, not
very large, and when a Stranger arrives there, 'tis quickly known to
every one: It is no wonder then that the next day after our Arrival, the
News of it was carry'd to Mr. Hubbard, the Minister of the Town."[75]

The modern community of Mineville and the colonial town expected news to spread quickly. Should a death occur at nine in the
morning, and a resident of Mineville not learn of it till late afternoon, his reaction was "I can't understand why I didn't hear that
sooner." John Valentine of Boston left his house one morning in 1724
but somehow returned to hang himself in the garret. By evening the
whole town was looking for him. Sewall plaintively noted that "notwithstanding all this Bustle, I heard not the least inkling of it before
the Lord's day morning, when Scipio came from Watching, and told
of it."[76] The Reverend Mr. Parkman stayed home at the last minute
from the Harvard commencement in 1751 and two days later was
not invited to a private prayer meeting. He had difficulty convincing

[73] *Diary*, I, 354, 359. Adams had earlier argued that "the good People in the
Country, whom in Journeys which I often take I have pretty carefully observed,
are more dilligent and attentive to their own Business" than the idle fellows in
the town of Boston (*ibid.*, p. 212).

[74] *Small Town Stuff*, p. 136.

[75] *Letters Written from New England*, p. 282.

[76] Blumenthal, *Small Town Stuff*, pp. 136–37; Sewall, *Diary*, MHS, *Coll.*, 5th
ser., VII, 329. See a similar incident on Jan. 9, *ibid.*, p. 328; for other examples of
Sewall's desire for information and intense curiosity, see *ibid.*, V, 97, VI, 402–3
(1715).

himself that the slight was inadvertent: "For possibly they know not I am in Town–tho I may think that enough has been Said to Spread the Knowledge of it."[77] With some difficulty an event in a town could be kept private. Even in the 1630's when Boston was still a small, closely knit town, an incident involving the stillbirth of a severely malformed child was concealed for several months. Rumors began to circulate quietly, but the story did not become public until Anne Hutchinson was questioned about the report at the time of her expulsion from the colony.[78]

Personal privacy in the form of anonymity led a precarious existence in the intimate colonial world. In the small colonial town a continued preoccupation with privacy may even have been considered disloyal to the collective and communal experience of daily life. Neighbors and the community represented a consistent challenge to its achievement. Although a degree of anonymity was surely not unobtainable, a person could never be certain what aspects of his life were the current subject of conversation or observation. Most lives were so humdrum that neighbors and the community took only casual notice. But anyone who stood out from the crowd faced just the opposite problem. An individual taking special precautions to protect his privacy might even incite others to try to pierce the mystery. In the twentieth century thousands of different things occupy popular attention and entertain the populace, even if the human thirst for gossip has not abated. The colonists lived in a much different world.

Achieving a balance between privacy and society was a problem that the New England colonists approached with their own set of values. John Cotton, Boston's leading minister, summed up a common preference in the early 1650's: "Society in all sorts of humane affairs is better than Solitariness."[79] Such a priority arose from a strong sense of the threat of loneliness and isolation in a wilderness society. Human gregariousness is normally a strong instinct, but it is even more intense in a culture where communication normally takes place only on a person-to-person basis. As a young minister in the 1720's, Ebenezer Parkman of Westborough was particularly susceptible to loneliness. "Lieutenant Lee being gone to Boston, It was very lonely During his Absence, for he was Sociable." In 1726 "so

[77] "Diary," AAS, *Proc.*, LXXV (1965), 88–89.

[78] Winthrop, *Journal*, I, 266–69.

[79] Cotton, *A Brief Exposition . . . upon . . . Ecclesiastes* (London, 1654), p. 85, quoted in *The Puritans: A Sourcebook of Their Writings*, ed. Perry Miller and Thomas H. Johnson (rev. paperback ed., New York, 1963), p. 183.

many of my Friends absent I was very lonely." In 1728 Parkman dismissed his servant after his first crops were in: "Now we are intirely alone having no Servant nor any one in the House. Our Loneliness gives Scope for Thought. God Sanctifie our solitude, and help us to improve in acquaintance with Himself."[80]

On October 4, 1731, the *Weekly Rehearsal* of Boston published an essay in praise of conversation that reflects the colonial view of the relationship between privacy and society in all its dimensions.

To avoid conversation is to act against the Intention of Nature. To live always in a Retreat we must be something above Men or below the Beasts. . . .

To live then as Men we must confer with Men; Conversation must be one of the greatest Pleasures of life. . . . There is nothing more useful, nothing more dangerous: for as too long a Retreat enfeebles the Mind, too frequent a Conversation will dissipate it. It is of use to retire sometimes into oneself; nay it is necessary to give an exact Account of our Words, of our Thoughts, and of the Advances we have made in Wisdom. To enjoy the Advantage of our Reading and Discourse, to improve upon what we have seen, there is a necessity of Silence, of Repose, and Meditation.

The essence of this colonial balance between isolation, privacy, and society was further stated in a collection of verse:

> Mine be the pleasures of a rural life,
> From Noise remote, and ignorant of strife.
>
> . . . .
>
> Yet not a real hermitage I'd chuse,
> Nor wish to live from all the world recluse;
> But with a friend sometimes unbend the soul
> In social converse, o'er the sprightly bowl.[81]

The colonists were willing to sacrifice some of their privacy in the interests of equally important values. To escape isolation, loneliness, and boredom the residents of New England sought the continuing society of small towns, even though this meant some diminution of the personal privacy available outside the confines of their home. Other factors also compensated for this limited sacrifice. Life in colonial New England was much more personalized, intimate, and communal than the fragmented and highly individualistic character of existence in an industrial society. Solitude was readily available when needed. Privacy could be sought in the retirement of the family.

[80] "Diary," AAS, *Proc.*, LXXI (1961), 101, 155, 220–21.

[81] W. Livingston, *Philosophic Solitude* (New York, 1747; rpt. Boston, 1762), pp. 14, 19.

The colonist felt less need to withdraw from the public sphere than we do. In some ways the communal nature of existence in any town made distinctions between public and private less meaningful. A tiny neighborhood and smalltown community were not alien and inscrutable but familiar and encompassing for its residents. The colonists lived in locales which assured meaningful personal relationships, a sense of participation, and a feeling of collective caring and responsibility for one another, characteristics often absent from the modern city, where anonymity can be so readily found. Such dichotomies once again indicate that privacy is not an absolute value but one that must be balanced against other desirable goals. Men in an urban, industrialized society are concerned about privacy because they have such difficulties finding and protecting it. Conditions were quite different in colonial New England. Nevertheless residents of this agricultural and preindustrial society needed, used, and sought personal privacy.

PART TWO
The Individual in Colonial Society

THIS part discusses the relationship between the individual and the major institutions in colonial society. The relative balance among privacy for an individual, physical surveillance, and compulsory disclosure is examined. To what extent did the colonial churches, governments, and courts require the disclosure of private matters by individual citizens? Did these institutions acknowledge the value of personal privacy? Could an individual colonist enjoy freedom from surveillance when he left the haven of his home to venture into society?

Chapter four deals with the ability of one individual to communicate with another without surveillance or interference. In the colonial period the mails were the only available nonverbal method of communication. The method of carrying and delivering mail is examined to determine if this service provided adequate protection for the privacy of letters. The degree of governmental interference with the mails is also investigated.

The following chapter considers a central institution of New England society, the local Congregational church. The centrality of Puritan ideology in the formulation of values makes this one of the most intriguing locales in which to examine the existing balance among privacy, disclosure, and surveillance. Did required Sabbath church attendance and the religious compulsions of the Puritan ministry create a climate that challenged the personal privacy of the general populace? Could full church members, the only ones who were subject to both admissions procedures and ecclesiastical discipline, enjoy privacy?

Chapters six and seven study the values that motivated the colonial governments in the formulation of laws respecting aspects of individual behavior and their enforcement. To what extent did they institutionalize surveillance of the populace and for what purposes? Was the desire for privacy considered inimical to the best interests of the state? What was the actual effect of legislation that at first glance legitimized intrusions into private lives? More particularly, and this is the burden of chapter seven, how effective were the instruments of law enforcement available to the colonial authorities?

Did the nature of law enforcement serve as a balancing force on behalf of personal privacy?

The last chapter in this part evaluates the degree of concern for the privacy of an individual that existed within the confines of the colonial courtroom. The willingness of a society to extend certain protections to suspects in criminal cases is one of the more delicate barometers of sensitivity to the dignity of the individual personality. To what extent did the colonial legal system authorize compulsory disclosure in the examination of citizens suspected of crimes? How did an inefficient system of law enforcement handle criminal suspects? Finally, were inquisitorial oaths or torture used to elicit private information from suspects and witnesses? Could a person successfully refuse to incriminate himself?

4. The Privacy of Letters

THE contemporary world is well aware of the need to protect the privacy of communications in the face of a technological onslaught that makes letters and conversations more and more susceptible to interference. In colonial America, of course, conversations could only occur in the physical presence of someone else. This chapter surveys the privacy of the colonial mails in the light of a popular opinion that in colonial America "there was no one legally accountable for the mail, and no law, anyhow to protect privacy; and there was nothing to prevent people from opening letters that were not addressed to them."[1]

THE SEVENTEENTH CENTURY

Prior to 1692 no regular postal service existed in the New England region, although individual colonies initiated short-lived projects.[2] Boston did have a Post House as early as 1639, primarily as a depository for overseas mail. In 1677 a group of Boston merchants successfully petitioned the General Court to establish once again a place where incoming letters could be taken to prevent their loss or miscarriage.[3] Finally in 1692 the Englishman Thomas Neale was awarded a royal patent for a twenty-one-year monopoly of the American postal service. Massachusetts, Connecticut, and New Hampshire recognized the Neale patent and promised support, while Rhode Island ignored the whole business.[4] Although post offices were established in major

---

[1] Elinore Denniston, *America's Silent Investigators* (New York, 1964), p. 19.

[2] See, for example, the 1672 attempt by Gov. Lovelace of New York, in Wesley Everett Rich, *The History of the United States Post Office to the Year 1829* (Cambridge, Mass., 1924), pp. 5–6.

[3] *Mass. Rec.*, I, 281; "Post Office Department Documents," MHS, *Coll.*, 3d ser., VII (1838), 49–50; also see *Mass. Acts and Res.*, VII, 430ff.

[4] Neale himself never came to America. MHS, *Coll.*, 3d. ser., VII (1838), 50–54; *Conn. Rec.*, IV, 123; "Laws New Hampshire, 1702," in *Documents and Records Relating to the Province of New-Hampshire*, ed. Nathaniel Bouton et al. (Concord, N.H., etc., 1867–1943), III, 190–92 (1692) (hereafter cited as *N.H. Provincial Papers*).

towns, service by 1700 remained slow and uncertain. Lack of profits and Neale's death led to the repurchase of the patent by the crown in 1707.

In the seventeenth century friends, acquaintances, ship captains, occasional travelers, or hired men conveyed almost all mail within the colonies and across the oceans. Anyone taking a trip called around the town to pick up letters. Private conveyance normally had the added quality of being free, at a time when available postal service was relatively expensive. Anyone who wanted to maintain a correspondence could do so without much difficulty. Governor John Winthrop, Jr., of Connecticut carried on an extensive family correspondence with his sons in New London and Boston in the 1660's and 1670's.[5] Matthew Boys, Jr., of London instructed Governor Richard Bellingham of Massachusetts in 1668 that "when you have any Letters to send to my father; and you have noe known friend to Send by; if you give your Letters to Mr. William Darvall marchant in Boston hee will Convey them Safely to me; I Live with one hee hath dealeing with Sometimes."[6]

When friends carried the mail the privacy of the contents was normally assured. Such was not the case for mail carried by the first mailmen or deposited in Boston from overseas. The appointment of John Hayward as the postmaster in Boston in 1677 was meant to prevent the loss of letters, since "many times letters are throune upon the exchange, that who will may take them up."[7] Samuel Sewall was suspicious of the domestic letter carrier and assumed that he had been opening his letters. Lord Cornbury, the governor of New York, complained to the Lords of Trade in 1704 that "our letters do not come safe by the way of Boston, I have had several letters by that way which have been broken open."[8]

The absence of a formal postal system was a basic flaw. In major towns bags were hung up in a tavern in which mail was deposited for overseas delivery. The curious could under some pretext peruse the contents of the bag. When mail arrived from overseas, it could be claimed from the ship's master by anyone or else dumped upon a

[5] He wrote at least thirteen letters to his sons between April 2 and Aug. 22, 1672 (Winthrop Papers, V, 69–74).

[6] Mass. Arch., LVII ("Letter Books, 1658–1779"), 53a.

[7] *Mass. Rec.*, V, 147–48.

[8] Rich, *History U.S. Post Office*, pp. 10, 19. Carelessness, leading to the loss of letters, was a characteristic of the early postal service and even of private carriers on occasion; see Fitz-John Winthrop's letters to Gov. Dudley of Mass., April 5, 1704, and to Cousin Reade in London, *ca.* 1702, in Winthrop Papers, VIII, 29, 9.

table in a tavern house and thumbed through by the inhabitants. Fitz-John Winthrop, the new governor of Connecticut, told a London acquaintance in 1698 that if he put any letters for him "into the bag of any ship bound to this country they will come safe."[9] The letters would presumably reach America, but that Winthrop would be notified of their arrival and actually receive them was much less certain, particularly since his letters had to be forwarded from Boston to New London by one of his family. Because receipt of a letter was still something of a rarity, letters were objects of intense curiosity.[10] An isolated population constantly sought news from abroad or even the nearest colony. The absence of newspapers in the seventeenth century added to such pressures.

Illiteracy contributed to the confidentiality of the mails and correspondingly decreased privacy of communication among those who could not write their own letters. A large minority of the male population and the overwhelming majority of women in colonial New England were not capable of reading or writing a letter.[11] Several episodes in the seventeenth-century Essex County court records support this conclusion. A husband who was encouraging his wife to leave England had to have another person read and write his letters, while in England his wife went to another for the same purposes. A young servant was published as a bride-to-be but tired of her intended mate; whereupon, as she told the court, "I got a young maide that lived in the house with mee to write a letter to him to desire him to come noe more to mee, because I founde I could not love him."[12] For

---

[9] Winthrop to William Cowper, Nov. 12, 1698, MHS, *Coll.*, 5th ser., VIII (1882), 356; see also a similar directive *ca.* 1702 in Winthrop Papers, VIII, 9.

[10] Commenting on the English postal situation in the 16th to 18th centuries, James W. F. Hill stated that "it was only the 'gentlemen and traders' who were much concerned with the posts; other folk neither sent nor received letters" (*Tudor and Stuart Lincoln* [Cambridge, 1956], p. 16). Arthur H. Cole has estimated that individual merchants in America between 1730 and 1775 wrote "perhaps 200–300" letters "a year, or roughly four to six a week," and received even fewer letters ("The Tempo of Mercantile Life in Colonial America," *Business History Review*, XXXIII [1959], 280–83). Even by 1800 letter-writing in America had not become a widely practiced art; according to Leonard White, "on the average each person in the country, for the period of five years ending with 1799, sent but 1 4/10 missives by the mails" (*The Federalists* [New York, 1959], p. 190, n. 17). Henry Adams claimed that in 1800 the postal system handled an average of one letter a year for every adult (*United States in 1800* [paperback rpt., Ithaca, N.Y., 1955], p. 44).

[11] The tentative conclusion of research in progress by Kenneth Lockridge, as reported in Demos, *A Little Commonwealth*, p. 22.

[12] *Essex Rec.*, V, 66–67, 229; also see *ibid.*, VI, 347–48, 352.

these persons illiteracy lessened their personal privacy, but it also prevented them from invading the privacy of anyone with a letter in transit.

A variety of interesting means were taken to protect the privacy of letters. An Irish correspondent sent John Winthrop, Jr., a coding device in 1635: "Herewith I send you a casement through which I thinke you may much more securely impart your minde then any other way. . . . And then you may reade my secrett minde. . . . I had written in the way wee agreed on, butt I fownd itt, in my judgment, more tedious, and less secrett."[13] Most writers sealed their letters with wax, although such seals could easily be broken or could fall apart in transit. Wait Winthrop of Boston wrote to his brother, the governor of Connecticut, in 1701: "I have your role of papers, the seale was open at one end and might have been taken all out but I suppose it was broke with the carriage, conecticot wax being good for nothing but crumbles all away."[14] Many correspondents also wrapped a blank sheet around very important letters before sealing them to prevent reading through the paper. In 1622 an English correspondent of Governor Bradford of Plymouth Colony sent his missive sewn into the sole of a new pair of shoes "for fear of intercepting." The fear was well-founded, for one of Bradford's enemies discovered the letter while on board ship. One of the numerous persons seeking medical advice from John Winthrop, Jr., asked him to "be myndfull of my wife's condition, to sende what you thinke may be meete, and may safely be sente by this bearer *modo hoc obsecro, ut si aliquid secreti scribas latine scriberes* [this I beseech you, to write in Latin anything of a private nature]."[15] Others employed codes, shorthand, or nicknames when writing to friends, particularly on political topics. When short-lived mail services were inaugurated between the colonies in 1673, the mail was packed in different bags, "according to the towns the letters are designed to, which are sealed up till their arrival with the seal of the secretarie's office. Only by-letters are in an open bag, to dispense by the wayes."[16] A spur to the establishment and maintenance of post offices in the late seventeenth and early eighteenth centuries was the threat "to the discovery of the Correspondencies and secrets of merchants" by individuals who

13 *Winthrop Papers*, III, 190–91.

14 Winthrop Papers, VII, 121 (Nov. 17).

15 Bradford, *Of Plymouth Plantation*, p. 104; Rev. James Fitch to John Winthrop, Jr., July 18, 1654, Winthrop Papers, XIII, 42.

16 A letter to Gov. John Winthrop, Jr., of Conn., quoted in Rich, *History U. S. Post Office*, p. 6.

boarded newly arrived ships and claimed letters that were not addressed to them.[17] Information about foreign markets was a strong temptation to a merchant's competitors.

Despite the casualness of delivery, there seems to have been little premeditated and malicious perusal of other people's mail, except perhaps on the part of colonial authorities. At least the infrequency of colonial complaints about such interference suggests that the privacy of the mails was fairly secure. No court cases were found in which persons were specifically indicted for opening someone's mail, but the courts revealed their attitude on several related occasions. In 1639 a court fined John Kitchen of Boston "for shewing books which hee was commanded to bring to the Governor, and forbidden to shew them to any other." In 1668 a Plymouth resident succeeded in having the court admonish three persons "for opening a certaine box in his house, wherin were his writings."[18] Both the secretary and the governor of Massachusetts had harsh words for Samuel Sewall in 1709 when he tried to read several letters on the secretary's desk during a Council meeting. *The School of Good Manners*, representative of the colonial attitude, instructed: "Touch not, nor look upon the Books or Writings of any one, unless the Owner invite or desire thee. . . . Come not near when another reads a Letter or any other Paper."[19]

THE EIGHTEENTH CENTURY

The English Post Office Act of 1710, which established a postal system in America, was the turning point for the colonial mail service. Post offices were organized in New London, Newport, Providence, Boston, Portsmouth, Salem, and Ipswich, and a postmaster-general was appointed to carry out the provisions of the act, which set the standards for the remainder of the colonial period. The postrider became an important man in the life of the towns that were fortunate enough to be on his established route. Service was weekly except in winter. By 1715 correspondents had all but abandoned private carriers in favor of the regular service, which also carried parcels and drove animals. The departure of the postrider at a precise hour introduced a new tyranny into the lives of letter writers, who were unaccustomed to such regularity and consistency. Yet the various Win-

---

[17] *Mass. Acts and Res.*, VIII, 281 (1699); MHS, *Coll.*, 3d ser., VII (1838), 83 (1715).

[18] *Mass. Rec.*, I, 269; *Plymouth Col. Rec.*, V, 10.

[19] Sewall, *Diary*, MHS, *Coll.*, 5th ser., VI, 255; *School of Good Manners*, p. 16.

throps in New London became upset when the postal service decided to visit New London only every second week: "It is a great Inconvenience to have it thus. Almost as good as none if it must be thus Stated. And Abundance of people that use to be good Customers to Campbels News papers, along this Road, are now Resolved to have no more. And they send all their Letters by Travellers now Rather then by the post."[20]

Cost militated against the writing of letters and in favor of private conveyance. Letter writing was too expensive for perhaps half the population and practiced with some caution by the remainder. Since the recipient paid the postage, such comments as the following were not unusual: "Lett me assure you I do not begrudge Postidge for my friends Letters."[21] "I expect my private opportunities will fail me soon, and should not chuse to put you to the expence of postage, without your *special* permission."[22]

Eighteenth-century postal service was efficient in the context of the times. Mails moved constantly from Maine to Georgia on a regular basis of once a week, or perhaps twice a month, depending on the season of the year. The major abuses involved tardy postriders, who carried more mail on their own private account than for the government and spent too much time carrying parcels.[23] Some areas of the country, such as the upper Connecticut Valley, had no postal service until the 1750's, and New Haven did not have a post office until 1755. Nevertheless mail was moving, and persons could communicate on a reliable basis to an extent unknown in the seventeenth century.

The Post Office Act of 1710 contained an important provision concerning the privacy of the mails: "No Person or Persons shall presume wittingly, willingly, or knowingly, to open, detain, or delay, or cause, procure, permit, or suffer to be opened, detained, or delayed, any Letter or Letters, Packet or Packets."[24] There was a twenty-pound fine for each offense. Thus it was against the law for any colonist to open the letters of another, except in a few specific instances.

[20] John Winthrop, FRS, to Wait Winthrop, Feb. 8, 1715, Winthrop Papers, IX, 25.

[21] Thomas Lechmere, Boston, to John Winthrop, FRS, New London, Sept. 24, 1711, *ibid.*, p. 81. For other Winthrop family comments on postal costs, compare *ibid.*, VIII, pt. 2, p. 33 (June 9, 1709), and IX, 68 (May 4, 1727).

[22] John Andrews, Boston, to William Barrell, Philadelphia, Sept. 4, 1774, Andrews-Eliot Papers, p. 42; see also pp. 6, 11.

[23] For an interesting survey of the state of the postal system on the eve of the Revolution, see Finlay, *Journal, passim*, but esp. pp. 32, 45–46.

[24] 9 Anne, cap. X, s. 40. The 1765 act was 5 George III, cap. 25. It supplanted only the part of the 1710 act that laid down rates.

The most detailed information concerning the privacy of the colonial mails dates from the tenure of Benjamin Franklin as postmaster-
general for America from 1753 to the Revolution. He and his associate, William Hunter, required new postmasters to follow a list of
instructions.[25] Everyone who worked in the post office, or who had
any connection with the receiving, sorting, marking, or delivering of
letters, was obliged to take the "Oath required by the Act of the Ninth
of Queen Anne." A copy of the oath was sent to the postmaster and
his associates, who subscribed to it before a justice of the peace. This
was the initial requirement for entering the postal service: "I A. B.
do swear, That I will not wittingly, willingly, or knowingly open . . .
or cause, procure, permit, or suffer to be opened . . . any Letter or
Letters . . . which shall come into my Hands, Power, or Custody, by
Reason of my Employment in or relating to the Post Office; except
. . . by an express Warrant in Writing under the Hand of one of the
principal Secretaries of State for that purpose."

Franklin and Hunter also attempted to deal with a perennial problem of the colonial post: "You are to keep your Office, in a Place to
be set apart for that Purpose . . . and not to suffer the Letters to lie
open in any Place, to which Persons, coming to your House, may
have Access; nor suffer any Person whatsoever, but such as you en-
trust in the Execution of your Office, to inspect or handle the Letters
at any Time, unless they are first delivered to them." This should
have terminated the indiscriminate shuffling of letters spread out on
an open table. One gathers from the recommendation of Hugh Finlay
in 1773–74, however, that Franklin's directions were not totally successful: "Every Deputy shou'd have an office, for when the publick
sees letters thrown carelessly about in an open room or store, for
every comer to handle it is natural to conclude and it is accordingly
concluded that letters are not safe under a deputy's care." Postmasters complained about inadequate resources. Finlay, who had
just completed a tour of postal establishments, suggested an extra
allowance that would allow postmasters to restrict access to "such as
may have taken the oaths of a Post officer." Finlay also reported that
the New London postmaster had established a separate office but
could not keep everyone out because his predecessor had maintained
an open-door policy.[26]

---

[25] Franklin had previously served as the postmaster of Philadelphia. These
instructions can be found in *The Papers of Benjamin Franklin*, ed. Leonard W.
Labaree *et al.* (New Haven, 1959–), V, 162–68, esp. nos. 1, 2, 5, 13, 22.

[26] Finlay, *Journal*, pp. 70–71, 34–35.

Other directives of Franklin and Hunter added significantly to the protection of privacy. When the mail came through a town, the post-master was not to allow any pouch to be opened except the one containing the town's mail. When individuals requested the return of posted letters from a post office, the postmaster was directed to demand several proofs to ensure that the person was the actual writer and sender. The postmasters were also warned to pay attention to seals on both the letters and the mail bags. They were to seal bags they sent off carefully and to check arriving sacks to ensure that the seals had not been broken.

After the British relieved Franklin of his office on the eve of the Revolution, William Goddard, a Baltimore newspaperman and printer, set out to organize an independent postal system that would protect the security and privacy of the mails. A Boston broadside of April 30, 1774, explained "the Plan for Establishing a New American Post-Office."

A set of Officers, *Ministerial* indeed, in their Creation, Direction and Dependance are maintained in the Colonies, into whose Hands all the social, commercial and political Intelligence of the Continent is necessarily committed; which, at this Time, every one must consider as dangerous in the extreme. It is not only our Letters that are liable to be stopt and opened by a Ministerial Mandate, and their Contents construed into treasonable Conspiracies.[27]

This new postal system was operating by the fall of 1774. The Continental Congress took it over a year later, at about the time the British post ceased to function in America. Goddard drew up "Model Rules for a Constitutional Post Office," which contained the following provision pertaining to privacy: "That the several mails shall be under lock and key and liable to the inspection of no person but the respective postmasters to whom they shall be directed, who shall be under oath for the faithful discharge of the trust reposed in them."[28]

In actual practice the colonists always demonstrated concern for the privacy of their letters by discretion and an awareness of the dangers involved in using the mails. In the first decade of the eighteenth century a Winthrop warned his cousin in New London: "Take care how you send Letters loose to the Posthouse they are all

[27] Quoted in Ward L. Miner, *William Goddard, Newspaperman* (Durham, N. C., 1962), p. 126.
[28] Rich, *History U. S. Post Office*, p. 45.

Either taken up or opened."[29] An Englishman wrote to the former lieutenant governor of New Hampshire in 1719:

Sir I have bin so unfortunate as to have a great many of my Letters intercepted and Several open'd before thay came to my hands, and I have just reason to Suspect that your Honours to me meet with the Same fate which makes me farefull least mine which I send to my friends should meet with the like misfortune So Sir you must pardon my Silence relateing to publick affairs but must leave it till I have the hapiness of seeing you.[30]

A Bostonian visiting London in 1742 commented on various matters in a letter to a Boston friend and then stated: "I'll say no more on this head, but When I have the Pleasure to See you again, shall Inform you of many Things too tedious for a Letter and which perhaps may fall into Ill hands, for I know there are many at Boston who dont Scruple to Open any Persons letters, but they are well known here."[31] One of the eighteenth century's famous criminals, Tom Bell, was expelled from Harvard for a series of thefts, "particularly of stealing private Letters out of Gray's study."[32] On a trip to Maine in 1774, John Adams wrote his wife: "I write you this Tittle Tatle, my Dear, in Confidence. You must keep these Letters chiefly to yourself, and communicate them with great Caution and Reserve. I should advise you to put them up safe."[33]

During the Revolution the privacy of the mails inevitably deteriorated. John Jay of New York wrote to a correspondent that "were I sure that this letter would reach you uninspected, I should commit many things to paper worth your knowledge, but which would give you little pleasure or surprise; but as it is uncertain who will be the bearer, they must be reserved for the present." Correspondents resorted to private ciphers and codes. Jay received another letter that suggested the extent to which this situation was a product of the war. "To the disgrace of Human Nature, it has become a common Practice to betray the Confidence we repose in each other, either by

[29] John Winthrop, FRS, to his cousin Livingstone, between 1700 and 1707, *Winthrop Papers*, IX, 6.

[30] William Tailer to John Usher in Mass., Sept. 10, 1719, Jeffries Family Papers, III, 135.

[31] Oliver Noyes to David Jeffries, Sept. 24, 1742, *ibid.*, XIII, 17. See the expression of a similar fear of committing certain things to paper in Edmund Trowbridge, Cambridge, Mass., to William Bollan in England, Nov. 1764, Dana Family Papers, 1674–1769, folder 1761–64.

[32] See the sketch of Bell's life by Clifford Shipton, *New England Life in the Eighteenth Century* (Cambridge, Mass., 1963), pp. 375ff.

[33] *Adams Family Correspondence*, I, 121; see also p. 129.

opening Letters, or not sending them to the Persons to whom they are directed. I have seen so many Instances of such Behaviour that I am determined to use more Caution hereafter." This outcry was an eloquent tribute to the degree of privacy usually anticipated in the colonial mails.[34]

GOVERNMENTAL INTERCEPTION

The role of the various levels of government in mail interception deserves some attention, both in terms of the motives used to justify such activity and the extent of the practice. Organized governmental interception of mail furnishes an opportunity to observe a major colonial institution trying to balance the values of privacy and civil security. The colonist did not fully control his privacy interests in this area, except to the extent that he refrained from letter writing or exercised great caution therein.

The year 1624 was one of crisis and conspiracy in the fledgling Plymouth Colony. Governor Bradford strongly suspected that the colony's first minister, the Reverend Mr. Lyford, an Anglican, and another person named Oldham, were organizing a faction against the Pilgrim church and preparing to carry their case to England.[35] "At length when the ship was ready to go, it was observed Lyford was long in writing and sent many letters." Fearing the effect of these letters in England, Bradford and his friends followed the ship a short distance to sea, boarded her, and opened the letters of Lyford and Oldham. Not only were slanders and false accusations revealed but also copies of letters originally written in England and sent to persons in Plymouth. Lyford could only have had access to these while coming over on a ship. When Bradford assembled the whole company of Plymouth, Lyford and Oldham denied all charges and required proof. Then Lyford's "letters were produced and some of them read, at which he was struck mute. But Oldham began to rage furiously because they had intercepted and opened his letters, threatening them in very high language, and in a most audacious and mutinous manner stood up and called upon the people" to rise and aid him.

[34] Jay to Gouverneur Morris, March 11, 1778, in Henry P. Johnston, ed. *The Correspondence and Public Papers of John Jay* (New York, 1890), I, 177; Robert Troup to Jay, July 22, 1777, Jay Papers, Special Collections, Columbia University; see also John Coffin, Quebec, to the Amorys in Boston, Nov. 3, 1779, and Nov. 20, 1780, Amory Papers, I (1698–1784), MHS.

[35] The entire episode is in Bradford, *Of Plymouth Plantation,* pp. 149–53.

Bradford immediately asked Lyford "if he thought they had done evil to open his letters; but he was silent, and would not say a word, well knowing what they might reply." Lest Oldham's attack win a sympathetic hearing, Bradford explained his position to the populace: "The Governor showed the people he did it as a magistrate, and was bound to it by his place, to prevent the mischief and ruin that this conspiracy and plots of theirs, would bring on this poor Colony." Bradford was also able to show that Lyford "had dealt treacherously with his friends that trusted him, and stole their letters and opened them."

This episode highlights the colonial attitude toward opening the letters of other individuals. During the precarious early years of settlement, and at a time of crisis, the governor of a colony felt obliged to explain why he had opened another's letters. He believed that security outranked privacy as a value under such circumstances. That a seventeenth-century New England governor felt even an element of uncertainty about the correctness of his action suggests an obvious assumption by the populace that the mails should be private.

This official uneasiness about opening the letters of others appeared at other times in the early history of New England. In 1629 the General Court of Massachusetts Bay was still meeting in London when letters arrived from New England written to private persons in the home country. A debate ensued whether "they should bee opened and read, or not." The decision was in the affirmative, because it was suspected the authors had defamed the country of New England, its governor, and its government.[36] In 1631 Governor Winthrop received a packet of letters from the governor of the Piscataqua region in Maine addressed to Sir Christopher Gardiner. Winthrop opened the letters and discovered information inimical to his colony. Some time after he had written his account of the incident, Winthrop inserted an explanatory paragraph in the margin of his journal. "These letters we opened, because they were directed to one, who was our prisoner, and had declared himself an ill willer to our government."[37]

The practice of permitting officials to intercept mail suspected of containing treasonable material had a solid legal foundation in English history.[38] The custom dated from the Tudor period and was based on an exercise of the royal prerogative. But the right to open mail was forbidden without an express warrant from a secretary of state,

[36] *Mass. Rec.*, I, 52–53.

[37] Winthrop, *Journal*, I, 64. Compare *ibid.*, pp. 285, 300.

[38] For the English background on which this account is based, see Kenneth Ellis, *The Post Office in the Eighteenth Century* (Oxford, 1958), pp. 60–77.

a requirement that was specifically restated in 1663. The Post Office Act of 1710 forbade opening someone's mail, "except by an express Warrant in Writing under the Hand of one of the Principal Secretaries of State for every such opening." The qualification was incorporated into the oath of a postmaster and applied to America as well as England.

In eighteenth-century Britain a specific institution handled official opening of mail. Any domestic and foreign mail could be perused in "the Secret Office," of whose existence few were even aware. Great volumes of mail were thus examined, and as Kenneth Ellis has remarked, "secrecy made legality unimportant. By custom, mail was opened freely on suspicion, or in search of designated letters." The Secret Office employees were so expert that few, including foreign governments, knew their mail was being tampered with. The public was generally ignorant about the extent of interception. In 1735 during a parliamentary debate on the post office several members of Parliament did complain that their letters were being opened.[39] The M.P.'s claimed that everyone knew this, and thus no traitorous individual would think of using the mails; therefore, "the Liberty given to break open letters at the post-office could now serve no purpose, but to enable the little clerks about that office to pry into the private affairs of every merchant, and of every gentleman in the kingdom." Sir Robert Walpole, who "was far from vindicating the practice of opening the letters of members," echoed this concern for privacy but defended the need to do so in special cases involving national security.

It can be assumed pending further investigation that the British practices outlined above were not unknown in America. Although there is little extant evidence of the opening of colonial letters by New England governors, other than the instances from early New England history, Ellis has noted that "colonial Letters, by custom opened by Governors in transit, were also in times of crisis seized on board, and opened on general warrants on arrival at the Inland Office."[40] One can cite the instance of the mail carrier John Perry, who was arrested by order of Jacob Leisler during the Revolution of 1689 and taken to New York, where his letters were perused. New Haven Colony had a law which would seemingly have permitted interception of mails:

---

[39] *Ibid.*, pp. 63–64; William Cobbett, *Parliamentary History of England* (London, 1806–20), IX (1733–37), 839–848.

[40] *Post Office in the 18th Century*, pp. 64–65.

And for that designes or practises tending to publique inconvenienc and mischiefe, are usually mannaged by letters or writings in a cunning secret way, the conspirators or actors not thinking it safe to meete often, it shall be in the power of the governor, or any magistrate, or other officer where there is no magistrate, upon just or probable grounds, to search or cause to be searched any mans house, study, closset, or any other place, for bookes, letters, wrightings, or any thing else, to discover and prevent such danger, and the like in case of murder, theft, and other enormioss crimes, that wee may live a quiet and peaceable life, in all godlines and honesty, which is the use and end of magistracy.[41]

This statute nicely balanced off a normal preference for privacy versus the occasional demands of security. Presumably most colonial governors followed such customs in times of crisis or when they felt a particular need to know the minds of certain of the inhabitants. In the interests of security the populace generally acquiesced in such limitations on their privacy.

On the eve of the Revolution control over the means of communication was a vital issue. A prime motivation of William Goddard, Sam Adams, and the Committees of Correspondence in fighting for an American post was the fear of having their letters opened by "a Ministerial Mandate." It was generally acknowledged that mails could be intercepted and used by governing authorities. The act of the Continental Congress creating a National Post Office in 1782 recognized this power by ordering that no postmaster or employee was to open mail without a direct warrant from the president of the Continental Congress.[42]

In general, the colonists demonstrated a well-developed and explicit concern for the privacy of their letters and correspondence. Indeed their concern and its motivation were remarkably similar to our attitudes several hundred years later. In this area the problems for protecting personal privacy have retained similar dimensions, at least so far as letters are concerned. Technological change has created the enormous problem of trying to protect the privacy of telephone conversations. The colonists expected complete privacy for their communications except under extraordinary circumstances.

[41] *New Haven Col. Rec., 1653–1665,* p. 198 (1656).
[42] *The Journals of the Continental Congress, 1774–1789,* ed. Worthington C. Ford (Washington, D.C., 1904–37), XXIII, 671 (1782). There was no provision for anyone to open mails under the terms of the federal statute of 1792 (see *The Statutes at Large,* I [Boston, 1845], Act of 2d Cong. 1st Sess., chap. 7, p. 236, sect. 16).

5. The Church

T HE Congregational church in many ways provides an ideal setting for an examination of New England public attitudes toward personal privacy and the practical conditions in society for its enjoyment. The nature and extent of an individual's relations with the church influenced the preservation of his personal privacy. As the primary institutional manifestation of the Puritan creed in the New World, the established church played significant direct and indirect roles in society. Its ministers were a highly visible and influential group. In each community the church had an impact on the general populace through Sabbath regulations and the surveillance obligations of its ministers and members. To what degree did such requirements and practices restrict the availability of solitude and anonymity for individuals? Only a segment of the populace voluntarily entered into an intimate relationship with the Congregational church by becoming full church members. Did the internal procedures for admission of new members and the carrying out of church discipline compel the disclosure of private matters and the regular acceptance of mutual surveillance? Did concern for privacy keep some colonists from full membership?

THE SABBATH

The Congregational churches influenced the personal privacy of the general population through the requirement of church attendance on the Sabbath. This day presented the colonists with a contradictory situation. The emphasis on discreet behavior and personal religious exercises encouraged withdrawal from the world, to the benefit of individual privacy. But the laws requiring church attendance, which were enforced as a matter of course during the colonial period, brought the residents of the town together for a good part of the morning and afternoon.[1] A month's absence from church normally

[1] From medieval times presence at Sunday services had been compulsory in England, and the various Acts of Uniformity in the 16th century had restated this obligation. Elizabeth and the Stuarts followed suit. Debates in England had

attracted the attention of the authorities, although there were isolated prosecutions in New Haven County in the 1720's and 1730's for neglecting public worship on a specific Sabbath.[2] Even a large town like Boston attempted to enforce this attendance requirement strictly until the Revolution. In the early eighteenth century Boston ordered its constables "to take turns to Walk in and about the said town on the Lords Day in the time of Divine Worship" to note absentees. Plymouth Colony required selectmen to investigate those who did not come to meeting.[3] When the Hampshire County court convicted a person for absence from public worship in 1734, it ordered someone "to Inspect him and See if he does Reform and Attend Diligently and steadily upon the Publick Worship of God."[4]

Expected presence in a small public assembly on each Sabbath could be detrimental to personal privacy in a variety of ways. Absences were readily noticeable, engendering curiosity as to the whereabouts and circumstances of the absentee. Speculation about missing persons lightened the burden of a tedious sermon. When Samuel Sewall did not appear at a Thursday evening lecture delivered by his son, "twas taken much notice of." In 1717 Sewall himself observed that Mrs. Winthrop missed the service on a Sabbath afternoon: "I enquire of Mr. Winthrop. He saith She was not well at Noon: but was better."[5]

The social aspect of the Sabbath services was also related to the question of personal privacy. In one sense the decision to attend church was a deliberate search for publicity and an opportunity for

---

focused on behavior during the remainder of the day (see W. B. Whitaker, *Sunday in Tudor and Stuart Times* [London, 1933], and *The Eighteenth-Century English Sunday: A Study of Sunday Observance from 1677 to 1837* [London, 1940]).

[2] New Haven Co. Co. Files, 1720–29, L-Y, bundle R-Rex (1720, 1726); *ibid.*, 1730–39, M-R, bundle Rex (1734). One month's absence from services was also sufficient grounds for prosecution in early Stuart England (see Lambarde, *Eirenarcha*, p. 204).

[3] Suffolk Co. Gen. Sess., 1702–12, p. 132 (1706), pp. 169–70 (1708); *ibid.*, 1712–19, p. 156 (1717); *ibid.*, 1719–25, pp. 137–38 (1722); *Plymouth Col. Rec.*, XI, 217–18, 228 (1666, 1670). The minute books of the Suffolk Co. court contain prosecutions for nonattendance at public worship until the Revolution. In 1644 the town of Salem established Sabbath patrols to seek out those at home or in the fields during services (see Upham, *Salem Witchcraft*, I, 40).

[4] Hampshire County General Sessions and Common Pleas, bk. A, no. 2 (1728–35), p. 315, Northampton. Ministers encouraged church attendance; see Cotton Mather, *A Monitory Letter* (Boston, 1702; 2nd ed., Boston, 1738), and Benjamin Wadsworth, *Assembling at the House of God* (Boston, 1711).

[5] *Diary*, MHS, *Coll.*, 5th ser., VII, 143, 151n.

social display, as evidenced by the recurrent disputes over exact seating plans. Visibility in the local meetinghouse reflected one's status in the community. Church attendance was both an ingrained habit and the most regular group activity in the community. It was a pleasant opportunity to meet with friends and acquaintances; the Sabbath service informed the populace about the world. Local news circulated, most of it harmless; yet some gossip affected the privacy of others. The social benefits of church attendance, not to speak of the religious, tended to offset any lessening of personal privacy inherent in the situation. The interval between services was particularly suitable for social pleasures, since those living at a distance retired to the homes of friends or remained near the meetinghouse. During this interval ministers tried to "divert them as much as may be, even from all unseasonable Discourses."[6]

Outside the time of public worship the requirement that the Sabbath was not supposed to lose its serious aspect could hinder a search for personal privacy. New England practice reflected English ways about the time the immigration to America began. In sixteenth-century England, Sundays had been relatively unregulated in terms of permissible behavior; the populace regularly enjoyed sports and games. But by 1600 reformers were beginning to question popular behavior on the Sabbath. Although the Declaration of Sports by James I in 1618 permitted lawful recreations, the Puritans favored a complete spiritualization of the day.

New England formally dedicated the Sabbath to works of religion, charity, and necessity. Working, traveling, walking, riding, loitering, assembling, swimming, hunting, gardening, and frequenting public houses were forbidden. According to Cotton Mather the Sabbath was to be a day of "Sacred Rest." "Not only our own works but also our own Words, yea, and our own thoughts, must on the Lords-day be Rested from." There was to be no "speaking of Impertinencies," no "vain thoughts." "Tis Gods Time and will not admit any Pastime. Sports on the Lords-day; Never did any thing sound more sorrowfully or more odiously." But the Sabbath should not be a day of complete rest. "The Lords-day is as often polluted by Idleness, as by any sort of Profaneness. We never do more Amiss, than when we do nothing at all. By Sins of Omission; By Sleeping immoederately; by

[6] C. Mather, *A Good Evening*, p. 9; see also *Records of the First Church at Dorchester . . . 1636–1734* (Boston, 1891), pp. 111–12 (1696); a letter from the Rev. Nathaniel Eells to his congregation, the South Society in Scituate, March 29, 1732, Cushing Papers, 1664–1780, MHS; and Parkman, "Diary," AAS, *Proc.,* LXXIII (1963), 433 (1748).

Walking only to take the Air." The young theologian Jeremiah Dummer echoed this admonition: "They are egregiously mistaken, who imagine they have nothing else to do on this Day of rest, but to go dozing about with folded arms, or sit still in their chairs, free from all exercise of body, or mind."[7] Many persons did not heed these warnings; Sunday was an ideal time for relaxation and privacy. As early as 1595 the English Puritan Nicholas Bownde denounced "that brutish mind that some are of, that know no other thing to do upon the Sabbath but to rest, and take their ease, and therfore lye many times at home sleeping most prophanely, and so their oxe and their asse in ceasing from their worke, keepe as good a Sabbath as they."[8]

The prohibition of many activities on the Sabbath could contribute to crowding in the home, since parents may have attempted to keep children and servants within doors.[9] On the one free day of the week the entire family could be forced to share the intimacy of the home. Yet Sabbath regulations could contribute to the preservation of privacy by discouraging noisy behavior in the environs of a home or in the neighborhood, while encouraging withdrawal from collective activities and the search for individual solitude. Sabbatarian goals also clashed with the practical realities of human existence, especially for younger persons. Even though Rhode Island prohibited "sports, and Labours on the First Day of the Week," commissioners had to urge towns in 1654 to appoint other days when the young could "recreate themselves."[10]

A person who pursued his pleasures in public on the Sabbath ran the risk of prosecution for profaning the day. Nevertheless the pattern of enforcement of Sabbath regulations was typical of law enforcement in colonial New England.[11] Between March and Sep-

[7] Mather, *The Day Which the Lord Has Made* (Boston, 1703; rpt. Boston, 1707), pp. 17–20; Dummer, *A Discourse on the Holiness of the Sabbath* (Boston, 1704), p. 41.

[8] *The Doctrine of the Sabbath* (London, 1595), p. 169. See also Whitaker, *Sunday in Tudor and Stuart Times.*

[9] See the attempts recorded in *New Haven Town Rec.*, I, 415 (1659); *The Records of the First Church in Boston, 1630–1868*, ed. Richard D. Pierce, Col. Soc. Mass., *Publications, XXXIX-XLI* (Boston, 1961), XXXIX, 92 (1691) (hereafter cited as *Boston First Church Rec.*).

[10] *R.I. Rec.*, I, 279–80; for the law see *ibid.*, III, 31; *Laws R.I., 1719*, p. 32; *ibid., 1730*, p. 27; *ibid., 1767*, p. 241.

[11] See chapter 7 *infra.* Joseph Bennett, an English visitor to New England in 1740, was most impressed with the strictness of the Sabbath observance and the evidence of precautionary measures by the authorities to maintain it. One senses that Bennett was exposed more to the façade than to the realities of personal behavior on the Sabbath. There were a number of activities of an inevitably public

tember, 1761, Richard Dana, a Boston justice of the peace, handled about twenty-five cases of "unnecessarily walking and loitering in the street on the Lords day."[12] But Dana's record book, extending from 1760 through 1772, shows that this number of cases was extraordinary; in fact, between 1765 and 1771 only one other such action came before Dana. The sudden and temporary flurry of activity in 1761 clearly resulted from the establishment that year of a system of twelve wardens in the town "to see the Observation of the Lord's Day, on Penalty of £100. The Wardens are to inspect the Streets of the Town in their respective Wards on the Lord's-Day, to examine Persons, and require them to repair to their several Abodes."[13] The creation of such officers presumably reflected a recognized need to control Sabbath violations. In other Massachusetts towns from two to six wardens were elected annually, with the instructive proviso that a person need serve only once in five years. When the town of Belfast in Maine despaired of legally restraining visiting on the Sabbath, the town voted "that if any person makes unnecessary Vizits on the Sabeth, They shall be Look't on with Contempt."[14]

On the Sabbath the colonist was discouraged from seeking solitude by a walk in the outskirts of the town and encouraged to remain around his home when not at church. There are few indications that such desires suited the popular tastes. Few churches could house the entire population of a town for any service, so that enforcement of the attendance requirement was never total. In the eighteenth century Boston had to maintain a Sabbath watch during the harvest season to try to prevent persons leaving the town.[15] Many wandered outside the town to gather apples and fruits. In any town it was impossible to police the fields, woods, and obscure places on the Sabbath. The continuing reaffirmation of Sabbath laws was a response to the lack of popular observance.

The revels of Sunday evening when the Sabbath had officially

---

nature, such as traveling or congregating on a main street, that a person could not do, but there was only slight chance of discovery if an individual retired to a private place ("The History of New England, 1740," pp. 138–40, Sparks MSS Houghton Library, Harvard University).

[12] Dana, "Minute Book, 1760–1767," for Boston, Suffolk Co., *passim;* and "Pleas before Richard Dana, Esq., Beginning January 6, 1768, Ending March 8, 1772," for Boston, Suffolk Co., *passim,* in Dana Family Papers, box 3, MHS.

[13] *County and Town Officer,* pp. 19, 131–32.

[14] Alice Morse Earle, *The Sabbath in Puritan New England* (8th ed., Boston, 1896), pp. 249–50 (1776).

[15] *Boston Town Rec.,* XIII, XVII, *passim.*

ended alleviated the impact of any repressive regulation of private lives on the Puritan Sabbath. Cotton Mather observed that "the Parents [were] on Rambles, the Children in Revels, the Servants in Cabals . . . escaping from the Tiresome Duties of the Day." Mather was convinced that "the licentiousness of our Lords Day evening" was one of the flagrant scandals providing material for "some Filthy Men who Write Base Things of New-England."[16] The Massachusetts act for the reformation of manners in 1712 specifically forbade sporting, playing, making a disturbance, or committing any rudeness "on the evening following the Lord's day."[17]

The majority of the colonists attended a religious service on the Sabbath because it was a pleasant and customary social and religious duty. Whether or not they came, residents were subjected to some surveillance. Outside the church services behavior obviously ranged from that of the strictly ordered family to the opposite extreme, perhaps more typical than is usually suggested, in which the adults patronized the alehouses while the children and servants cavorted in the streets and fields. A proclamation by the royal governor of Massachusetts in 1699 complained that despite the laws for the sanctification of the Sabbath, "it is observed that not only Children and Youth, but many persons of riper years, do too often prophane the said Day by frequenting of Taverns and Ale-houses for Tipling and Drinking, Walking abroad in the streets and fields for diversion and recreation, and otherwise mispend the said holy Time."[18] The clash of promptings to conformity with the desires of human nature benefited privacy.

MINISTERS

The London Confession of 1589 had carefully described the duties of a Puritan pastor: "Hee must alwaies be carefull and watchfull over the flock whereof the Lord hath made him an overseer, . . . doing his duetie to everie soule, as he will aunswer before the chief Shepheard. . . . Hee must guyde and keep those sheep . . . thereby drawing them to him, thereby looking into their soules, even into their most secret thoughtes."[19] In Boston in 1673 the Reverend Increase Mather still

16 *A Good Evening*, pp. 13, 15; see also Mather's preface to T. Symmes, *A Monitor for Delaying Sinners* (Boston, 1719), p. i.
17 *Mass. Acts and Res.*, I, 681.
18 *A Proclamation* (Boston, 1699).
19 Walker, *Creeds and Platforms*, pp. 35–36.

considered himself the "Watchman" whom the Lord had charged "to blow the Trumpet, that sinners may have warning of their danger."[20] Such attitudes officially encouraged a Puritan minister to undertake a significant surveillance over his parishioners, with seemingly ominous effects on their privacy.

Certain Congregational ministers intruded in many ways into the private lives of their flocks. In the mid-seventeenth century the pastor of Roxbury overlooked the local tavern from his study window. When he saw town dwellers tippling, he would go over and warn them away.[21] Joseph Green, the minister of Salem, "admonished" his congregation "for drunkenness" on a Sabbath in 1708 and a year later specifically "acquainted the Church with the intemperate drinking of Jno. Martin and his wife."[22] But an incident in 1744 involving the Reverend Ebenezer Parkman's participation in the raising of a large barn in Westborough best illustrates both the scope and problems of ministerial supervision.

At Supper there were So many to be entertain'd that we were kept till 10 o'Clock. I manifested so much uneasiness that we were so detain'd that I concluded everybody would retire home as Soon as they might, but it prov'd otherwise. Many tarried long after I was got home and the Time run off; among the rest 3 of my own Family. After 12 I walk'd away towards the House again. Ebenezer and Thomas Needham were returning home—upon which I went to my Bed—but understanding that there were many yet behind and among them Some Heads of Family. I rose very uneasy and went down to the House, and having acquainted Captain Maynard with what Time of Night it was, I ask'd him whether he did not Consent to my going in among the Company that were Still diverting themselves at this unseasonable Time, I went in and admonished them, and sent them home. . . .

This Exerting my Authority gave me great uneasiness, but I was resolute to Shew Impartiality and not be partaker of other Mens Sins, as likewise to discharge my own Duty as Watchman in this Place and as having the Care of their Souls.[23]

This episode sensitively depicts the self-doubts of ministers of

20 *Wo to Drunkards* (Cambridge, Mass., 1673; 2d ed. Boston, 1712), "To the Reader."

21 This was Samuel Danforth, whose activities in this realm were hardly typical (*Sibley's Harvard Graduates* [Boston, 1873–], I, 89–90). A century later the minister of Westborough still periodically concerned himself with the drinking habits of his parishioners (Parkman, "Diary," AAS, *Proc.*, LXXV [1965], 120–21 [1751], 137–38 [1752]).

22 "Diary," Essex Institute, *Hist. Coll.*, X (1869), 81–82.

23 "Diary," AAS, *Proc.*, LXXII (1962), 181–82. Parkman was regularly inef-

eighteenth-century New England. Parkman's uneasiness at an action almost unparalleled in his recorded life contrasts sharply with the attitudes of some of his seventeenth-century predecessors.

The practice of family visitations channeled some ministers' inclinations toward surveillance. The Massachusetts ministers' convention of 1704 urged as a remedy for the lamentable decay of religion that pastors "do take up that Laborious, but engaging Practice, of making their Personal Visits unto all the Families that belong unto their Congregations."[24] Many kept their afternoons free for such visits, when social and religious obligations were blended in a private setting. In Newport, Ezra Stiles tried to visit his 130 families at least four times a year.[25]

Since ministers tended to settle in their offices for life, the combination of visits and a simple process of assimilation furnished them with intimate knowledge of a town. In Plymouth, for instance, only six pastors served before 1800, three in the eighteenth century. In colonial New Hampshire a twenty-year term as minister was typical.[26] Nevertheless, there were considerable limits to pastoral surveillance. In the country parishes the population was typically scattered over a large area after the first decades. Population growth dramatically increased the number of persons for whom a minister was responsible, even in the earliest years of settlement. There was one minister for every 260 Connecticut inhabitants around 1636, but only one for every 430 by 1662.[27]

Some ministers were little interested in regulating behavior among their flock by the processes of church discipline.[28] A minister who

---

fectual in his pleas for good behavior when a new barn, or even a meetinghouse, was raised (see *ibid.*, LXXIV [1964], 64–65 [1749], LXXV [1965], 76–77 [1751]).

[24] Walker, *Creeds and Platforms*, p. 483; see also Cotton Mather, *The Rules of a Visit* (Boston, 1705).

[25] Morgan estimated that Stiles made eighteen to twenty pastoral visits per week (*Gentle Puritan*, pp. 130, 191–92).

[26] Daniel H. Calhoun, *Professional Lives in America* (Cambridge, Mass., 1965), pp. 119–20.

[27] Benjamin Trumbull, *A Complete History of Connecticut* (Hartford, 1797), I, 292, 300.

[28] See, for example, the careers of John Cotton in Boston until 1652, Andrew Eliot in Boston of the 1750's, and Ezra Stiles in Newport at the same period (Larzer Ziff, *The Career of John Cotton: Puritanism and the American Experience* [Princeton, N.J., 1962], pp. 239, 252; Shipton, *New England Life*, p. 402; Morgan, *Gentle Puritan*, pp. 174, 191). In addition many towns had difficulty even finding ministers. Plymouth was without a minister from 1655 to 1667, Sandwich from 1653 to 1675 (George D. Langdon, Jr., *Pilgrim Colony* [New Haven, 1966], p. 119).

subordinated his moralistic duties to his other activities provided direct and indirect benefits for individual privacy in the locality. His attitude could have significant influence on the mass of the congregation. Security in office made some ministers lazy and others ineffectual when it came to the surveillance of personal behavior. They were never wholly freed from the burdens of maintaining existence, since salaries were rarely generous. Parkman found himself in a typical conflict when he scheduled a church lecture and the supervision of a hired plowman for the same day. "So perplexing is it to have the Affairs of the Ministry and of a Farm to manage together."[29] Few ministers could maintain for any lengthy period the religious hypertension demanded of the conforming Puritan minister and congregation, as the periodic cries for reform and revival in colonial New England testified. The changes affecting religiosity in the latter half of the seventeenth century created a less conducive atmosphere for all ministerial activities. Ministers always had enough problems in their ministry to make the delicate task of supervising personal behavior an attractive area to neglect, especially in the case of non-church members. Cotton Mather used strong language against these kinds of ministers in 1704: "A Pastor that can see Sin prevailing among his People, but is afraid of Reproving it, lest he lose his Gain from his Quarter, he may call himself a Shepherd, but God calls him, a Dumb Dog."[30] When a minister did try to oversee discipline, attention of an unpleasant sort often focused on him, especially by the eighteenth century. At an ordination sermon in Colchester, Connecticut, in 1732 the Reverend Thomas Clap reported that:

The Management of Church Discipline is become one of the standing Matters of Controversy and Contention in our Churches, fills the Heads and Hearts of Ministers with pressing Troubles and Distress, and is the greatest Means through the Instigation of Satan, of stirring up the Clamour and Ill-Will of People against them. One sad Effect and Consequence of all which is, that Ministers being under the Difficulties which this Part of their Work exposes them to, are under a Temptation to neglect or at least to perform it, in too overly a Manner, and not to deal faithfully with Men. So that Church Discipline is under an apparent Decay; the dealing with Offenders (which is so very necessary to preserve the external Purity of Religion) is but too slightly performed, and many Scandals pass over without a Reproof, and so Iniquity abounds amongst us.[31]

[29] "Diary," AAS, *Proc.*, LXXII (1962), 425–26.
[30] *A Faithful Monitor* (Boston, 1704), p. 380.
[31] *The Greatness and Difficulty of the Work of the Ministry* (Boston, 1732), p. 13.

If ministers were having this many problems with the disciplining of church members, their enthusiasm for broader supervision of the local populace was no doubt even more limited.

The changing status of the Congregational clergy in the local community by the early eighteenth century is well illustrated by a letter in 1721 from Samuel Sewall to the Reverend Benjamin Colman, the leading Boston clergyman, who had been collecting money for some religious purpose. Sewall wrote:

> I am Sorry to hear there is Such a deficiency in the Contribution; It puts me on asking the favor of You Never to Use Any Argument with any One of my giving orders that my part Should continue to be Contributed, for Although I am Conscious to my Selfe that It is my duty (by the Ingagements I am under, as representative of a proprietor and One of the church and Congregation; and as this distresst time brings a much greater burthen on the ministers) yet we live in Such An Age that It's too Often a flouting expression to be called a Ministerial man, but however I am fully of Opinion that the present Contempt of Our Ministry carries with it a Very Ill Omen; I'm sure Its a Very great Degeneracy from Our Forefathers, who always had that Order of men highly in Esteem, and We never were happier than when we were So Sweetly Guided by the hands of Moses and Aaron without the Least Jarr or discord.[32]

Sewall requested Colman to burn the letter, claiming that he had not planned to speak on the topic, "but Its what I have often thought of and dreaded the Consequence."

The minister's position as an employee of the congregation on which he was dependent for support further diminished his zeal. Only a strong man could far outdistance the mood of his congregation in the drive for sanctity. The experience of Jonathan Edwards in Northampton in 1750 suggests that even the exception ran into eventual obstacles.[33] He was dismissed from his pulpit when he tried to return to the seventeenth-century practice of restricting full church membership, and especially the privilege of participation in the Lord's Supper, to those who could publicly furnish evidence of a conversion experience, that is, of their sanctity. The population saw the minister as their religious advisor and granted him no official voice in the temporal affairs of either the church or the town. Even the pastor's control over the discipline of full church members was shared with the elected elders of the church. Solomon Stoddard of Northampton touched on some further problems: "The Calling of a Minis-

---

[32] Sewall, Medford, to Colman, Boston, Sept. 12, 1721, B. Colman Papers, I.
[33] See Ola E. Winslow, *Jonathan Edwards (1703–1758)* (New York, 1940), chaps. 11 and 12.

ter lay him open to great Temptation, especially thro' a Spirit of Fear
to neglect his duty. Sometimes he is called to Preach such Truths as
will be offensive to some . . . some are his friends and he is loth to of-
fend them, he has a dependance upon some, and it is dangerous cross-
ing them."[34] Such pressures, which affected all officials charged with
the regulation of private lives, served to create a climate in which the
need not to infringe too greatly on personal privacy was given due
consideration.

An incident in Westborough during the pastorate of Ebenezer
Parkman illustrates a concern for privacy in actual ministerial practice. When he was called late one evening in 1727 to visit a dying
woman, Parkman asked her a series of questions about her religious
life in the presence of the family and close friends. One relative later
took great exception to the questions asked, particularly in front of the
group. Parkman sought to justify his procedure: "The person being
look'd upon as near expiring I thought not to thrust those persons
So well acquainted with the woman . . . out of the room, and Seeing
my discourse was generall and what anyone might hear. Yet when
under any of those heads any particular private matters have occur'd
it has then been usuall with me to desire the Company to withdraw."
The woman had never done anything scandalous, and her answers
could only be edifying to those present: "Were I examining a person
that had been notoriously vicious and demanding a particular confession and before so many witnesses it had been another thing."[35]
This is but one example of the sense of privacy normally attached to
the conduct of many church activities. The colonial ministers brought
their duty of surveillance and their flock's demands for privacy into
some kind of practical equilibrium.

THE RELATION

The novel procedures for admission to full membership in the Congregational church had implications for personal privacy. Since only
full church members were admitted to the Lord's Supper, they were
expected to be Visible Saints. Anyone who wished to join the elect
church from the general congregation had to be carefully scrutinized
for proof of a conversion experience. This scrutiny, as institutionalized

[34] *The Presence of Christ with the Ministers of the Gospel* (Boston, 1718),
p. 6.
[35] "Diary," AAS, *Proc.*, LXXI (1961), 186–91; for another instance of Parkman's concern for privacy, see *ibid.*, LXXIII (1963), 100.

after 1633 in the Relation,[36] required a person seeking admission to testified regenerate membership to be interviewed by the elders. The latter were in charge of the admission process until the decline of their office in the late seventeenth century; thereafter the minister himself interviewed candidates for the Relation. According to the Puritan leader Thomas Hooker, the elder was "to enquire diligently, and carefully to inform himself, touching the uprightnesse of the persons carriage and conversation from the testimony of others, who know him intimately, and will in reason deale nakedly and sincerely therein."[37] If no unsatisfactory information was uncovered, the elders informed the congregation of his desire to enter into full communion so that any who objected could express their views.

When the final ceremonies arrived, the applicant made a Relation of the work of God on his soul. Edward Johnson, a layman who participated in the formation of a church at Woburn, Massachusetts, in the 1640's, described the Relation as follows:

Then publikely he declares the manner of his conversion, and how the Lord hath been pleased by the hearing of his Word preached, and the work of his Spirit in the inward parts of his soul, to bring him out of that natural darkness, which all men are by nature in and under, as also the measure of knowledg the Lord hath been pleased to indue him withal. And because some men cannot speak publikely to edification through bashfulness, the less is required of such, and women speak not publikely at all, *for all that is desired*, is to prevent the polluting the blessed Ordinances of Christ by such as walk scandalously.[38]

This address of about one quarter hour was a time for spiritual autobiography. A person guilty of scandalous behavior concluded his Relation by alluding to these sins and his subsequent repentance.

[36] Scholars debate whether the Relation altered the essential character of Congregationalism or was simply a "technical adaptation" of the earlier admission standards to new circumstances (see Raymond R. Stearns and David H. Brawner, "New England Church 'Relations' and Continuity in Early Congregational History," AAS, *Proc.*, LXXV [1965], 13–46).

[37] *A Survey of the Summe of Church-Discipline* (London, 1648), pt. 3, p. 4.

[38] Quotation is from Johnson, *Wonder-Working Providence*, pp. 217–18 (my italics). On the question of church admissions, see Thomas Lechford, *Plain Dealing; or, Newes from New-England* (London, 1642), in MHS, *Coll.*, 3d ser., III (1833), 65–69, 108; Edmund S. Morgan, *Visible Saints: The History of a Puritan Idea* (New York, 1963), esp. pp. 51–63, 88–92; *New Haven Col. Rec., 1638–1649*, p. 16; Hooker, *Survey of Church-Discipline*, pt. 3, pp. 4–6; *A Platform of Church Discipline Gathered out of the Word of God, and Agreed Upon by the Elders, and Messengers of the Churches Assembled in the Synod at Cambridge in New England* (Cambridge, Mass., 1649; rpt. London, 1653), chap. 12 (hereafter cited as *Cambridge Platform of Church Discipline*).

Then the elders asked whether the Relation had satisfied the church members. Probing questions were in order if fuller explanations were desired. Finally the applicant made a formal profession of faith and subscribed to the local church covenant.

An individual thus submitted to a searching investigation of his past behavior and then publicly told the story of his conversion.[39] The application of Jehabal Loomis for membership in the First Church of Windsor, Connecticut, in 1734, exemplified the extent to which the private life of an applicant could be probed. The church met to consider some "credible Reports" respecting his "ill Conversation" two years before with the wife of Stephen Loomis. It took evidence from persons who knew about the affair at the time and concluded "that he is Guilty to Scandal of Lascivious Carriage in said Private Converse and to not to be accepted without Publicke Reflexion on himselfe therein."[40] In this unusual case acceptance was predicated upon a demonstration of abasement and humiliation before the community. During the admission process anyone could provide information detrimental to an applicant. In 1713 Abraham Skinner of Chelsea heard that Thomas Parker planned to join the church at Malden. Skinner wrote the pastor to report "that I have known this Thomas Parker to be guilty of falsifying or lying." In 1749 a Negro tried to join the Chelsea church but was rejected after the pastor of Mansfield wrote that he had earlier suspended the man for obnoxious conduct. Chelsea voted not to admit the applicant until he had satisfied Mansfield church.[41]

The procedures for admission to membership kept some persons out of the church. As early as 1640, Thomas Lechford, a Boston resident unsympathetic to the Puritans, wrote that "here is required such confessions, and professions, both in private and publique, both by men and women, before they be admitted, that three parts of the

[39] The whole procedure was a trying personal experience. Two recent writers have referred to the Relation as "a psychological probe" and a "seventeenth-century forerunner of the Rorschach, or ink-blot test, by which a trained technician can make a sketchy but comprehensive assessment of the salient features of his subject's personality" (Stearns and Brawner, "New England Church Relations," p. 32). The Relations also fulfilled an emotional need for the listeners (see Lewis M. Robinson, "A History of the Half-Way Covenant," [Ph.D. diss., University of Illinois, 1963], pp. 72, 59).

[40] First Congregational Church, Windsor, Conn., Records, 1636–1932, vol. XV ("Church Discipline, 1723–1747"), Dec. 27, 1734, CSL.

[41] Chelsea church records, M. Chamberlain, *A Documentary History of Chelsea* (Boston, 1908), II, 204, 270.

people of the Country remaine out of the Church."[42] Men especially did not appreciate such practices, if one can judge from the usual predominance of female members. English men and women were not accustomed to admissions procedures, since everyone in England automatically belonged to the state church. Thus the pursuit of membership in a Puritan church was not at first glance an attractive prospect. The procedures seem to have authorized compulsory disclosure of intimate matters and searching forays into private lives. Even English and Continental contemporaries became concerned with the character of church admissions in early New England.[43]

The leading ministers of New England responded to criticism with expositions explaining and defending their methods and furnished a somewhat different picture of the nature of the Relation. Thomas Hooker set forth his moderate views of the admission process in *A Survey of the Summe of Church-Discipline*.[44] His initial point, an important one for privacy, was that no person was forced to join the church against his will: "Faith is not forced." Applicants voluntarily agreed to make Relations in the interests of a higher good. The preconditions for admittance only involved the avoidance of scandal, open sins, and neglect of duty, coupled with some reasonable statement of conversion. "This rule being received and agreed upon, it would marvailously facilitate the work of Admission, without any trouble, and prevent such curious inquisitions and niceties, which the pride and wantonnesse of mens spirits hath brought into the Church, to disturb the peace thereof, and to prejudice the progresse of God's Ordinances." Hooker's version of these matters presumed careful concern for the privacy of those involved.

In 1645 John Norton, the Ipswich minister, finished a work about New England church practices in response to the questions of a

---

[42] *Plain Dealing*, pp. 122–23.

[43] See Rev. R. Stansby, Suffolk, to Rev. John Wilson, Boston, April 17, 1637, *Winthrop Papers*, III, 390; and Thomas Gostlin, Groton, to John Winthrop, Boston, *ibid.*, IV, 211.

[44] A brilliant preacher and among the ablest English ministers of his generation, Hooker had been a leading Puritan before his immigration to Massachusetts in 1633. In 1636 he led the foundation of Connecticut, where he ruled as a virtual dictator until his death in 1647. One historian has suggested that Hooker left Massachusetts partly because he found the admissions policy too strict there (Norman Pettit, *The Heart Prepared: Grace and Conversion in Puritan Spiritual Life* [New Haven, 1966], p. 100). Hooker treated church admissions in *Survey of Church-Discipline*, pt. 3, pp. 3–6. The work was written in 1644–45 and approved by the ministers of New England at Cambridge in 1645.

Dutch colleague. He too was sensitive to criticisms of harshness, arguing that "the judgment of charity" should prevail in the admissions procedure: "Nothing beyond the strength of any faithful adult using his reason is required in the candidate's confession or for the criterion in general. Nothing is required in this confession which is not shared by all faithful men. *There is no place here for private matters.* Extraordinary beliefs are not sought after. . . . All must be done in a spirit of gentleness and prudence, with thought for *the dignity* of the candidate."[45] Such statements indicate a well-developed awareness of the need to safeguard personal privacy.

The Cambridge Platform of Church Discipline in 1648 was the culmination of the early development of Congregational practices in New England. It remained the guide to usage for the rest of the colonial period. The product of a synod of New England ministers, the Platform explicitly called for moderation and compassion in the admission process: "The weakest measure of faith is to be accepted in those that desire to be admitted into the church. . . . The Lord Jesus would not quench the smoaking flax, nor breake the bruised reed, but gather the tender lambes in his arms, and carry them gently in his bosome. Such charity and tenderness is to be used, as the weakest christian if sincere, may not be excluded, nor discouraged. Severity of examination is to be avoyded."[46]

The utilization of the Relation to discern saving grace underwent modification during the colonial era. Changes making admission to full membership easier began as early as 1645. Some persons desiring to become church members, especially the children and grandchildren of members, could not produce evidence of a regenerate religious experience. The Half-Way Covenant of 1662 permitted a major shift in the standards of admission.[47] As acceptance of the Half-Way Covenant gradually spread after 1675, the children of full church members were baptized and were permitted to have their children baptized, but fewer and fewer attempted to reach the exclusive summit of church membership, participation in the Lord's Supper, by making a Relation. A form of open Communion became associated

[45] *The Answer to the Whole Set of Questions of the Celebrated Mr. William Apollonius* (London, 1648), ed. and tr. Douglas Horton (Cambridge, Mass., 1958), pp. 26–27, 39, 42 (my italics). Norton came to Massachusetts in 1635 and served in Ipswich from 1638 to 1652. In the latter year he succeeded John Cotton to the leading pulpit in New England.

[46] *Cambridge Platform of Church Discipline*, p. 17.

[47] See Robert G. Pope, *The Half-Way Covenant* (Princeton, N.J., 1969), pp. 142–47, 251–58, 265–69.

with a series of Connecticut, Massachusetts, and Plymouth churches in the late 1660's and then with the name of Solomon Stoddard in 1677 in Northampton. The latter was much imitated in the Connecticut Valley in subsequent years. The practice of open Communion permitted Half-Way Covenant members to partake of the Lord's Supper without making a Relation. The significance of the Relation gradually declined. In fact, Lewis Robinson has argued that the Relation was more responsible for the Half-Way Covenant than any other single factor.[48] Persons did not relish making such a public appearance before the congregation, even if they could make claims of receiving saving grace. Perry Miller argued that the Half-Way Covenant embodied Puritan recognition that "religion was practically confined to the inner consciousness of the individual. He alone needed to be concerned about the assurances of election. The churches were pledged in effect not to pry into the genuineness of any religious emotions, but to be altogether satisfied with decorous semblances."[49] The prominent minister John Higginson, who was pastor of the Salem church for almost a half century after 1660, concluded: "He that is privie to his owne wickedness and knows himselfe to be one that hates to be reformed, should not present himselfe to a Church for admission ps. 50: 16: 17, yet if such an one doo present himselfe the church ought to admit him as Judas, because the Church Judgeth not of Secret Things."[50] The Congregational churches generally recognized the limited extent to which they could or should penetrate the privacy of an applicant for admission.

From an early date the methodology of the Relation evidenced concern for privacy, and subsequent changes lent even more privacy to the procedures. In 1633 the Reverend John Cotton, a leading exponent of Congregationalism, asked that his wife "not be put to make open confession, etc., which he said was against the apostle's rule, and not fit for women's modesty." When a Dedham woman fainted several times in public, she was examined in private and only acknowledged the Relation in full assembly.[51] In the 1640's Thomas Hooker wrote concerning women that "we find it by experience, the feebleness in some, their shamefac'd modesty and melanchollick

---

[48] "History of the Half-Way Covenant," p. 47.

[49] "The Half-Way Covenant," *NEQ*, VI (1933), 703.

[50] In his undated account Higginson was opposing the necessity of making a Relation (Misc. Coll. [bound], I [n.d.-1662], fol. 1, 1629, MHS).

[51] Winthrop, *Journal*, I, 107; Dedham church records, *Dedham Historical Records Series* (Dedham, Mass., 1888), II, 21 (1639); see also Salem (1629), in *Chronicles of the Pilgrim Fathers*, pp. 100–101.

fearsomenesse is such, that they are not able to expresse themselves in the face of a Congregation." He reported that it was common practice to receive the Relations of all women "in private" and only "make report of them to the Congregation."[52] The Cambridge Platform generally extended this practice of leniency toward bashful men and women to any that "through excessive fear, or other infirmity, be unable to make their personal relation of their spirituall estate in publick." John Norton described a further modification: "If one of the brethren asks for further elucidation of some point than has been given in a confession of the object and work of faith, we judge it expedient that the question be not directly asked by that brother himself. With the approval of the eldership, it is put to the candidate indirectly by one of the elders, because elders are the mouthpiece of the church."[53] This last measure prevented embarrassing personal confrontations.

Local practices surrounding the making of Relations in the mid-seventeenth century have been little known, but some information does exist about the pastorate of the Reverend John Fiske in Wenham and then in Chelmsford, Massachusetts. An initial question after the organization of the Wenham church in 1644 was whether women should make their Relations themselves, since some churches did not permit it. Wenham decided in the affirmative, "because the whole Church is to judge of your meetnes, which cannot so well be if she speake not herselfe." Twelve years later the new church in Chelmsford reached the opposite conclusion, declaring "that the officer should repeate and declare the Relation of the Women to the Church."[54] In 1644 the Wenham church also debated whether the examination of new members, the hearing of their Relations, and church discipline cases should be conducted before the entire congregation. Because of concern for privacy, they decided that only church members and specially admitted persons could be present: "We reason because church members being men, and men haveing these weaknesses and weake men wilbe apt to show their weaknesses, that these may not be knowne or manifested. We [see] no reason to cry our weaknesses, but hide them for this for the honor of our husband, and head Christ: not to give occasion to others, to speake reproachfully of the church. . . . Nor is there the freedom of speaking: for some, nor in some cases, before a mixt multitude."[55] In December

[52] *Survey of Church-Discipline*, pt. 3, p. 6.
[53] *Cambridge Platform of Church Discipline*, p. 17; *Answer*, p. 42.
[54] Fiske, "Notebook of Church Matters," pp. 28, 181.
[55] *Ibid.*, p. 29.

of the same year, the Wenham church reaffirmed that initial investigations of candidates for church membership should be before the church in private. "Here some reasons alledged for it, because 1. the preserving of the good name of the party 2. that the things that be private, be kept private 3. the preserving the honor of the gospel and the providing of the great peace and safety of the church."[56] The Wenham church thought of itself as a familial unit, in which full church members enjoyed a special intimacy. Yet privacy was essential in all activities and against the outside world.

The practice of making public Relations was controversial enough as a stumbling block to church membership to attract the attention of a man charged with an examination of major issues in New England. An English commissioner appointed to investigate New England in the 1660's wrote about one of his associates to a fellow commissioner, who was also the governor of New York: "Colonel Sarles, I hear, is to be made a [church] member, and a magistrate; it is certain that they have agreed that the members upon their admission must make no more publick confessions in their meeting houses, but in private, and they say, this order was made in relation to him."[57]

By 1700 men had been extended the traditional female privilege of making their Relation in private to the elders and then having it read in public. The Dorchester church adopted this custom as early as the mid-1660's, after the elders reported that "ther weer severall yong men in the Towne who would be willing to Joyne to the Church if they might have ther Confession taken in privat by wrighting and declared publickly to the Church, they standing forth and owneing what was declared." After some opposition the church concluded that such a practice was permissible, although some remaining hesitancy was expressed in the instruction that if the elders "judged any man able to make a publick relation by his owne mouth they should endeavor to p'swad him soe to doe."[58] The First Church of Boston recognized the possibility of a written Relation in 1679, and the Charlestown church did so in 1685, concluding that "mens relations (their own pronouncing them having been constantly found inconvenient) be for the future *read*."[59] There was serious debate in the

---

[56] *Ibid.*, pp. 47–48. The Chelmsford church also decided in 1656 that church members would meet alone for the initial investigations of prospective members (*ibid.*, p. 181).

[57] Col. George Cartwright, Boston, to Col. Richard Nicolls, New York, Jan. 30, 1665, Gay Transcripts, State Papers, II, 4.

[58] *Dorchester Church Rec.*, pp. 45–46; vote renewed in 1672, p. 67.

[59] *Boston First Church Rec.*, Col. Soc. Mass., *Publications*, XXXIX, 75; *Rec-*

Old South Church in 1685 when two men sought "to come into the Church without making any Relation at all; or having Mr. Willard report the Substance of what they said to him." They finally had to make Relations themselves, but only after the church decided that the general congregation would be excluded at such times.[60]

Over the course of the late seventeenth century, some Congregational churches ceased to require Relations, and the majority of remaining churches hedged the Relation with even more protections for privacy. The battles over the necessity of the Relation were carried out on two levels: colonywide, with the leading clergymen sounding salvos, and in the individual independent churches where the dispositions of pastor and laity always held sway. The only common pattern was that the form of the Relation, before whom it should be made, and whether it should be required, eventually became subject to debate in most churches, leading in the end to the complete abolition of the practice. Personal privacy was a basic issue underlying this concern.

The Reforming Synod of 1679–80 in Massachusetts declared that "it is requisite that persons be not admitted unto Communion in the Lords Supper without making a personal and publick profession of their Faith and Repentance, either orally, or in some other way, so as shall be to the just satisfaction of the Church."[61] Edmund Morgan has pointed out that this was an equivocal statement, since it could be construed to mean that only a profession of faith was required. A majority of those in attendance refused to endorse a statement by Increase Mather "that persons should make a Relation of the work of Gods Spirit upon their hearts."[62]

In the 1690's the debate flared anew as the Mathers attempted to hold the line on Relations against liberal innovators, especially the founders of the Brattle Street Church in Boston. The Manifesto of this church maintained the standard of "visible Sanctity," but "we assume not to our selves to impose upon any a Publick Relation of their Experiences."[63] The pastor should satisfy himself privately on such subjects. Cotton Mather admitted there had been "unjustifiable Severity, in Imposing Circumstantials not Instituted, whereby some

---

ords *of the First Church in Charlestown, Massachusetts, 1632–1789* (Boston, 1880), p. ix.

[60] Sewall, *Diary*, MHS, *Coll.*, 5th ser., V, 92, 94–95.

[61] Walker, *Creeds and Platforms*, p. 433.

[62] Quoted in Morgan, *Visible Saints*, p. 147.

[63] From a Manifesto in *Records of the Church in Brattle Square, Boston, 1699–1872* (Boston, 1902), pp. 4–5.

truly Gracious Souls have been Discouraged from Offering themselves to joyn in Fellowship with such Churches."[64] Increase Mather
recognized that the Relation was not absolutely necessary for reasons
indicative of a definite sensitivity about personal privacy:

The natural Tempers and Infirmities of some are such as make them un-
capable of relating publickly what God has done for them. Some have a
natural Hesitance of Speech. Others are of very bashful Tempers. . . . It
is possible that the Occasion of a mans Conversion may have been something not fit to be publickly related. . . . It may be some Secret Sin which
himself has been guilty of . . . but this he ought not to tell the World of.[65]

But he still argued that the Relation by those seeking full church
membership edified the listeners and honored God. His critics re-
asserted that Relations were a creation of man that should be dispensed with: "The more meek and fearful are hereby kept out of
Gods House, while the more conceited and presumptuous never
bogge at this, or any thing else."[66]

In 1697 the church in Cambridge held several meetings about the
Relation; liberal innovators were evidently trying to make changes.
At first the church agreed that the elders could question a person
privately about his religious experiences and then communicate the
answers publicly. Two months later the church agreed "that the
making a Relation be not imposed upon any that Offer themselves
for Communion with us at the Lord's Table"; no mention was made
of the public report of a private Relation. Several meetings ensued
because some of the congregation were upset. The pastor and elders
were asked to communicate to the church something of the applicant's spiritual fitness. The minister agreed that this was to continue
"so long as the peace of the Church calls for it; They would then be
satisfyed and give no further Trouble."[67] Obviously the subject of
the Relation caused great controversy, with personal privacy often
a central issue.[68] Yet substantial progress was made in protecting the
privacy of the minority actively seeking admission to full Communion by the relation of a conversion experience.

By the time Cotton Mather produced his monumental study of

[64] *Ecclesiastes: The Life . . . of Jonathan Mitchell* (Boston, 1697), p. 6 and,
for the whole argument, pp. 6–25.
[65] *The Order of the Gospel* (Boston, 1700), pp. 29–30, 32.
[66] Anon., *Gospel Order Revived* (New York, 1700), pp. 6, 9.
[67] *Records of the Church of Christ at Cambridge in New England, 1632–
1830*, ed. S. P. Sharples (Boston, 1906), pp. 121–23.
[68] The churches of western Massachusetts and the Connecticut Valley turned
to open Communion without Relations partly under the influence of Solomon
Stoddard (see Stoddard, *An Appeal to the Learned* [Boston, 1709]).

Congregational practices in 1726, the process of admission to full Communion had been shorn of all its tendencies to invade privacy. In many churches the pastor examined a candidate alone and asked him a series of questions about his education, religious knowledge, and resolutions about piety. Only one standard question bordered on the invasion of privacy: "Is every Sin Grievous and Odious to you? And is there no known Sin wherein you indulge your self?" The pastor briefly reported the results of his examination to the church. Mather concluded that Relations in public were no longer necessary and surmised that "there is now generally a great Relaxation of several Severities, in the Modes of these Matters, formerly required in some of the Churches."[69] Although the inevitable reaction later appeared in the person of the prominent minister Jonathan Edwards, who wanted to reinstitute strict standards for admission to full Communion,[70] the process of liberalization continued.

The making of Relations remained a controversial question in eighteenth-century New England. A succession of additional churches finally abandoned the custom or made it optional. In 1714 the minister of Medford refused to reject applicants who would not make Relations.[71] Beverly, Natick, and Harvard discontinued Relations around 1730.[72] They were made optional in the next twenty years by Hull, Brewster, Quincy, Weston, and Chelsea. Weston did so because "some serious Persons may have Scruples in their minds about Making a Relation of their Experience or Convictions . . . as thinking they are not obliged thereto by the Gospel."[73] The Lynnfield church only did away with the required Relation in 1784.[74] Most of these churches still allowed a person to make a Relation if he so desired.

The evolution of admission practices in the Plymouth church typi-

---

[69] *Ratio Disciplinae*, pp. 85–89.

[70] Edwards, *An Humble Inquiry . . . Concerning the Qualifications Requisite to a Compleat Standing and Full Communion in the Visible Christian Church* (Boston, 1749).

[71] Emil Oberholzer, Jr., *Delinquent Saints: Disciplinary Action in the Early Congregational Churches of Massachusetts* (New York, 1956), p. 23.

[72] Beverly First Church records, Essex Institute, *Hist. Coll.*, XXXVI (1900), 301; Oberholzer, *Delinquent Saints*, p. 23; Shipton, *New England Life*, pp. 290–91.

[73] Oberholzer, *Delinquent Saints*, pp. 23, 273–74; Town of Weston, *Church Records, 1709–1825* (Boston, 1901), pp. 530, 548; Chamberlain, *Doc. Hist. of Chelsea*, II, 265, 290.

[74] Lynnfield First Church records, Essex Institute, *Hist. Coll.*, XXXIV (1898), 161.

fied the growth of concern for personal privacy. Even in the 1640's their requirements assumed a respect for privacy. According to the sometime governor Edward Winslow, the Plymouth churches wanted "to see the grace of God shining forth (at least seemingly, leaving secret things to God) in all we admit into church fellowship with us, and to keep off such as openly wallow in the mire of their sins."[75] By 1669 the Plymouth custom was for men to make oral Relations in the presence of the entire congregation, while women had their Relations written in private and read in public by the pastor. In 1677 "the church condescended soe far as to take in private the relation of Samuel Cutbert, and the Elder the next Sabbath declaring some part of it in the publick congregation, he was admitted to full communion." By 1688 the church members were told that "divers men who offered themselves to church-fellowship were bashfull and of low voices and therefore not able to speak in publick to the edification of the congregation, nor to the hearing of the whole church." The members decided to hear these Relations in private; they were undetermined whether to communicate them later to the whole congregation. By 1705 Plymouth had followed the lead of the other eastern Massachusetts churches and capitulated on the matter of written Relations. They agreed that an oral Relation "might be an hindrance to Some Gracious Soules and that it might hinder the growth of the Church," undoubtedly a minimization of the problems encountered by the church. Subsequently a Relation could be written and then acknowledged as it was read to the church. This practice remained standard in Plymouth until at least the Revolution.[76]

There are indications that Connecticut churches were less forward in dispensing with Relations, although traditionally less strict on admission to church membership. The First Church of Norwich voted in 1717 to continue to require Relations from applicants. In 1732 the church agreed that Relations could be written out in advance and read before the full church members only. Finally in 1745 Relations were no longer required for admission to the Norwich church. In 1751 the First Church of New Haven simply decided that Relations should be made before the church members and not the entire congregation. In 1775 the First Church of Windsor accepted as current practice their desire "that those that Joyn in full Communion with this Church

[75] Quoted in Langdon, *Plymouth Colony*, p. 128.
[76] *Plymouth Church Records* (New York, 1920–23), I, 145, 154, 163, 201, II, 371.

would make Relations, but at the same time this Church do not make it a term of Communion."[77]

Although most congregations retaining the Relation required the applicant for full membership to step up to the front during the public ceremonies, some of these churches eventually introduced a further protection for personal sensibilities. In 1757 some members of the Cambridge church proposed to end the practice of persons standing in front, "alledging that it was disagreeable and Surprizing to Some Persons and had been offered by way of objection by some Persons and had been such a Stumbling Block to them as to prevent the offering themselves for admission and Considering it was but a meer Circumstantial thing and a matter of indifference, and considering allso that the Practice of other Churches allowed persons to Stand in their own proper Places att the time of admission." The church agreed to end the requirement, insisting only that the applicant "be fairly before the Pastor and in view of the assembly." Weston ended the same practice in 1783 although the church had insisted upon it in 1751.[78] The public confession of particular past offenses as part of the Relation was the last aspect of the admission process to attract attention. This was required in those churches that kept Relations until after the Revolution.[79] It was one part of the admission procedure that in theory could become intensely personal. Yet even the mid-seventeenth-century Relations reveal that although every applicant had some sins to repent, these tended to be dull in comparison with some other incidents known to have occurred in the society. Persons reported doubts that they would persevere or concern about the danger of hypocrisy. No one proceeded to narrate tales of adultery, bestiality, or drunkenness. The selectivity of the process meant that such sinners rarely applied for church membership. The many Relations summarized by the Reverend John Fiske between 1640 and 1675 were autobiographical but contained almost no intimate details. Even this formalized custom died out after the Revolution. The Weston church decided in 1794 that "where persons have been guilty of notorious violation of God's law, instead of a particular

[77] J. M. Bumsted, "Revivalism and Separatism in New England: The First Society of Norwich, Connecticut as a Case Study," *WMQ*, 3d ser., XXIV (1967), 595, 602–603; First Congregational Church of New Haven, Records, 1639–1926, I ("Minutes of Church Meetings and Proceedings, 1644–1806"), 13; First Cong. Church, Windsor, Rec., XV, 35, 38.

[78] *Cambridge Church Rec.*, p. 215; Weston, *Church Rec.*, pp. 542, 533.

[79] See list of churches abandoning the practice in Oberholzer, *Delinquent Saints*, pp. 24, 274.

confession to the church, specifying their faults, as has been usual, heretofore, in some cases, a confession of sin in general terms in their relation, and procession of repentance and sorrow, shall be deemed satisfactory."[80] In most churches this had always been the practice.

The making of a Relation was always hedged with significant protections for personal privacy. In fact the opposition to the Relation that was encountered and the changes carried out further to protect privacy are a most revealing aspect of the whole practice. By 1700 it was relatively easy to become a full member of a New England church. The admissions process no longer presented any apparent problems for privacy. An appreciation of the need to safeguard personal privacy played a significant part in this evolution.

CHURCH DISCIPLINE

When Robert Brown was reducing Congregational principles to writing in the late sixteenth century, he included the statement that "we must all watch one another."[81] Full church members in New England agreed "to submitt to the order, discipline and governement of Christ in this his church . . . and to the brotherly watch of fellow members."[82] These Visible Saints were obligated to help their brethren remain in visible sanctity. As Thomas Hooker wrote, "I stand charged in a most peculiar manner, to prevent all taint of sin in any Member of the Society, that either it may never be committed; or if committed, it may speedily be removed, and the spirituall good of the whole preserved."[83] This applied not only to the observation of an offense but to the implementation of disciplinary action. When a Chelmsford man encouraged the church to quash a case in 1663, he was reminded that "sin must not be so smothered, but our brother having broke the Rule must see it."[84] When certain members of the Plymouth church generated concern in 1677 by spending too much time in taverns, all agreed that "in case they saw or heard of any such carriage in any of the church for the future, to demand a reason of the party why he

---

[80] Fiske, "Notebook of Church Matters," *passim;* Weston, *Church Rec.,* p. 543.

[81] Walker, *Creeds and Platforms,* p. 22; see also p. 67 for the Second Confession of the London-Amsterdam Church, 1596.

[82] From the Covenant in Beverley First Church rec., (1667), Essex Institute, *Hist. Coll.,* XXXV (1899), 182–83; see also Salem, 1665, Walker, *Creeds and Platforms,* p. 121; and Chelsea church rec., (1715), in Chamberlain, *Doc. Hist. of Chelsea,* II, 198–99; *Plymouth Church Rec.,* I, 233 (1726).

[83] *Survey of Church-Discipline,* pt. 3, p. 3.

[84] Fiske, "Notebook of Church Matters," pp. 286–87.

soe did, and that wee would satisfy the demands of each other in such a case, and if any did not give satisfying answers to such sober, christian demands, it should be accounted just matter of offence." In the 1750's Andrew Sergant of Gloucester saw Mrs. Tabitha Luskin and a friend in the pasture at dusk in an adulterous situation. "As he was going to Meeting the next Sabbath (it being Sacrament day) he saw said Tabitha Going to Meeting. She being a Communicant. He told her if she Tarried to partake of the Sacrament he would Speak out and tell the Church what he had Seen and heard on Which she Turned back and went home."[85] The concept of watchfulness seems to have subjected church members to a substantial degree of mutual surveillance.

Church discipline was not an invention of the Puritans. The Anglican church in Elizabethan and early Stuart England had ecclesiastical courts that supervised the morality and ecclesiastical views of the entire population. These courts became generally corrupt and ineffectual, primarily concerned with persecuting those of Puritan inclination for such offenses as neglecting the Book of Sports or not wearing surplices.[86] Thus church courts were anathema to the Puritans; there were no ecclesiastical courts in colonial New England. The disappearance of such zealous and invidious English officials as the apparitors, whose semiclerical enthusiasm for the enforcement of morality far surpassed that of any New England secular officials, made a significant contribution to the preservation of individual privacy.

The disciplinary procedures of the Congregational churches affected only those in the general population who volunteered to participate. Thomas Hooker wrote that these full church members "have speciall power one over another, and that by vertue of the Covenant; for by free and mutuall consent, they who were free to joyn in any other Society, they willingly yeelded themselves unto this, to walk one with another in all the Ordinances of Christ, and to be subject one unto another, to be proceeded judicially against, in case they should wrong that society." In the 1760's John Adams made a similar argument in an action where a church member sued another for libel and slander, after a church complaint was brought against him:

[85] *Plymouth Church Rec.*, I, 153; Court Files Suffolk, no. 129735, p. 43.

[86] See F. Douglas Price, "The Abuses of Excommunication and the Decline of Ecclesiastical Discipline under Queen Elizabeth," *English Historical Review*, LVII (1942), 106–15; Ronald A. Marchant, *The Puritans and the Church Courts in the Diocese of York, 1560–1642* (London, 1960), *passim;* C. Hill, *Society and Puritanism*, chap. 8.

A Church is a voluntary society of Christians. Voluntary, because no Man is compellable to join with the Church. . . . One End of Church society, and Government is mutual Watch and Jealousy over each other, mutual Advice, Admonitions Censures, and that all evil Examples may be suppressed. . . . Thus the fundamental Principle of Ecclesiastical Polity is that as every Member is a Volunteer, if he will not submit to their Rules he shall be cut off.[87]

Any individual retains the right to submit to potential limitations on his privacy in pursuit of another personal value.

Since the Saints only formally supervised the behavior of one another in the early years, a large proportion of the congregation escaped church discipline. John Adams asked: "Is it common for the worst Men to be Church Members. By no Means. Church Members are generally much more virtuous, and benevolent than others."[88] The limited scope of essential supervision removed the threat of surveillance from the unregenerate, who were almost always a substantial percentage of the congregation.[89] It simplified the task of church members, who instead of watching over a congregation of perhaps four hundred might be collectively responsible for only one hundred Saints. However, with the gradual opening of the gates to church membership after 1662, anyone admitted to baptism under the Half-Way Covenant was subject to church discipline. Yet, if only a handful of the church members were enthusiastic about discipline, as increasingly became the case, strict controls could hardly be maintained. Similar problems arose when membership in a particular church became too large. Although selectivity meant that church

[87] Hooker, *Survey of Church-Discipline*, pt. 3, p. 2; *Legal Papers of John Adams*, II, 30. Adams lost the case.

[88] *Legal Papers of John Adams*, II, 31.

[89] The number of full members varied widely from one independent church to another. Churches with relaxed admissions standards had more full church members. In the early 1670's the Rev. Increase Mather stated that in New England "the Generality of the Inhabitants" were "in the condition of Infidels" (*The First Principles of New England* [Cambridge, Mass., 1675], p. iv). In 1676 Edward Randolph reported to the English government that in New England "the number of the church members and freemen compared with the rest of the inhabitants . . . is very inconsiderable, not being reckoned above one sixth part" (Thomas Hutchinson, *The Hutchinson Papers: A Collection of Original Papers Relative to the History of the Colony of Massachusetts-Bay* [Boston, 1769; rpt. Albany, 1865], II, 219). For numerical estimates, see Morgan, *Gentle Puritan*, pp. 185–86, and "New England Puritanism," *WMQ*, 3d ser., XVIII (1961), 240; also Charles W. Akers, *Called unto Liberty: A Life of Jonathan Mayhew, 1720–1766* (Cambridge, Mass., 1964), p. 58. In general, see Pope, *Half-Way Covenant*, passim.

members were less likely to engage in behavior that would stimulate the invasion of their privacy, the obligation of mutual observation remained a latent threat.

The Puritans limited the kinds of offenses that deserved the attention of church disciplinary procedures. In a book first published in 1630 the eminent theologian William Ames asked what kinds of sins required church attention. "Not those infirmities which are common, almost to all Beleevers; for the singular care, or reforming of those, neither can be expected, nor exacted of them who are subject to the same, or like imperfections."[90] The true wrath of the church should be reserved for scandalous offenses. This limitation obviously minimized the challenge of disciplinary obligations to the privacy of the average church member.

One can readily create a detrimental picture for privacy by exaggerating the terrors of church discipline. Calvin had earlier warned of the need for moderation: "Unless this gentleness is maintained in both private and public censures, there is danger lest we soon slide down from discipline to butchery."[91] Thomas Hooker set down definite rules in the 1640's for dealing with both private and public offenses. Positive evidence had to be available before any accusations could be made. "If yet it be not so cleer, but doubtfull to us onely, though our thoughts and apprehensions lead that way; it is not yet ripe for any Church processe." The elders were to keep public charges under firm control. "It is in their power to suppresse such petty occasions which are not worthy the time, pains and disturbance that must be spent upon them." In addition, "such humaine infirmities, which unavoidably attend the best Saints breathing upon earth, while they carry a body of death about them, are not to be taken as matter of offence intended by our Saviour, nor have we any just cause to stumble at such straws, or be taken with distaste against the carriage of a Brother in that case."[92]

Concern for personal privacy specifically appeared in the elaborate procedures developed to deal with disciplinary cases when the offense was not public knowledge. Again according to Cotton Mather:

Where a Scandalous Transgression is known only to One or Two, the Proceedings of the Persons that know it, are the same, that they are in the case of a Personal Injury: The Steps directed in the XVIII Ch. of Mathew.

[90] *Conscience,* bk. 4, p. 86.
[91] *Institutes of the Christian Religion,* ed. John T. McNeill (Philadelphia, 1960), p. 1238.
[92] *Survey of Church-Discipline,* pt. 3, pp. 33–38.

He that knows the Offence, first of all himself goes to the Offender, and seriously endeavours to bring him to Repentance. If the Offender be Obstinate, he then (having Proof to convict him) takes one or two Brethren with him, and renews his Endeavours. . . . If this be ineffectual, They carry the Complaint unto the Pastor. . . . If the Man does now Relent, and the Offence be still in a sure Way to be kept private, the Satisfaction thus privately given is taken up withal. But if either the Man continue Impenitent, or the Matter have so taken Air, as to be a Matter of common Fame, and the Talk of the People, then it falls into the Course, that such a Matter is to be treated withal.[93]

There was probably a definite attempt to handle most cases in a private manner, which may account for the paucity of disciplinary actions in church records. If the person gave private satisfaction the case was forgotten and no record kept.

The need for maintaining the privacy of private offenders was constantly reiterated. According to Thomas Hooker "private offences appear only to few, one or more; and therefore they onely are to proceed against them, in covering and hiding them from the apprehension of others, as much as may be." In 1644 the newly organized Wenham church insisted that the initial admonitions of offenders and "private offences betwene brethren" should be handled in a private setting: "That all agitations receive privacy against the churches order, or wherin differences of mens judgments may be likely to appear, be in private."[94] When the Lancaster church renewed its covenant in 1708, the members agreed to "walk in Love one towards another . . . and warning any Brother or Sister which offendeth not divulging private offences Irregularly, but heedfully following the Precepts laid down for Church dealing Matth. 18, 15, 16, 17."[95] When the church at Leicester removed their pastor from office in 1729, one of the charges against him was "bringing cases of private Offence before the Church."[96]

Strict procedures for bringing charges before the church further served to maintain a sense of reserve and to protect against devastating personal encounters. When a Chelmsford man spoke out suddenly against a person about to be elected to church office, he met with a

---

[93] *Ratio Disciplinae*, pp. 148–49. A private offense involved only one or two witnesses. See also the London Confession of 1589 in Walker, *Creeds and Platforms*, pp. 39–40; *Cambridge Platform of Church Discipline*, p. 21; *Plymouth Church Rec.*, I, 182 (1697).

[94] Hooker, *Survey of Church-Discipline*, pt. 3, p. 34; Fiske, "Notebook of Church Matters," pp. 47–48, 29.

[95] *Lancaster Rec.*, p. 170.

[96] Chamberlain, *Doc. Hist. of Chelsea*, II, 234.

chilly reception. The church convicted him of breaking "a received rule of order in bringing his offence, grievance or dissatisfaction that day to the church, before he had consulted 1st with the officer." Nor was his defense of the spur of conscience accepted. The relevant rules of order established two years before, in 1661, required strict adherence to the disciplinary procedures outlined in Matthew.[97] Nothing about a private offense could be made public until an accuser had exhausted the several steps leading to private correction. Whenever this order was not followed, the accusation became ecclesiastically invalid. A church council at Norton in 1722 stated that complaints should be submitted in writing, as a hindrance to hasty, malicious, or intemperate action.[98] Such regulations extended a veil of privacy over most disciplinary questions.

The church member whose transgressions became publicly known forfeited his claim to personal privacy in the investigation of his offense. The procedure in such cases was straightforward, as depicted in Cotton Mather's handbook of 1726: "If one under the Covenant and Government of the Church, fall into a Scandalous Transgression against the Laws of our Holy Redeemer, and the Transgression be at once, and at first a Matter of Publick Fame, the Pastor upon the Cry, reckons it his Duty to Enquire into it, and bring it immediately under an Ecclesiastical Cognizance. . . . The Pastor sends for the Delinquent, and usually he desires a few of the chief Brethren to be with him in the Action."[99] Personal privacy was hardly at issue since the offense had been a matter of public knowledge in the first place. Such public sins might include Sabbath-breaking, fornication, and drunkenness, the most common items in the church discipline records.

Only the recalcitrant private offender and the public offender forfeited their right to privacy and had their suits aired in public. In 1644 several members of the New Haven church tried with mighty efforts to settle in private a disciplinary case involving the wife of the governor. But as they explained to the church: "Thus we are compelled to bring sundry particulars of which she was privately admonished into the public notice of the Church, because she refused to hear us in a private way, according to the rule in Matt. XVIII, 17." In 1657 Nathaniel Shipley of Chelmsford, accused of "Notorious Lying," was "called before the church haveing been dealt with before in private by the pastor in the presence of 4 or 5 Brethren." In

[97] Fiske, "Notebook of Church Matters," pp. 284, 286–87 (1663), 254–55.
[98] *Dorchester Church Rec.*, p. 136.
[99] *Ratio Disciplinae*, pp. 141–42, 144.

1748 a parishioner sought the Reverend Mr. Parkman's advice on some misbehavior that had occurred: "I advised him to keep it as private as he could but to go and discourse with the yoangsters themselves and with their parents. I refused to know who they were till he should take these steps and if these steps were not successful it would then be time enough to expose them."[100]

Another episode in Parkman's career suggested that there was a continuing movement, especially in the eighteenth century, to handle even public offenses as privately as possible. At Grafton in 1774 the church considered a fornication charge against one Wheeler. Parkman, who had prodded the Grafton minister for not dealing with the case, wrote that on the eve of the assembly he had informed the minister "how much rather I chose to have Wheeler labour'd with in private and that he would prevent public Ecclesiastical process."[101] Only the full church members seem to have then heard the case. The times were no longer congenial for the public treatment of even public offenses.

The church gathered to hear reports on public disciplinary cases from either a committee or the pastor. The offenders were summoned to "show Cause (if they can) why they should not be Censured."[102] In 1671 the Chelmsford church meeting dealt with the case of Brother Martin "for Idleness and his neglect of his particular calling, or liveing disorderly not employing himself in any lawful outward employment."[103] After discussing the charge the church voted unanimously that he was guilty and should be publicly admonished. Some churches met at regular intervals to consider disciplinary cases. In the late seventeenth century the Plymouth church members agreed "to meet statedly twice in a year for the express purpose of attending more specially to the Matter of Discipline—and to examine into the conduct of its Members."[104] In the normal course of events church discipline cases became just as tiresome and repetitive as those in the

[100] N. Smyth, ed., "Mrs. Eaton's Trial in 1644," New Haven Colony Historical Society, *Papers*, V (1894), 137–38; Fiske, "Notebook of Church Matters," pp. 196–98; Parkman, "Diary," AAS, *Proc.*, LXXIII (1963), 402–3.

[101] *Ibid.*, LXXII (1962), 181.

[102] See the case of Widow Eades in Charlestown in 1698, *Charlestown Church Rec.*, pp. xi–xii; *Dorchester Church Rec.*, p. 135 (1722); also case of Sarah Balch in Beverly First Church rec. (1714), Essex Institute, *Hist. Coll.*, XXXVI (1900), 155–56, 160; and Lydia Cushman in Plymouth, 1727–29, *Plymouth Church Rec.*, I, 237–38, 240.

[103] Fiske, "Notebook of Church Matters," p. 344.

[104] *Plymouth Church Rec.*, I, 145, 154, 370.

secular courts. A sense of religious duty was the chief motivation of those members who actively participated in the process. Curiosity seekers found only occasional fulfillment in the monotonous strivings to convince a sinner of his waywardness. Over a twenty-year period the Chelmsford church had only one case with sexual overtones, that of Joshua Fletcher in 1658, accused of often climbing to the window of a young lady and entering her bedroom in the darkness of the night.[105] The church convicted him of incivility and immodesty for courting the young woman without her parent's consent, a charitable, limited judgment for mid-seventeenth-century Puritans.

A person whose offense had required public discussion due to his recalcitrance or its public nature normally made a public confession as the final step in his exoneration. This practice was the most obvious example of the required forfeiture by church members of personal privacy. As Cotton Mather described the process, the offender

Is put either upon Writing of his Acknowledgement, (which is most usual), or upon speaking of it, as 'tis foreseen will be most for Edification. And then in some Congregations of the Faithful, either the Church alone (which is thought most Advisable where the Neighbourhood is very Populous, and full of Strangers) or the Rest of the Neighbourhood staying with the Church (which is the Custom in most Places;) the Pastor gives the Church a true Report of the Scandal, and adds his Hope of the Man's having Repented of it: who now appears before them, to testify it with a Confession proper to the Occasion, which is then exhibited. . . . This being done the Pastor puts it unto the Vote of their uplifted Hands, whether they accept the Satisfaction which has been thus offered by the Repenting Brother before them.[106]

The church judged the quality of the repentance and sought further enlightenment if necessary. After a public confession at Charlestown in 1667, "liberty was given . . . to the brethren to object, if any of them had any thing materiall to say . . . . And after a little further inquiry by some made . . . he was restored." On a Sabbath in 1709 Samuel Sewall was surprised to hear a woman confess to fornication and be immediately reinstated. "I think it is inconvenient, when persons have so fallen, not to give the Church some previous notice of it; that the Brethren may have Opportunity to enquire into the Repentance. An ignorant Consent is no Consent." The minister agreed to give more warning in future. The most stringent action by a church was to postpone the readmittance of the member, "The Confession ap-

105 Fiske, "Notebook of Church Matters," p. 323a.
106 *Ratio Disciplinae*, pp. 144–45.

pearing somewhat hopefull yet not so full, nor convincing to the world as was desired," or, as in another instance, "after Considerable debate about his acknowledgment, whither it were sufficient for his being restored."[107]

Once public sin had tarnished the sanctity of a church member, the Puritans were primarily concerned with the need for repentance; the penitent offender was welcomed back into the fold. As the Reverend Mr. Robbins of Plymouth, a firm disciplinarian, wrote in 1771, "the *falling into Sin* is just Cause of Shame–but 'tis *no Shame to Confess it* but a lasting shame not to confess it."[108] Form had to be maintained, and the collective sanctity of the church vicariously refurbished. A public offense required a public show of repentance; those exposed to evil example should be given notice of the repentance of the sinner. The confession was a moral and almost a physical expurgation. Another Plymouth pastor commented on a 1727 confession: "Tis very Remarkable that she was brought to this Confession by being followed for some time with Lingering Sickness and such Strong Convictions and Distresses of Conscience that she could receive no Ease till she had Confessed her Complicated and Aggravated guilt."[109] Yet only public offenses required such purgative treatment. As Cotton Mather commented, "would it not be Another Sin, and an Open Sin, for men to Publish their Secret Sins, the Sins which have been kept Secret by the Providence of God."[110] Public confession was not merely the main hurdle in an obstacle course. It was an opportunity for the member to imbibe a peculiar help from his fellow members.[111] Within the familial context of church mem-

---

107 *Charlestown Church Rec.*, p. vi; Sewall, *Diary*, MHS, *Coll.*, 5th ser., VI, 267; Beverly First Church rec., (1669), Essex Institute, *Hist. Coll.*, XXXV (1899), 188; and Chelsea church rec. (1734), in Chamberlain, *Doc. Hist. of Chelsea*, II, 242.

108 *Plymouth Church Rec.*, I, 147 and 287 (1674).

109 *Plymouth Church Rec.*, I, 240; compare this comment by E. Adamson Hoebel: "Among the Central Eskimos of Canada and those of West Greenland confession in a public gathering purges the soul. . . . Covillagers form a background chorus to his chanting–washing the polluted soul clean with their cries for forgiveness. . . . That a confessional cure is theatrics and fun for the local group who makes up the audience–a welcome diversion in an Arctic world–can scarcely be doubted. . . . The action on the part of the sinner is 'voluntary' and no compulsive legal sanctions are indicated when complete and abject confession is forth coming" (*The Law of Primitive Man* [Cambridge, Mass., 1954], pp. 71, 73).

110 *Religion of the Closet*, p. 15.

111 Calvin, *Institutes*, pp. 600–601, 630, 634–35.

bership, the offender revealed himself in all his wretchedness. His individual efforts could thereby again be joined with the march of the predestined toward eternity. Once again a person agreed to sacrifice some privacy for a higher goal.

Public confessions occurred regularly but not so often as to stultify the curiosity of the listeners. The confession was not always written, particularly in the early days. It might be lengthy and formalized and not even make direct mention of the offense. But the example of self-abasement and shame, as well as oblique references to sexual transgressions, probably held the attention of the audience. Mary Modesly was called before the Dorchester church in 1681 "to answer for her sine of fornication. She did appear but being put to it to speak by way of acknowledgment of the sin, she gave noe answer but weept whether for the shame or the sin that was not known." A Plymouth woman charged with the same offense in 1689 "manifested much sorrow and heavynesse by words and teares."[112] These were dramatic experiences in the lives of the listeners. In 1784 the Spanish traveler Miranda attended a Congregational service on Long Island: "A poor young man, who had been married a few months and had received a son before the nine, brought the child to be baptized. The preacher refused to administer this Sacrament until the father confessed publicly his sin. So see you here this poor fellow in front of the entire congregation declaring loudly that he had covered his wife before marrying her. I have never in my life suffered greater shame. What barbarity!"[113] In most instances the procedures for the implementation of church discipline guarded against such a scene.

Two eventual changes in the formula for public confessions provided more personal privacy for the offender. By the late seventeenth century most confessions were written in advance and read in public by the pastor. The Dorchester woman who was unable to speak when she came before the church in 1681 was later allowed to make a written confession. The second common change was the limitation of the audience to church members. An early attempt at Plymouth in 1684 failed, but a church meeting at Beverly in 1704 agreed "that such as had been scandalous Among us, If they made their confession before the church only it Should be Accepted, If they desired It." The Old South Church in Boston took a similar stand in 1717, much to the dismay of Samuel Sewall. Other churches gradually changed their position, although it was not until the 1790's, and indeed well into the nineteenth century, that the entire concept of public confessions

112 *Dorchester Church Rec.*, p. 87; *Plymouth Church Rec.*, I, 265.
113 *Travels*, p. 129.

met great opposition.[114] For the fallen Saint a short period of debasement seemed a small price for readmission to full fellowship.

The impact of church discipline on individual privacy in New England society can be easily exaggerated. Discipline generally applied only to a minority of the population, and enforcement of discipline was a problem even among this select group, particularly in the face of the changes taking place in New England society during the colonial era. One need not accept the post-1660 jeremiads at their face value to agree with Increase Mather that "there is a great decay as to the power of godliness amongst us." He added that "we can now see little difference between Church-members and other men." Church members agreed to "watch over one anothers Souls: But how little is that Christian and Brotherly Watchfulness attended ever after? Indeed, if men fall out one with another, then they can watch for Haltings, and prosecute to the utmost, which is to serve themselves, and their own vile lusts and passions. . . . But otherwise there are too many that can see one another sin, and never attend the Rules of Christ appointed for the healing of every sinning, offending Brother."[115] Similar problems were encountered in secular law enforcement.

Church discipline was responsive to the tenor of the times. In the Dorchester church, for example, the records reveal only one case of church discipline between 1660 and 1675. Around this latter date the colony became excited about war, gross sins, God's provocation by Massachusetts, and the laxity of church discipline and family instruction. During the next ten years the Dorchester church had many discipline cases, eventually tapering off in the 1690's. The records varied from church to church. In another instance in the 1730's the Cambridge church bewailed the decay of religion and especially the neglect of "Christian watchfulness." In 1737 the church established a committee to be specifically responsible for "watchfulness," by inquiring into any evil reports about professing Christians. The committee was organized annually until the Revolution with the same members serving year after year. Yet during a forty-year period this committee handled only five recorded cases of church discipline; the church records dealt far more with problems of finance.[116] Most

---

[114] *Plymouth Church Rec.*, I, 159; Beverley First Church rec., Essex Institute, *Hist. Coll.*, XXXVI (1900), 149; Sewall, *Diary*, MHS, *Coll.*, 5th ser., VII, 123, 126–27; for a survey of the rise of opposition to public confessions, see Oberholzer, *Delinquent Saints*, pp. 36–37, 135–36, and 239ff.

[115] *The Day of Trouble* (Cambridge, Mass., 1674), pp. 22–24. See also C. Mather, *A Faithful Monitor*, p. 45.

[116] *Dorchester Church Rec.*, pp. 69–106; *Cambridge Church Rec.*, 128–252.

churches had greater activity without special committees. The typical church had a pattern of scattered cases until the Revolution and in most instances beyond.

In the eighteenth century a Congregational minister had an additional motive for being light-handed in the enforcement of church discipline. Individuals who disliked the Congregational admission or disciplinary procedures could escape to one of the growing number of Anglican churches in New England. In Windham County, Connecticut, in the 1730's the council of the county's Congregational churches censured a husband and wife for immoralities. The Reverend Thomas Clap, a stern disciplinarian, visited the couple to admonish them. In response the pair went to the Anglican minister in New London, who received them into his church. Clap sought the advice of the eminent Benjamin Colman in Boston, suggesting that "we must Conclude either to lay aside all Discipline and never Pretend to Deal with any men for their Faults at all (and then we shall presently grow as loose and Corrupt as they are) or else to begin to Deal with men, and when they say they are Churchmen [Anglicans] to let them alone, and by this means it is probable that in a little time a great part of the Country under such Temptations will say they are Church-men."[117]

The ministerial attitude toward church discipline always helped to determine the zealousness with which it was enforced. The Plymouth church was running against the trend during the pastorate of Chandler Robbins, 1760–99, when more disciplinary actions were recorded than during any other ministerial term. Since Robbins believed in public admonitions and public confessions, Plymouth remained strict until after his death.[118] Emil Oberholzer has described the slow death of church discipline in his excellent study.[119] The existence of disciplinary procedures far outlived the course of their practical influence on individual privacy.

The Puritan church is not the most obvious place to discover substantial evidence of concern for personal privacy in colonial New England. Yet even the Saints saw no need to forfeit their natural right to privacy as human beings. Customs that on the surface sug-

[117] Clap, Windham, to Rev. B. Colman, Boston, Dec. 8, 1735, John Davis Papers, 1627–1747, II, 66, MHS; also see Bruce E. Steiner, "New England Anglicanism: A Genteel Faith?" *WMQ*, 3d ser., XXVII (1970), 122–35.
[118] See *Plymouth Church Rec.*, I, 334–39 (1770) and 370–71 (1792); for another example of the revival of discipline, Weston, *Church Rec.*, p. 543 (1794).
[119] *Delinquent Saints*, pp. 239ff.

gest a complete disdain for privacy, such as the requirements of a Relation, mutual surveillance, and public confession, were either initially or gradually circumscribed with protective directives and practices that embodied respect for the individual and his rights. In their admissions procedures the Congregational churches virtually declared from the beginning that they could only be concerned with the overt manifestations of a person's religious life and could not legitimately pry into his private life. The Puritans operated their churches and practiced their religion with significant concern for personal privacy. Within an inevitable framework of demands and compromises, they recognized privacy as a vital value. The institutionalized manifestations of Puritanism did not significantly lessen the availability of personal privacy in colonial society.

6. Government and the Law

IN late-twentieth-century America the various levels of government represent a major threat to the personal privacy of individuals, who have to defend themselves and be defended against such an institutionalized challenge. Such perilous conditions were less prevalent in early America. Colonial lawmakers did justify certain intrusions into private lives in the interests of public security and the maintenance of good order. The extent of legislated surveillance is examined particularly at this point, because it is primarily through the observation of individuals that a government can challenge personal privacy. To what degree did the New England governments choose to regulate the lives of their citizens through statutes, especially in terms of what they could and could not do in private?

REGULATION IN NEW ENGLAND LIFE

It is important to delineate the various attitudes associated with authoritarianism and the ideology of Puritanism that the colonial authorities brought to the enactment and enforcement of laws affecting individuals. Governments in both the Old and New Worlds in the seventeenth century were authoritarian in the regulation of personal behavior. Wallace MacCaffrey in his study of the English town of Exeter, for example, has stressed the "authoritarian" nature of society. Regulation of private lives was considered an excellent defense against economic and social ills. Sexual morality was vigorously enforced, despite the late appearance in Exeter of the distinguishing characteristics of Puritanism. "It is probably necessary to look elsewhere for the roots of this policy. . . . In the eyes of the magistrates, moral offenders were a danger to civil society of the same kind as vagabonds . . . we must suppose that a strong infusion of a general religious sentiment strengthened the policy. Nevertheless, it remained primarily a matter of law enforcement rather than one of the moral direction of society."[1] Such close governmental reg-

[1] *Exeter, 1540–1640: The Growth of an English County Town* (Cambridge, Mass., 1958), pp. 97, 72.

ulation of personal behavior was a basic feature of sixteenth- and seventeenth-century social life. In one of his first directives in 1606, Chief Justice Coke reminded the constables of England that "all unlawful games, drunkenness, whoredom, and incontinency in private families [are] to be reported, as on their good government the commonwealth depends."[2]

It is essential not to label as Puritan those statutory enactments of the first settlers that were primarily a reflection of the authoritarianism of seventeenth-century governments. According to Perry Miller, if "we wish to take Puritan culture as a whole, . . . about ninety per cent of the intellectual life, scientific knowledge, morality, manners and customs, notions and prejudices, was that of all Englishmen."[3] Although the advent of Puritan ideology in England infused a new source of strength into the movement for moral reform, this movement itself was by no means a new phenomenon. Motivated more often by economic and social considerations than by religious impulses, local English authorities had long been implementing the kinds of measures that have been branded as wholly Puritan in derivation when enacted in colonial New England. The values that New Englanders embodied in their criminal laws were a combination of typical authoritarian attitudes and the particular world view of a Puritan. The peculiar governmental challenges to personal privacy in New England grew out of the addition of a particular zealousness to an already authoritarian ethic.

In theory the authorities scrutinized the covenanted Puritan of the first generation in New England to ensure success in the godly venture. Internal and external conformity to a prescribed mode of living was a basic requirement. The state totally regulated the conduct of life. The well-led personal life contributed to the essential corporate thrust of the community. Both would be judged by God under the covenant. Thus in a metaphysical sense personal privacy did not have a place among the dominant values of a Puritan government. The impact of Puritan ideology had to be cushioned before the desire for personal privacy could fully reassert itself in New England society. Although there were some intensely private aspects of Puritan practices, the true believer could fear privacy as a shield for wrongdoing, at least for others.

The struggle to establish a Puritan stronghold in the New World

[2] Quoted in Davies, *Enforcement of English Apprenticeship*, p. 233; also see Eleanor Trotter, *Seventeenth Century Life in the Country Parish* (Cambridge, 1919), pp. 178, 88.
[3] *The Puritans*, ed. Miller and Johnson, p. 7.

meant that a wide variety of activities attracted governmental regulation. Undertaking a new settlement in a strange land required
especially high standards of public behavior. John Robinson, the
pastor of the Leyden congregation, wrote the Pilgrims: "The Lord
call[s] us in a singular manner upon occasions of such difficulty and
danger as lieth upon you, to a both more narrow search and careful
reformation of our ways in his sight. . . . Let every man repress in
himself and the whole body in each person, as so many rebels against
the common good, all private respects of men's selves, not sorting
with the general conveniency."[4] Such a collective venture required
everyone to interest himself in the life of his neighbor.[5] The Reverend
Thomas Hooker described the duties of the "true Convert": "What
ever sins come within his reach, he labors the removal of them, out of
the familyes where he dwells, out of the plantations where he lives,
out of the companies and occasions, with whom he hath occasion to
meet and meddle at any time."[6]

A person shared the responsibility for sins he observed, unless he
reported such offenses to the magistrates. The Reverend Solomon
Stoddard stated the matter plainly in his 1703 Massachusetts election
sermon: "The Country is not Guilty of the Crimes of particular Persons, unless they make themselves guilty; if they countenance them,
or connive at them, they make themselves guilty by participation:
But when they are duely witnessed against, they bring no publick
guilt."[7] New Hampshire warned its law enforcement officials in 1657
"to take care herein that wee may prosecute all such exsesse drinkinge
and other sins which els will bringe the Judgment of god upon us."[8]
Such an attitude was widespread among public authorities for a good
part of the seventeenth century. Sinful activities, they believed, attracted the wrath of God in the form of Indian attacks, storms, fires,
and other misfortunes. In 1675 the Massachusetts General Court de-

[4] *Mourt's Relation: A Journal of the Pilgrims at Plymouth,* ed. Dwight B.
Heath (New York, 1963), pp. 10, 12.

[5] These sentiments were expressed in a sermon by Robert Cushman at Plymouth in 1621, in *Chronicles of the Pilgrim Fathers,* pp. 236–37.

[6] *The Application of Redemption* (London, 1659), p. 684, quoted in Morgan,
Puritan Family, p. 6.

[7] *Way for a People,* p. 8. On the concept of watchfulness see J. Linzee Coolidge, "Aspects of Puritan Morality: Personal Conduct and Civil Authority in
Hampshire County, Massachusetts, 1660–1727" (Master's thesis, Columbia University, 1964), p. 12. See the use of the term *watchfulness* by Bradford, *Of
Plymouth Plantation,* p. 345.

[8] "New Hampshire Court Records, 1640–1692," in *N.H. Provincial Papers,*
XL, 134.

clared that God had raised up the Indians against them.[9] If God was
to bring judgment on everyone for the sins of a few, then the community felt justified in efforts to stamp out such offenses by legislated
intrusions into private lives. The notion of reporting sins represented
a serious theoretical challenge to the privacy of colonial man. A
zealous Puritan should have been constantly on the alert for offenses
committed by his fellows.

Yet in the actual interactions of privacy and watchfulness, some
important qualifications emerged. Many of the New England laws
that threatened personal privacy were not consistently and conscientiously enforced in any colony. These laws were primarily the handi-
work of the Puritan leadership and found only sporadic response
from law enforcement officials. The progress of time and the succession of generations further cooled the Puritans' ardor for enforcement of particular laws. Even in the early years the mass of the New
England population never ardently espoused the Puritan way of life,
especially in the area of the regulation of personal behavior, where
the Puritan movement represented an attempt at repression from
above. The inhabitants were divided into the elect and the unre-
deemed sinners. According to one estimate, "the provable elect were
a minority, probably no more than one fifth of the total population."[10]
This lessened the ability of the Puritan elite to control behavior in
society, even though laws passed throughout the seventeenth century
bore the stamp of their anticipation of or response to some form of
illicit activity. In times of high tension, especially the period of war
in the mid-1670's, they continued to launch campaigns "to suppresse
vice and immorallitie." But after the first generation had passed on,
such episodes were only temporary revivals of Puritanism. They were
an inaccurate reflection of actual behavior in society, at least in terms
of the observance of such legislation.

For a practical estimate of the availability of personal privacy in
the face of seventeenth-century governmental regulation, one must
also evaluate the conflict between "pretend rules" and genuine law in
New England society. Judge Jerome Frank has written that "all
groups have their pseudo-standards, their 'pretend rules'; it is part
of the rules of any group to break some of its own rules. Greeks and

---

[9] *Mass. Rec.*, V, 59. Connecticut had the same experience (*Conn. Rec.*, IV,
28–29).

[10] *The Puritans*, ed. Miller and Johnson, p. 191. The percentage of full church
members varied greatly from one independent Congregational church to another
and from decade to decade in the 17th century. This figure rarely approached
50%, unless admissions procedures were relaxed.

Trobrianders, New Yorkers and Hottentots, not only preserve but currently produce . . . rules which they circumvent or openly violate but which they refuse to abandon."[11] Both residents and visitors noted a consistent dichotomy between the zealous moralism that the seventeenth-century Puritans brought to the enactment of laws and the practical results. Governor Bradford of Plymouth Colony described this ambivalence in 1642:

Marvelous it may be to see and consider how some kind of wickedness did grow and break forth here, in a land where the same was so much witnessed against and so narrowly looked unto, and severely punished when it was known, as in no place more, or so much, that I have known or heard of. . . . And yet all this could not suppress the breaking out of sundry notorious sins. . . . 3. A third reason may be, here (as I am verily persuaded) is not more evils in this kind . . . but they are here more discovered and seen and made public by due search, inquisition and due punishment; for the churches look narrowly to their members, and the magistrates over all, more strictly than in other places. Besides, here the people are but few in comparison of other places which are full and populous and lie hid, as it were, in a wood or thicket and many horrible evils by that means are never seen nor known; whereas here they are . . . brought into the light and set in the plain field, or rather on a hill, made conspicuous to the view of all.[12]

Bradford's explanations for the continuing existence of serious offenses were in effect an early recognition of the limitations inherent in regulation of private lives. John Dunton, a London visitor to New England, commented on this situation in the 1680's: "Their Laws for Reformation of Manners, are very severe, yet but little regarded by the People, so at least as to make 'em better, or cause 'em to mend their manners."[13]

The changes that took place in New England society in the last half of the seventeenth century altered the impact of the Puritan movement on legislation, law enforcement, and popular attitudes. The religious ideology of Puritanism ceased to be the spark of an experiment and became the creed of an ordinary community, as the inhabitants of New England gradually abandoned certain of the enthusiasms of the first generation in the New World and settled down to the normal patterns of life in an agricultural, preindustrial society. New England did not cease to be Puritan in general outlook and religious belief in the late seventeenth century. But the Puritan move-

[11] Quoted in Hoebel, *The Law of Primitive Man*, pp. 29–30.
[12] *Of Plymouth Plantation*, pp. 316–17.
[13] *Letters*, p. 71.

ment was purged of its harsher elements, especially those which challenged personal privacy. By 1704 Cotton Mather was lamenting: "How much would Religion Revive and Flourish, if the Watchfulness of Christians over one another, were more Conscientiously Maintained among us!" At the same time he issued some warnings about reproving an erring neighbor. The reprover should be sure of his facts, avoid mistakes and malice, and speak lovingly and in a prudent manner. He significantly qualified traditional Puritan theory about those he called "the Scorners, of whome we have no Hopes to do any good upon them": "Suppose we see or hear a Person, doing amiss; are we bound alwayes to give a Verbal Reproof unto him? No; if there be any likely Hopes, of doing him any Good, Reprove him; If not, Then say nothing." Even without such conscious encouragement, the number of "Scorners" in New England society was increasing rapidly.[14]

In the eighteenth century the original Puritan zealousness had evaporated to a point where ardent moralism had become the responsibility of an ever smaller minority. Around 1700 Edward Ward, an English pamphleteer who had toured New England, wrote that "they are very busie in detecting one anothers failings; and he is accounted, by their Church Governers, a Meritorious Christian, that betrays his Neighbours to a Whipping-Post." Ward then narrated this lesson in the protection of privacy:

A good Cudgel apply'd in the Dark, is an excellent Medicine for a Malignant Spirit. I knew it once Experienced at Boston, with very good success, upon an Old rigged Precisian, one of their Select, who used to be more then ordinary vigilant in discovering every little Irregularity in the Neighbourhood; I happening one Night to be pritty Merry with a Friend, opposite to the Zealots dwelling, who got out of his Bed in his Wast-coat and Drawers, to listen at our Window. My Friend having oft been serv'd so, had left unbolted his Cellar Trap-door, as a Pit-fall for Mr. Busie-Body, who stepping upon it, sunk down with an Outcry like a distressed Mariner in a sinking Pinnace. My Friend having planted a Cudgel ready, run down Stairs, crying Thieves, and belabour'd Old Troublesome very sevearly before he would know him. He crying out I am your Neighbour.[15]

In 1704 Madam Knight of Boston was told that the Connecticut inhabitants "were formerly in their Zeal very Riggid in their Administrations towards such as their Lawes made Offenders, even to a harmless Kiss or Innocent merriment among Young people."[16] The

---

[14] *A Faithful Monitor*, pp. 32, 29–31, 27.

[15] *Trip to New England*, p. 43.

[16] *Journal*, pp. 33–34.

Scotch traveler Burnaby reflected in 1759 that "the character of the inhabitants of this province is much improved, in comparison of what it was; but puritanism and a spirit of persecution is not yet totally extinguished."[17]

A member of the first generations in New England had to find some grounds of coexistence with the ostensible Puritan moral ethic, as embodied in statutory regulations and requirements for surveillance. To the extent that this was done, one could resume the normal pattern of living of non-Puritan England. In that culture personal privacy had an established place as a dominant value in all areas of life, with individual variations because of cultural outlook, social class, and economic position. In seventeenth-century New England both the ardent Puritans and the unregenerate among the population ultimately shared a similar practical concern for privacy. A Puritan sought the various forms of privacy at specific times and expected some degree of privacy in his general mode of living. There was a gap between his theoretical acceptance of brotherly surveillance and the extent to which he would accept such practices in everyday life.

RESIDENCE REQUIREMENTS

No one could settle in a New England town without the permission of the inhabitants or their representatives. The law governed the movement of persons from overseas, neighboring colonies, and other towns within the colony. Such a law restricted personal freedom; in the process of enforcement it also affected privacy. Residency laws had a long tradition in England, where their primary motivation was protection from economic competition, social evils, and the burden of supporting the poor. Balancing competing values, the populace accepted some limitations on their privacy in the long-term interests of the community. Exeter instructed its aldermen to watch for strangers, vagabonds, and generally suspect persons in their wards. In early Stuart Lincoln, "the parish underconstables were ordered weekly to notify the mayor or a justice overseeing the parishes of all persons seeking settlements, with a view to their removal."[18]

Residence requirements existed from the early days of the New England colonies. Each colony's General Court first passed such laws to apply to every town in the colony; most of the towns later es-

---

[17] *Travels*, pp. 108–9.

[18] MacCaffrey, *Exeter*, p. 91; J. W. F. Hill, *Tudor and Stuart Lincoln*, p. 137; see also Lord Hugh A. W. Leconfield, *Petworth Manor in the Seventeenth Century* (Oxford, 1954), pp. 35–36.

tablished their own by-laws.[19] As late as 1767 Boston declared that
no person could become an inhabitant without appearing before the
selectmen to make known his intentions and eventually securing ap-
probation at a town meeting.[20] There are thousands of examples in
the colonial town and court records of enforcement of these residence
requirements. The usual method was to "warn out" any person who
tried to reside in a town without permission.[21] This formal process of
enforcement began in the 1650's and continued unabated in the
eighteenth century.[22]

An applicant ordinarily appeared before the selectmen. In Lancaster the selectmen "apoynted him a day when he might come and
have a full meeting, and be heard." In similar fashion the Boston selectmen often granted leave to a person to "become an Inhabitant."
In 1658 New Haven, still a tiny independent colony, had a "committee setled for admitting of planters." When one Brother Cowper
nominated a young man, the committee desired Cowper "to enquire
after his conversation, and if he find that, that satisfies him, then he,
with the rest of the Townsmen, to give such encouragement as they
see meet, he being allowed a planter by the above said Committee."[23]
In some instances the town required that an individual bring a certifi-
cate of good character from his previous residence.[24]

Residency laws affected personal privacy at several points, especially in the approval process. The committees on admission wanted

19 *Mass. Assistants Rec.*, II, 4 (1630); *Plymouth Col. Rec.*, XI, 26 (1637);
New Haven Col. Rec., 1638–1649, p. 25 (1639); *Conn. Rec.*, I, 351 (1660).
For the towns, see *The Records of the Town of Cambridge, 1630–1703* (Cambridge, Mass., 1901), p. 50 (1633); *Boston Town Rec.*, IV, 8, 95 (Dorchester,
1634); *Watertown Rec., Town Proc.*, p. 1 (1636); Dedham (1636) and Med-
field (1650) in Josiah H. Benton, *Warning Out in New England* (Boston, 1911),
pp. 32–34; *R.I. Rec.*, I, 53 (Portsmouth, 1638); *Records of the Town of Braintree, 1640–1793*, ed. Samuel A. Bates (Randolph, Mass., 1886), pp. 2, 6, 19–20
(1641); *The Early Records of Groton, 1662–1707*, ed. Samuel A. Green (Groton,
Mass., 1880), p. 60 (1680); *Boston Town Rec.*, VII, 134 (1679).

20 *Mass. Acts and Res.*, IV, 912.

21 According to Josiah Benton, the Connecticut laws were "more elaborate,
complicated, and severe, than that of any other New England Colony or State"
(*Warning Out*, p. 63; this is the only competent work on residence requirements).

22 See *Boston Town Rec.*, XIII (1716–36), *passim*; Plymouth Co. Gen. Sess.,
1749–60, *passim*.

23 *Lancaster Rec.*, p. 90 (1671); *Boston Town Rec.*, II, 35, 39 (1638–39), for
example; *New Haven Town Rec.*, I, 356–57.

24 See, for example, *Town Records of Derby, Conn., 1655–1710* (Derby,
1901), p. 8 (1673); Winthrop, *Journal*, I, 54 (1630); MacLear, *Early New
England Towns*, p. 135.

to know the elementary facts about prospective residents. Boston in 1723 complained that there were many newcomers in the town "whose Circomstances and Condition are not known." Every such person was directed to "come and Enter his name and Occupation with the Town Clerk, and if marryed the number and Age of his Children and Servants." Persons entertaining such newcomers were to send their names to authority, "with their Circomstances as far as they are able." In Portsmouth in 1668 the county court asked a newcomer where he came from, why he came to this country, and whether he brought any estate with him.[25] Even at this early date, the dominance of the economic inquiry was apparent. The selectmen of Manchester found Thomas Chick, his wife, and three children "to be in a poare condision not haveing wherewith to suply the present nesesity of himselfe and his family neither for food nor Raiment" and ordered them expelled.[26]

Moral uprightness was a prerequisite for admission to residency in a town in the early days. A prominent resident of Newbury summarized "the godly intents" of the Massachusetts residency law of 1637, "which was as well to keepe out such whose lives were publickely prophane and scandalous as those whose judgements were Corrupt Least by the one the Comfortable societye of godes people might be disturbed and by the other the judgments of god procured."[27] When Edward Johnson played an active role in the organization of Woburn around 1650, he reported that "seven men have power to give and grant out land unto any persons . . . this they did without any respect of persons, yet such as were exorbitant, and of a turbulent spirit, unfit for a civil society, they would reject, till they come to mind their manners."[28] In the attempt to build a community of Saints, such rejections may have occurred frequently. Muddy River wanted only such newcomers "as may be likely to be received members of the congregation." Boston accepted persons "upon the usuall Condition of Inoffensive carryage," and "he carrying himself without Scandall." Plymouth wanted "houskeepers of honest life."[29]

---

[25] *Boston Town Rec.*, VIII, 177; "N.H. Court Rec.," *N.H. Provincial Papers*, XL, 240–41.

[26] *Essex Rec.*, VII, 271 (1679).

[27] Edward Rawson to Gov. John Winthrop, Feb. 7, 1639, *Winthrop Papers*, IV, 97; see similar sentiments in *ibid.*, III, 216.

[28] *Wonder-Working Providence*, p. 213.

[29] *Muddy River and Brookline Records, 1634–1838* (n.p., 1875), p. 12 (1675); see also *Lancaster Rec.*, p. 28 (1653); *Boston Town Rec.*, II, 34 (1638), 55 (1640), 112 (1652); *Records of the Town of Plymouth* (Plymouth, Mass., 1889–1903), I, 107–8 (1668).

After 1660 every edition of the Connecticut laws ordered "that no person shall be received an Inhabitant into any Town in this Colony but such as are known to be of an honest conversation and accepted by the major part of the Town."[30] Dancing masters, wigmakers, and the like never found it easy to gain formal admittance.[31] When the townsmen of Canton, Massachusetts, inquired about a newcomer in 1734, they discovered "he has several hundred acres of land in Connecticut, but that a glass of good liquor stands a very narrow chance when it lies in his way."[32] Yet it was troublesome to perpetuate moral uprightness as an official condition of residence. Towns had no investigative machinery other than the statements of the prospective resident. Financial probity was of much greater concern, and there was a corresponding lack of emphasis on sanctity once religious considerations ceased to be a major influence in the direction of town life in the late seventeenth century.

Since newcomers were never enthusiastic about meeting committees, the authorities tried to devise a series of methods whereby newcomers might not escape observation. This created another slight obstacle to the achievement of personal privacy. Ship captains were sometimes required to report the names of their newly arrived passengers to the authorities.[33] Town inhabitants had to inform officials whenever they gave lodging to a stranger,[34] which further encouraged some residents to observe one another: "Ralph Houghton aged about 47 yeares. Witnesseth that the last Spring of the yeare, I met with William Lincorne in our towne and he being a stranger I inquired of him what his ocasion was their and he told me he was about to hire a farm of Master Kimball in the towne, and I told him of our towne orders . . . and advised him to goe to the townsmen and have their aprobation before he made any contract with master Kimball."[35] In the largest towns it became necessary to appoint special officials to keep watch for strangers. In 1670 Salem had to appoint an officer to go from house to house once a month to inquire

[30] *Conn. Rec.*, I, 351 (1660); *Laws Conn., 1673*, p. 36; *ibid., 1702*, p. 58; *ibid., 1750*, p. 99; *ibid., 1784*, p. 103.

[31] *Mass. Assistants Rec.*, I, 197 (Boston, 1681); Suffolk Co. Gen. Sess., 1712–19, pp. 108–9 (1716), 111.

[32] Benton, *Warning Out*, p. 58.

[33] "N.H. Court Rec.," *N.H. Provincial Papers*, XL, 240–41.

[34] *Boston Town Rec.*, VIII, 102, 104 (1714), XVII, 299–300 (1753); *Early Records of the Town of Worcester*, ed. Franklin P. Rice, Worcester Society of Antiquity, *Collections*, II–IV (1879–82), IV, 118 (1765). For Lexington, see Benton, *Warning Out*, p. 62.

[35] *Lancaster Rec.*, p. 90.

whether any strangers "had come or had privily thrust themselves into the town, and to give notice to the selectmen." Boston appointed such officials in the mid-eighteenth century, a reflection of the unwillingness of citizens to become much involved in this activity.[36]

The problems of enforcing the residence requirements were great, especially in a town the size of Boston, or in any of the increasingly large eighteenth-century towns. As early as 1662 the Boston selectmen complained about newcomers "shifting from house to house" to avoid warning out. In 1733 the town erected two hundred posters warning the inhabitants not to entertain persons contrary to law. In 1758 Boston could not keep track of those who had been once warned out and ordered a list made of persons warned out of the town in the past ten years.[37] The Connecticut legislature noted similar problems eleven years later, when it complained of newcomers "set to Work by those who live in the Skirts and obscure Places of said Towns, out of the view and Observation of the Officers of the Town."[38] This is interesting evidence of the limited capabilities of official surveillance.

Residence requirements were a hindrance to the privacy and liberty of some individuals but were never very repressive in practice. Mobility within New England was never great in the seventeenth century, nor was immigration excessive after the first twenty years. Thus residence requirements affected a small fraction of the population, and then perhaps only once in their lifetimes. Except in Boston, appearances before admissions committees were not daily occurrences. The practical difficulties of enforcing such laws increased, particularly as substantial population growth and mobility occurred in the mid-eighteenth century. Decisions became more and more impersonal and wholly dependent on financial evaluation. Moral considerations disappeared from the eighteenth-century records. Enforcement also depended on the support of town residents. The strident reiterations of the residence laws in the eighteenth century suggests that many New Englanders considered rigid compliance anachronistic and bothersome. Eighteenth-century communities were no longer assemblages of Puritan Saints. In fact, Darrett Rutman has shown that as early as the 1640's few new Bostonians bothered to go through the process of formal admission. They could live in Boston unmo-

[36] Quoted in MacLear, *Early New England Towns,* p. 132; for Boston, see *Boston Town Rec.,* XVII, 299–300 (1753), XIX, 49 (1756), 55 (1757), 188 (1762), 198 (1762).

[37] *Boston Town Rec.,* VII, 7, XIII, 240, XIX, 83–84, 130.

[38] Quoted in Benton, *Warning Out,* p. 67.

lested, except during the infrequent periods when the law was enforced.[39]

Solitary Living

The seventeenth-century custom of forbidding persons to live alone and ordering them to submit to family government is another significant instance of the state's regulation of private lives. When it became necessary to enact a statute on this matter, the law was primarily directed against young single persons, although it was enforced against widows on occasion. Such a law deserves careful attention, since it seems to embody a massive indifference to the personal privacy that individuals might want to achieve by living alone. The opposition to the solitary life, however, was motivated, not by lack of concern for privacy, but by traditions, practicality, and an underlying fear of sin.

The English immigrants did not come from a tradition that encouraged solitary dwelling. Even in Greece, Rome, and the medieval world one was expected to belong to a family.[40] Living under a family roof was considered essential to a healthy economy and an orderly society in the sixteenth and seventeenth centuries.[41] Vagrancy, pauperism, and social disorders were the anticipated consequences of single living. Thus the town of Salem concluded that "it would be a bad president to keep hous alone," when it refused Debora Holmes land in 1636, although Taunton granted land to single men after its settlement in 1638.[42] The authorities expected a person to live within his family until such time as he or she left to form a new family. The unmarried remained with their family while it was intact and then

[39] *Winthrop's Boston*, pp. 196–98.

[40] See Willystine Goodsell, *A History of Marriage and the Family* (rev. ed., New York, 1934), pp. 116–17.

[41] For discussion of single men in England, see Davies, *Enforcement of English Apprenticeship*, pp. 193–96; Keith Thomas, "Women and the Civil War Sects," *Past and Present*, no. 13 (1958), p. 42; Laslett, *World We Have Lost*, p. 11. Lawrence Towner has pointed out the provisions against single living in the Statute of Artificers of 1562–63 and has suggested that earlier commentators on the New England laws have exaggerated their Puritan nature ("A Good Master Well Served: A Social History of Servitude in Massachusetts, 1620–1750" [Ph.D. diss., Northwestern University, 1955], p. 91n).

[42] Benton, *Warning Out*, p. 32 (Salem); Langdon, *Pilgrim Colony*, p. 49 (Taunton).

lived with other relatives. This custom in part accounted for the large number of persons living under any colonial roof.

Common sense was a primary hindrance to solitary living in an agricultural society. Embarking on their first task, building houses, the Pilgrims in 1620 "took notice how many families there were, willing all single men that had no wives to join with some family, as they thought fit, that so we might build fewer houses."[43] When the Massachusetts Bay Company sent over its first servants in 1629, artificial families were created to encourage religion and to prevent disorders, but primarily "for the better accommodation of businesses."[44] The burden of domestic duties further encouraged persons to live in families. George Homans has pointed out that few persons in a primitive society lived alone because "the need for co-operation in getting and preparing food makes it convenient for a single person to join another household."[45] In light of the domestic labor involved, most colonists did not even want to live alone, for reasons unrelated to attitudes toward personal privacy.

The Puritan opposition to the solitary life also had a moral basis. Individuals living alone, or several single persons together, were considered closer to the ways of the devil than those safely ensconced under the watchful eye of a family head. In 1672 the Hampton court discussed the Haverhill man who "lay in a house by himself contrary to the law of the country, whereby he is subject to much sin and iniquity, which ordinarily are the companions and consequences of a solitary life."[46] Many seventeenth-century indictments for solitary living significantly included the adjective "disorderly." The law was a particularly handy tool against single persons living together who behaved in unconventional fashion.

In 1668 both Plymouth and Massachusetts indicated concern over solitary living, obviously in response to a growing problem. The law formally enacted by Plymouth in that year singled out the "great Inconvenience [that] hath arisen by single persons in this Collonie being for themselves and not betakeing themselves to live in well Gouverned famillies."[47] The selectmen, however, could grant per-

---

[43] *Mourt's Relation*, p. 42 (1622).

[44] Alexander Young, *Chronicles of the First Planters of the Colony of the Massachusetts Bay, from 1623 to 1636* (Boston, 1846), pp. 167, 176–77.

[45] *The Human Group* (New York, 1950), p. 207.

[46] Such cases were unusual; hence this episode has become well known through frequent citation (see *Essex Rec.*, V, 104). See also, for example, two "disorderly" prosecutions in *Plymouth Col. Rec.*, I, 118.

[47] *Plymouth Col. Rec.*, XI, 223, 32.

mission for an individual to live alone. The Massachusetts statute requiring young persons to live under family government was clearly directed at those few who did "not serve their parents or masters as children, apprentices, hired servants, or journey men ought to do, and usually did in our native country being subject to their commands and discipline."[48] In a stratified, authoritarian society one had to fit into such a category or be a threat to it. Living alone as a young person was presumptive evidence of disorderliness, and towns ordered their constables to compile lists of such delinquents.

The passage of these laws in 1668 was an Old World response to changes created by differing conditions in the New World. From at least the time of the Statute of Artificers in England in the 1560's, the authorities had assumed that young and unmarried men and women would continue to live under family government. Prior to the 1668 enactment Massachusetts had simply stated that towns should settle their single men in service;[49] either they served or were served. Now some young persons were finding it desirable and possible to live alone, primarily because of economic abundance in the New World. This was a significant innovation in the life of Western societies.

Of the approximately sixty-five prosecutions for living alone noted in Massachusetts, all but three occurred between 1668 and 1677–that is, within a decade of the enactments of the General Court. The towns of Dedham and Dorchester were particularly strict. On three occasions between 1669 and 1677 the Dedham selectmen met "to setel the younge persons in such familyes in the Town as is most sutable for thier good." The selectmen assigned them to a family or approved their choice of a family. In Dorchester in 1669 "the Constable brought in a list of the yong men that where not under the Gouvernment of famelys according as the law enjoyns."[50]

There were no cases of the successful enforcement of this law against solitary living after King Phillip's War in the mid-1670's, although it is possible that town officials handled this matter, keeping instances out of the court records. In the eighteenth century the laws against solitary living reappeared as part of the Poor Laws, but with significant changes. Only single persons under twenty-one years of age were not permitted to live alone, "for the better preventing of

[48] *Mass. Rec.*, IV, pt. 2, pp. 395–96; *Laws Mass.*, 1660, pp. 259–60 (1668).
[49] *Laws Mass.*, 1660, p. 76; *ibid.*, 1672, p. 148.
[50] *Early Records of the Town of Dedham, Massachusetts*, ed. Dow G. Hill (Dedham, 1892–99), IV, 170, and V, 53–54; for Dorchester, see *Boston Town Rec.*, IV, 158. Twenty-one men were listed.

idleness and loose or disorderly living." The Poor Law passed in 1692 did not even have a clause relating to this matter. Its inclusion in 1703 was no longer a Puritan measure but simply one facet of the safeguards against poverty and disorder. The Massachusetts statutes repeated this restriction for the remainder of the colonial period and expected the Court of General Sessions or the justices of the peace to enforce it, but there is no record of its use against solitary living.[51] Officials as well as citizens found these laws too unpalatable or irrelevant and let them fall into disuse, along with other restrictions on liberty and privacy that gradually disappeared in the late seventeenth century and thereafter.

Laws against solitary living appeared earlier in the Connecticut region and Rhode Island than in Massachusetts and Plymouth. The Connecticut statute of 1636 stipulated that "no man that is neither married, nor hath any Servant, nor is a publick Officer shall keep house of himself without consent of the Town where he lives." The New Haven Colony code of 1656 contained a similar law, which had been enforced at an even earlier date.[52] Rhode Island passed a law against solitary living in 1656. It implied that individuals could live alone unless "they shall live disorderly," probably the tacit understanding in all the New England colonies.[53] Every Connecticut legal code until 1750 contained a statute against solitary living.[54] Its omission in that year's edition was an explicit reflection of the nascent secularization of society in the eighteenth century, which was so favorable to personal privacy. The Connecticut laws against solitary living were rarely enforced. Less than a half-dozen cases were found between 1651 and 1683. "In the calamitous time of New England's distresse by the war with the Indians," that is, during King Phillip's War, the General Court was "moved to make some lawes for the suppression of some provoakeing evills which were feared to be groweing up amongst us." These evils included "young persons shakeing off the goverment of parents or masters." In 1684 the court admitted that these laws had not been successful and urged law enforcement officials to greater zeal. They repeated the same

---

[51] *Mass. Acts and Res.*, I, 538 (1703); for 1692, see *ibid.*, I, 67; for subsequent repetitions from 1706 to 1780, see *ibid.*, I, 587, 654, II, 73, 183, 580, 1054, III, 488, IV, 324, V, 86, 458, 1121.

[52] *Conn. Rec.*, I, 8, 105, 538–39; *New Haven Col. Rec.*, *1653–1665*, p. 608; *ibid.*, *1638–1649*, pp. 47, 70.

[53] *R.I. Rec.*, I, 332. New Hampshire had a similar statute ("N.H. Court Rec.," *N.H. Provincial Papers*, XL, 269 [1671]).

[54] *Laws Conn.*, *1673*, p. 47; *ibid.*, *1702*, pp. 74–75; *ibid.*, *1750*, p. 152.

encouragement in 1690. No prosecutions under these reinvigorated laws have been found, except a stray case in Hartford County in 1709, when a grand jury presented a Windsor man "for breach of law, by his living alone."[55] The court discharged the accused when the evidence did not fully prove the charge. This prosecution was the last one discovered in New England.

In general, these laws against solitary living had only an inter-mittent and indirect effect on the desire for privacy. In the seven-teenth century enforcement was spasmodic, depending on the zeal of the particular group of town officials in office, and then ceased altogether. The residents of seventeenth-century New England re-garded the desire to live alone with suspicion. Morality and the eco-nomic interests of the state were better served if everyone lived in a family. Yet this was not an expression of total hostility to the value of privacy. Living alone was so untraditional and made so little sense that anyone seeking to do so appeared to be challenging the good order of society. This was unacceptable behavior during a good part of the seventeenth century. By the latter part of that century experi-ence in America had shown that it was possible to live alone and not become a burden on the community. After this time the solitary liv-ing laws were never rigidly enforced but were kept on the law books for infrequent use against indigent or disorderly youths. Eighteenth-century New England society was prepared to accept the person who wanted to live alone because he enjoyed the privacy this way of living provided. One suspects the custom remained uncommon for practical reasons.

MORAL LEGISLATION

Association of the Puritan movement with repressive moral legis-lation is largely responsible for the common assumption that privacy was not a Puritan concern. Since the New England Puritans had laws regulating disorderly houses, idleness, drinking, gaming, tobacco, and cursing,[56] how could such a society also foster respect for indi-

55 *Conn. Rec.*, III, 147–48, IV, 28–29 (1675–76); Hartford Co. Ct. Rec., bk. G, no. 7, p. 90.

56 Other American colonies had laws on most of these same matters. See, for example, a Virginia act of 1691 and its several renewals: "An Act for the more effectuall suppressing the several sins and offences of swaring, cursing, pro-faineing Gods holy name, Sabbath abuseing, drunkenness, fornication, and adultery" (William W. Hening, comp., *The Statutes-at-Large, Being a Collec-tion of All the Laws of Virginia, 1619–1792* [New York, etc., 1819–1823; rpt. Charlottesville, Va., 1969], III, 71–75, 137–40, 168–71, 358–62).

vidual privacy? In order to discover what influence such statutes had on the availability of personal privacy, one must understand them in a proper historical perspective and investigate the question of their enforcement. The ethical regulations enacted by the Puritans were part of a continuing stream of such statutes from medieval times. Practically every item of moral legislation enacted in New England had direct English antecedents.

The attempt to regulate disorderly conduct in a private home is one example of such legislation. This practice did not involve a host of officials keeping close watch on each home and making presentments for minor offenses. For the Puritans a disorderly house meant approximately what the term has denoted in later times. The problem of prostitution plagued Boston from the 1650's, through the time of Alice Thomas in the 1670's, to the mid-eighteenth-century Hannah Dilley, the wife of a feltmaker, who "permitted men and other suspected persons . . . to Resort to her said husbands house and Carnally to lye with whores, which the said Hannah then and there procured for them."[57] There were presentments for such disorders in the home as drunkenness, "swearing Cursing and Damning one another," and entertaining "lewd dissolute and disorderly persons, suffering them to be and remain there rioting and profanely Cursing Swearing etc."[58] These were serious breaches of the peace of the community. Town officials did not go out of their way to oversee behavior in households. Regulation of disorderly houses, for instance, had almost no effect on the enjoyment of privacy by the general populace.

The Puritan dislike of idleness has served as a popular sign of the authoritarianism of their society and its disregard of personal privacy. Yet presentments for "idleness" were common on both sides of the ocean in the colonial period.[59] Connecticut passed a law in 1702 that "no person, Householder or other, shall spend their time idly, or

[57] See *Suffolk Rec.*, pp. 82–83 (1672), 125, 443; Suffolk Co. Gen. Sess., 1749–54, April 30, 1753; see also *ibid.*, 1702–12, p. 248 (1712); and *ibid.*, 1769–73, Oct. 6, 1772. For the English experience, see MacCaffrey, *Exeter*, p. 91.

[58] *Mass. Assistants Rec.*, II, 89 (Boston, 1639); *Maine Ct. Rec.*, V, 138 (York Co., 1713); Suffolk Co. Gen. Sess. 1712–19, p. 215 (1718); Rhode Island Gen. Ct. of Trials, 1725–41, p. 24 (1725); Suffolk Co. Gen. Sess., 1754–58, Jan. 23, 1756; *ibid.*, 1769–73, Nov. 14, 1769.

[59] *Watertown Rec., Town Proc.*, pp. 33 (1653), 113 (1672); "N.H. Court Rec.," *N.H. Provincial Papers*, XL, 186 (1663); *Maine Ct. Rec.*, II, 288 (York Co., 1674); *Suffolk Rec.*, p. 844 (1677); Middlesex Co. Ct. Rec., 1681–86, p. 59. See the comments on idleness in William Lambarde, *The Duties of Constables* (Rev. ed., London, 1614; rpt. London, 1619), p. 28. C. Hill stresses the great benefit to society of this dislike of idleness (*Society and Puritanism*, pp. 126–38).

unprofitably."⁶⁰ Massachusetts legislators often bewailed the sin of idleness and eventually ordered the selectmen and overseers of the poor to put the idle to work. In Boston in the 1760's Justice of the Peace Richard Dana handled several cases in which persons were convicted of being "a vagabond strolling and idle person." He found one widow "to be an idle person, wandering about from town to town mispending her time and neglecting her calling and business."⁶¹ In fact idleness was often the colonial term for vagrancy. Prosecution served to discourage persons from becoming a burden on the community. Prohibitions against idleness did not apply to the ordinary person who was enjoying desirable relaxations or the pursuit of privacy.

Regulation of drinking was another characteristic New England practice. This once again reflected customary English attitudes in the seventeenth century, when many bills were introduced "against excessive and common drunkenness."⁶² New England efforts were ordinarily limited to controls over the sale of liquor. The Puritans attempted to restrict the time one could spend in a tavern and, according to John Josselyn, sent officers into the ordinaries to see that people did not drink too much, but this was primarily a curiosity of the first decades of settlement.⁶³ Public drunkenness remained a normal item in the court records, much as it has to the present day, and was often combined with an assault on a constable or tythingman.

The regulation of tippling involved some invasion of privacy when the authorities sought to control drinking within the home. Several colonies had laws in the seventeenth century against "drunckenes in private howses."⁶⁴ These included penalties for the homeowner who

---

⁶⁰ *Laws Conn., 1702*, p. 53. See the subsequent enforcement in Hartford Co. Ct. Rec., bk. G, no. 7, p. 91 (1709); Inferior Ct. Hartford, Conn. Arch. Crimes and Misdemeanors, II (1707–24), docs. 104–5 (1715).

⁶¹ For example, see General Court, *Mass. Rec.*, V, 62 (1675); 1703 act in *Mass. Acts and Res.*, I, 538; Richard Dana, "Minute Book, 1760–1767," 1761–62, cases 86, 216, 221, 223, in Dana Family Papers, box 3.

⁶² For a thorough discussion of the English scene, see Frances E. Baldwin, *Sumptuary Legislation and Personal Regulation in England* (Baltimore, 1926), pp. 244–45, 270–72; see also 1 James I, c. 9 (1604); 4 James I, c. 5 (1606); 21 James I, c. 7 (1623).

⁶³ See Middlesex Co. Ct. Rec., 1649–63, p. 128 (1657); Josselyn, *Two Voyages*, pp. 132–33.

⁶⁴ *Plymouth Col. Rec.*, I, 13 (1633); *Mass. Rec.*, III, 359 (1654), IV, pt. 1, p. 203; *Laws Mass., 1660*, p. 165; *ibid., 1672*, p. 81; *Conn. Rec.*, I, 333 (1659); *Laws Conn., 1673*, p. 21. Note the passage of a similar law by the Quakers around 1690 (*Charter and Laws of Pennsylvania*, ed. George Staughton *et al.* [Harrisburg, Pa., 1879], p. 195).

allowed his friends to get drunk. The Connecticut statute provided that "if any person be found Drunk in any private Family or House, he shall forfeit twenty shillings." Perhaps individuals tried to escape the wrath of the authorities by drinking with friends in their homes. However, the vast majority of seventeenth-century prosecutions for suffering persons to drink in one's home were not against the home-owners themselves for drinking, but against their permitting others to do so, probably in return for money.[65] Unlicensed retailing of liquor was a continual problem, and the main reason for prosecutions in this area.

In the eighteenth century an incident in the life of magistrate Samuel Sewall illustrates the lack of concern with social drinking in private houses. He was summoned one Saturday evening in 1714 to cope with a large party in a Boston tavern. Although the rules for Sabbath behavior began at sundown on Saturday, the company refused to disperse and continued drinking toasts. Finally Sewall prevailed upon a senior resident to set a good example: "Upon this he invited them to his own House, and away they went."[66] Sewall recognized that such social activity was tolerated in a private house but not in public.

On occasion the authorities published lists of known tipplers as a part of the regulation of drinking habits. In 1679 Ipswich ordered "that no person should sell or give to John Browne, the glazier, any strong drink . . . and should any ordinaries suffer him to come or stay in any of their houses . . . they would do it at their peril." Notices of the order were posted at the meetinghouse and taverns. In Boston in 1711 and 1727 lists of "reputed Drunckard and Common Tiplers" were drawn up and posted.[67] Most of the seventeen on the latter list were artisans. Since such notices were rarely posted, although required by law, one can assume that they offended the sensibilities of the townspeople.[68]

[65] Boston, *Mass. Rec.*, I, 168, 284 (1639) and *Mass. Assistants Rec.*, II, 131–39 (1643–44); Haverhill, *Mass. Rec.*, III, 290 (1652); Charlestown, Middlesex Co. Ct. Rec., 1649–63, p. 197 (1659); Salem Commissioner's Ct., *Essex Rec.*, VII, 109, 251 (1678–79); New London Co. Ct. Rec., III, 136 (1679); York Co., *Maine Ct. Rec.*, III, 77 (1681).

[66] *Diary*, MHS, *Coll.*, 5th ser., VI, 419–20.

[67] *Essex Rec.*, VII, 184; *Boston Town Rec.*, XI, 126–32, XIII, 171.

[68] The law was included in *County and Town Officer*, p. 98. In response to a petition "of sundry Inhabitants" in 1754, the Boston town meeting nullified a decision of the previous year to permit the overseers of the poor to exhibit annually a list of all such persons who received support from the town's money (*Boston Town Rec.*, XIV, 244–46, 225, 254–55).

The Massachusetts tobacco laws followed the pattern of the moral legislation already considered.[69] The consumption of tobacco was at first completely prohibited. Then in 1637 "all former lawes against tobacco are repealed, and tobacco is set at liberty." Less than a year later the General Court noted that abuses in the use of tobacco had increased and put limited prohibitions into execution. The main purpose was fire prevention, for tobacco was forbidden near any house or barn, as well as in the fields, except on a journey or at mealtime.[70] Although the codes of 1660 and 1672 repeated these idealistic rules, less than a dozen presentments were found for smoking tobacco.[71] In each instance the accused was smoking too close to houses or barns. The pattern of prosecutions suggested intermittent enforcement, due perhaps to some zealous individual who came into office and either prosecuted this offense or prodded subordinates into action. Connecticut's 1647 law regulating the use of tobacco was similar to the Massachusetts statute, but it does not seem to have been enforced at all.[72] The enforcement of tobacco regulations did not involve extensive surveillance of the populace, such as might have threatened personal privacy on a regular basis.

In 1601 the English House of Commons debated a bill forbidding "usual and common swearing." Laws were later passed against cursing and swearing, and as late as 1679 the Lord Mayor of London issued a proclamation against these offenses.[73] The New England colonies also outlawed cursing and swearing. Official interest in repressing such practices did not die out in the seventeenth century, for as late as 1747 and 1761, respectively, Massachusetts and New Hampshire passed acts "more effectually to prevent profane Cursing

[69] The laws regulating gaming did not have any influence on the availability of personal privacy (see David H. Flaherty, "Privacy in Colonial New England" (Ph.D. diss., Columbia University, 1967), pp. 215–17).

[70] The Mass. tobacco laws can be found in *Mass. Assistants Rec.*, II, 28; *Mass. Rec.*, I, 126, 206, 241–42; *The Laws and Liberties of Mass.*, ed. Max Farrand (Cambridge, Mass., 1929), p. 50; *Laws Mass., 1660*, p. 75; *ibid.*, *1672*, p. 146. No formal attempts were made to regulate the use of tobacco in England, although James I spoke and wrote against the practice, providing further evidence that being against tobacco had little to do with Puritanism.

[71] *Essex Rec.*, I, 414 (1656), II, 70 (1658); Middlesex Co. Ct. Rec., 1649–63, p. 172 (1659); *Suffolk Rec.*, p. 995 (1679); Hampshire County General Sessions and Common Pleas, no. 1 (1677–1728), p. 61 (1682), Northampton.

[72] *Conn. Rec.*, I, 153.

[73] See Baldwin, *Sumptuary Legislation*, pp. 240–69, 270; 21 James I, c. 20, "An Act to prevent and reform profane Swearing and Cursing," continued by 3 Charles I, c. 4 (1627) and 16 Charles I, c. 4 (1640); see also the strongly worded act of 6 and 7 William III, c. 11 (1695).

and Swearing."[74] New Hampshire made this law perpetual in 1764. Although convictions for cursing were always common in the New England courts, fines were minimal and individuals rarely debated their guilt.[75] As late in the colonial era as 1767 a resident of Kingston in Plymouth County was fined thirteen shillings for using the phrases "damn you," "God damn you," and "by God," and repeating the same "ten different times." Cursing presentments were reserved for individuals who violently lost their tempers in public, usually during a fight. Officials did not bend their ears to the keyhole to discover offenders.

This short survey of New England moral legislation has made several things apparent. In the first place, laws against disorderly houses, drinking, and the like bore little relationship to the enjoyment of privacy, if one defines it in terms of solitude, family intimacy, and anonymity in public. Such statutes embodied a traditional antipathy to specific kinds of behavior. Persons were being arrested for most of the same offenses in late-nineteenth-century Boston.[76] The colonial laws were relatively moderate in conception and execution. Few institutionalized any consistent intrusions into private life. The long-term impact of Puritan moral legislation on personal privacy was negligible. The relationship of the Puritan movement and privacy did not begin or end with moral legislation; the latter simply presents a false detour on the path to understanding the actual influence of the Puritan movement on personal privacy in the seventeenth century.

SUMPTUARY LAWS

In seventeenth-century New England the authorities restricted specific types of clothes and accouterments to precise classes of the citizenry. Silk hoods, for example, could only be worn by the better classes. Lace was forbidden on the clothes of the poor. Such sumptuary laws had a long tradition in medieval and Renaissance history.[77]

[74] See, for example, *Laws Mass., 1660*, p. 74; *Mass. Acts and Res.*, III, 318 (1747); *Temporary Acts and Laws of His Majesty's Province of New Hampshire* (Portsmouth, 1761), pp. 3–7; *Laws N.H., 1771*, p. 259.

[75] See, for example, Dana, "Minute Book, 1746–1748," Middlesex Co., Cambridge, cases 9, 11, 13, 19, 20 in Dana Family Papers, box 3; "Minute Book, 1757–1760," Suffolk Co., Boston, *passim, ibid.*

[76] See Roger Lane, *Policing the City: Boston, 1822–1885* (Cambridge, Mass., 1967), pp. 230–31, 232–34.

[77] This discussion is based on Baldwin, *Sumptuary Legislation, passim*; Stone, *Crisis of the Aristocracy*, pp. 28–29; MacCaffrey, *Exeter*, p. 93.

Until the sixteenth century the main intent was to oppose extravagance and maintain class divisions, but such laws multiplied in the
era of the Reformation. During the reign of Elizabeth no less than
ten proclamations were issued enjoining the enforcement of the 1533
Sumptuary Act. Yet sumptuary legislation was not enforced. The end
result was the repeal of apparel statutes in 1604; later attempts to
pass new laws failed. The English Puritans passed no sumptuary laws
during the Interregnum. John Milton summed up the situation in his
Areopagitica: how absurd it would be to refer "our garments . . . to
the licensing of some more sober work-masters to see them cut in a
lesse wanton garb," as ridiculous as it would be to regulate music
and dancing.[78]

The American colonies thus were founded at a time when sumptuary legislation had disappeared in England. The tide of opinion
had turned against such minute regulation of a personal matter. This
did not prevent sumptuary laws from making an early appearance in
Massachusetts and, by automatic extension in the seventeenth century, Maine and New Hampshire. In 1634 the General Court drew
up the first rules against using lace, silver, gold, slashed clothes, and
the like. By an order of 1636 lace was not to be made or sold, and one
in 1639 encouraged officials to zealous enforcement. But no cases of
the enforcement of these laws were found. Not only were the problems of law enforcement formidable, but public opinion did not support such enforcement. In 1638 the Massachusetts General Court and
the churches agreed to redress "the great disorder general through
the country in costliness of apparel, and following new fashions."
At a subsequent conference "little was done about it; for divers of the
elders' wives, etc., were in some measure partners in this general disorder."[79] In 1644 "all those former orders made about apparrell and
lace" were repealed.[80] Massachusetts made subsequent experiments
with sumptuary legislation in 1651, 1662, and 1675.[81] Each reenact-
ment was prefaced with a lament that the "wholesome lawes already
made" were not being enforced. The statutes ordered selectmen to
take notice of the apparel of their inhabitants, a form of surveillance
which could have been seriously detrimental to privacy, and threatened them with dire punishment if they did not do their duty.

There have been two studies of the pattern of enforcement of this

[78] 1644; rpt. Chicago, 1952, p. 394.
[79] Winthrop, *Journal*, I, 279.
[80] *Mass. Rec.*, I, 126, 183, 274-75, II, 84.
[81] *Ibid.*, III, 243-44 (1651); *Laws Mass.*, *1660*, p. 3; *Mass. Rec.*, IV, pt. 2,
p. 41 (1662); *Laws Mass.*, *1672*, p. 5; *Mass. Rec.*, V, 59-60 (1675).

sumptuary legislation. Norman H. Dawes discussed attire in his study
of "Social Classes in Seventeenth-Century New England." Essex
County enforced each of the laws of 1651, 1662, and 1675 for a short
period after its enactment—in 1652–53, 1663, and 1674–76. In other
years the laws seem to have been ignored. Dawes concluded that
"except for a few scattered prosecutions, no noticeable attempt at
enforcement is indicated by the records after 1677."[82] Linzee Coolidge
paid similar attention to sumptuary legislation in Hampshire County.
No cases were recorded from the establishment of that county in
1662 till almost 1675, but many prosecutions occurred in the three
wartime years following passage of the 1675 law. Coolidge concluded
that "the laws met with opposition and indifference during the brief
period the county court attempted to enforce them."[83] An event in
the county court in 1682 supports his conclusions. The selectmen of
Springfield, Northampton, Hadley, Hatfield, and Westfield were presented "for not assessing of the Several Persons of their Inhabitants
that are Excessive in their apparel."[84] The court ordered the selectmen to enforce the sumptuary laws, but they did nothing.

The court records of other counties add support to the above conclusions. There are indications that only Hampshire and Essex counties enforced the law with periodic vigor. The Watertown selectmen
only threatened to do so in 1659. When a grand jury menaced the
Dedham selectmen with indictment, "if they take no effectuall care:
that law be prosicuted refering to excess in aparall," the selectmen decided that persons would be rated for tax purposes by the clothing
they wore; but no cases of subsequent enforcement were found. For
the decade 1671–80 the Suffolk County court records reveal only one
presentment for sumptuary law violation.[85] The printed Maine court
records contain no such presentments for the seventeenth century.
The Reforming Synod of 1679–80 generally concluded that "pride in
respect to Apparel hath greatly abounded. Servants, and the poorer
sort of People are notoriously guilty in the matter, who (too generally) goe above their estates and degrees, thereby transgressing the
Laws both of God and man."[86]

[82] Ph.D. diss., Harvard University, 1940–41, pp. 340–48. Perry Miller agreed
with Dawes's conclusion (*The New England Mind: From Colony to Province*
[New York, 1953], pp. 50–51).

[83] "Aspects of Puritan Morality," pp. 50–52. See also Judd, *Hadley*, pp.
99–100.

[84] Hampshire Co. Gen. Sess. and Common Pleas, no. 1, p. 61.

[85] *Watertown Rec., Town Proc.*, p. 62; *Dedham Rec.*, V, 33 (1675); *Suffolk
Rec.*, p. 751 (1676).

[86] Walker, *Creeds and Platforms*, pp. 427–28.

Connecticut passed laws concerning apparel in 1641 and 1676. The problem confronting the authorities was stated in their 1641 complaint that "notwithstanding the late Order conserneing the restraynt of excesse in apparrell, yet divers persons of severall ranks are obsearved still to exceede therein." When public opinion did not support laws, enforcement was almost impossible. This probably accounted for the complete absence of presentments for breach of the sumptuary laws in Connecticut, except for a solitary case in New Haven County in 1679.[87] New Haven and Plymouth colonies did not have such laws while they were independent.

Some colonists actively resented sumptuary legislation. When the selectmen of Watertown investigated John Willington in 1664 for the fashion of his apparel, he condemned the town "as haveinge no power to deale with him: for his apparill." In 1674 the Hampton court prosecuted Samuel Weed "for giving retorting and saucy language to the president of the court in saying that he might wear silver buttons if he paid for them as well as any man in the country."[88] If such expressions reached the official records, they represented a significant body of opinion in the country.

By the eighteenth-century sumptuary legislation, like most of the Puritan laws that interfered too much with the private lives of the people, was no longer enforced. Daniel Neal's *History of New England*, published in London in 1720, contained an "Abridgment of the Laws and Ordinances of New England." His preface to the volume added this qualification about the list of laws: "It must be observed, that some of the more Ancient Ones, relating to Fashions, Dress, etc. are obsolete." Persons were free to dress, chew tobacco, and play games as they wished. Peter Harrison epitomized the new era when he sent his new wife two pairs of pink worsted stockings, "which they tell me, in England is all the mode."[89] Even a cleric like Ebenezer Parkman, who occasionally preached against "the growing extravagance of Velvet and scarlet among people of low rank," was distressed when he lost a "pair of Gold Buttons" from his sleeve and rejoiced when presented with "a Wigg of Considerable Price."[90] This

---

[87] *Conn. Rec.*, I, 64, II, 280–83; New Haven Co. Ct. Rec., I, 115; see also Dawes, "Social Classes in 17th-Century New England," pp. 342–43n.

[88] *Watertown Rec., Town Proc.*, p. 84; *Essex Rec.*, V, 409.

[89] Quoted in Carl Bridenbaugh, *Peter Harrison* (Chapel Hill, N.C., 1949), p. 30. Family manuscript collections of the 18th century abound with references to the purchase of clothes of the latest fashion (see, for example, John Winthrop, FRS, to Fitz-John Winthrop, *ca.* 1700–1707, Winthrop Papers, IX, 8).

[90] "Diary," AAS, *Proc.*, LXXI (1961), 445, 448 (1738), LXXII (1962), 219 (1744), 428 (1746).

relative secularization of society, as evidenced in the decline of the enforcement of so much moral legislation, provided a suitable climate for the enjoyment of personal privacy under normal circumstances.

This chapter has assessed the extent of regularized statutory intrusions into the private lives of New England citizens. It is essential for an understanding of how interests affecting privacy are balanced to recognize why this intrusion should even have been possible. All governments enact regulations for the maintenance of good order, public health and safety, and public security. Individual preferences normally have to give way in these instances. The New England governments at various times thought it important to control such matters as the admission of new inhabitants to a community, the circumstances in which single persons lived, and the prevalence of drunkenness and other social disorders. Since all governments then were authoritarian and repressive with respect to such matters, these laws were not unusual. The Puritan social ethic lent even stronger societal support for such regulations in the early years, for reasons that went beyond the usual motives of civil authorities. In some instances the regulations temporarily limited the degree to which a person could secure solitude, intimacy, or anonymity without interruption. If he wanted to settle in another town, a limited amount of screening was essential. A person who sought to live alone might be left unbothered, but he was certain to receive more attention from the authorities because of the suspicions his unusual behavior naturally aroused. In the same way public drunkenness, foul language, idleness, or disorderly conduct would sometimes result in the forfeiture of privacy. Only a small proportion of the population faced such a forfeiture at any point in their lives. Whatever the laws may have stated, persons had to engage in some flagrant violation to attract the attention of the authorities in most cases. If an individual chose to engage in antisocial behavior, this preference could mean forfeiting his usual enjoyment of privacy. If a person lived up to certain minimal norms, the law ignored him; for that matter the law had great difficulty in finding out if he did not.

7. Law Enforcers

L
AW enforcement officials can jeopardize personal privacy by
widespread surveillance of individuals. On the other hand ju-
dicious interpretation and execution of their duties permit
officials to acknowledge a right of privacy in everyday life. Some
colonial laws could have hindered the search for privacy if rigorously
implemented, but such laws are of little consequence when they are
not executed. Colonial New England had a structured system of local
law enforcement. It might be assumed that such organization and
the assistance of paid informers automatically resulted in a well-
regulated society, wherein the enacted statutes accurately reflected
personal behavior. The conduct of the officials designated to enforce
these statutes is thus a significant consideration in an evaluation of
the preservation of personal privacy.[1]

As the previous chapters have shown, the practice of surveillance
techniques was clearly recommended to local officials. In 1673 Increase Mather, the pastor of Boston's North Church, lamented the
prevalence of drunkenness: "And there are some that ought to do
more than merely to pray against it; . . . it concerns those that have
any Civil Power in their hands, to bear witness against it in their
way. . . . Townsmen, Constables, Grand Jurymen, etc. Behold the
Word of the Lord is upon you in particular this day. . . . Especially
see that you keep a vigilant eye over these private, dark alehouses."
The Connecticut General Court in the late seventeenth century made
several similar pleas for stricter law enforcement, recommending
that officials "use all circumspection and dilligence to suppresse the
abuses . . . that so our government and rulers may be a terror to evill

---

[1] This chapter focuses on those officials actively involved in the law enforcement process at the local level. This excludes, for example, the selectmen who
generally played a minor role in the actual enforcement of laws designed to regulate personal behavior and requiring surveillance activities. As members of the
social and economic elite, their interests centered much more on the over-all direction of the town and the administrative problems facing it. Land problems
were more significant to them than the minutiae of town morality (see Flaherty,
"Privacy in Colonial New England," pp. 229–34).

doers as in our first times."[2] Such directives make plain the Puritan expectation that law enforcers could, or should, stamp out sin. The establishment of an elaborate hierarchy of local law enforcement officials testified to the Puritan authorities' intention to scrutinize their fellow residents. This represented a threat to the enjoyment of privacy.

The Puritan elite could enact almost any laws they desired for a good part of the seventeenth century, but enforcing them was another matter even in the early years. To what extent were surveillance procedures actually implemented? What was the attitude of the enforcement arm to the implementation of these laws? Did the acknowledged moralism and authoritarianism of the seventeenth century create an atmosphere in which the individual was under constant scrutiny by law enforcers? How did the gradual changes in the impact of the Puritan movement on society affect attitudes toward privacy in this sphere?

CONSTABLES

In 1658 the Massachusetts General Court listed the "office and power" of a constable under twenty-six titles.[3] Although the majority of the tasks were administrative, constables were also primarily responsible for the general maintenance of law and order in their locality. Idlers, drunkards, thieves, nightwalkers, and Sabbath breakers came within the scope of their scrutiny. This responsibility and capacity for immediate supervision of behavior placed the constable in a position of control over the availability of personal privacy in his community. Nicholas Boone of Boston wrote in a handbook for constables in 1710 that they "have great Power for the Suppressing of Prophaneness and Debauchery." In 1655, for example, the Middlesex County court ordered the Charlestown constables to "take speciall inspection into the Manners of the said Mansfield and wife."[4] At an earlier date the General Court of Connecticut requested constables to "obsearve and take notice of any particular person" who broke the apparel laws. Massachusetts laws required constables to inform

[2] Mather, *Wo to Drunkards*, p. 29; *Conn. Rec.*, III, 202–3 (1686), IV, 28–29 (1690).

[3] *Mass. Rec.*, IV, pt. 1, pp. 324–27; also *Cambridge Rec.*, pp. 351–52.

[4] Boone, *The Constable's Pocket Book; or, A Dialogue, between an Old Constable and a New* (Boston, 1710), p. 8. Middlesex Co. Ct. Rec., 1649–63, pp. 89–90.

the courts about newcomers who had settled in the town without permission.[5]

How diligently did the constables carry out their duties? In the absence of intensive studies of the constable in colonial New England, the English experience with petty constables is relevant. The duties of these officials on both sides of the ocean were similar, except for some of the short-term and esoteric duties imposed by the mid-seventeenth-century Puritan leadership on the New England constables.[6] In general the English constable was a person of low social status, overwhelmed by the burden of office, disinterested in certain aspects of his work, and with little motivation to be zealous in his duties. Boone was probably reacting to just such conditions when he described the office of a New England constable as "a very trouble-some one." In their classic study of *English Local Government* the Webbs noted a general disinclination to hold local office and concluded that "the post most objected to was that of Petty Constable, which was either abandoned to humble folk, attracted by its perquisites, or else invariably filled by a substitute."[7] Michael Dalton, whose handbook was indispensable for English and American justices of the peace in the seventeenth century, reported that "constables chosen out of the meaner sort are either ignorant what to do; or dare not do that they should; and are not able to spare the time to execute this office." Margaret Davies has also pointed out that the "constable had to put first his own business of getting a living, whether at a craft or trade or as a husbandman who had to be the 'most part of the day in the fields.' The demands made upon his time and energy fully to carry out his multifarious duties under the many statutes were impossible to meet."[8] The English petty constable thus led a troubled existence. He held office for a short time, often had to report on or deal with his social betters, and could jeopardize his relations with neighbors by overzealous enforcement

[5] *Conn. Rec.*, I, 64 (1641); Code of 1648, *Laws and Liberties Mass.*, p. 49; *Laws Mass., 1660*, pp. 73–74; *ibid., 1672*, p. 144.

[6] See Willcox, *Gloucestershire*, pp. 212–13; Trotter, *17th Century Life in the Country Parish*, p. 88; Sidney and Beatrice Webb, *English Local Government: The Parish and the County* (London, 1906), pp. 470–71.

[7] Boone, *Constable's Pocket Book*, p. 1; Webb, *English Local Government: Parish and County*, p. 18. See Shipton, *New England Life*, p. 274, for the story of attempts to get gentlemen to serve as constables. Fines for refusal to serve as constables were common in New England.

[8] Dalton, *The Countrey Justice* (London, 1618; later ed., London, 1635), p. 47; Davies, *Enforcement of English Apprenticeship*, p. 187.

of the law.[9] Internal and external pressures encouraged him to mind his own business.

The New England town constable was the victim of similar considerations. By the late seventeenth century no one in Massachusetts could be compelled to serve as a constable twice in seven years, a provision indicative of the unpopularity of the office and its ultimate ineffectuality.[10] The constable's responsibilities for the enforcement of moral legislation, for example, were either ignored, of an occasional nature, or liable to become a serious threat to privacy only in the hands of overly zealous individuals. Such an excess of zeal was not typical of the colonial law enforcer.

One of the surveillance obligations of constables, their function as searchers, especially of unlicensed houses, could have led to invasion of privacy. In Massachusetts and Connecticut the law authorized constables to enter homes suspected of selling alcohol without permission or of housing drunkards.[11] Since unlicensed houses were always a major concern of the New England legislators, all officials, including tythingmen, grand jurors, and constables, were charged with ferreting them out. These cases did not require a warrant; the law could have been interpreted as a blanket permission to enter private homes at will. But the constables rarely entered a private house in this fashion. There were two actions in Suffolk County in 1674, and another in Ipswich four years later, when the Andover constable was himself convicted of having persons drinking in his home.[12] By the 1690's in Massachusetts the legislators had carefully qualified this power of entering homes. Officials could enter suspected houses without a warrant only if the resident had been convicted of the same offense within the previous year.[13] An incident recorded by Governor Winthrop in 1644, while Puritan zeal was still at its peak, sheds some light on the delicate position of constables with respect to privacy. An Englishman who had recently arrived in Boston was carried drunk to his lodgings. "The constable, (a godly man, and zealous against such disorders,) hearing of it, found him out, being

[9] See Willcox, *Gloucestershire*, pp. 54–55; Thomas G. Barnes, *Somerset, 1625–1640: A County's Government during the "Personal Rule"* (Cambridge, Mass., 1961), pp. 76–77; Davies, *Enforcement of English Apprenticeship*, p. 186.

[10] *Mass. Acts and Res.*, I, 65 (1692).

[11] *Mass. Rec.*, II, 171–72 (1646); Code of 1648, *Laws and Liberties Mass.*, p. 13; *Essex Rec.*, VII, 70 (1678); *Conn. Rec.*, I, 333 (1659); *Laws Conn.*, 1673, p. 15; *ibid.*, 1702, pp. 20–21; *ibid.*, 1750, pp. 22–23.

[12] *Suffolk Rec.*, p. 435; *Essex Rec.*, VI, 439–40.

[13] *Mass. Acts and Res.*, I, 224; *County and Town Officer*, pp. 69–70, 129.

upon his bed asleep, so he awaked him, and led him to the stocks." A great furor ensued when the man's friends came to the rescue. The next day the magistrates soothed the ruffled feelings. Winthrop concluded: "The constable was the occasion of all this in transgressing the bounds of his office." Winthrop was especially unhappy with the act of "fetching a man out of his lodging that was asleep upon his bed, and without any warrant from authority." His last words were re-revealing: "Such are the fruits of ignorant and misguided zeal."[14] Succeeding generations were not more demanding than Winthrop in such matters. A constable was primarily charged with upholding basic law and order, not with interfering at his own discretion in the private lives of the citizenry.

NIGHTWATCH

The duties of the nightwatch also included scrutiny of the populace, since seventeenth-century Puritan authorities thought people should not leave their homes at night without good reason. The Connecticut General Court specified in 1663 that "in case they meet with any persons walking in the streets unseasonably," the nightwatch were "to examine them, and in case they cannot give a good accompt of their occasions," to take them into custody. New Haven Colony empowered the watch "to bring to the court of guard any person or persons whom they shall finde disorderly or in a suspitious manner within dores or without, whether English or Indians or any straingers whatsoever." Both the generalized Massachusetts laws and the specific Boston regulations were similar to those in Connecticut.[15] Boston directed that the watchmen "walke Silently and Slowly, now and then to Stand Still and Listen in order to make discovery."[16]

By the eighteenth century the nightwatches' duties had been substantially refined. They no longer were to examine "known, sober, orderly householders or inhabitants";[17] they were to be concerned mainly with fire prevention and the apprehension of Negroes and mulattoes, who stood little chance of explaining away their presence

[14] *Journal*, II, 191–92.

[15] *Conn. Rec.*, I, 404; *New Haven Col. Rec., 1638–1649*, p. 34 (1640); *Mass. Rec.*, III, 282 (1652); *Mass. Acts and Res.*, I, 699 (1712); *Boston Town Rec.*, XII, 138–40 (1736).

[16] *Boston Town Rec.*, XIII, 113 (1723).

[17] *Mass. Acts and Res.*, I, 699 (1712).

if found outside after dark. In Boston, Negroes were believed responsible for thefts, disorders, and riots, and there was a strong effort to keep them in their masters' homes at night. It was a liberalization of policy when Boston directed in 1769 that Negroes and other such servants were excused if "carrying Lanthorns with light Candles" and able to give good reason for being out.[18]

Not all towns had nightwatches, probably because of the effort involved when the duty devolved upon ordinary citizens in rotation. It was difficult to stay up all night and then work at the shop or farm the next day. Most inland towns found watches unnecessary. Boston, New Haven, Hartford, and Cambridge kept more constant watches in the colonial period. But even in the seventeenth century Boston did not maintain a watch during the winter, except in times of war. In the next century Boston instituted a year-round watch with hired watchmen, another obvious indication of the secularization of society.

The nightwatches were sometimes efficient in maintaining law and order. They occasionally reported persons for having boisterous drinking parties in homes.[19] In 1723 the Boston watch displayed unusual ability by discovering two couples shut up in a barn. Sewall's experience at two o'clock one morning, while escorting a midwife to her home, was perhaps more typical of their seventeenth-century duties: "Met with the Watch at Mr. Rockes Brew house, who bad us stand, enquired what we were. I told the Woman's occupation, so they bad God bless our labours, and let us pass."[20]

On the other hand lack of the kind of zeal that could be a threat to the privacy of the populace was a particular affliction of the nightwatch. In the seventeenth century New Haven watchmen wandered off to eat peaches, went to bed, sat drinking, or were accused of nightwalking with others. Eighteenth-century Boston had trouble with sleepy and unruly hired watchmen and appointed inspectors to supervise them, either permanently or on unannounced nights. In 1742 the door of a watchhouse was twice stolen while the occupants were asleep.[21] The normal colonial night was so dark and dull that staying awake seemed a senseless task. MacCaffrey commented in his study

[18] *Boston Town Rec.*, XXIII, 45.

[19] *New Haven Town Rec.*, II, 186 (1666); *Suffolk Rec.*, p. 226 (1673).

[20] Suffolk Co. Gen. Sess., 1719–25, p. 283; Sewall, *Diary*, MHS, *Coll.*, 5th ser., V, 40.

[21] *New Haven Col. Rec., 1638–1649*, pp. 488–89 (1649); New Haven Co. Ct. Rec., I, 168; *Boston Town Rec.*, XIII, 175, 242–44, 253, XIX, 9. Carl Bridenbaugh relates the door incident in *Cities in the Wilderness* (New York, 1938), p. 378.

of the English town of Exeter that "the watch was an institution proverbially ineffective."[22]

The instructions prepared for the Boston watch in 1662 neatly demarcated the narrow path between overzealousness and laxity that they were expected to tread. The nightly charge directed them to walk "silentlie but vigilantlie." When they saw lights in homes they were "to make discreett inquiry, whether there be a warrantable cause." If they heard noises or disorderly carriages in any house, they were "wisely to demand a reason of it." The shore was to be watched "vigilantlye," those that came and went from the ships to be "prudentlie" taken account of, but at the same time no one was to be hindered "in theire lawfull affaires." When the watch encountered persons "not of known fidellitie," they were to "modestly demand the cause of theire being abroad, and if it apeare that they are upon ille minded imployment then to watch them narrowlye." Finally the instructions read:

For as much as the watch is to see to the regulateinge of other men actions and manners, that theirefore they be exemplary themselves neither useing any uncleane or corrupt language, nor unmanerlye or unbeseming tearmes unto any, but that they behave themselves soe that any person of quallitye, ore strangers that are uppon occation abroad late, may acknowledge that our watch neglects not due examination, nor offers any just cause of provcation.[23]

These instructions evidenced an attempt, even at this early date, to instill a certain sensitivity into the delicate operations of the watch.

TYTHINGMEN

The establishment in Massachusetts between 1675 and 1679, during the time of King Phillip's War, of the medieval office of tythingman, responsible for the moral supervision of ten families, symbolized the fundamental failure of early Massachusetts law enforcement in the field of Puritan morality. The tasks assigned to the tythingman were not totally new; they had previously been the responsibility of various other officers. In this time of crisis, the Puritans attempted to assuage the wrath of God by reinvigorating the law enforcement arm. The tythingman was not a constable or nightwatchman charged with general supervision; he was obliged only to oversee ten of the neigh-

[22] *Exeter*, p. 91.
[23] *Boston Town Rec.*, VII, 8–9.

boring families. His duties, as well as his practices, had significant import for the enjoyment of individual privacy.[24]

The 1675 laws concerning tythingmen were directed toward discovering private unlicensed houses of entertainment. To make the task easier "the selectmen of every towne" were directed to "choose some sober and discreete persons . . . , each of whom shall take the charge of ten or twelve families of his neighborhood, and shall diligently inspect them." The term *tythingman* did not appear until May 1677, when his power was extended to include apprehension of "all Saboath breakers and disorderly tiplers." In October 1677 a statute extended the initial grant of power to the right "to inspect publicke licensed houses, as well as private, and unlicensed houses." In October 1679 the duties of tythingmen received their fullest expression:

The tythingmen are required diligently to inspect the manner of all disorderly persons, and where by more private admonitions they will not be reclaimed, they are from time to time to present their names to the next Magistrate . . . as also they are in like manner to present the names of all single persons that live from under Family Government, stubborn and disorderly children and Servants, nightwalkers, Typlers, Sabbath breakers, by night or by day, and such as absent themselves from the publick Worship of God on the Lords dayes, or whatever else course or practice of any person or persons whatsoever tending to debauchery, Irreligion, prophaneness, and Atheism amongst us, whether by omission of Family Government, nurture, and religious dutyes, and instruction of Children and Servants, or idle, profligate, uncivil and rude practices of any sort.[25]

Towns in Massachusetts, the region of Maine, and eventually Plymouth and New Hampshire soon had tythingmen, and as new towns came into existence they chose such officers.[26]

Some county courts welcomed the tythingmen with great enthusiasm. Hampshire County added elaborate instructions to those of the General Court. Tythingmen were enjoined "faithfully to act in their Inspecting of their Neighbors, so as that sin and disorder may be prevented and Suppressed in their Several precincts." The Hampshire court also asked the tythingmen "to have a vigilant eye upon all persons that shall without just and necessary Cause be unseason-

[24] Connecticut and Rhode Island did not have tythingmen. Nothing very satisfactory or comprehensive has been written about the tythingman; H. B. Adams's *The Saxon Tithingman in America* (Baltimore, Md., 1883) is useless.

[25] For the legislation, see *Laws Mass.*, *1672*, pp. 235, 249–50, 259, 270; and *Mass. Rec.*, V, 61–62, 133, 155, 240–41, 373.

[26] For further details, see Flaherty, "Privacy in Colonial New England," p. 246.

ably abroad in the Evenings from their parents or masters houses or familyes." The town of Springfield initially established the exact jurisdiction of each tythingman, although mutual help was encouraged: "Samuel Bal to inspect the families from Mr. Glover's house to John Clarke his house inclusively."[27]

As is the case with other local officials, there is some difficulty in evaluating the practical effectiveness of the tythingmen. The occasions when they may have relied on private admonitions were not recorded. But instances when tythingmen appeared in the court records provide an enlightening commentary on New England law enforcement. The overwhelming number of these cases occurred in the first years after the institution of the office. Tythingmen were active in the Essex County court from 1677 to 1682. They dealt with drinking offenses, inspected "suspicious houses" to find those staying home from Sabbath service, and apprehended others who broke the Sabbath.[28] In Hampshire County the few cases involving tythingmen occurred between 1680 and 1692.[29] In two of the four examples individuals were indicted for resisting the tythingman in the execution of his office. In 1682 a tythingman was brought to court for selling liquor without a license. Justice William Pynchon advised him to pay a fine at once "rather then have the matter brought out further, he being a tithingman. He replyed he would appeale to the Countie Courte, and there would be tryed by the jury." The court convicted him. Joseph Smith has found few presentments by tythingmen in the lower courts for Springfield and vicinity in the last quarter of the seventeenth century. He surmised "that the tithingmen adopted a live-and-let-live attitude to the neglect of their sworn duties."[30] In the town of Dorchester and the courts of Maine the only cases occurred in 1681.[31]

Certain aspects of Boston's experience with tythingmen are also illustrative. The town responded to the first law about tythingmen by choosing 73 in 1676.[32] Selection of tythingmen occurred irregularly

[27] Hampshire Co. Gen. Sess. and Common Pleas, no. 1 (1677–1728), pp. 8–9, 27.

[28] *Essex Rec.*, VII, 248, VIII, 232, 293, 367.

[29] Hampshire Co. Gen. Sess. and Common Pleas, no. 1, pp. 42–43, 59, 69, 160.

[30] *Colonial Justice in Western Massachusetts (1639–1702): The Pynchon Court Record*, ed. Joseph H. Smith (Cambridge, Mass., 1961), p. 136 (hereafter cited as *Pynchon Ct. Rec.*). Smith suggested that tythingmen may have concentrated their efforts at the county court level. Research for this study found no evidence of this practice.

[31] *Boston Town Rec.*, IV, 251 (Dorchester); *Maine Ct. Rec.*, III, 77.

[32] The lists of tythingmen can be found in Robert Francis Seybolt, *The Town Officials of Colonial Boston, 1634–1775* (Cambridge, Mass., 1939).

for a number of years thereafter; not until 1693 did Boston begin to select tythingmen on an annual basis; a practice that continued into the first half of the eighteenth century. The 73 men originally chosen in 1676 may have made possible assigning one tythingman to each ten families, but that was the only year such a practice was feasible. Only 50 were picked in 1680, 37 in 1681, 25 in 1684, and about 35 in 1685, 1686, and 1690, before the average number settled to 16 to 20 after 1693. In practice this made short shrift of a one-to-ten ratio. Around 1720 Boston had approximately one tythingman for every 187 houses, or about one tythingman for every one thousand persons.

Another practice in Boston also reflected on the effectiveness of the tythingmen. If they had remained in the office a long time, diligent tythingmen would soon have known much more than an average citizen about the private lives of their neighbors. But if tythingmen served only short terms, the cumulative influence on personal privacy was negligible. The Boston experience suggests that even in the 1680's few tythingmen served more than one year. Only one man from the 1684 list served in 1685 or 1686; in 1686 only 10 men from the 1685 list of 34 returned to office, but then no tythingmen were selected until 1690. Between 1705 and 1714 141 men served as Boston tythingmen. Only 18 served more than once; of the 14 who were in office for two years, not all served consecutively; and only four served more than two years. A cursory examination of the available lists from other towns reveals few who served more than one year. On several occasions tythingmen were excused from this elective position because they "had lately served in that place" or were "but few years before chosen to that Service."[33] The rotation of tythingmen in office was a useful protection for personal privacy, especially in the late seventeenth century when they were still charged with their original duties. The short term in office exemplified the attitude of the populace to the position. Tythingmen did not relish supervising the private lives of their neighbors; in a small community such a position was almost untenable.

The original conception of the tythingman as the immediate supervisor of the morality of his neighbors underwent rapid change. This was most apparent when the Massachusetts laws relating to the office were reenacted in 1694.[34] Tythingmen now became responsible mainly for searching out people selling liquor without a license. There was a peripheral reference to their duties to apprehend idlers,

[33] *Boston Town Rec.*, VII, 227 (1697), VIII, 36 (1706).
[34] *Mass. Acts and Res.*, I, 155, and 257 (1696), 328–29 (1698). Also see the list of their restricted activities in *County and Town Officer*, pp. 129–31.

cursers, and Sabbath breakers, but the moral vitality in the 1679 legislation disappeared from this secularized revision. The tything-men no longer had explicit jurisdiction over single persons living alone, or disorderly children, or any other offenders whose appre-hension would involve intimate surveillance of a family. The 1694 act said nothing about the necessity of one tythingman for every ten families, one of the central stipulations pertaining to personal privacy in the original legislation. Finally, after 1694 the tythingmen were allowed the financial benefits of informers when they apprehended lawbreakers. With the status of informers tythingmen obtained one-half of the particular fine, whereas they had only received an allow-ance of one-third under the earlier legislation. Not relying on this secular stimulus to service alone, a 1696 law strengthened the earlier provisions against refusal to serve as a tythingman. Not only was a refusal countered by a more substantial fine, but the offender could be seized and imprisoned until his goods could be forfeited and sold to the amount of the fine. By the 1690's the moral zealousness that had stimulated the creation of tythingmen in an atmosphere of war-time crisis had disappeared. At the same time the new tythingman had become a minimal threat to the personal privacy of his fellow citizens.

Even after the modifications of 1694 some Bostonians refused to serve as tythingmen.[35] Often the records reported no reasons for such refusals, but there were hints that many disliked the required oath, whereby one swore to "faithfully endeavour and intend the duty of your office, according to law. So help you God."[36] In 1701 the town meeting instructed its Representatives to "Endeavour to git a modiga-tion of the Oath and Law about Tithing men." In a 1710 court case six tythingmen were fined for "refusing to take the Oath by Law appointed." In 1723–24 the town established a committee "to Draw up Somthing Relating to the Tything men for this Town." The com-mittee reported in May 1724, "having met and Considered the Ob-jections made by Persons chosen to that Office against taking the Oath by Law Prescribed." The "main Difficulty pretended" was "the tythingmans Obligation to Inform against all Persons Selling Drink without Licence." In their opinion this was not a valid objection, since that duty had now devolved upon the commissioners of excise. The General Court should specifically release the tythingmen from

[35] *Boston Town Rec.*, VII, 218 (1694), 228 (1698), 242 (1701), VIII, 38 (1706); Suffolk Co. Gen. Sess., 1702–12, p. 207 (1710).

[36] *Mass. Acts and Res.*, I, 155 (1694). For the Puritan sensitivity about the serious nature of oaths, see chapter 8 *infra*.

this obligation (the original reason for instituting the system) and broaden the powers of tythingmen to deal with tumults and disorders, prophaners, cursers, and the like.[37]

Cotton Mather, with his fine eye for the crucial problems of early-eighteenth-century society, had sought to cope with the problem of the tythingman's oath in a 1704 pamphlet.[38] His larger concern of the moment was to stamp out existing disorders, a task in which tythingmen could be most helpful. He recognized that there had been increasing disenchantment with holding the office of tythingman. "What shall we do, that our Tything-Men, may have a better Heart, for the Task imposed on them?" First he denied that their oath required them to leave their callings "and to do nothing else but find out, and present Offences." Tythingmen should do their best while following their regular occupations. "But that which most of all staggers many in the Oath is this; Because it seems to require, that the Delinquent must be Presented in every Case, without any room left for a Christian admonition." It was Mather's opinion that the tythingman was not bound to present an offense to which the offender was not commonly addicted, or an offense that was not a capital crime, did not involve others in its consequences, and was not so open as to have scandalized others. If the offender repented upon an admonition and gave indications that he would never err again, an officer might well be obliged to conceal the offense. The tythingman should exercise a "conscientious Discretion" in "the Concealing of a Punishable Fault." Mather's honest effort to refine the tasks of the tythingmen represented a significant reduction in the expectations that led to the creation of the office in the 1670's.

The General Court apparently did not respond to the popular dissatisfaction with the tythingman's duties. In 1726 the Boston town meeting again asked the selectmen "to prepare a Draft of a Bill about the Duty and power of Tything men and lay it before the Town at their next general meeting for their Consideration." There is every reason to believe that by 1729 the selectmen had presented a negative report on the necessity for tythingmen, since 1728 was the last year Boston chose such officers. In 1732, 1734, and almost every year during the next decade, the town meetings voted down proposals to select them.[39] Bostonians clearly had developed an adversion to the

[37] *Boston Town Rec.*, VII, 244; Suffolk Co. Gen. Sess., 1702–12, p. 207; *Boston Town Rec.*, VIII, 170, 182, 185.

[38] *A Faithful Monitor*, pp. 52–53.

[39] *Boston Town Rec.*, VIII, 204, XII, 28, 58, 129, 157, 190, 213, 293 (1732–43), XIV, 8.

whole idea of tythingmen, ever as limited censors of the behavior of their neighbors. If such they were, then the city's populace did not want tythingmen.

The restricted activities of the tythingmen in the eighteenth century make them elusive in the extant records. Some towns ceased to choose them, and they appear infrequently in the county court records, although the offices of persons making presentments often were not listed.[40] Tythingmen do occasionally appear in the records of the justices of the peace. Braintree tythingmen presented several men to Justice John Quincy for drunkenness in 1725 and 1733, but there were no known cases between those years. In Watertown in 1755 a tythingman brought a servant before Justice Nathaniel Harris for fishing on the Sabbath day evening. This was the only time the records of the Harris court attributed such a title to an official.[41] Where tythingmen did continue to function in the eighteenth century, they served as ordinary upholders of public order, especially the liquor laws, both legally and in practice abandoning their earlier duties as censors of morals.

The Grand Jury

The settlers of New England established grand juries partly in an effort to involve more of the populace in the actual enforcement of criminal legislation. The grand jury met several times a year at the county courts to inform "of the breaches of any order, or other misdemeanours, that they shall knowe or heare to be committed by any person."[42] They did not simply screen complaints but made presentments of matters that had come to their personal attention, at least in the seventeenth century. Each grand juror was expected to function as an observer of behavior in the town he represented.[43]

[40] See the Boston tythingmen's presentment of several persons for liquor violations in 1715 (Suffolk Co. Gen. Sess., 1712–19, pp. 99–100).

[41] John Quincy, J.P., "Quincy, Braintree Cases, 1716–1758" (Suffolk Co.), p. 22, Quincy MSS, MHS; *Records of the Court of Nathaniel Harris . . . J.P. for Middlesex County at Watertown, 1734–1761* (Worcester, Mass., 1938), p. 86 and *passim* (Hereafter cited as Harris, *Small Causes Watertown*).

[42] *Mass. Rec.*, I, 143 (1635); see also *Laws Mass., 1660*, p. 167.

[43] Every town did not have a grand juror. Eight towns were represented on the grand jury for York Co. in 1658, six on the New London Co. 1678 jury, eight for Hampshire Co. in 1693, and thirteen for Plymouth in 1765 (*Maine Ct. Rec.*, II, 69–70, 74–75; New London Co. Ct. Rec., III, 110; Hampshire Co. Gen. Sess. and Common Pleas, no. 1, p. 164; Plymouth Co. Gen. Sess., 1760–82, p. 137).

In the usual oath, such as that used in Plymouth, Maine, or Rhode Island, the grand juror swore to make presentment of all offenses that came to his attention.[44] Massachusetts and Connecticut, the Puritan strongholds, attached a significant qualification to the oath. The Massachusetts passage read: "It is Ordered by this Court; That no Magistrate, Juror, Officer or other man shall be bound to Inform Present or Reveal any private Crime or Offence, wherein there is no peril or danger to this Colony, or any Member thereof, when any necessary tye of Conscience grounded on the Word of God binds him to secresie, unless it be in case of Testimony lawfully required."[45] The Massachusetts law had the added marginal notation, "jurors not bound to reveal Secrets," while the Connecticut one noted, "private offences when they may be kept secret." These provisions applied to every inhabitant of these colonies. They soften the image of the Puritan as an individual obliged to report every token of misbehavior he observed, and recognize that knowledge based on an intimate relationship could be privileged; its forced revelation in all cases would only destroy rewarding personal relationships, perhaps even the intimacy of a family.

Grand jurors were not constantly on the prowl seeking grounds for presentments. The information they brought to court was firsthand in the sense that it came to them from the town in which they lived. But except when grand jurors presented an individual on the basis of chance observation or common knowledge of an offense, such as the numerous cases of bastardy or children born within eight months of a marriage,[46] persons sought out the local juror with a grievance. The increasing size of local populations made reliance on complaints inevitable. The Essex County court records abound with such examples. After Samuel Harris beat his wife in 1673, his daughter and another woman "informed two of the jury of it." When Goodman

---

[44] See, for example, *Plymouth Col. Rec.*, XI, 85; *Maine Ct. Rec.*, I, 223; *R.I. Laws, 1719*, p. 16; *ibid., 1730*, p. 196; *ibid., 1767*, p. 58.

[45] The qualification appears in the Massachusetts Body of Liberties, 1641, no. 61, in *Laws Mass., 1660*; Code of 1648, *Laws and Liberties Mass.*, pp. 47, 58; *Laws Mass., 1660*, p. 167; *ibid., 1672*, p. 86. The qualification is not in Code of 1650, *Conn. Rec.*, I, 546, but can be found in *Laws Conn., 1673*, pp. 54, 64; *ibid., 1702*, pp. 88, 105; *ibid., 1750*, p. 177; *ibid., 1784*, p. 184.

[46] See, for example, in 1718 when two New Haven grand jurors presented Thomas Dawson and his wife Hannah of Easthaven, who "have been lately guilty of the sin of fornication . . . . The fact is matter of common fame . . . . The said Hannah was delivered of a Child the night after marriage." The couple later pleaded guilty in court (New Haven Co. Ct. Files, 1700–1719, N-Z, bundle Rex-S; New Haven Co. Ct. Rec., III, 90).

Prince abused his wife in 1675, she went "weeping" to the grand juryman. In 1681 "Henerie Russell of Marvellhead testified that when he was on the grand jury, Joseph Bubie came into his house with the skin of his face torn away and desired deponent to present Roben Cox for beating him."[47] These examples illustrate an important aspect of law enforcement in colonial America. Until the appearance of police forces in the nineteenth century, officials generally did not seize the initiative in law enforcement.

Nevertheless a great deal of discretionary power over private lives remained in the hands of the grand juryman. It was often his decision whether or not to enforce a particular law, or to publicize a particular offense. Grand jurors could warn an offender privately, although the admonished did not always heed advice. A York County grand juryman warned Gowan Willson in 1657 to stop wandering around with Mrs. Joan Andrews, but to no avail. The juror for Lancaster informed Edmund Parker in 1673 "that if he did not Reforme his not coming to meeting he must present him."[48] The occasional laxness of grand jurors in the enforcement of a particular law sometimes contributed to the protection of privacy. In 1675 the Massachusetts General Court ordered the fining of grand jurors if they did not enforce the apparel laws. The New London County court in 1679 denounced "the Grandjurymen's Neglect of attending the duty of their place attending to Law to the great disservice of the County." The Hampshire court ordered grand jurors to come to court to take their oaths of office, "for the better takeing notice or to stir up said Persons or Grand-Jurors to a more careful and studious attendance to Search and find out al misdemeanours and breaches of the Laws of this Jurisdiction."[49] The conscientiousness of grand jurors obviously could not be taken for granted. A Maine court summoned certain grand jurors to inquire "why some persons were omitted in their presentments, who by some publique reports did deserve to bee presented." They lamely answered that they did not know the truth of the reports. A more blatant episode involved a tailor from Plymouth County who bribed a grand juryman in 1764 to treat his fellows so they would not return an indictment against the tailor.[50]

[47] *Essex Rec.*, V, 221, VI, 116, VIII, 147–48; see also *ibid.*, VIII, 315 (1682), V, 25 (1672).

[48] *Maine Ct. Rec.*, II, 55–56; *Lancaster Rec.*, p. 95; see also *Boston Town Rec.*, IV, 84 (1657).

[49] *Mass. Rec.*, V, 59–60; New London Co. Ct. Rec., III, 127; Hampshire Co. Gen. Sess. and Common Pleas, no. 1, p. 66 (1861).

[50] *Maine Ct. Rec.*, III, 204 (1684); Plymouth Co. Gen. Sess., 1760–82, p. 217.

The rotation of the role of grand juror among a town's populace also served to protect personal privacy. No one was in office long enough to build up a significant body of information about the activities of the inhabitants. Massachusetts legislation in the 1690's on the duties of grand jurors stipulated that "no grand juror shall be compelled to serve more than one year in three."[51] There were no repeaters on the twelve grand juries sworn in for Suffolk County from 1672 to 1674, or among the twelve or thirteen persons annually chosen for the Maine grand jury between 1683 and 1685.[52]

An anonymous author published a pamphlet entitled *Grand Jurors Duty Considered* in Boston in 1724 which implied that all was not well with the grand jury system at this stage of New England history. Not enough grand jurors realized the seriousness of the oath they had taken, nor were they motivated by "the good of our Country" and the desire "to prevent misery and calamy coming upon our Land." Instead grand jurors found themselves exposed to varied temptations: "If a Friend deserves to be presented, we are in danger of being tempted to spare him: or if an adversary transgress, we are in danger of presenting him for envy, hatred or malice. If a rich man transgress, we are in danger of being tempted to spare him, from a secret hope of reward. We may be tempted also to spare others from sinful fear."[53] Such problems were familiar to colonial law enforcers.

An anecdotal illustration further brings into appropriate perspective some of the dilemmas involving the privacy of others faced by both grand jurymen and ordinary citizens in the course of enforcing the law. In 1663 Henry Greenland of Ipswich, a man of great local reputation, was having an affair with Mrs. Mary Roffe. When her mother, Rebecca Bishop, became aware of this, she insisted that "these things are not to bee kept private, [lest] wee may Justly Provoake God." The daughter assured her she had been to see Goodman Emery, the grand juryman, "and hee have promised to bee a father to mee, and hee saith it is best to keep it private seeing there is no harm done." The mother insisted that "Goodman Emery beeing grand Juryman must present them." At this point Emery met with the mother: "Wee fell into discourse about it, Hee Advised to keep it Close and warranted there should bee no more harm done. . . . I then asked Goodman Emery how hee could dispence with his oath being Grandjuryman. He answered, That I cann doe very well, I see no harm in none of them." After further reflection Mrs. Bishop, who was obvi-

[51] *Mass. Acts and Res.*, I, 194.
[52] *Suffolk Rec.*, pp. 31, 127, 195, 271, 347, 457; *Maine Ct. Rec.*, III, 109, 120.
[53] Pp. 8–9 and *passim* (copy available at the Boston Public Library).

ously a more zealous Puritan than the grand juryman, dared "not keep such things as these private upon my owne head." She told the story "to a wise man in the Towne," who arranged for the matter to come before the courts.[54] This episode evidences the problems of balancing the competing values of privacy and the public good.

INFORMERS

In modern societies law enforcement has become an activity in which the average citizen has little part. Such was not the case in early New England. Although a small number of individuals were officially charged with law enforcement, much greater reliance had to be placed on ordinary inhabitants to help uphold the law. This dependence was embodied in large measure in the process called informing, whereby a colonist was expected to make known to the authorities any misdeeds he witnessed or of which he became aware. Such a requirement could have stimulated widespread mutual surveillance by fellow citizens.

The process of informing received its strongest support from religion, since the Puritan church taught that God would judge New England harshly if it permitted sin to reign unchecked. Anyone who sheltered offenders shared in the guilt. Governor Winthrop of Massachusetts stated this clearly during his controversial exchange with Anne Hutchinson in 1637: "Say, that one brother should commit felony or treason, and come to his other brother's house, if he knows him guilty, and conceals him, he is guilty of the same. . . . So if you do countenance those that are transgressors of the law, you are in the same fact."[55] The Boston pamphlet in 1724 on the duties of grand jurors reminded them that even before officially taking the oath of office, "if we know of any wickedness committed by Persons who ought to be presented . . . we are as much obliged to inform of it, as any other private person is."[56] This notion that the colonist was responsible for the unreported sins of his neighbors was a latent challenge to privacy. The threat was greatest from the zealously religious, of whom there were always a numerically insignificant but active number, especially in the seventeenth century.

The law codes were drawn up in such a fashion that informing was an important and integral part of the enforcement system. The

[54] *Essex Rec.*, III, 51–53, 65–66.
[55] Peleg W. Chandler, *American Criminal Trials* (Boston, 1841–44), I, 12.
[56] *Grand Jurors Duty Considered*, p. 7.

process of informing was essential for the prosecution of private offenses. It was hard to detect card playing in private homes; hence such laws were passed as the one in Massachusetts in 1670 outlawing playing cards and dice: "And if any person that hath played or gamed, and shall give Information thereof, he shall be freed from the penalty of the Law to pay treble damage." Connecticut made the head of the home where the game was played equally responsible.[57]

The custom of allowing informers to share in fines furnished the only real impetus to the system. Whereas religion may have served as an incentive for the elect, money was more stimulating to the unregenerate. Liquor violations were prime areas of application, although monetary rewards were sometimes extended to informing on a broad scale, even to persons who informed against hucksters in Boston.[58] Some remarkable individuals broke the liquor laws and informed on themselves in order to claim a share of the fine and thus have their total fine lessened. Usually such an informer reported on his friends as well to broaden his share base.[59] Presumably such individuals knew they were about to be turned in by others. John Farrell has suggested that most criminal offenders in mid-eighteenth-century Connecticut went to the justice of the peace and confessed voluntarily.[60] This self-reporting, inspired by a hint from the local law enforcer, saved the culprit as much as two-thirds of court costs, since the constable did not have to be paid for bringing him to justice. This explanation is at least in accord with the notion that law enforcers had to maintain a delicate balance in their relations with fellow inhabitants.

New Englanders who knew of some misdeed also may have been encouraged to report it to the authorities to avoid the penalties that were occasionally meted out to concealers of offenders. When the governor of New Haven reported his Negro for drunkenness in 1647, the court praised the "governers zeale and faithfullnes" for "not conniving at sinn in his owne family." On the other hand, a servant of the Reverend John Davenport, Sr., in New Haven "was much blamed for his unfaithfullnes in keepeing theyr Counsell and not discovering

[57] *Laws Mass., 1672,* p. 58; rather similar *Mass. Rec.,* II, 180 (1646); *Laws Conn., 1673,* pp. 26–27; *Conn. Rec.,* I, 289; *Laws Conn., 1702,* p. 44; *ibid., 1750,* p. 81; *ibid., 1784,* p. 89.

[58] *Mass. Rec.,* II, 171–72 (1646), V, 375 (1682); Boston, *Boston Town Rec.,* VIII, 105 and *passim,* XII, 240.

[59] *Pynchon Ct. Rec.,* pp. 369–70 (1701); two cases in 1728 in Hampshire Co. Gen. Sess. and Common Pleas, no. 1, p. 353.

[60] "The Administration of Justice in Connecticut about the Middle of the 18th Century" (Ph.D. diss., Yale University, 1937), pp. 137–38.

it," after some of his fellow servants were arrested.[61] A father who allowed his son to live with a married woman in his home was made "accessory to the fornication."[62] Others were brought into court for concealing drunkenness, cursing, and card playing.[63] A New Haven man had obviously decided to forget about his affair with a married woman in 1674, but she went into court to accuse him of adultery. He was able to prove that she had seduced him but was then denounced for not complaining to the authorities.[64] Of course there is no record of those who failed to inform on themselves and others and escaped discovery.

This insistence on informing occasionally extended to the punishment of persons who had themselves been the victims of abuse. In Boston in 1638 John Bickerstaffe was whipped for committing fornication with Alice Burwoode. The latter was similarly punished "for yielding to Bickerstaffe without crying out, and concealing it 9 or 10 dayes." Apparently the Puritan court lacked sympathy for the young woman who may not have wanted to be discovered at such a time or to have others know about it later. Around the same date a Connecticut servant girl who had been subjected to sexual abuse was punished "for Concealing it soe long." When Blanche Hull went to the Plymouth court in 1656 to report an assault, she was presented for not crying out at the time.[65] These examples document the zealousness of the Puritan movement of the first few decades and the court's desire to stimulate informing by making examples of those who failed to do so.

In England informing was a professional occupation, a by-product for the most part of the introduction of many new misdemeanors into law by the Tudors. In the absence of a police force the common informer became primarily responsible for the enforcement of these laws. Despite their importance to the system, informers were victims of abuse and lack of support from local officials.[66] A Star Chamber

[61] *New Haven Col. Rec., 1638–1649*, pp. 335–36; *New Haven Town Rec.,* II, 65–71.

[62] Suffolk Co. Gen. Sess., 1712–19, p. 151 (1717); see a similar case in Middlesex Co. Ct. Rec., 1671–80, p. 75 (1673).

[63] *Mass. Rec.,* IV, pt. 1, p. 51 (1651); *Suffolk Rec.,* p. 751 (1676); Plymouth Co. Gen. Sess. of the Peace, 1760–82, no. 3, p. 202 (1767).

[64] New Haven Co. Ct. Rec., I, 80.

[65] *Mass. Assistants Rec.,* II, 79; *Records of the Particular Court of Connecticut, 1639–1663,* Conn. Hist. Soc., *Coll.,* XXII (Hartford, 1928), p. 3; *Plymouth Col. Rec.,* III, 97.

[66] Barnes, *Somerset,* pp. 54–55; G. R. Elton, "Informing for Profit," *Star Chamber Stories* (London, 1958), pp. 78–113.

comment about Sir John Stafford, a justice of the peace who made a
habit of being a common informer, illustrates this ambivalent attitude. He "was greatly blamed by the court that being so worthy a
gentleman, so honorably descended, and otherwise so well deserving
in himself, that he would stoop to so base an office as to be an informer, who albeit they be necessary in every well-governed state,
yet for the most part they are of the meaner and worst kind of people."[67] The English informer was generally of odious reputation, and
the term became synonymous with the words *liar* and *villain*. They
were often subjected to physical abuse. This situation even endured
when attempts were made to give a moral impetus to informing,
as in the 1690's, during a movement for widespread moral reform in
England.[68]

Informing in New England soon fell into equally low repute despite the consistent attempt to make it a religious duty. Even the
Puritan leadership was not unanimous about the scope of the religious obligation to inform. The Reverend Thomas Hooker acknowledged a significant distinction between the treatment afforded a
church member and the nonelect:

If I tell another Christian of his fault, if he refuse to hear, I am not necessarily bound to follow this law against him; and if I do take one or two
to fasten his conviction, if he should refuse, I must leave him. But against
Brethren we have expresse law, by which I am bound to pursue their
conviction, and they are bound and will be necessitated to attend, and
either come unto a reformation or else suffer a just censure for their
obstinacy.[69]

When a leader of the importance of Hooker held such an opinion,
the general populace was unlikely to subscribe to a stricter view of
their religious duty to involve themselves with the offenses of others.
In addition, the standard seventeenth-century Puritan handbook on
ethics stated that "no man is always bound to reveale a secrete crime
of anothers, of which no ill report went before. For hee, whose offence
is hidden, has hee as yet right to preserve his fame, that it should not
rashly bee layed open."[70] The author of this statement, the Englishman William Ames, who had great influence on Puritan New Eng-

[67] Quoted in Willcox, *Gloucestershire*, p. 57 (1600).

[68] See especially Dudley W. R. Bahlmann, *The Moral Revolution of 1688*
(New Haven, 1957), pp. 47–50; and for the general place of the English informer, Davies, *Enforcement of English Apprenticeship*, pp. 156, 47.

[69] *Survey of Church-Discipline*, pt. 3, pp. 2–3.

[70] Ames, *Conscience*, bk. 5, pp. 280–81.

land, demonstrated a subtle awareness of the individual's right to personal privacy.

In addition the oath taken by grand jurymen and all other office-holders limited the requirement for informing on "any private Crime or Offence."[71] This important legal qualification was primarily a protection for personal privacy in the society, since persons were not required to report to officials in indiscriminate fashion. It was particularly beneficial for those individuals of tender conscience who saw informing as a duty. They could distinguish between offenses observed in the public sphere and those discovered because of one's privileged position relative to the offender. Presumably such a qualification protected the privacy of the communications of husbands and wives, which were recognized as privileged by the common law. According to Dalton's famous handbook, "the wife is not to be bound to give evidence, nor to be examined against her husband; for by the lawes of God, and of this Land, she ought not to discover his counsel, or his offence, in case of theft (or other felony, as it seemeth)."[72] A curious case in Massachusetts in 1634 suggests that the restriction extended to protect the privacy of the other members of the observer's family. John Winthrop reported that "a godly minister, upon conscience of his oath and care of the commonwealth, discovered to the magistrates some seditious speeches of his own son, delivered in private to himself; but the court thought not fit to call the party in question then, being loath to have the father come in as a public accuser of his own son, but rather desired to find other matter, or other witness against him."[73] The moral pressure to inform was counteracted by the need to protect the intimacy of a family, although the government did not thereby abandon its desire to prosecute the offender, an action typical of the early Puritan movement.

Individuals who concealed thefts or received stolen goods were frowned upon by the law and made subject to penalties. The lawmakers added a similarly restrictive phrase to the clauses encouraging persons to report thefts and stolen goods: reporting was obligatory, "except the Fact be private, or committed by some Member of

[71] For the oath, see p. 202 and note 45 *supra*. Commenting in 1704 on the qualifications limiting the duty of tythingmen to inform on their fellows, C. Mather added this clarifying phrase: "Nor are the Tyes of Nature neither in such a Case to be superseded" (*A Faithful Monitor*, p. 53).

[72] *Countrey Justice*, chap. 111, p. 296. This statement also appeared in the editions of 1655, 1677, 1727, and 1742.

[73] *Journal*, I, 126.

his own Family."[74] This exception modified informing to the extent
that there were obviously certain things one did not have to report,
even in such a serious matter. As a result the only cases prosecuted
regularly in the courts were for concealing stolen goods. In the 1730's
Francis Fane, the English counsel to the Board of Trade who was
charged with the review of colonial legislation, commented on the
Connecticut statute of 1702: "The clause against the concealers of
Theft is a very good one, but the exception relating to the privacy of
the fact, etc., seems a very unnecessary and extraordinary one, and
proper to be left out."[75] But no action was ever taken on the basis of
Fane's *Reports*, and Connecticut retained this remarkable evidence
of concern for personal privacy in its statutes throughout the eighteenth century.

In many court cases the manner in which the offense was reported
was not recorded; informers must have accounted for some of these
prosecutions. A few presentments were specifically based on information. Most were for liquor offenses and smuggling, fields in which
a degree of professionalism existed. The various county collectors of
excise on spiritous liquors in eighteenth-century Massachusetts were
professional informers. From 1758 to 1766 Thomas Fletcher held this
position in Suffolk County. The first five years he made a substantial
number of complaints against persons for selling liquor without a
license, receiving an average share of over one pound per fine. But
for the next four years Fletcher seems to have ceased to bring complaints, perhaps as a concession to opposition.[76]

Informing of offenses committed in private was unusual, as is evidenced by the number of incidents which were common knowledge
yet took years to reach the courts.[77] In 1744 two ministers awoke in
an inn to the sight of a young man leaving a girl's bed. They "kept the
matter for the Parents for the Time," rather than making an immedi-

[74] *Laws Mass., 1660*, p. 128; *ibid., 1672*, pp. 13–14; *Laws Conn., 1702*, p. 12;
ibid., 1750, p. 237; *ibid., 1784*, p. 245 (wording of the Connecticut law of 1784
is important for interpretation.)

[75] *Reports on the Laws of Connecticut*, ed. Charles M. Andrews (New Haven,
1915), p. 63.

[76] Fletcher remained in Boston as a merchant until he went to St. Croix in
the early 1770's. The cases are in Richard Dana, JP, "Suffolk: Records of Judgments and Proceedings before Me in the County of Suffolk Beginning the 20th
Day of April 1757, Ending the 18th of April 1760" (Boston), and Dana, "Minute
Book, 1760–1767," Dana Family Papers, box 3. It was unlikely that Fletcher
transferred his presentments to another justice after 1762.

[77] See Rex v. Atwater, New Haven Co. Ct. Rec., III, 38off.; New Haven Co.
Ct. Files, 1730–39, M-R, bundle Rex; and chap. 2 *supra*.

ate presentment.[78] Informing was simply not a pleasant task for the colonist living in a closely knit community. Friends did not react favorably to the news that their neighbor had reported them to the authorities, and it was difficult for an informer to maintain anonymity. Solomon Stoddard discussed the matter fully in 1722:

We may suppose that Magistrates and Ministers, were they informed, would bear a due Testimony against Drunkenness, Sabbath-breaking, and other sins. But such things are seldom punished, for want of information. Many persons are bound by Oath, to inquire into Disorders, and give information. But many times there is a fame of such things, but seldom complaint is made to Authority. Possibly, some Persons are obnoxious to themselves, and are afraid that if they bring out others, that they shall be brought out . . . [and] are afraid that others will be disgusted, that it will be a foundation of ill-will and Contention.[79]

Private persons were even more apt to be discouraged from informing by such considerations. During a tour of the North American postal establishment in 1773, Hugh Finlay recorded the following conversation with the New Haven postmaster: "He complains much of the Post riders; he begs that the complaints may not appear to have come from him, because the riders being of service to the people on the road have many friends in the country as well as in town, and the name of informer (which his official representations would incur from his neighbours) wou'd hurt him in his business, but in conscience he looks on himself as obligated to represent the following matters."[80] This ambivalent attitude toward informing was typical of the colonial outlook and greatly ameliorated the potential impact of the legal requirement on personal privacy.

THE CHARACTERISTICS OF LAW ENFORCEMENT

In colonial New England the characteristics of law enforcement furnished a significant protection for personal privacy in society as a whole. Moral legislation, calling for intrusions into private lives at many points, required careful surveillance by officials but actually received only intermittent attention. The General Courts often lamented that criminal laws were not being enforced, especially in the

[78] Parkman, "Diary," AAS, *Proc.*, LXXII (1962), 163.

[79] *An Answer to Some Cases of Conscience* (Boston, 1722), p. 10; see also Stoddard, *Way for a People*, pp. 21–22.

[80] *Journal*, p. 40. The Salem postmaster said an informer would be tarred and feathered and no jury would find the fact.

late seventeenth century, when the attempt to maintain a strict Puritan moral order was collapsing. During this period many types of censorious legislation ceased to be implemented. At a special session in 1685 the Massachusetts General Court took "notice of the great neglect that there is found in severall persons who are intrusted to see the observation of such orders as from time to time hath binn enacted, especially such as have a tendency to the reformations of such evills as are found amongst us." The Connecticut General Court observed in 1684 that the laws passed in 1675–76 for the reformation of social evils, "for want of due prosecution of offenders that are guilty of the breach of them, have little prevayled to the suppressing of the growth of sayd evills amongst us." By 1690 the General Court admitted the failure of its 1684 encouragements: "Instead of the reformation sincerely aymed at, vice and corruption of maners, in most places rather abound and increase more than ever." Once again it was urged that "all the sayd lawes be duely, constantly and impartially executed."[81]

Clerical writers also complained frequently that many laws were not enforced and some offenses not reported to the authorities. In the seventeenth century Increase Mather believed the enforcement of the moral code in the Boston area was lax. He claimed that strangers reported more drunkenness in New England in six months than they had seen in England in a lifetime. Solomon Stoddard complained in 1705 that "there be many gross immoralities in the Land, as Swearing, Drunkenness, Fornication; these things are indeed punished when they do appear: but a great deal never comes to light." The Reverend Mr. Eliot in 1753 decried the prevalence of known acts of uncleanness: "But may we not fear, that many Deeds of Darkness are kept secret from men?"[82]

In Boston in the first decade of the eighteenth century Cotton Mather recognized that the local law enforcement apparatus needed reinforcement. Inspired by recent English initiatives in this sphere, he decided early in 1702 to organize a "Society for the Suppression of Disorders" in Boston.[83] His goal was a membership of twelve to fourteen persons, including a justice of the peace to whom offenders could

[81] *Mass. Rec.*, V, 469–70; *Conn. Rec.*, III, 147–48, IV, 28–29. The Reforming Synod of 1679–80 also denounced the lack of enforcement of existing laws (see Walker, *Creeds and Platforms*, p. 435).

[82] "Diary of Increase Mather," MHS, *Proc.*, 2d. ser., XIII (1900), 358 (1676); Stoddard, *Danger of Speedy Degeneracy* (Boston, 1705), p. 19; Eliot, *Evil and Adulterous Generation*, p. 18.

[83] Unless otherwise noted, all references to the societies are from *Diary of*

be reported. In December 1703 Mather prepared a short pamphlet, *Methods and Motives for Societies to Suppress Disorders,* which he forwarded to specific individuals in "all Parts of the Countrey." His motives were most revealing: "A Small Society may prove . . . an invaluable Blessing to a Town, whose Welfare shall become the object of their Watchful Enquiries. . . . Offenders against those Laws, may be kept under such a Vigilant Inspection, that they shall not escape a due Chastisement."[84] Membership should be small, select, and secret. These seems to have been little organized response outside Boston. It had three societies by 1706 with less than forty members drawn from three churches. The town at that time had a population of more than 7,000. Mather himself made few references to the actual work of the societies.[85] By 1711 one had disbanded; none was functioning in January 1714, despite Mather's recurrent resolutions to stimulate activity. He made plans for the reforming societies to check on houses of prostitution and to admonish the patrons. His repeated references to the necessity for this effort suggested that little progress was made. In 1714 Mather spoke of reviving a society, "leaving out . . . some unworthy and improper members." If such had found their way into his select company, the result of secular recruitment for similar purposes could hardly be more successful. The societies died out after a brief life span, although the void they sought to fill remained. As late as 1724 Mather admonished himself to organize and revive such a society.

Later in the eighteenth century clerical laments about inadequate law enforcement became uncommon. The old morality was no longer proclaimed with pristine vigor. Colonial officials charged with law enforcement reported only the most flagrant and basic offenses against the mores of the community. Fornication (usually associated with the subsequent birth of a child), swearing, thefts, murders,

---

Cotton Mather, ed. Worthington C. Ford (rpt. New York, 1957), I, 418, 500, 516–17, 531, II, 42, 123, 160, 206, 229, 235, 275–76, 283, 767. In general see Robert Middlekauf, *The Mathers* (New York, 1971), pp. 269–73.

[84] Boston, 1703, pp. 6–7. Mather repeated part of this appeal in 1710 in *Bonifacius,* pp. 133–37.

[85] A series of pamphlets published during this period appear to have been a part of Mather's movement to reform disorders. See Mather, *A Faithful Monitor: Offering an Abstract of the Lawes in the Province of the Massachusetts-Bay, New England, against . . . Disorders* (Boston, 1704); Samuel Danforth, *Piety Encouraged* (Boston, 1705), with a preface by Mather; Mather, *Private Meetings Animated and Regulated* (Boston, 1706); William Williams, *The Danger of Not Reforming Known Evils* (Boston, 1707); Samuel Danforth, *The Duty of Believers to Oppose the Growth of the Kingdom of Sin* (Boston, 1708).

and assaults were the offenses that filled the pages of the court records. The petty indictments often cited as evidence of seventeenth-century Puritan moralism had disappeared.

An observation by Solomon Stoddard in 1701 clearly sets forth the reasons why laws potentially detrimental to individual privacy were not enforced. His analysis of the human factor was particularly acute:

> Sometimes there is a great deal of iniquity in the Land, and yet there is little testimony born against it; those that know the thing will not complain: they will talk of it, and blast the names of others; but don't take care that the thing may be punished. If they know a thing in a man they are angry with, they will complain: but, if he be a Friend, they won't. Sometimes the man is above them, and they are afraid to do it; sometimes the man knows as much by them, and they dare not.[86]

The same charges could be brought against those formally responsible for the enforcement of colonial criminal laws. The burden of office, ignorance, corruption, fear, friendship, and indifference were detrimental influences on law enforcement.

The burden of office was a primary reason for the nonenforcement of moral legislation and the absence of intensive surveillance even in the seventeenth century. For communities of their size the New England colonies had substantial law codes and a mass of legislation. According to William Weeden, Massachusetts gradually discovered in the seventeenth century "that even the Lord's people could not carry this enormous and complicated legislation into perfected and wholesome practice."[87] The overwhelmed official created a hierarchy of values in his own mind, enforcing the most essential laws first and then, if ever, implementing the most recent and intricate offerings of the General Court. It was an arduous task, for example, to discover the mind of the Massachusetts General Court on sumptuary legislation at any specific time before 1675. The most elementary legal requirements were met first. Peace and good order had to be maintained, murderers sought, and thefts solved.

The various officials in a town were busy men. Selectmen had to run towns and constables to execute myriad duties for the courts. Since few officials were paid for their services, most had to run their farms or their businesses at the same time. This was a full-time occupation at many seasons of the year, and the duties of elected office

---

[86] *The Necessity of Acknowledgment* (Boston, 1701), p. 8; see also Stoddard, *Way for a People*, pp. 21–22.

[87] Weeden, *Economic and Social History*, I, 60.

often became a secondary consideration.[88] During the first years of settlement, town officials were too preoccupied with the multiple details of creating a viable community to become very involved in the strict enforcement of moral legislation, and thereafter they were not much interested. In many cases persons refused to serve when elected. In the 1670's Salem had trouble finding constables, since those who refused were only fined small sums.

At any time in the colonial period it was burdensome to bring someone to justice. Officials sometimes ignored what passed as minor in their eyes. A grand juror, for instance, was not enthusiastic about leaving his shop, farm, or tavern and riding several miles to obtain details about a supposed offense. There was no way of ensuring even that he would hear about an incident. Attendance at the regular courts was time consuming for the grand juror, informer, or constable. Weighty duties dulled the zealousness of seventeenth-century officials; a definite malaise and routineness made its appearance. Public sentiment, as well as human inertia, argued against any drastic revisions, either by an overactive or zealous new town official or in response to the most recent directives of a General Court, especially if Boston or Hartford were far away. No effective supervisory system existed to ensure that constables, tythingmen, and grand jurors performed their tasks with ardor and thoroughness. Officials did not have to be church members. Some may have felt distaste for the more moralistic offerings of the seventeenth-century Puritan General Courts. As Cotton Mather well stated: "What can the Magistrates do, . . . if there be no Informers?" In his study of seventeenth-century Hampshire County, Coolidge concluded that "although informing, snooping, gossiping, and suspicion may have been inherent in small-town Puritan life, these tendencies remained largely absent from the official activities of the civil authority in Hampshire county."[89]

Ignorance of the laws was a further impediment to official zeal as laws changed and were frequently modified. The Massachusetts House of Representatives complained in 1706 that "many chosen to

[88] Coolidge concluded that the Hampshire County officials were too busy with their own private affairs to become much involved in the enforcement of codes of morality ("Aspects of Puritan Morality," p. 111). For a thorough discussion of such problems as the burden of office, which led to the nonenforcement of apprenticeship legislation, see Davies, *Enforcement of English Apprenticeship,* pp. 248–51.

[89] Mather, *A Faithful Monitor,* p. 50; Coolidge, "Aspects of Puritan Morality," p. 103.

the Office of Tythingmen, are not furnished with Law Books, where-by to be Informed of the Duty of their Office."[90] They ordered the sundry acts collected and reprinted. Many of the statutes that could have negatively influenced the preservation of privacy in a community were of a minor character to begin with. Some towns sent no representatives to many General Courts, and it took some time for knowledge of the latest statutes to be communicated to them. Isolation and independence became enemies of local law enforcement. Interruptions created the same effect. During wars frontier towns were able to deal in rough fashion with only the worst offenders against justice. During the Andros regime in New England in the 1680's the Puritan moral code suffered a mortal blow through years of neglect. The Massachusetts government issued a broadside from Boston dated March 13, 1690, ordering "that the Laws of this Colony against Vice . . . (which Laws have too much lost their edg by the late Interruption of the Government) be now faithfully and Vigorously put in Execution." But it was now difficult to revive certain kinds of laws that had fallen into disuse, or had traditionally been moribund.

The venality of local officials was another problem. In 1671, for example, witnesses claimed there had been much heavy drinking at Hathorne's public house in Lynn on Christmas Day. Joseph Collins was said to have drunk seventeen quarts of rum, and his wife had to be carried to bed: "The reason why it was 'smothered up' was because Mrs. Laton had a daughter among them." Thomas Laughton was a selectman of Lynn. In the Worcester County court in 1733 the grand jurors presented Rachel Wilder of Lancaster, a spinster, on a fornication charge. There was no further disposition of the case, although others indicted for the same offense were fined. Joseph Wilder was a justice of the peace at this session, and the Wilders were a leading family in Lancaster.[91] Edward Ward in his account of a journey to New England in the late seventeenth-century made this comment about tythingmen: "Every Tenth Man is chose as one of the Select [tythingmen], who have Power, together, to Regulate and Punish all disorders that happen in their several Neighbourhoods. . . . But get your Select Member into your Company and Treat him, and you may do either [drunkenness or cursing and swearing] without offence." A Maine grand jury presented the tythingmen of Kittery

[90] Mass. Arch., XLVII ("Laws, 1645–1774"), 248.
[91] *Essex Rec.*, V, 60; *Worcester Rec.*, Worcester Soc. of Antiquity, *Coll.*, II, 79, and other cases on p. 107.

for not enforcing the liquor laws in 1681. A committee in Boston reported in 1761 that several watchmen had been bribed to refrain from giving evidence against persons they had originally reported to the authorities.[92]

The threat of economic or physical reprisal was a further discouragement to conscientious law enforcement. The colonists duplicated the English custom of frequently choosing men from the lower classes for such posts as constables, nightwatchmen, and grand jurors. Their sense of deference discouraged the annoyance of their betters by petty presentments or interference in their private lives, while force of habit extended this privilege to their peers. Violence was also never far below the surface of colonial society; constables, nightwatchmen, and tythingmen could not be certain of emerging unscathed when they tried to intervene in a fight or enforce a particular law.[93] Verbal abuse was normal. Submission to minor local officials was not an outstanding characteristic of the colonists.

Friendship also affected the way certain kinds of laws were enforced. An official normally preferred not to report his friends, and in a closely knit colonial community, friendship encompassed a goodly segment of a town's population. In her study of aspects of life in Elizabethan and early Stuart England, Margaret Davies observed that "the close intimacy of country life, if it made for better knowledge of one's immediate neighbors, must have tended to turn the business of presenting their misdeeds into personal problems of strained relations, petty grudges, even a threat to security of livelihood for an unlucky juror or constable."[94] In a Connecticut election sermon in 1715 a minister warned the civil authorities that it was their duty to punish breaches of the penal laws "without fear of offending any but God; and without indulgent affections on the score of consanguinity or Affinity."[95] In an enlightening episode at New London in the 1770's persons were accustomed to having free access

[92] Ward, *Trip to New England,* p. 42; *Maine Ct. Rec.,* III, 78; *Boston Town Rec.,* XVI, 62.

[93] See, for example, *Essex Rec.,* II, 245–46 (1660), VIII, 101–2 (1681); Suffolk Co. Gen. Sess., 1712–19, pp. 76–78 (1715); Massachusetts Superior Court of Judicature, 1760–62, fol. 180 (Boston, 1761), SCCH; Suffolk Co. Ct. Rec., 1680–92, p. 108; "Quincy, Braintree Cases," pp. 21–22 (1733), Quincy MSS.

[94] *Enforcement of English Apprenticeship,* p. 249. See also Blumenthal, *Small Town Stuff,* pp. 194–95.

[95] Joseph Moss, *An Election Sermon* (New London, Conn., 1715), p. 11. See a similar comment with respect to church discipline by C. Mather, *A Faithful Monitor,* p. 45.

at all times to the post office. The new postmaster, Mr. Miller, "attempted to break this custom, but he finds he cannot, without quarreling with his friends." A desire not to quarrel with one's friends was an important influence in many other situations.[96]

"Let every one meddle with his own Business" ran a proverb in a colonial almanac.[97] Many colonial officials charged with local law enforcement shared this attitude. The man who tried to enforce every law necessarily would find himself interfering in the private affairs of others. Persons were only too happy to remind any official who forgot the proverb and his sense of balance. When Richard Barnum of Boston was engaged in some disorders in his home, he made "reflective speeches to the constable that made inquiry about it." In Marblehead three of the Gatchell family were at home one night when the watchmen inquired about the noise and told them to put out their lights: "My brother Joseph went to the doore and saide who are you: and they saide wee are the watch: and hee saide you may goe aboute your busnes Into the Kings high way: and they saide they would not but they would Cary hem with them and hee saide they were Rogues and not the watch: and hee tooke a Lighte and opend the geate and bid them begon."[98]

Even better guides were at hand for the colonial official who was determined to serve with as little unnecessary disturbance as possible to the private lives of his fellows. The best example was Dogberry, the constable who instructs the nightwatch in Shakespeare's *Much Ado about Nothing* (III.3). The English historian W. E. H. Tate called Dogberry "the most distinguished member" of the class of low-ranking officials in his light-hearted approach to his duties.[99] Dogberry is seen instructing the nightwatch. What if an accosted vagrant will not stop? "Why, then take no note of him, but let him go; and presently call the rest of the watch together and thank God you are rid of a knave." A similar approach is recommended for those found drinking in alehouses and thieves discovered in the night. Dogberry's final comment is "keep your fellows' counsels and your own; and good night." Since colonial towns did not have persons who made a real career of law enforcement, the pressures were great to let sleeping dogs lie.

[96] Finlay, *Journal,* pp. 34–35.
[97] Daniel Travis, *An Almanack . . . 1722* (Boston, 1722).
[98] *Suffolk Rec.,* p. 22 (1671); *Essex Rec.,* VIII, 377–78 (1682).
[99] *Parish Chest,* p. 186.

8. *The Courts*

T HE treatment of defendants and witnesses in the colonial courtroom reflected the development of certain legal aspects of the right of privacy. It was generally agreed that a preliminary examination or a trial provided magistrates with an opportunity to discover evidence. Were there recognized limits on the methods that could be used for this purpose? Could forms of compulsion or denial of rights be utilized? Were torture and oaths used to discover incriminatory information from defendants? The seventeenth century had also begun to recognize a general privilege against self-incrimination for defendants and witnesses. Did the colonial courts accept such protections for the privacy of the individual as the right against self-incrimination?

At the most general level the New England courts showed a definite sensitivity about the privacy of individuals in the conduct of judicial business. Although county courtrooms were generally open to the public, the court reserved the right to meet in private for consultation and the hearing of cases. Doors were closed when delicate matters, usually involving sexual irregularities, came before the courts. At New Haven in 1653 six boys were brought before the governor and magistrates for filthy and corrupt wickedness: "They were examined in a private way, and their examinations taken in wrighting, which were of such a filthy nature as is not fitt to be made known in a publique way."[1] A justice of the peace usually settled most minor criminal cases in the privacy of his home with only the principals and witnesses present. Judge Pynchon in seventeenth-century Hampshire County kept a particularly lewd offense private because the two men who reported the case had done so. He personally gave the culprit "private Correction with a rod on his bare back six lashes well set on." But when a man was accused of tussling with three girls in a yard and calling for help because "he could not serve three at once," the New Haven court decided the news had "spread farr, therefore ought not to be ended in private."[2]

[1] *New Haven Town Rec.*, I, 179; see also *Pynchon Ct. Rec.*, p. 107n.
[2] *Pynchon Ct. Rec.*, pp. 224, 205; *New Haven Town Rec.*, I, 455–56 (1660).

Judges also displayed some sensitivity when dealing with witnesses whose concern for their own privacy would not permit them to speak about some matter. At Fairfield in 1665 a woman told Justice Nathan Gold during an examination about the paternity of her child that she had known upon awaking in the morning that "she had been abused: Mr Gold asked her how shee could know that shee was abused considering that shee was at that time Drunk and was asleep, the abovenamed Mary answered shee had some reasons in her selfe but shee was not willing to speake them: Mr Gold then Did Desire Mrs. Gold and Mrs. Beatrice Risdon to aske the said Mary in private what her reasons were."[3]

TORTURE

Torture was one method of forcing persons to incriminate themselves and others in a fashion manifestly destructive of personal privacy. In England torture could not be inflicted in the ordinary course of common-law justice, but the practice still occurred under the aegis of the royal prerogative. According to nineteenth-century writer David Jardine, before 1640 "torture was always used as a matter of course in all grave accusations, at the mere discretion of the king and Privy Council, and uncontrolled by any law besides the prerogative of the Sovereign." The accused did have to be under "vehement suspicion" of guilt. The early Stuarts reserved torture for state offenses, a refinement from its wholesale use during the reign of Elizabeth. By the time of the migrations to New England the practice of torture was dying out in the home country. The last recorded instance was in 1640, with only a handful of cases occurring after 1600.[4]

In colonial New England both the legal codes and public opinion were adverse to the employment of torture. According to the Massachusetts Body of Liberties of 1641: "No man shall be forced by Torture to confesse any Crime against himselfe nor any other unlesse it be in some Capitall case where he is first fullie convicted by cleare

[3] Mary's reasons satisfied the women (Conn. Arch., Crimes and Misdemeanors, I, pt. 1, p. 21); see the notation of a woman's modesty in *ibid.*, III (1724–36), doc. 218a.

[4] *A Reading on the Use of Torture in the Criminal Law of England, Previously to the Commonwealth* (London, 1837), esp. p. 13. See also G. R. Elton, ed., *The Tudor Constitution* (Cambridge, 1960), pp. 169–70; and Leonard W. Levy, *Origins of the Fifth Amendment: The Right against Self-Incrimination* (New York, 1968), pp. 33–35, 326–27.

and suffitient evidence to be guilty, After which if the cause be of that nature, That it is very apparent that there be other conspiratours, or confederates with him, then he may be tortured, yet not with such Tortures as be Barbarous and inhumane."[5] Henry Charles Lea considered it "rather remarkable" to find torture legalized even in such a limited form, although he concluded this was "a limitation on a preexisting, more general use of torture."[6] This Massachusetts provision corresponded to the English notion of "vehement suspicion." No examples have been found where this proviso was put into effect. A Connecticut law of 1673 contained a forthright denunciation of torture, declaring that "no man shall be forced by Torture to confess any Crime against himself."[7]

In the rape case involving the Humfrey children in Massachusetts in 1641–42 the clerical consultants disapproved of torture to obtain evidence, except for the Reverend Charles Chauncy, who would have allowed it in much the same circumstances as the Massachusetts statute permitted. Cotton Mather advised one of the Salem witchcraft judges how to obtain confessions but added that "I am farr from urging the un-English method of torture."[8] During the examinations at Salem, Bridget Bishop replied to a series of threatening remarks by suggesting that the judges could not employ compulsory means to obtain evidence: "You may threaten, but you can do no more than you are permitted. I am innocent of a witch."[9]

Despite the laws and opinions against torture that operated in support of personal privacy, threats of punishment did not disappear from either colonial or English judicial proceedings. Much evidence could be secured without actual physical torture. Threats encouraged the hesitant to incriminate themselves in some instances. In New Haven in 1663 the court labored unsuccessfully to have a runaway servant confess his offenses. "The Court therefore did Commit him to the Care of the Marshall that soe he might be brought to a sight of his sin in a way of suffering, seeing it could not bee attained otherwise."[10] The servant confessed "after the court was risen up," pre-

[5] No. 45, in *Laws Mass.*, 1660; Code of 1648, *Laws and Liberties Mass.*, p. 50; *Laws Mass.*, 1660, p. 187; *ibid.*, 1672, p. 129.

[6] *Superstition and Force: Essays on the Wager of Law, the Wager of Battle, the Ordeal, Torture* (4th ed. rev., Philadelphia, 1892), pp. 569–70n.

[7] *Laws Conn.*, 1673, p. 65.

[8] Mather to John Richards, 1692, "The Mather Papers," MHS, *Coll.*, 4th ser., VIII (1868), 394.

[9] *Records of Salem Witchcraft*, ed. W. Elliott Woodward (Boston, 1864), I, 142–45.

[10] *New Haven Town Rec.*, II, 23–25.

sumably once the marshall had discoursed with him about sin and suffering. There was a further instance of the threat of torture during the Salem witch trial of Margaret Jacobs. When she later recanted her confession, she described how the judges "told me, if I would not confess, I should be put down into the dungeon, and would be hanged, but if I would confess, I should have my life; the which did so affright me, and . . . made me make the confession, I did, which confession . . . is altogether false and untrue."[11]

Torture was employed in several instances during the Salem witchcraft trials to force persons to confess their guilt. In several cases the accused were tied with their neck and heels together for a period of time.[12] The Salem outbreak was unique, and suspected witches had always been an exception in England when it came to the use of torture. Lea noted that "sorcery and witchcraft were regarded as crimes of such peculiar atrocity, and the dread they excited was so universal and intense, that those accused of them were practically placed beyond the pale of the law, and no means were considered too severe to secure the conviction which in many cases could only be obtained by confession."[13] Dalton's *Countrey Justice* did not treat witchcraft as an ordinary felony. His long directions for the better discovery of witches were not omitted until the 1742 edition, after a statute of George II prohibited such prosecutions. The Reverend Richard Bernard's *A Guide to Grand-Jury Men* provided detailed instructions for the examination of suspected witches. "If none of these will work to bring them to confesse, then such as have authority to examine, should begin to use sharp speeches, and to threaten with imprisonment and death. And if the presumptions be strong, then if the Law will permit (as it doth in other countries in this case) to use torture, or to make a shew thereof at least, to make them confesse, as many have done hereupon in other Countries."[14] Despite these English precedents the utilization of a form of torture at Salem should not be dismissed lightly. In most criminal cases resort to torture would have been unthinkable because of the relative pettiness of the offenses. But the one time a locality became

[11] Chandler, *American Criminal Trials*, I, 90–91.

[12] There is evidence that a few accused persons were tied with their necks and heels together to encourage confession (see *Narratives of the Witchcraft Cases,* pp. 363, 180–81; Chandler, *American Criminal Trials,* I, 112). The matter of torture is discussed in Chadwick Hansen, *Witchcraft at Salem* (New York, 1969), pp. 175–77.

[13] *Superstition and Force*, pp. 570–71.

[14] 2d ed., London, 1629, pp. 235–36.

extremely aroused about particular offenses, there was recourse to this form of forced self-incrimination.[15]

Torture was not normally employed in colonial New England. It had no effect on the availability of personal privacy for the typical defendant. In addition to a general ideological aversion, there was little need to use torture; other methods for obtaining the required evidence were available. Even in England torture was reserved for crimes against the security of the state by the seventeenth century. Such offenses did not figure prominently in the judicial records of the New England colonies. In fact, questions of privacy were hardly relevant in the vast majority of ordinary criminal cases, where the external evidence for conviction or a confession already existed. It required an extraordinary case, such as that of the Humfrey children or the witch scare at Salem, to stimulate serious consideration of compelling disclosures by such means as torture or an oath. Since the common law did not even recognize the utilization of torture, there was little question of introducing it in America. The inquisitorial practices of the colonial judiciary remained the most likely and effective method of obtaining evidence from a defendant.

OATHS

In England the oath *ex officio* had served as an efficient weapon for securing evidence in the operation of the prerogative courts. The New England settlers thus owed their opposition to incriminatory oaths of any kind to the political and religious clashes of the early seventeenth century, and especially the Puritan resistance to the oath *ex officio* used by the court of the Star Chamber and the ecclesiastical courts. By this particular oath the suspect swore to answer all

[15] The most cited example of judicial atrocity in colonial New England was the pressing to death of Giles Cory during the Salem trials. This punishment was the medieval penalty *peine forte et dure,* the attempt to force an individual to enter a plea upon his indictment for a felony. Rocks were piled on the accused until he either agreed to plead or expired. Cory may have refused to plead to save his estate for his descendants, since it might have been confiscated after his conviction and execution in a witchcraft trial. Chadwick Hansen claims Corey's death was his protest against the methods of the Special Court of Oyer and Terminer. A refusal to plead, however, has no relevance to self-incrimination, to privacy in the courts, or to the normal meaning of torture (see Sewall, *Diary,* MHS, *Coll.,* 5th ser., V, 364; Chandler, *American Criminal Trials,* I, 122; *Narratives of the Witchcraft Cases,* p. 367 and n; Starkey, *Devil in Massachusetts,* pp. 9–12; Hansen, *Witchcraft at Salem,* pp. 198–99).

questions before he knew the charges and his accusers, which could lead to self-incrimination and an obvious invasion of privacy. John Cotton, writing around 1646, listed the English resort to the oath *ex officio* as the major reason for the Puritan immigration to America.[16] Such oaths to tell the truth were particularly useful weapons against Puritans because of their abhorrence of a false oath. To put a Puritan under an inquisitional oath was to force him to incriminate himself if he was guilty. Calvin had taught that perjurers would be punished in the next world if not discovered in the present.[17] Even the secular law dealt severely with perjurers in New England.

An early episode aptly illustrates the sensitivity of colonial New Englanders about oaths in general. During her trial before the Massachusetts General Court in 1637, Anne Hutchinson made a surprise demand that the ministers who appeared as witnesses against her be sworn upon oath. Many denounced the idea in the debate that ensued. In the opinion of a deputy from Watertown, "an oath is of a high nature, and it is not to be taken but in a controversy, and for my part I am afraid of an oath and fear that we shall take God's name in vain."[18] Both former Governor John Endicott and Mrs. Hutchinson agreed that "an oath is the end of all strife," a summation of the general Puritan belief that an oath taken by a witness or a defendant demanded an immediate statement of truth. Even in the more secularized mid-eighteenth century a writer argued against employing oaths in the collection of a new excise tax, because "oaths are so awful and sacred, and the Welfare of Society so much depends on cultivating a religious Reverence for them, they ought not to be too frequently used, nor adopted into every trifling Concern."[19]

An incident at the trial of John Wheelwright during the Antinomian controversy of 1637 strikingly illustrates the specific fear of the English oath *ex officio* as an incriminating device. Wheelwright wanted to know his accusers. Someone answered for the Massachusetts General Court that his sermon was his accuser, and since he acknowledged it, they might proceed *ex officio*. "At this word great exception was taken, as if the Court intended the course of the High Commission." Hastily the court tried to explain away the reference: "It was

[16] In his preface to Norton, *Answer*, p. 10.

[17] C. Hill, *Society and Puritanism*, p. 394. For oaths and Puritans in England, see *ibid.*, pp. 382–419, and Levy, *Origins of the Fifth Amendment*.

[18] C. F. Adams, ed., *Antinomianism*, pp. 257–58, 263.

[19] Cooper, *The Crisis* (1754), pp. 7–8, 6; see the similar argument in John Lovell, *Freedom the First of Blessings* (Boston, 1754), p. 5.

answered that the word *ex officio* was very safe and proper, signifying no more but the authority or duty of the Court, and that there was no cause of offence, seeing the Court did not examine him by any compulsory meanes, as by oath, imprisonment, or the like."[20] This denunciation of compulsory means was an important indication of the limitations accepted by the Puritans in the search for evidence. New England Puritans were obviously just as sensitive to the oath *ex officio* as their coreligionists in England.

Ordinarily an accused person in New England was not examined under an oath of any kind. The privilege of a person not to be forced thereby to accuse himself was accepted. Massachusetts "ordered and decreed . . . that no man shall be urged to take any oath, or subscribe any Articles, Covenants, or remonstrance of publick and civil nature but such as the General Court hath considered, allowed and required."[21] Three Plymouth ministers who corresponded with Governor Bellingham concerning the Humfrey case were generally opposed to oaths: "It is not safe, nor warranted by God's Word, to extract a confession from a delinquent by an oath in matters of life and death."[22] Two mentioned specific opposition to the oath *ex officio*, the most direct threat to privacy, which was not used in New England.

Several incidents illustrate the problems of generalizing about the specific use of oaths in judicial examinations. At New Haven in 1667 a Stratford man was accused of sexually assaulting Mary Linley, a lame servant girl. Little evidence was available, and the court repeatedly emphasized the importance of revealing the truth. Finally the court asked the girl if she would confirm her testimony with an oath? "She answered that Shee would, Shee was told the weight of an oath and the danger of misinforming in such a matter."[23] Then attention shifted to the accused who "againe denied it etc. That he was as cleared from it as any man in the world, god knows his heart. . . . Then Mary Linley was called to take her oath." The court then had

[20] This episode is from Winthrop's account in C. F. Adams, ed., *Antinomianism*, p. 194.

[21] Body of Liberties, 1641, no. 3, in *Laws Mass., 1660;* Code of 1648, *Laws and Liberties of Mass.,* p. 43; *Laws Mass., 1660,* p. 62. George Lee Haskins noted that this provision effectively barred the oath *ex officio* since the General Court could never have allowed it at this time (1640's) (*Law and Authority in Early Massachusetts* [New York, 1960], pp. 201–2). On the use of oaths for accused and witnesses, see the *Pynchon Court Record,* p. 146.

[22] See Bradford, *Of Plymouth Plantation,* pp. 404–13.

[23] New Haven Co. Ct. Rec., I, 10–11.

no doubts about the guilt of the accused. In a second case at Hartford in 1700 Jonathan Biglow was suspected of stealing a colt. The judge asked a series of questions culminating in the following:

5. Do you not know who took away this colt last night.
   Answer. No he did not either directly or indirectly.
6. Can you make oath to the truth of that.
   Answer. Yes I can bot at present I shall not.[24]

Here the judge sought to test the substance of the accused's evidence by asking him to make an oath. Perhaps such an informal request was a regular tool in inquisitorial examinations. Biglow never actually took the oath; he was later found guilty. An instance when an oath was used to compel self-incrimination occurred in New Haven in 1702. The court was trying the case of a mutilated horse. A suspect was "sworne to answer directly to what interrogatories the Court should put to him respecting the case. The said Ebenezer Riggs after many equivocal and indirect answers did owne that he abused a horse. . . . The Court considering his great evill did sharply reprove him for trifling with the oath of God."[25]

The colonists perhaps overcame the slightly irrational Puritan fear of oaths that marked the first years of settlement. Problems of law enforcement without a professional police force became more acute with each passing decade. Necessity may have overshadowed some qualms about oaths in the minds of certain of the judiciary. In 1711 Cotton Mather proposed writing an essay on the nature of an oath, "because, the *Fear of an Oath*, is too much laid aside, and forgotten among us; our Courts have too much inconsiderate Swearing in them."[26] Some judges obviously resorted to oaths on occasion during examinations. In one area of the law an oath of a peculiar type was required if the defendant wished to prove himself innocent. If an Indian accused a white man of selling him liquor, the accusation was tantamount to conviction unless the suspect cleared himself by an oath of purgation. Until he swore that the charge was untrue, the court considered him guilty. Several colonies had such laws in the seventeenth century.[27] Refusal to take this oath of purgation there-

[24] Conn. Arch., Crimes and Misdemeanors, I, pt. 2, p. 224.

[25] New Haven Co. Ct. Rec., II, 98–99.

[26] *Diary of C. Mather*, II, 110; see Mather, *The Religion of an Oath* (Boston, 1719).

[27] *Laws Mass.*, 1660, p. 236 (1666); *Laws Mass., 1672*, p. 78; *Mass. Acts and Res.*, I, 151; *The Book of the General Laws of the Inhabitants of the Jurisdiction of New-Plimouth* (Cambridge, Mass., 1672), p. 45; *The Book of the General*

fore resulted in self-incrimination.[28] The problem of securing evidence in such cases, as well as the heinous nature of the crime, which could result in death for white settlers, perhaps seemed to justify the use of such an oath. In most cases the authorities did not attempt to use oaths to compel self-incrimination.

JUDICIAL EXAMINATION

The suspect in an ordinary criminal proceeding was brought before a local magistrate or justice of the peace, who conducted a pretrial examination into the details of the offense before settling a minor matter himself or sending the accused to trial at the county court. This examination afforded an opportunity to elicit evidence or a confession. As a result inquisitorial techniques characterized such interrogations until the era of the American Revolution.[29] As Leonard Levy has commented, "in the preliminary examination prior to indictment and arraignment, it was still ordinary practice to press a suspect to confess his guilt; and in the prosecution of an accused person before a jury, his interrogation was still the focal point of the trial, the objective to trap him into damaging admissions."[30] At this court level the magistrates were both judge and prosecutor, with primary emphasis upon obtaining and evaluating the evidence rather than protecting the rights of the accused.

By eliciting voluntary disclosures, the magistrates preserved a formal respect for individual privacy. So long as the accused or witnesses volunteered information, or the inquisitorial talents of judges managed to extract material from the suspect, there was no invasion of privacy. Examinations by one magistrate were usually private af-

---

Laws . . . of New-Plimouth (Boston, 1685), p. 40; Laws Conn., 1673, p. 41.

[28] In 1692 the Rev. Gershom Bulkeley of Connecticut was aware that this oath in liquor cases permitted self-incrimination and cited it as an example of a Connecticut law contrary to those of England, since by the laws of England, "nemo tenetur prodere se ipsum" ("Will and Doom," Connecticut Historical Society, Coll., III [1895], 115).

[29] By the close of the 16th century preliminary examinations in England had become very inquisitorial; they retained that characteristic into the 18th century (see Levy, Origins of the Fifth Amendment, pp. 35, 41, 325). On the cessation of such practices in America, see William E. Nelson, "Emerging Notions of Modern Criminal Law in the Revolutionary Era: An Historical Perspective," New York University Law Review, XLII (1967), 469, 478.

[30] Origins of the Fifth Amendment, p. 282.

fairs with only the accused, a complainant, and perhaps some witnesses present.[31] The justice of the peace was the most eminent man
of the neighborhood, in whose presence and from whose questions
nothing should be kept hidden. The magistrate who questioned a
pregnant single woman in Plymouth in 1769 received answers to such
questions as who the father was, whether any other men had intercourse with her, and "where was the place he had Carnal Knowledge
of your Body?"[32] When more than one judge took part in a pretrial
examination, the pressures on the suspect to provide private information voluntarily were even greater. In 1751 Joshua Hempstead of
New London "went with Mr Chapman, Capt Hurlbut and Adams
Selectmen to John Roger's to take the examination of a Nancy an
Irishwoman great with Child by fornication."[33] In a deferential society only the habitual offender was indifferent to the status of such
leading men of the town; they would certainly intimidate a servant
girl. In a small community, incurring the animosity of such a gentleman as the leading magistrate was not a prospect to be treated lightly. The suspect was less likely to refuse to answer incriminatory questions or confess under such circumstances. Since the justice of the
peace in the average town knew most of those brought before him, at
least by family reputation, he also had some idea whether a particular
individual was likely to be guilty and could proceed accordingly.
Under such conditions the government's refusal to sanction the use
of methods for compulsory disclosure did not usually hamper the
judicial process.

In England justices of the peace considered it their duty to secure
a confession from an accused felon. Christopher Hill has written that
"J.P.'s would normally try to extort a confession from the humbler
suspects whom they examined; when dealing with simple folk it was
the easiest method of procedure."[34] John Wigmore and William
Holdsworth both have emphasized that the habit of "questioning
and urging the accused died hard—did not disappear indeed till the
eighteenth century had begun." Holdsworth continued: "In spite of
the rule that a person need answer no question which tended to incriminate him, the statutes which required the justice of the peace to

---

[31] Jury trials in criminal cases were rare in the 17th century (see *Pynchon
Ct. Rec.*, p. 144; and Mark Howe, Jr., "Records of the Suffolk County Court,"
NEQ, VII [1934], 307–10).

[32] *Legal Papers of John Adams*, I, 322.

[33] *Diary of Joshua Hempstead of New London*, New London County Historical Society, *Collections*, I (New London and Providence, 1901), 563.

[34] *Society and Puritanism*, p. 385.

examine persons charged with crime, and the witnesses for the prosecution, were still in force. No one seems to have suggested that the privilege was inconsistent with these examinations of an accused person till the eighteenth century."[35]

The treatment of persons accused as witches at Salem in 1692 furnishes a case study of the conduct of examinations and trials. Although the hysteria surrounding this episode made it unique, the local judges who conducted many of the pretrial examinations, as well as the members of the specially appointed court of oyer and terminer, were representative of the New England judiciary. In a packed and tense courtroom these judges subjected the accused to relentless questioning, disregarding any of their answers until they had finally admitted their guilt. Hardly a question was not of the most incriminating sort: "How can you know, you are no witch."[36] Time after time the judges brushed aside protestations of innocence and continued the interrogations, implying that only a guilty plea would satisfy them.

Since most of the accused at Salem were women, this method was singularly successful; few had the stamina to prolong resistance. The confessions of others were used to encourage the timorous. When one woman protested that she knew nothing about witches, the judges answered: "No, have you not heard that some have confessed." The court reminded a husband that the "afflicted" had stopped their moanings and torturings after his wife and daughter had confessed: "Can you still deny that you are guilty?"[37] Thomas Brattle, the treasurer of Harvard, described the plight of those who tried to maintain their innocence:

Others of them denied their guilt, and maintained their innocency for above eighteen hours, after most violent, distracting, and draggooning methods had been used with them, to make them confesse. Such methods they were, that more than one of the said confessours did since tell many, with teares in their eyes, that they thought their very lives would have gone out of their bodyes; and wished that they might have been cast into the lowest dungeon, rather than be tortured with such repeated

[35] See William S. Holdsworth, *A History of English Law* (London, 1926), IX, 200–201. In reported English trials magistrates did not object to confessions that were improperly obtained until the 18th century (E. M. Morgan, "The Privilege against Self-Incrimination," *Minnesota Law Review*, XXXIV [1949–50], 15–16). Research in New England court records has not revealed any rejections of confessions because they were secured under nonphysical duress.

[36] *Records of Salem Witchcraft*, I, 142.

[37] *Ibid.*, I, 145, 185.

buzzings and chuckings and unreasonable urgings as they were treated withal.[38]

One of the accused, Margaret Jacobs, recanted her confession in a letter to her father from the dungeon of Salem prison: "The reason of my Confinement is this, I having, through the Magistrates Threatnings, and my own Vile and Wretched Heart, confessed several things contrary to my Conscience and Knowledg. . . . I was forced to confess the truth of all before the Magistrates, who would not believe me [until I confessed]"[39] Robert Calef, a Boston merchant, further described the pretrial examinations at Salem: "There are numerous Instances . . . of the tedious Examinations before private persons, many hours together; they all that time urging them to Confess (and taking turns to perswade them) till the accused were wearied out by being forced to stand so long, or for want of Sleep, etc. and so brought to give an Assent to what they said."[40]

The ability of colonial judges to obtain a confession from the suspect, despite his initial reluctance, has probably been underestimated. A judge held the upper hand in the process. In an episode in New London in 1750, Jedidiah Ashcraft was asserting his innocence of a counterfeiting charge before a justice of the peace: "Here I stopt him (having in my hand the ten pound bill . . .) set forth to him the improbability if not the impossibility of his story—showed him the bill, etc. Now he weeps. After a pause, he like a true penitent acknowledged he had spoken that which was false."[41] When persons were recorded as confessing "voluntarily," no mention was made of how much interrogation and intimidation by the judge preceded the confession. Occasionally a court did indicate that this approach had not worked. In New Haven in 1671 a man was accused of trading with the Indians. "The Court after much labouring with him for an ingenious confession and acknowledgment of the truth in the case but little prevailed."[42] This episode also illustrates the differing conditions of the courtroom experience at the county level, where the assembled judges played a more passive role in the prosecution of a case than at solitary pretrial examinations. Publicity, the presence of juries, and the various rules of evidence made it easier for an individual to resist interrogation in the county courtroom, although he

[38] *Narratives of the Witchcraft Cases*, p. 189.

[39] *Ibid.*, p. 365.

[40] *Ibid.*, pp. 374–76 (written in 1700).

[41] Superior Ct. Files, New London Co., March 1750, as quoted in Farrell, "Administration of Justice in Connecticut," p. 105.

[42] New Haven Co. Ct. Rec., I, 52–53. He was eventually convicted, although he would not admit his guilt.

still received much encouragement to confess. In New Haven in 1687, for example, an individual vigorously denied a paternity suit; then "the said Joseph Russell after much labouring with him for conviction and owning the truth both by the court and others of his friends and relations, he did confesse and owne that what the said Jane Blackman had charged and accused him with was true."[43] However, the courts were normally prepared to dismiss a case for lack of sufficient evidence and to release the accused without attempting to force a confession if a pretrial examination or an actual trial did not produce an admission of guilt. In some cases the suspect, like Anne Hutchinson, who was accused of heretical beliefs in 1637, could "tell when to speak and when to hold her tongue."[44]

By the early eighteenth century members of the developing colonial bar gave the accused advice and support during major trials and examinations at the county court level and above. Occasionally an individual requested counsel and was assigned a lawyer by the court.[45] Lawyers could help the accused resist judicial interrogation. By 1710 Cotton Mather felt it necessary to warn lawyers that in the pleading of causes, "you will abominate the use of all unfair arts, to confound *evidences,* to browbeat *testimonies,* to suppress what may give light in the case."[46] Whether obeying these precepts or not, a lawyer was sure to encourage a careful concern for the rights of a suspect by the judiciary.

Judicial examinations were conducted in an atmosphere that made concern for the personal privacy of the suspect a secondary consideration. The main desire of the judges was to settle a criminal case quickly, so that they could return to other pressing personal or public interests. The heavy case load at the intermittent county courts also encouraged haste; but at the same time it provided fewer opportunities for extensive examinations of suspects. Many criminal offenders haled before the courts had been seen in the act by an individual charged with law enforcement or by an available witness, so that there was little doubt about guilt. In other cases the accused had small encouragement to refuse to admit his guilt in the light of the evidence against him; and if he did have obstreperous notions, a dim realization of the possible consequences served its purpose.

Concern for the privacy of a suspect was not very relevant during a judicial examination. The accused was more fortunate in several

---

[43] *Ibid.,* p. 168; see also *ibid.,* p. 136 (1682).

[44] Gov. Winthrop's description in C. F. Adams, ed., *Antinomianism,* p. 245.

[45] Hampshire Co. Gen. Sess. and Common Pleas, bk. B, no. 3 (1735–40), p. 51.

[46] *Bonifacius,* p. 127.

other developments that supported any claims he cared to make for personal privacy in the courtroom.

THE PRIVILEGE AGAINST SELF-INCRIMINATION

During an examination conducted by judicial officials, a colonist could have recourse to several legal devices to protect his privacy. The most important of these was the right not to accuse himself in response to incriminatory questions. This privilege had developed over a long period of time in England, culminating in its fairly widespread acceptance during the Stuart period as a by-product of Puritan opposition to the crown and its courts. By the mid-seventeenth century Englishmen had begun to claim that no man was bound to incriminate himself under any circumstances.

The earliest colonial legislation concerning the right against compulsory self-incrimination appeared indirectly in the Massachusetts Body of Liberties of 1641. A statute forbade the ordinary use of torture to force anyone "to confesse any Crime against himselfe nor any other."[47] There is some question whether this provision, which subsequent Massachusetts codes repeated, was a meaningful recognition of the right against self-incrimination, in the sense in which it was then recognized in England.[48] But the existence of such a right need not be fully predicated upon this statute, which after all was enacted at a date when uncertainty prevailed in England on the same issue.

The 1673 edition of the laws of Connecticut also contained a forthright denunciation of self-incrimination by torture.[49] In 1698 Connecticut further declared that witnesses could be forced to testify, "provided that no person required to give testimonie as aforesaid shall be punished for what he doth confesse against himselfe when under oath."[50] These two Connecticut laws provided more substantial statutory recognition that a right against self-incrimination did exist. The formal extension of the privilege to witnesses was an

---

[47] Body of Liberties, 1641, no. 45, in *Laws Mass., 1660*; Code of 1648, *Laws and Liberties Mass.*, p. 50; *Laws Mass., 1660*, p. 187; *Laws Mass., 1672*, p. 129. One can reasonably assume that the privilege was taken for granted in noncapital cases.

[48] This provision is frequently cited to prove the early acceptance of the privilege in America (see R. Carter Pittman, "The Colonial and Constitutional Privilege against Self-Incrimination in America," *Virginia Law Review*, XXI [1935], 776).

[49] *Laws Conn., 1673*, p. 65.

[50] *Conn. Rec.*, IV, 236.

implicit acknowledgment of the general existence of the privilege.

There were no subsequent legislative enactments of this right in the New England colonies until Massachusetts and New Hampshire included the privilege against self-incrimination in the Bill of Rights section of their new constitutions drawn up during the Revolution.[51] Article Twelve of the Massachusetts Constitution of 1780 declared that "no subject shall . . . be compelled to accuse, or furnish evidence against himself."[52] The privilege against self-incrimination was thus asserted because it had been a recognized form of protection for individual rights during the eighteenth century.

The most significant colonial debate concerning the right against self-incrimination occurred in Massachusetts in 1641–42. The stimulus came from the extraordinary case of the Humfrey children, both under ten, who had been sexually molested. After the incident came to the attention of the authorities, John Winthrop recorded the ensuing developments. "The offenders, being brought to examination presently confessed all but entrance of her body; and being committed to prison, and the judgment of the case referred to the General Court, it was a great question what the kind of this sin was."[53] Since the rape statute did not anticipate the involvement of such young persons, it was difficult to determine the nature of this crime. In their dilemma the General Court decided to seek the advice of the ministers of New England. Because it was also troublesome in this case to prove penetration of the girls' bodies, the General Court specifically asked the ministers "how far a magistrate may extract a confession from a delinquent to accuse himselfe of a capital crime, seeing *nemo tenetur prodere seipsum?*" This last phrase was an explicit recognition that "no man is bound to accuse himselfe." Why then ask such a question? The General Court was either worried by the methods used to obtain the original confessions or, more likely, was seeking support to proceed to other forms of examination in order

[51] The Connecticut Constitution of 1776 was only four paragraphs long and included no stated privilege against self-incrimination. The Connecticut Constitution of 1818 contained the privilege.

[52] Benjamin P. Poore, comp., *The Federal and State Constitutions, Colonial Charters, and Other Organic Laws of the United States* (Washington, D.C., 1877), p. 958. This was essentially the same wording as had been submitted in the draft constitution of September 1779. There is no record of debate on this part of Article 12 in the *Journal* of the Convention except about a grammatical correction.

[53] Winthrop, *The History of New England from 1630 to 1649*, ed. James Savage (Boston, 1826), II, 46–47. This case is expurgated from J. K. Hosmer's edition of Winthrop's *Journal* (New York, 1908).

to substantiate a charge of rape. For Puritans keenly aware of the current struggles to establish the privilege in England, this unusual case was a real dilemma.

Assuming that "extraction" of a confession involved some form of torture, it was perhaps surprising that procedures so destructive of privacy were even contemplated. Governor Bellingham, for example, possessed practical experience in the administration of English criminal justice.[54] He should have been aware that the common law did not recognize the use of torture and that Michael Dalton as early as the 1619 edition of his widely used *Countrey Justice* had included the privilege against self-incrimination in his section on examination of felons. Perhaps it was due to men like Bellingham that the subject was left open for debate under these special circumstances. Perhaps the shocking nature of the offense put public pressure on the magistrates to secure the necessary evidence by any means and punish the offenders in this instance. Asking the question also indicated prevailing uncertainty about the privilege. In England it was only at this period that the right began to be invoked by the accused during trials and allowed by judges.[55] Persons were claiming it in famous trials, such as that of John Lilburne; but the matter had yet to become common knowledge.

The answers submitted by the ministers after several months of reflection represented the considered opinions of the clerical leadership.[56] John Rayner, one of two ministers in the town of Plymouth, made three distinct points. His initial assumption concerning judicial examination was that the "magistrate cannot without sin neglect diligent inquisition into the cause brought before him."

Secondly, if it be manifest that a capital crime is committed, and that common report or probability, suspicion or some complaint (or the like), be of this or that person, a magistrate ought to require, and by all due means to procure from the person (so far already bewrayed) a naked con-

[54] A contemporary described him as "learned in the Lawes of England" (Johnson, *Wonder-Working Providence*, p. 97). Stefan A. Riesenfeld argues that Bellingham accepted the famous maxim as law ("Law Making and Legislative Precedent in American Legal History," *Minnesota Law Review*, XXXIII [1949], p. 120). Several other magistrates had a working knowledge of English law, including John Winthrop himself.

[55] On the English background, see Levy, *Origins of the Fifth Amendment*, esp. chaps. 9 and 10.

[56] Only the replies of the Plymouth ministers have survived (quoted in full in Bradford, *Of Plymouth Plantation*, appendix, pp. 404–13). No other replies have been located.

fession of the fact. . . . For, though *nemo tenetur prodere seipsum*, yet by that which may be known to the magistrate by the forenamed means, he is bound thus to do or else he may betray his country and people to the heavy displeasure of God.

Thirdly, this confession of a capital crime must not be extorted by "punishment" or an oath "ex officio." Rayner recognized the privilege against self-incrimination but relied on the magistrate's inquisitorial talents to ensure that the obviously guilty did not employ the right successfully. This was a moderate view in the mid-seventeenth century.

The Reverend Ralph Partridge of Duxbury in Plymouth Colony was a graduate of Cambridge. To the question "how far may a magistrate extract a confession of a capital crime from a suspected and an accused person," Partridge answered:

I conceive that a magistrate is bound, by careful examination of circumstances and weighing of probabilities, to sift the accused; and by force of argument to draw him to an acknowledgment of the truth. But he may not extract a confession of a capital crime from a suspected person by any violent means, whether it be by an oath imposed, or by any punishment inflicted or threatened to be inflicted, for so he may draw forth an acknowledgment of a crime from a fearful innocent. If guilty, he shall be compelled to be his own accuser when no other can, which is against the rule of justice.

This admirable statement of the meaning of the privilege was perfectly suited to both colonial and English practice and was a satisfactory protection for the privacy of the individual involved.

The Reverend Charles Chauncy, also a Plymouth minister, has been called the most learned man of the Puritan migration, for he had been a fellow and lecturer at Cambridge. He too opposed the use of oaths and torture and advocated reliance upon voluntary confession. He allowed only one exception: "I conceive that in matters of highest consequence, such as do concern the safety or ruin of states or countries, magistrates may proceed so far to bodily torments, as racks, hot irons, etc. to extract a confession, especially where presumptions are strong; but otherwise by no means." In England torture was applied under just these circumstances as late as 1640, in a situation where political leaders felt justified in sacrificing privacy for national security.

The three Plymouth ministers recognized the right of individuals not to incriminate themselves. They represented the libertarian strain in the Puritan tradition that contributed substantially to the acceptance of a colonial right of personal privacy. But the religious leaders also emphasized the duty of magistrates to discover the guilty and have them "voluntarily" confess. Since the privilege must not be a shield for the guilty, judicial examination was the answer.

By the time the replies of the various ministers had been received, John Winthrop was again the governor of Massachusetts. He summarized all the answers received:

> Another question was, how far a magistrate might extract a confession from a delinquent in capital cases? To this it was answered by the most, that where such a fact is committed, and one witness or strong presumptions do point out the offender, there the judge may examine him strictly, and he is bound to answer directly, though to the peril of his life. But if there be only light suspicion, etc. then the judge is not to press him to answer, nor is he to be denied the benefit of the law, but he may be silent, and call for his accusers. But, for examination by oath or torture in criminal cases, it was generally denied to be lawful.[57]

Winthrop's stringent personal beliefs and the gravity and uniqueness of this particular case probably shaped the construction of this brief summary. However, the entire debate furnished substantial evidence that the New England colonists were prepared to acknowledge an individual's right not to incriminate himself, an integral element in the protection of privacy.

In the light of ministerial involvement in this debate over self-incrimination and the harsh procedures of English ecclesiastical courts, a discipline case in the Wenham church in 1645 has a particular importance. Persons wondered whether an accused church member should be asked such questions "as may tend to the making good their accusations by his owne confession, and so to entrap him upon meere suggestions; to bring a brother by this meanes into a snare; seemes besids the rule." It was further added that "tis against the law of nature for a man to be forced to accuse himself."[58] Such an episode strongly evidences an existing recognition of the right against self-incrimination.

There are solid legal grounds to expect that the right to be silent existed in practice in colonial New England. The English handbook normally used as a reference by colonial magistrates, Dalton's *Countrey Justice*, stated in the section on "examination of felons, and

[57] *History of New England*, ed. Savage, II, 47.
[58] Fiske, "Notebook of Church Matters," p. 59 (Jan. 1645). The spelling and punctuation have been slightly modernized in the interests of intelligibility.

evidence against them," that "the offender himself shall not be examined upon oath, for by the Common Law, *Nullus tenetur seipsum prodere*: Neither was a mans fault to be wrung out of himselfe (no not by examination onely) but to be proved by others, untill the stat. of 2. and 3. P. and M. cap. 10 gave authority to the Justices of Peace to examine the felon himselfe."[59] While acknowledging the obligation to question suspects closely during the pretrial examination, Dalton still accepted their right not to be forced to incriminate themselves at this stage of proceedings.[60] Since the common law did not recognize torture, Dalton implicitly rejected it. Oaths were ruled out, and only judicial questioning could be employed to elicit confessions. Dalton represented the standard British attitude toward the privilege until the eighteenth century. In 1647 the Massachusetts General Court ordered two copies of Dalton's work from England "to the end we may have the better light for making and proceeding about laws." Justice Pynchon in seventeenth-century frontier Massachusetts was familiar with Dalton, and in mid-eighteenth-century Worcester County a small-town minister sought a copy of Dalton when he needed legal enlightenment.[61]

The first recorded claim of the privilege against self-incrimination in New England occurred in 1637 during a preliminary examination of the minister John Wheelwright before the Massachusetts General Court. After the court calmed the furor over its ill-advised reference to the term *ex officio*, the examination continued. As Governor Winthrop described it:

The question then put to him was, whether before his Sermon he did not know, that most of the Ministers in this jurisdiction did teach that doctrine which he in his Sermon called a Covenant of works; to this he said, he did not desire to answer, and hereupon some cried out, that the court went about to ensnare him, and to make him accuse himselfe, and that this question was not about the matter of his Sermon, etc. Upon this he refused to answer any further, so he was dismissed till the afternoone; The

[59] This statement appeared in the editions of 1619, 1635, 1655, 1677, 1727, and 1742.

[60] William Lambarde, Dalton's predecessor, had stated in his 1614 and 1619 editions that "at the common Law, *Nemo tenebatur prodere seipsum*, and then his fault was not to be wrung out of himselfe but rather to bee discovered by other meanes and men" (*Eirenarcha*, p. 213). The phrase first appeared in the second edition of 1588. Lambarde was also used in New England into the 18th century.

[61] *Mass. Rec.*, II, 212; *Pynchon Court Rec.*, p. 31; Parkman, "Diary," AAS, *Proc.*, LXXII (1962), 171.

reason why the Court demanded that question of him, was not to draw matter from himselfe whereupon to proceed against him, neither was there any need, . . . the court might soone have convinced him by witnesses, if they had intended to proceed against him upon that ground.[62]

The court records preserve other assertions of this right not to incriminate oneself. In the New Haven County court in 1666, John Tharpe was named in a paternity suit. He "was called and asked what he had to say heareing what he was Charged with? He answered, that he Could not accuse himselfe . . . [and] denied the fact charged."[63] In a case before the Hampshire County court in 1671 John Stewart "refused to confess against himself though also he denyeth not the fact."[64] In New Haven in 1709 two individuals suspected of robbing a house refused to admit they had entered a particular home, "saying they came not there to accuse themselves."[65] It was significant that these various claims all occurred in ordinary cases and during trials in the lower courts. In both England and America in the seventeenth and eighteenth centuries the rights of the accused received more consideration in an actual trial than in a pretrial examination.[66] Such concern was also characteristic of the rare criminal cases in the superior courts in New England. Several of the accused at the Salem witch trials even claimed the privilege against self-incrimination. During two examinations the accused replied to a series of incriminating questions by shouting, "would you have me accuse myself?"[67] The answer of the judges in both cases was "Yes if you be guilty." This reply well illustrates the judiciary's general lack of enthusiasm for the privilege in the light of other priorities, as well as the gradualness of full acceptance of the right.

The privilege against self-incrimination figured in the heated debate over the Massachusetts Excise Bill of 1754. Defenders of the bill argued that excise officers seeking an account of the rum consumed by families would not have the power of visitation in homes but only "to demand an Account upon Oath." "But," wrote one pamphleteer, "will anyone presume to say, that this will be no Dimi-

---

[62] See above, p. 224; C. F. Adams, ed., *Antinomianism*, pp. 194–95.

[63] *New Haven Town Rec.*, II, 184. He was later convicted on the basis of other evidence. See a similar case in 1670 in New Haven Co. Ct. Rec., I, 35.

[64] *Pynchon Court Rec.*, p. 146.

[65] New Haven Co. Ct. Rec., II, 396–97; see also *ibid.*, I, 35 (1683).

[66] Levy has stated that in England for all practical purposes "the right against self-incrimination scarcely existed in the pre-trial stages of a criminal proceeding" (*Origins of the Fifth Amendment*, p. 325).

[67] *Records of Salem Witchcraft*, II, 33; Chandler, *American Criminal Trials*, I, 88.

nution of our Liberties, if it be an essential Part of our Constitution, that No Man is held to convict himself in any Affair whereof he is accus'd?"[68] The author implied that the right against self-incrimination was "essential" and was commonly recognized as such.

The treatment of witnesses was an important aspect of the development of the privilege against self-incrimination. Should witnesses enjoy this privilege, or should they be forced to testify and granted immunity from prosecution in the event that they did incriminate themselves? There is some evidence that colonial courts fined persons who refused to give testimony but did permit them not to testify.[69] In England the privilege against self-incrimination was first extended to an ordinary witness in 1649.[70] In Connecticut the General Assembly may have backslid on the matter in 1698:

Whereas oftentimes when upon complaint of misdemeanors, persons being called to give evidence in cases that are of a capitall or criminall nature, or of breach of a penall lawe, doe refuse to give evidence therein, whereby justice in punishment of those that are offenders is hindred; . . . for the future . . . whatsoever person shall be called by civill authority to give evidences in any such cases as aforesaid, and shall refuse to make answer so farre as he is capable to such questions as shall be demanded respecting the case in question, and also refuse to make oath that he will declare all and whatsoever he knowes or hath cognisance of respecting the case or matter in question, shall . . . be committed to the countie gaole, there to remain untill he will make oath that he will give evidence as aforesaid . . . always provided that no person required to give testimonie as aforesaid shall be punished for what he doth confesse against himselfe when under oath.[71]

This description of current practices in Connecticut suggests that witnesses in that colony were aware of their rights in the area of self-incrimination and nicely illustrates the competing values. This new law compelling testimony aroused opposition. The limitation whereby a person was forced to incriminate himself but not held liable was removed in 1703, and a further qualification was added. The individual now must testify "so farre as it concernes any other person besides himselfe, (unless any religious tye of conscience bottomed on the word of God bind him to the contrary)."[72] This extension of the privilege to witnesses in Connecticut was a significant step. It im-

[68] Cooper, *The Crisis,* p. 6.
[69] See, for example, New Haven Co. Ct. Rec., I, 167 (1687); Plymouth Co. Gen. Sess., 1686–1721, p. 63.
[70] Levy, *Origins of the Fifth Amendment,* p. 313.
[71] *Conn. Rec.,* IV, 236.
[72] *Ibid.,* 410.

plied that the privilege was fully accepted in its original application to the accused.

Joseph Smith has observed that no person in Judge Pynchon's magistrate's court in seventeenth-century western Massachusetts claimed the privilege against self-incrimination.[73] There were actually few occasions for persons to claim the privilege in this minor court. A person was normally not arrested for such common criminal offenses as drunkenness or a theft unless clear evidence to support a conviction was at hand. Even at the county courts methods of conviction were unpretentious in most criminal cases. The inquisitorial techniques in the courtroom were not geared to the employment of the privilege in ordinary cases. A man who claimed the privilege in such a case was disturbing the deliberate equilibrium of arrest and conviction. Yet individuals could and did refuse to incriminate themselves. The right was accepted and defended on occasion, whether one's motives in claiming it was the protection of personal privacy or an attempt to escape the consequences of an untoward act. The acceptance of the privilege against self-incrimination in colonial New England was predicated upon a fundamental respect for individual human dignity, with consequent benefits for personal privacy in society as a whole.

The colonist who was brought to trial before a colonial court could choose not to incriminate himself and was not likely to be burdened with an inquisitional oath or the infliction of torture. Suspects had an acknowledged right to protect their privacy and to have their case judged on external evidence. At the same time their judges wanted to settle the case at hand. Because of the nature of law enforcement activities in colonial America, a man was not likely to be brought to court in a criminal case unless he had been apprehended in the commission of a misdeed. If evidence was readily available, the personal privacy of the accused was both safe from intrusion and irrelevant. A colonist knew that his criminal case would be judged on the evidence produced by witnesses or elicited from him by a skillful judge during examination. In general no one could force him to reveal anything about himself that he cared to keep private. In many ways it was irrational to extend such a right to a suspected criminal; the fact that the extension was made indicates the degree of respect for privacy that existed in colonial society. Recognition of the privilege against self-incrimination evidenced societal and governmental con-

---

[73] *Pynchon Ct. Rec.*, p. 146.

cern for the dignity of the individual colonist. Puritan-inspired notions of man's freedom and innate rights encouraged this custom to develop in the first instance. Man by his very nature deserved such treatment. In the long run these notions overcame Puritan concepts less beneficial to privacy. Even in the face of the problems involved in the maintenance of public order and public security, society was not willing to legitimize compulsory disclosure of private matters.

Epilogue

T HE New England colonists' desire for personal privacy was not a novel demand in the New World but a part of their traditional English heritage. The residents of colonial New England valued privacy. Probably every resident sought a measure of privacy at some point in every day. Only the intensity with which an individual searched for it differed from person to person. Individuals sought as much privacy as their personalities demanded and tried to ensure that a sufficient amount was available to them.

The contemporary notion that we are the first people to want privacy and to be concerned about its preservation is misleading. Western civilization has recognized the value of some personal privacy from time immemorial. In fact, the desire for some degree of privacy is as near as one can come to naming a constant of human nature in Western civilization. It is a unique value with a biological basis in the demand for life space as well as social, intellectual, and cultural rationales. Rarely has a society or the individuals that compose it demonstrated total disdain for privacy. This concern for privacy is so closely tied to the most elementary needs of all humans and is so much taken for granted that its desirability often is not articulated, or its availability recognized. By the seventeenth century, in the English-speaking world, privacy had become an integral part of a total value system that included freedom, material comfort, achievement, success, and the work ethic—a system within which we still live. This valuation of privacy has not changed drastically since that time, except that changed conditions make privacy more passionately sought today, since it is less readily available.

Conditions in colonial New England for the enjoyment of personal privacy remained stable in many ways. The colonists generally enjoyed the beneficial effects of large home lots in well-laid-out towns or spacious farms in the peaceful countryside. The architecture of homes featured a substantial style that protected the family from outside observation, together with some gradually introduced internal improvements for the benefit of privacy. Within most homes the physical conditions of daily life were less amenable to the enjoyment of privacy. Large families, the presence of servants and lodgers, and the sharing of houses by several families effectively decreased the availability of solitude and sometimes family intimacy in many instances. Curtained beds and the practice of bundling represented searches for privacy within the home. The colonists also sought privacy for sexual relations and generally obtained it. Spending a good part of the day in fields and shops alleviated crowded conditions in most homes, and privacy was always available outdoors and during periods of darkness.

The conception of the home as a castle formalized the prevailing expectation of privacy for the family in the home. The colonists expected to be left alone by outsiders when they were within their houses. Outside the home, the smallness of towns in which everyone knew almost everyone else restricted anonymity; yet at the same time the general paucity of population in such a large area made solitude available at almost any time with minimum effort.

In the twentieth century the various levels of government play a decisive role in the protection of personal privacy and often in institutionalizing its invasion. This was much less the case in the colonial era. The authoritarian character of seventeenth-century governments did encourage attempts to regulate private behavior extensively. But in practice the colonial governments presented a minimal threat to the privacy of the individual in comparison to that existing in modern times. The Puritan attitude toward sin encouraged surveillance by public authorities and the strict regimentation of private lives, at least in the mid-seventeenth century. Yet once again mitigating factors existed, as the changes in the impact of the Puritan movement on society encouraged the preservation of privacy.

It is misleading to associate lack of privacy with Puritan moral legislation. Most of these regulations did not relate to the enjoyment of solitude or intimacy within the family. Fathers, clergy, and law enforcement officials have always served as the agents of society in maintaining some forms of surveillance over the behavior of the general population. Despite an apparent institutionalization of this surveillance by colonial governments, the various law enforcers did not subject the population to rigorous supervision. A wide variety of human considerations mitigated this requirement. The mores of daily existence demanded respect for the privacy of others, while protections for personal privacy were also built into the legislation outlining the duties of law enforcers.

Of the New England institutions, the Congregational churches presented the most substantial threat to the privacy of the inhabitants through the processes of admission and discipline. Yet real concern for privacy was evident in both areas, which were hedged about with significant protections for personal sensibilities. The situation in the colonial courtroom paralleled that in the churches, with the privilege against self-incrimination furnishing significant protection for individual privacy.

Puritanism was not the only source of the attitudes that affected the availability of privacy in colonial New England. Certain other ideas that have since disappeared or grown to maturity made positive contributions to the preservation of privacy. If the ideology of Puritanism did not survive in the New World in its pristine form, neither did other fundamental values or attitudes that the colonists brought with them. In many ways the fate of Puritanism was closely intertwined with some of these Old World values, since the Puritan movement was one of the chief reasons for their migration to America. These values had their own independent encounter with conditions in America, and in the process of change liberated alternative norms. Three major examples are the authoritarianism associated with all seventeenth-century governments, the patriarchal attitude to family government, and the communal ethic associated with the early years of settlement. As the impact of each of these values gradually softened, a desire for privacy could surface more readily. The results were visible by the eighteenth century in all the colonies. Governments generally ceased trying to regulate private lives in intimate fashion; parents became more tolerant in the upbringing of their children; the search for privacy played a more important part in the location of homes.

If the New World was not a healthy climate for some Old World notions, other values thrived in the new environment. Individualism became a much more viable concept in a world of plenty and independence. Families acquired considerable freedom in initial settlement and subsequent relocations. If, as historians are inclined to assert vaguely, Puritanism served as a stimulus to nascent individualism in seventeenth-century English society, the spur grew even stronger in the New World. As the significance of Puritanism changed, individualism was well launched on its career as a permanent trait of the American character and a continuing impetus to the search for personal privacy. A basic process of secularization took firm root in the New World, primarily in association with the changes in Puritanism. Since privacy is in many respects a secular value, such a development gradually made its own contribution to legitimizing claims for privacy.

Perceptibly improving conditions of life also contributed to the availability of greater privacy. The accumulation of capital over several generations and the improvement in the general standard of living as a by-product of gradual economic growth meant that more and more persons could afford privacy. The ability to build large houses became more widespread. Population growth broke down the sense of forced intimacy in some communities and gave residents a choice of environments in which to live. The increasing availability of anonymity, and many other developments, enabled the enjoyment of a substantial degree of personal privacy to become an accepted characteristic of colonial life.

The colonists and colonial society achieved a balance of privacy interests in innumerable ways. Individuals in their private lives and society as a whole took into account a whole series of concerns, conditions, and competing values. Crowded and noisy living conditions, the burden of poverty, and the surveillance goals of governments represented environmental, economic, and political considerations that upset the privacy balance at particular times and in individual lives. The cultural norms of the society and an individual's status affected the way he would choose between privacy and disclosure. The norms of privacy changed, particularly with the alterations in Puritanism and the Puritan movement, permitting a return to the older values such as privacy in an improved environment. In all of these instances a temporary or more permanent equilibrium prevailed. When the privacy balance was seriously disturbed in the life of an individual or society, a process of restoration of normality ultimately occurred. Such an imbalance could be the product of either too much solitude or intimacy or too much surveillance and exposure. Solitude was ever plentiful, overbearing intimacy was a prevailing threat, reserve was most subject to individual control, and anonymity was less of a concern than in more modern times.

The ready availability of some personal privacy in colonial New England meant that positive demands for it only infrequently became strident. Consciousness of privacy's importance surfaced primarily in response to an invasion of privacy. Thus it was not a highly publicized or articulated concept in colonial America. Unlike such political values as freedom and democracy, privacy was rarely the focus of any intense struggles. It did not encounter such challenges until the late nineteenth and twentieth centuries. The colonial concept of privacy, like so many rights and privileges, was essentially a negative one. The colonists expected to be left alone in their homes and families. They did not anticipate interference in their private lives by government, the churches, and the courts so long as they abided by the accepted norms of their society.

Human nature has remained relatively the same in its elemental concern for privacy, while the conditions surrounding man have changed. Some changes since the colonial era have made privacy more readily available, and others have hindered its enjoyment. In the nineteenth century modern technology and industrialization at first markedly improved the situation for privacy in many areas, especially within the home. Factories removed shops from private homes, and the acquisition of various appliances gradually led to the disappearance of domestic servants. At the same time the forces of democratization in the nineteenth century liberated many antiprivacy elements in the American psyche, in marked contrast to one benefit of a deferential society. The advent of professional police forces and the utilization of modern technology in law enforcement has made possible serious governmental threats to the preservation of privacy. Solitude, perhaps too readily available in preindustrial times, has become increasingly difficult to find in modern mass societies. Whereas a need for some privacy seems innate in human beings, impediments to the enjoyment of privacy seem inherent in human societies. It perhaps stands to reason that the current generation always considers its peculiar imbalances unusually severe.

Contemporary Americans are much more conscious of the value of privacy than the New England colonists were, in part because mass society has subjected personal privacy to so much abuse. A colonial farmer who had been alone in the fields all day was less concerned about privacy in the evening than the employee of the modern corporation. The slow pace of life in an agricultural society made privacy less important as a source of rest and recuperation than it is today. Although it is an individually desired cultural value that is usually defended on a personal rather than societal level, the challenge to personal privacy is now so great that the government and the courts must intervene. The individual can no longer totally protect his own privacy. Privacy was not under such attack in colonial America. With the assistance of developments in the social and behavioral sciences, we are also more cognizant than the colonists were of the importance of privacy. The modern challenge to privacy has led to the articulation of a concept that was once taken for granted. Yet earlier societies demonstrated their own sense of the importance of privacy.

Twentieth-century concern for personal privacy has sought relief in the form of legal recognition for a right of privacy, especially in the courts. The serious nature of contemporary challenges to privacy has made such legal efforts of paramount importance. The contrast with the situation in colonial New England is readily apparent. Most colonists enjoyed an adequate level of personal privacy in its various states. The challenges to privacy that they encountered were of a traditional nature for the most part. Prying servants or neighbors, for example, could be handled on a personal basis and by an occasional resort to the courts. Individual choice governed participation in most activities that threatened personal privacy. The levels of privacy that persons enjoyed and expected were relatively fixed and stable.

The contrast between the colonial scene and today was most marked in the area of a person's relations with the government on the local and colony-wide level. A colonial government was only a minor challenge to privacy; one did not normally need recourse to the courts to defend oneself against governmental intrusion. But when necessary, such as during the Massachusetts Excise Bill controversy in 1754, the colonists were prepared to assert their rights to a private life against the government. There was a marked degree of popular resistance to close governmental supervision of family life and interference with individuals. Existing moral legislation did not provoke consistent intrusions into private lives under ordinary circumstances. The disappearance of sumptuary laws and the failure to enforce laws against solitary living had a direct connection with public concern for individual privacy. Colonial laws that interfered too much with the lives of the people were simply not enforced. Even law enforcers enjoyed statutory limitations on the extent to which they had to conduct surveillance. The state of technology severely limited governmental activities in this area. The inadequacy of colonial law enforcement guaranteed the protection of personal privacy and insulated the individual from serious and extensive surveillance. Although there was some governmental regulation, colonial governments recognized strict limitations for the most part in their contacts with residents. Searches of private homes and the serving of legal papers were restricted activities. Popular outcries and legal challenges greeted real or envisioned governmental breaches of the security of the home. In those areas where it became necessary, the colonists discovered adequate legal means of redressing privacy grievances against the government and the major institutions in society. The government for the most part demonstrated a marked regard for privacy. The courts disdained modes of compulsory disclosure of private matters and recognized the privilege against self-

incrimination. The privacy of communication through the mails was
legally protected.

A right of privacy existed in colonial America that was both traditional and customary. The existence of that right was clearly recognized during the revolutionary times of the second half of the
eighteenth century; the manifest challenges to privacy that emerged
in this era produced the most developed legal defenses of the right
to privacy. The legal resources available for the assertion of a right
to privacy were perfectly suitable to the level of challenges that
privacy encountered in the colonial setting. Although the claim of
privacy as a *legal* right has developed slowly in Western history, the
courts in colonial New England protected privacy in indirect or
derivative fashion, by prosecuting trespassers, limiting search and
seizure, entertaining defamation cases, and protecting the privileged
communications of husbands and wives in the courtrooms. The limited character of these legal protections is apparent, yet they were
adequate for the times. Men are still protecting their privacy in derivative fashion. Courts are not and never have been the sole recourse for the protection of privacy. Even today many invasions of
privacy are not actionable at law. In fact, there are only limited areas
in which laws can usefully be enacted for the protection of privacy.
The editor of a recent symposium on privacy reminded readers that
"privacy still remains primarily a nonlegal concept." It is "a cultural
norm which has been introduced into a variety of legal issues and
which serves the purpose of providing a rallying point for those
concerned about the encroachments of mass society on the individual."[1] The American colonists had several ways to secure redress in
the courts for an invasion of privacy and few unfulfilled needs. When
they encountered obstacles to their enjoyment of privacy, they could
respond directly and personally.

In *Griswold* v. *Connecticut*, Justice William O. Douglas for the
United States Supreme Court asserted a right of privacy older than
the Bill of Rights.[2] The several amendments to the Constitution,
Douglas argued, explicitly and implicitly embodied a series of legal
protections for privacy. The Constitution guarantees recognized
zones of privacy. The constitutional arguments embodied in the
Griswold opinions recognizing the right of marital privacy have been
greeted with scepticism in some quarters. But as William M. Beaney
has commented, "the disagreement of members of the majority as to

[1] Clark C. Havighurst, "Foreword," *Law and Contemporary Problems*, XXXI
(1966), 251–52.
[2] Griswold v. Connecticut, 381 U.S. 479 (1965).

the constitutional underpinning of the claim is less important than the fact that they agreed that a right to privacy had a constitutional basis."[3] This study basically supports Justice Douglas's majority opinion in its major contention that a constitutional right of privacy exists. Even Justice Hugo Black's strong dissent recognized that "there are, of course, guarantees in certain specific constitutional provisions which are designed in part to protect privacy at certain times and places with respect to certain activities."[4] The Supreme Court sensed the true dimensions of the colonial and revolutionary situation with respect to privacy, even though the existing scholarly literature did not shed much light on the matter. The colonists believed they had a general right to privacy and had asserted it long before the writing of the Bill of Rights; it flourished in the eighteenth century on an individual basis. The Bill of Rights, and in particular the First, Third, Fourth, Fifth, and Ninth Amendments, incorporated those aspects of the right of privacy that had acquired formal legal recognition to the time in question. Several common law protections for privacy in the courts also continued in existence. The Founding Fathers had no reason to anticipate the consequences of modernization that would require a much more comprehensive development of legal protections for the right of personal privacy. Privacy received as much protection in the Bill of Rights as was needed at that time; the various amendments have remained the starting point as the American legal system has sought to respond to the vastly increased number of serious challenges to personal privacy in modern American society.

[3] William M. Beaney, "The Right to Privacy and American Law," *Law and Contemporary Problems,* XXXI (1966), 263. See also Beaney, "The Griswold Case and the Expanding Right to Privacy," *Wisconsin Law Review,* 1966, pp. 979–95.
[4] 381 U.S. 508.

Select Bibliography

PRIMARY SOURCES

Public Records

Laws

Court Records

Town Records

Church Records

Personal and Family Papers

Contemporary Works

Statistics

SECONDARY SOURCES

Architecture and Town Planning

Social History

Legal History

Religious History

English History

Select Bibliography

THE following is a list of the valuable primary and secondary materials used in the course of research for this volume. Two excellent bibliographies of New England colonial history are included in: *English Historical Documents: American Colonial Documents to 1776*, ed. Merrill Jensen (New York, 1955); and *The Puritans: A Sourcebook of Their Writings*, ed. Perry Miller and Thomas H. Johnson, 2 vols. (rev. paperback ed., New York, 1963). Charles Evans, *American Bibliography*, 12 vols. (Chicago, 1903–34), is the basic list of titles printed in colonial America. This should be supplemented by Clifford K. Shipton and James E. Mooney (eds.), *National Index of American Imprints through Eighteen Hundred: the Short Title Evans*, 2 vols. (Barre, Mass., 1969). An annotated version of the bibliography that follows is available in David H. Flaherty, "Privacy in Colonial New England" (Ph.D. diss., Columbia University, 1967).

PUBLIC RECORDS

Connecticut. *The Public Records of the Colony of Connecticut.* Ed. J. Hammond Trumbull and Charles J. Hoadly. 15 vols. Hartford, 1850–90.

Massachusetts. Massachusetts Archives. Vol. IX, "Domestic Relations, 1643–1774." State Archives, State House, Boston.

    Records of the Governor and Company of the Massachusetts Bay in New England. Ed. Nathaniel B. Shurtleff. 5 vols. in 6. Boston, 1853–54.

New Hampshire. *Documents and Records Relating to the Province of New-Hampshire.* Ed. Nathaniel Bouton *et al.* 40 vols. Concord, N. H., etc., 1867–1943.

New Haven. *Records of the Colony and Plantation of New Haven, from 1638 to 1649.* Ed. Charles J. Hoadly. Hartford, 1857.

    Records of the Colony or Jurisdiction of New Haven, from May, 1653, to the Union, Together with the New Haven Code of 1656. Ed. Charles J. Hoadly. Hartford, 1858.

Plymouth. *Records of the Colony of New Plymouth in New England.* Ed. Nathaniel B. Shurtleff and David Pulsifer. 12 vols. Boston, 1855–61.

Rhode Island. *Records of the Colony of Rhode Island and Providence Plantations in New England.* Ed. John Bartlett. 10 vols. Providence, 1856–65.

LAWS

The Early American Imprints Series, edited by Clifford K. Shipton, makes available on microcard all legal codes published between 1639 and 1800.

Connecticut. Bibliography. Albert C. Bates. *A Bibliographical List of Editions of Connecticut Laws from the Earliest Issues to 1836.* Hartford, 1900.

"Fundamental Orders of 1639." In *The Public Records of the Colony of Connecticut.* Ed. J. Hammond Trumbull. Hartford, 1850. I, 20–25.

"Ludlow's Code of 1650." In *ibid.* Pp. 509–63.

The Book of the General Laws for the People within the Jurisdiction of Connecticut. Cambridge, Mass., 1673. Rpt. Hartford, 1865.

Acts and Laws of His Majesties Colony of Connecticut in New-England. Boston, 1702. Rpt. Hartford, 1901. Rev. eds. (with slightly varying titles), New London, 1715, 1750, 1754, 1769, 1784.

Massachusetts. *The Laws and Liberties of Massachusetts.* Cambridge, Mass., 1648. Facsimile rpt. Ed. Max Farrand. Cambridge, Mass., 1929.

The Colonial Laws of Massachusetts Reprinted from the Edition of 1660, with the Supplements to 1672, Containing Also, The Body of Liberties of 1641. Ed. William H. Whitmore. Boston, 1889.

The Colonial Laws of Massachusetts, Reprinted from the Edition of 1672 with the Supplements through 1686. Ed. William H. Whitmore. Boston, 1887.

The Acts and Resolves, Public and Private, of the Province of the Massachusetts Bay. Ed. A. C. Goodell. 21 vols. Boston, 1869–1922. Vols. I–V contain the Province laws, 1692–1780.

New Hampshire. "Laws of the Province of New-Hampshire, from 1692–1702." In *Documents and Records Relating to the Province of New Hampshire.* Vol. III. Ed. Nathaniel Bouton. Manchester, N.H., 1869.

Laws of the Province of New-Hampshire, Passed by the Assembly at the Session Begun at Portsmouth August Seventh, 1699. Boston, 1699.

Acts and Laws Passed by the General Court or Assembly of His Majesties Province of New-Hampshire. Boston, 1706. Rev. eds. (with slightly varying titles), Boston, 1716, 1726, and Portsmouth, 1761, 1766, 1771, and 1780.

New Haven Colony. *Records of the Colony and Plantation of New Haven, from 1638 to 1649.* Ed. Charles J. Hoadly. Hartford, 1857. Contains the laws of 1639 and 1643.

Records of the Colony or Jurisdiction of New Haven, from May, 1653, to the Union, Together with the New Haven Code of 1656. Ed. Charles J. Hoadly. Hartford, 1858.

Plymouth Colony. *Records of the Colony of New Plymouth in New England.* Ed. David Pulsifer. Boston, 1861. Vol. IX contains the code of 1636, pp. 6–24, and the revision of 1658, pp. 71–121.

The Compact, with the Charter and Laws of the Colony of New Plymouth. Ed. William Brigham. Boston, 1836. Includes all 17th-century Plymouth laws.

The Book of the General Laws of the Inhabitants of the Jurisdiction of New-Plimouth. Cambridge, Mass., 1672.

The Book of the General Laws of the Inhabitants of the Jurisdiction of New-Plimouth. Boston, 1685.

Rhode Island. *The Proceedings of the First General Assembly of "the Incorporation of Providence Plantations," and the Code of Laws Adopted by That Assembly in 1647.* Ed. William R. Staples. Providence, 1847.

Laws and Acts Made from the First Settlement of Her Majesties Colony of Rhode Island and Providence Plantations. Providence, 1705. Rpt., with an introduction by Sidney S. Rider. Providence, 1896.

The Charter and the Acts and Laws of His Majesties Colony of Rhode-Island and Providence Plantations in America, 1719. Providence, 1719. Ed. Sidney S. Rider. Providence, 1895.

Acts and Laws of His Majesty's Colony of Rhode Island, and Providence Plantations in America. Newport, 1730. Rev. eds. (with slightly varying titles), Newport, 1730, 1737, 1745, 1752, 1767, and 1772.

COURT RECORDS

With the addition of titles listed below, two printed bibliographies list the substantial body of court records used in this study.

Bibliography. Flaherty, David H. "A Select Guide to the Manuscript Court Records of Colonial New England." *American Journal of Legal History,* XI (1967), 107–26.

Jeffrey, William, Jr. "Early New England Court Records: A Bibliography of Published Materials." *American Journal of Legal History,* I (1957), 119–47.

General. Chandler, Peleg W. *American Criminal Trials.* 2 vols. Boston, 1841–44.

Howell, T. B. *Complete Collection of State Trials . . . from the Earliest Period to . . . 1783.* 34 vols. London, 1816–28.

Massachusetts. Divorces, 1760–1786. 1 vol. Office of the Clerk of the Supreme Judicial Court, New Suffolk County Court House, Boston.

New Hampshire. "New Hampshire Court Records, 1640–1692." In

Documents and Records Relating to the Province of New-Hampshire.
Vol. XL. Ed. Otis G. Hammond. Concord, N.H., 1943.

Boston. *Records Relating to the Early History of Boston.* Ed. William H.
Whitmore *et al.* 30 vols. Boston, 1876–1909. Vols. I–XXII issued as
Reports of the Record Commissioners of the City of Boston.

Braintree. *Records of the Town of Braintree, 1640–1793.* Ed. Samuel A.
Bates. Randolph, Mass., 1886.

Brookline. *Muddy River and Brookline Records, 1634–1838.* n.p., 1875.

Cambridge. *The Records of the Town of Cambridge, 1630–1703.* Cambridge, Mass., 1901.

Dedham. *Early Records of the Town of Dedham, Massachusetts.* Ed. Dow
G. Hill. 5 vols. Dedham, 1892–99.

Derby. *Town Records of Derby, Connecticut, 1655–1710.* Derby, 1901.

Dorchester. *Dorchester Town Records: Fourth Report of the Record Commissioners of the City of Boston.* Boston, 1880. (Vol. IV of Boston,
Records.)

Dudley. *Town Records of Dudley, Massachusetts, 1732–1794.* 2 vols. in 1.
Pawtucket, R.I., 1893–94.

Duxbury. *Old Records of the Town of Duxbury, Massachusetts, 1642–
1770.* Plymouth, Mass., 1893.

Fitchburg. *The Old Records of the Town of Fitchburg, Massachusetts.*
Comp. Walter A. Davis. 4 vols. Fitchburg, 1898–1913.

Groton. *The Early Records of Groton, 1662–1707.* Ed. Samuel A. Green.
Groton, Mass., 1880.

Lancaster. *The Early Records of Lancaster, Massachusetts, 1643–1725*
Ed. Henry S. Nourse. Lancaster, 1884.

New Haven. *New Haven Town Records, 1649–1684.* Ed. Franklin B.
Dexter. 2 vols. New Haven, 1917–19.

Plymouth. *Records of the Town of Plymouth.* 3 vols. Plymouth, Mass.,
1889–1903.

Watertown. *Watertown Records Comprising the First and Second Books
of Town Proceedings. . . .* Watertown, Mass., 1894.

Worcester. *Early Records of the Town of Worcester.* Ed. Franklin P. Rice.
3 vols. Worcester Society of Antiquity, *Collections,* vols. II–IV. Worcester, Mass., 1879–82.

Massachusetts

Bibliography. Oberholzer, Emil, Jr. *Delinquent Saints.* New York, 1956.

Pp. 337–55. The records of the following Massachusetts churches were consulted in the course of research for this volume: Beverly, Boston (Old South), Cambridge, Charlestown, Chelsea, Dedham, Dorchester, Groton, Lynnfield, Plymouth, Sharon, and Weston. They are listed by title in Oberholzer's volume under the name of the town.

In addition the following Massachusetts church records were examined:

Boston. *Records of the Church in Brattle Square, Boston, 1699–1872.* Boston, 1902.

    The Records of the First Church in Boston, 1630–1868. Ed. Richard D. Pierce. 3 vols. Colonial Society of Massachusetts, *Publications,* vols. XXXIX–XLI. Boston, 1961.

Connecticut

Bibliography. *List of Church Records on Deposit at Connecticut State Library.* Connecticut State Library, Bulletin no. 19. Hartford, 1951.

New Haven. First Congregational Church of New Haven. Records, 1639–1926. Vol. I. "Minutes of Church Meetings and Proceedings 1644–1806." Connecticut State Library.

Windsor. First Congregational Church, Windsor, Connecticut. Records, 1636–1932. Vol. XV. "Church Discipline, 1723–1747." Connecticut State Library.

Personal and Family Papers

Bibliography. "The Manuscript Collections of the Massachusetts Historical Society: A Brief Listing." *M.H.S. Miscellany,* no. 5. Boston, 1958.

Amory Papers, 1698–1784. 1 vol. Massachusetts Historical Society.

Andrews-Eliot Papers, 1771–1811. 1 vol. MHS. Pp. 1–58 are the letters of John Andrews, Boston to William Barrell, Philadelphia, 1771–76. Partially reprinted in Massachusetts Historical Society, *Proceedings,* VIII (1865), 316–412.

Benjamin Colman Papers, 1697–1763. 2 vols. MHS.

Dana Family Papers and Dana Manuscripts. Several boxes. MHS.

John Davis Papers, 1627–1747. 2 vols. MHS.

Dow Papers, 1643–1825. 1 vol. MHS.

Jeffries Family Papers. 33 vols. MHS.

Thomas Prince Papers. 1 vol. MHS.

Winthrop Papers. *Ca.* 65 vols. for the colonial era. MHS.

Winthrop Papers. Ed. Allyn B. Forbes *et al.* 5 vols. to date. Boston. 1929–.

Contemporary Works

Bibliography. *American Diaries: An Annotated Bibliography of American*

Diaries Written Prior to the Year 1861. Comp. William Matthews. Berkeley, Calif., 1945. Rpt. Boston, 1959.

Adams, Charles Francis (ed.). *Antinomianism in the Colony of Massachusetts Bay, 1636–1638.* Boston, 1894.

Adams, John. *Diary and Autobiography of John Adams.* Ed. L. H. Butterfield *et al.* 4 vols. Cambridge, Mass., 1961.

——. *Legal Papers of John Adams.* Ed. L. Kinvin Wroth and Hiller B. Zobel. 3 vols. Cambridge, Mass., 1965.

American Husbandry. 2 vols. London, 1775. Ed. Harry J. Carman. New York, 1939.

Ames, William. *Conscience with the Power and Cases Thereof . . . Translated out of Latine into English.* London, 1643.

Barnard, Sir John. *A Present for an Apprentice.* London, 1740. Rpt. Boston, 1747.

Bennett, Joseph. "The History of New England, 1740." Sparks Manuscripts, Houghton Library, Harvard University. Partially reprinted in Massachusetts Historical Society, *Proceedings*, V (1860–62), 108–26.

Bernard, Rev. Richard. *A Guide to Grand-Jury Men.* 2d ed., London, 1629.

Birket, James. *Some Cursory Remarks Made by James Birket.* New Haven, 1916.

Boone, Nicholas. *The Constable's Pocket Book; or, A Dialogue, between an Old Constable and a New.* Boston, 1710, Rpt. 1727.

Boston. *A Compleat Body of the Rules, Orders and By-Laws of the Town of Boston, to This Present Time.* Boston, 1758.

Bownde, Dr. Nicholas. *The Doctrine of the Sabbath.* London, 1595. 2d ed., London, 1606.

Bradford, William. *Of Plymouth Plantation.* Ed. Samuel E. Morison. New York, 1952.

Burkitt, William. *The Poor Man's Help, and Young Man's Guide.* Boston, 1731. Rpt. of 8th English ed. of 1693.

Burnaby, Rev. Andrew. *Travels through the Middle Settlements in North America, in the Years 1759 and 1760; with Observations upon the State of the Colonies.* 3d ed. rev., London, 1798.

Calvin, John. *Institutes of the Christian Religion.* Ed. John T. McNeill. 2 vols. The Library of Christian Classics, vols. XX–XXI. Philadelphia, 1960.

Cambridge. Synod, 1648. *A Platform of Church Discipline Gathered out of the Word of God, and Agreed Upon by the Elders, and Messengers of the Churches Assembled in the Synod at Cambridge in New England.* Cambridge, Mass., 1649; rpt., London, 1653.

Chastellux, Marquis de. *Travels in North America in the Years 1780,*

1781 and 1782. Tr. and ed. Howard C. Rice, Jr. 2 vols. Chapel Hill, N.C., 1963.

Chronicles of the Pilgrim Fathers. Everyman's Library. London, 1910–11.

Clap, Rev. Thomas. *The Greatness and Difficulty of the Work of the Ministry.* Boston, 1732.

Clarke, John. *Paroemiologia Anglo-Latina . . . ; or, Proverbs English and Latin.* London, 1639.

Cleaver, Robert. *A Godlie Forme of Household Government.* London, 1598. Rpt. London, 1603.

Cooper, Samuel. *The Crisis.* Boston, 1754.

The County and Town Officer. Boston, 1768.

Cummings, Abbott L. (ed.). *Rural Household Inventories, 1675–1775.* Boston, 1964.

Dalton, Michael. *The Countrey Justice, Containing the Practice of the Justices of the Peace out of Their Sessions, Gathered for the Better Help of Such Justices of Peace As Have Not Been Much Conversant in the Studie of the Lawes of This Realme.* London, 1618. Numerous editions to 1742.

Danforth, Samuel. *The Duty of Believers to Oppose the Growth of the Kingdom of Sin.* Boston, 1708.

———. *Piety Encouraged.* Boston, 1705.

Dummer, Jeremiah. *A Discourse on the Holiness of the Sabbath Day.* Boston, 1704. Rpt. Boston, 1763.

Dunton, John. *Letters Written from New England, A.D. 1686.* Ed. William H. Whitmore. Boston, 1867.

———. *The Life and Errors of John Dunton.* London, 1705.

Edwards, Jonathan. *An Humble Inquiry . . . Concerning the Qualifications Requisite to a Compleat Standing and Full Communion in the Visible Christian Church.* Boston, 1749.

Eliot, Andrew. *An Evil and Adulterous Generation.* Boston, 1753.

Finlay, Hugh. *Journal Kept by Hugh Finlay, Surveyor of the Post Roads on the Continent of North America, during His Survey of the Post Offices between Falmouth and Casco Bay in the Province of Massachusetts, and Savannah in Georgia; Begun the 13th September 1773 and Ended 26th June 1774.* Brooklyn, 1867.

Fiske, Rev. John. "Notebook of Church Matters, 1637–1675." Typescript. Essex Institute. Salem, Mass.

Hamilton, Dr. Alexander. *Gentleman's Progress: The Itinerarium of Dr. Alexander Hamilton, 1774.* Ed. Carl Bridenbaugh. Chapel Hill, N.C., 1948.

Hempstead, Joshua. *Diary of Joshua Hempstead of New London, Connecticut Covering a Period of Forty-Seven Years from September,*

1711, to November, 1758. New London County Historical Society, *Collections*, vol. I. New London and Providence, 1901.

The Holyoke Diaries, 1709–1856. Ed. George F. Dow. Salem, Mass., 1911.

Hooker, Thomas. *A Survey of the Summe of Church-Discipline.* London, 1648.

Hutchinson, Thomas. *The History of the Colony and Province of Massachusetts Bay.* Ed. Lawrence Shaw Mayo. 3 vols. Cambridge, Mass., 1936.

Johnson, Edward. *A History of New England: The Wonder-Working Providence of Sions Saviour in New England.* London, 1654. In *Original Narratives of Early American History.* Ed. J. Franklin Jameson. New York, 1910.

Josselyn, John. *An Account of Two Voyages to New England Made during the Years 1638, 1663.* London, 1675. Rpt. Boston, 1865.

Kalm, Peter. *Peter Kalm's Travels in North America: The English Version of 1770.* Ed. Adolph B. Benson. 2 vols. New York, 1937.

Knight, Sarah Kemble. *The Journal of Madam Knight, 1704.* Ed. George P. Winship. Boston, 1920.

Lambarde, William. *The Duties of Constables, Borsholders, Tythingmen, and Such Other Lowe and Lay Ministers of the Peace.* London, 1583, Rev. ed., London, 1614.

———. *Eirenarcha; or, Of the Office of the Justices of Peace, in Foure Bookes.* London, 1581. Rev. ed., London, 1614. Rpt. 1619.

Lechford, Thomas. "Note-Book Kept by Thomas Lechford, Esq., Lawyer, in Boston," 1638–41. *Transactions and Collections of the American Antiquarian Society*, VII (1885).

———. *Plain Dealing; or, Newes from New-England.* London, 1642. In Massachusetts Historical Society, *Collections*, 3d ser., III (1833), 55–128.

Livingston, William. *Philosophic Solitude; or, The Choice of a Rural Life. A Poem.* New York, 1747. Rpt. Boston, 1762.

Mather, Cotton. *Bonifacius: An Essay upon the Good.* Boston, 1710. Ed. David Levin. Cambridge, Mass., 1966.

———. *The Day Which the Lord Has Made.* Boston, 1703. Rpt. Boston, 1707.

———. *The Diary of Cotton Mather.* Ed. Worthington C. Ford. 2 vols. Massachusetts Historical Society, *Collections*, 7th ser., VII–VIII (1911–12). Rpt. New York, 1957.

———. *Ecclesiastes: The Life . . . of Jonathan Mitchell.* Boston, 1697.

———. *A Faithful Monitor.* Boston, 1704.

———. *A Family Well-Ordered.* Boston, 1699.

———. *A Good Evening for the Best of Days.* Boston, 1708.

———. *A Good Master Well Served.* Boston, 1696.

——. *Magnalia Christi Americana*. London, 1702. Ed. Thomas Robins. 2 vols. Hartford, 1853–55.

——. *Methods and Motives for Societies to Suppress Disorders*. Boston, 1703.

——. *A Monitory Letter*. Boston, 1702. 2d. ed., Boston, 1738.

——. *Private Meetings Animated and Regulated*. Boston, 1706.

——. *Ratio Disciplinae Fratrum Nov-Anglorum. A Faithful Account of the Discipline Professed and Practised in the Churches of New England*. Boston, 1726.

——. *The Religion of An Oath*. Boston, 1719.

——. *The Religion of the Closet*. Boston, 1705. 2d ed., Boston, 1706.

——. *The Rules of a Visit*. Boston, 1705.

——. *Winter-Meditations*. Boston, 1693.

Mather, Increase. "The Autobiography of Increase Mather." Ed. Michael G. Hall. American Antiquarian Society, *Proceedings*, LXXI (1961), 271–360.

——. *The Day of Trouble*. Cambridge, Mass., 1674.

——. *The First Principles of New England*. Cambridge, Mass., 1675.

——. *The Order of the Gospel*. Boston, 1700.

——. *Wo to Drunkards*. Cambridge, Mass., 1673. 2d. ed., Boston, 1712.

Miranda, Francisco de. *The New Democracy in America: Travels of Francisco de Miranda in the United States, 1783–1784*. Tr. Judson P. Wood. Ed. John S. Ezell. Norman, Okla., 1963.

Morton, Nathaniel. *New England's Memorial*. Cambridge, Mass., 1669. In *Chronicles of the Pilgrim Fathers*. Everyman's Library. London, 1910–11. Pp. 1–224.

Morton, Thomas. *New English Canaan*. Amsterdam, 1637.

Mourt's Relation: A Journal of the Pilgrims at Plymouth. Ed. Dwight B. Heath. New York, 1963.

Narratives of the Witchcraft Cases, 1648–1706. Ed. George L. Burr. New York, 1914.

Norton, John. *The Answer to the Whole Set of Questions of the Celebrated Mr. William Apollonius, Looking toward the Resolution of Certain Controversies Concerning Church Government Now Being Agitated in England*. London, 1648. Ed. and tr. Douglas Horton. Cambridge, Mass., 1958.

Parkman, Ebenezer. "The Diary of Ebenezer Parkman," 1719–. Ed. Francis G. Walett. American Antiquarian Society, *Proceedings*, LXXI (1961), 93–227, 361–448, LXXII (1962), 31–233, 329–481, LXXIII (1963), 46–120, 386–464, LXXIV (1964), 37–203, LXXV (1965), 49–199, LXXVI (1966), 71–201.

Penn, William. *Some Fruits of Solitude*. 8th ed. Newport, 1749.

"Post Office Department," Documents, 1639–1775. Massachusetts Historical Society, *Collections*, 3d ser., VII (1838), 48–89.

Prince, Thomas. *The Vade Mecum for America; or, A Companion for Traders and Travellers.* Boston, 1731.

Records of Salem Witchcraft, Copied from the Original Documents. Ed. W. Elliott Wodward. 2 vols. Boston, 1864.

Reyce, Robert. *Suffolk in the Seventeenth Century: The Breviary of Suffolk, by Robert Reyce, 1618.* London, 1902.

The School of Good Manners. New London, Conn., 1715. Rpt. Boston, 1772.

Seccombe, Joseph. *Business and Diversion Inoffensive to God, and Necessary for the Comfort and Support of Human Society.* Boston, 1743.

Sewall, Samuel. *The Diary of Samuel Sewall.* Massachusetts Historical Society, *Collections*, 5th ser., V–VII. Boston, 1878–82.

Stiles, Ezra. *A Discourse on the Christian Union.* Boston, 1761.

——. *Extracts from the Itineraries and Other Miscellanies of Ezra Stiles, D.D., LL.D., 1755–1794, with a Selection from His Correspondence.* Ed. Franklin B. Dexter. New Haven, 1916.

Stoddard, Solomon. *An Answer to Some Cases of Conscience Respecting the Country.* Boston, 1722.

——. *An Appeal to the Learned.* Boston, 1709.

——. *The Danger of Speedy Degeneracy.* Boston, 1705.

——. *The Duty of Gospel Ministers to Preserve a People from Corruption.* Boston, 1718.

——. *The Necessity of Acknowledgment.* Boston, 1701.

——. *The Presence of Christ with the Ministers of the Gospel.* Boston, 1718.

——. *Way for a People to Live Long in the Land That God Hath Given Them.* Boston, 1703.

Symmes, Thomas. *A Monitor for Delaying Sinners.* Boston, 1719.

Two Centuries of Travel in Essex County, Massachusetts: A Collection of Narratives and Observations Made by Travellers 1605–1799. Ed. George F. Dow. Topsfield, Mass., 1921.

Wadsworth, Benjamin. *Assembling at the House of God.* Boston, 1711.

——. *An Essay to Do Good: By a Dissuasive from Tavern-haunting and Excessive Drinking.* Boston, 1710.

——. *The Well-Ordered Family.* Boston, 1712. 2d. ed., Boston, 1719.

Walker, Williston. *The Creeds and Platforms of Congregationalism.* New York, 1893. Rpt. Boston, 1960.

Ward, Edward. *Boston in 1682 and 1699: A Trip to New England by Edward Ward and A Letter from New England by J. W.* London, 1699. Ed. George P. Winship. Providence, 1905.

Ward, Nathaniel. *Simple Cobler of Aggawam*. London, 1647. Rpt. Boston, 1713.

Winthrop, John. *The History of New England from 1630 to 1649*. Ed. James Savage. 2 vols. Boston, 1826.

——. "A Short Story of the Rise, Reign, and Ruine of the Antinomians." London, 1644. In *Antinomianism in the Colony of Massachusetts Bay, 1636–1638*. Ed. Charles F. Adams. Boston, 1894. Pp. 71–233.

——. *Winthrop's Journal: "History of New England," 1630–1649*. Ed. James K. Hosmer. 2 vols. New York, 1908.

Young, Alexander. *Chronicles of the First Planters of the Colony of the Massachusetts Bay, from 1623 to 1636*. Boston, 1846.

STATISTICS

The Massachusetts Census of 1764 listed the following information for each of 200 towns in the Massachusetts Bay Colony, which included what is now the state of Maine: number of houses; number of families; number of white males under and over 16 years of age; number of white females under and over 16 years of age; number of male and female Negroes; number of male and female Indians; number of male neutrals (Acadians) under and over 16 years of age; number of female neutrals (Acadians) under and over 16 years of age. This census was begun in 1763 and finished in 1764. No known compilation of the data existed until a manuscript copy was found in 1822, the Dana MS. Another manuscript copy, the Crane MS, was not discovered until the twentieth century. Benton argued convincingly that the Crane MS was a more complete version of the original returns. The data employed in this study, exclusive of any totals, was derived principally from the Crane MS, as printed in Josiah H. Benton, Jr., *Early Census Making in Massachusetts (1643–1765) with a Reproduction of the Lost Census of 1765* (Boston, 1905). Some data missing in the Crane MS was found in the Dana MS as printed in Joseph B. Felt, "Statistics of Population in Massachusetts," *American Statistical Association, Collections*, I (1845), pt. 2.

From the census data information was obtained by town, county, and colony and employed in Tables 3–4, 6–7, and 9 for each of the following items: total population; average number of white persons per family; average number of all persons per family; average number of all persons per house; average number of families per house; percentage of families living in dual-occupancy homes. The methodology to be employed was clear, except in the last instance. The definition of a family employed by the census takers is unclear from the official record. It appears that the term connotes a nuclear family, normally composed of husband, wife, and children. A widow or widower and children also were a family. In almost all towns the number of families was more than the number of houses. I figured the surplus of families over houses as a percentage of the total families in the town, and then multiplied this percentage of surplus families by two to obtain the percentage of families living together in dual-occupancy homes in any one town. This assumed that no more than two families ever lived together; each of the surplus families shared the home of a family for which a house was available. This assumption seems relatively safe, although not totally accurate for reasons discussed in the text of this study.

ARCHITECTURE AND TOWN PLANNING

Bridenbaugh, Carl. *Peter Harrison: First American Architect*. Chapel Hill, N.C., 1949.

Brightman, Anna. "Window Curtains in Colonial Boston and Salem." *Antiques*, LXXXVI (1964), 184–87.

Brown, Ralph H. *Historical Geography of the United States*. New York, 1948.

Cady, John Hutchins. *The Civic and Architectural Development of Providence, 1636–1950*. Providence, 1957.

Chermayeff, Serge, and Christopher Alexander. *Community and Privacy: Toward a New Architecture of Humanism*. Garden City, N.Y. 1963.

Connally, Ernest Allen. "The Cape Cod House, an Introductory Study." *Journal of the Society of Architectural Historians*, XIX (1960), 47–56.

Cummings, Abbott Lowell. *Architecture in Early New England*. Sturbridge, Mass., 1958.

Downing, Antoinette F., and Vincent J. Scully, Jr. *The Architectural Heritage of Newport, Rhode Island, 1640–1915*. Cambridge, Mass., 1952.

Eberlein, Harold D. "The Seventeenth-Century Connecticut House." *White Pine Series of Architectural Monographs*, V (Feb. 1919), no. 1, 3–14.

Gardner, George W. "Some Early 'Single Room Houses' of Lincoln, Rhode Island." *Pencil Points*, XVI (Feb. 1935), 93–108.

Garrett, Wendell D. (ed.). "Note on 'Plan of an American Country Town,' 1769–1770." *Old Time New England*, LIII (1962), 11–16.

Garvan, Anthony N. B. *Architecture and Town Planning in Colonial Connecticut*. New Haven, 1951.

Greven, Philip J., Jr. "Old Patterns in the New World: The Distribution of Land in 17th Century Andover." Essex Institute, *Historical Collections*, CI (1965), 133–148.

Isham, Norman M., and Albert F. Brown. *Early Connecticut Houses*. Providence, 1900.

——. *Early Rhode Island Houses*. Providence, 1895.

Kelly, John Frederick. *The Early Domestic Architecture of Connecticut.* New York, 1924.

Kennedey, Robert Woods. *The House, and the Art of Its Design.* New York, 1953.

Kimball, Sidney Fiske. *Domestic Architecture of the American Colonies.* New York, 1922.

Morris, F. Grave. "Some Aspects of the Rural Settlement of New England in Colonial Times." In *London Essays in Geography.* Ed. L. D. Stamp and S. W. Woldridge. London, 1951. Pp. 219–27.

Morrison, Hugh S. *Early American Architecture, from the First Colonial Settlements to the National Period.* New York, 1952.

Reps, John W. *The Making of Urban America: A History of City Planning in the United States.* Princeton, N.J., 1965.

Rogers, Meyric R. *American Interior Design: The Tradition and Development of Domestic Design from Colonial Times to the Present.* New York, 1947.

Roos, Frank J., Jr. *Writings on Early American Architecture: An Annotated List of Books and Articles on Architecture Constructed before 1860 in the Eastern Half of the United States.* Columbus, Ohio, 1943.

Scofield, Edna. "The Origin of Settlement Patterns in Rural New England." *Geographical Review,* XXVII (1938), 652–63.

Shurtleff, Harold R. *The Log Cabin Myth: A Study of the Early Dwellings of the English Colonists in North America.* Cambridge, Mass., 1939.

Thwing, Annie H. *The Crooked and Narrow Streets of the Town of Boston, 1630–1822.* Boston, 1930.

Thompson, Edmund B. *Maps of Connecticut before the Year 1800: a Descriptive List.* Windham, Conn., 1940.

Trewartha, Glenn T. "Types of Rural Settlement in Colonial America." *Geographical Review,* XXXVI (1946), 568–96.

Waterman, Thomas Tileston. *The Dwellings of Colonial America.* Chapel Hill, N.C., 1950.

Waters, Thomas Franklin. "The Early Homes of the Puritans." Essex Institute, *Historical Collections,* XXXIII (1898), 45–79.

Whitehill, Walter Muir. *Boston: A Topographical History.* Cambridge, Mass., 1959.

Social History

Adams, Charles Francis. *Three Episodes of Massachusetts History.* 2 vols. 5th ed., Boston, 1896.

Ariès, Philippe. *Centuries of Childhood: A Social History of Family Life.* Tr. Roger Baldick. New York, 1962.

Bailyn, Bernard. *The New England Merchants in the Seventeenth Century.* Cambridge, Mass., 1955.

Baker, Herschel C. *The Image of Man: A Study of the Idea of Human Dignity in Classical Antiquity, the Middle Ages, and the Renaissance.* Cambridge, Mass., 1947.

Bash, Wendell Hubbard. "Factors Influencing Family and Community Organization in a New England Town, 1730–1940." Ph.D. diss. Harvard University, 1941.

Battis, Emery. *Saints and Sectaries: Anne Hutchinson and the Antinomian Controversy in the Massachusetts Bay Colony.* Chapel Hill, N.C., 1962.

Benton, Josiah Henry. *Warning Out in New England.* Boston, 1911.

Blumenthal, Albert. *Small Town Stuff.* Chicago, 1932.

Bowen, Richard Le Baron. *Early Rehoboth: Documented Historical Studies of Families and Events in This Plymouth Colony Township.* 4 vols. Concord, N.H., 1945–50.

Bridenbaugh, Carl. *Cities in Revolt: Urban Life in America, 1743–1776.* New York, 1955.

——. *Cities in the Wilderness: The First Century of Urban Life in America, 1625–1742.* New York, 1938.

Bushman, Richard Lyman. *From Puritan to Yankee: Character and the Social Order in Connecticut, 1690–1765* (Cambridge, Mass., 1967).

Calder, Isabel M. *The New Haven Colony.* New Haven, 1934.

Calhoun, Arthur W. *A Social History of the American Family.* 3 vols. Cleveland, 1917–19.

Clark, Charles E. *The Eastern Frontier: The Settlement of Northern New England, 1610–1763.* New York, 1970.

Cole, Arthur H. "The Tempo of Mercantile Life in Colonial America." *Business History Review,* XXXIII (1959), 277–99.

Coolidge, J. Linzee. "Aspects of Puritan Morality: Personal Conduct and Civil Authority in Hampshire County, Massachusetts, 1660–1727." Master's thesis. Columbia University, 1964. Copy at Massachusetts Historical Society.

Dawes, Norman H. "Social Classes in Seventeenth-Century New England." Ph.D. diss. 2 vols. Harvard University, 1940–41.

Demos, John. "Families in Colonial Bristol, Rhode Island." *William and Mary Quarterly,* 3d. ser., XXV (1968), 40–57.

——. *A Little Commonwealth: Family Life in Plymouth Colony.* New York, 1970.

——. "Notes on Life in Plymouth Colony." *William and Mary Quarterly,* 3d. ser., XXII (1965), 264–86.

Doten, Dana. *The Art of Bundling.* New York, 1938.

Dow, George Francis. *Domestic Life in New England in the Seventeenth Century*. Topsfield, Mass., 1925.

——. *Every Day Life in the Massachusetts Bay Colony*. Boston, 1935.

Dunn, Richard S. *Puritans and Yankees: The Winthrop Dynasty of New England, 1630–1717*. Princeton, N.J., 1962.

Earle, Alice Morse. *The Sabbath in Puritan New England*. 8th ed., Boston, 1896.

Erikson, Kai T. *Wayward Puritans: A Study in the Sociology of Deviance*. New York, 1966.

Friis, Herman R. "A Series of Population Maps of the Colonies and the United States, 1625–1790." American Geographical Society Mimeographed and Offset Publication no. 3. New York, 1940. Rev. ed., New York, 1968.

Goodsell, Willystine. *A History of Marriage and the Family*. Rev. ed. New York, 1934.

Grant, Charles S. *Democracy in the Connecticut Frontier Town of Kent*. New York, 1961.

Greene, Evarts B., and Virginia Harrington. *American Population before the Federal Census of 1790*. New York, 1932.

Greene, Lorenzo J. *The Negro in Colonial New England, 1620–1776*. New York, 1942.

Greven, Philip J., Jr. "Family Structure in Andover." *William and Mary Quarterly*, 3d ser., XXIII (1966), 234–56.

——. *Four Generations: Population, Land, and Family in Colonial Andover, Massachusetts*. Ithaca, N.Y., 1970.

Hall, Edward T. *The Hidden Dimension*. Garden City, N.Y., 1966.

Halmos, Paul. *Solitude and Privacy*. London, 1952.

Handlin, Oscar and Mary. *The Dimensions of Liberty*. Cambridge, Mass., 1961.

Hansen, Chadwick. *Witchcraft at Salem*. New York, 1969.

Howard, George E. *History of Matrimonial Institutions*. 3 vols. Chicago, 1904.

Jones, Mary Jeanne Anderson. *Congregational Commonwealth: Connecticut, 1636–1662*. Middletown, Conn., 1968.

Judd, Sylvester. *History of Hadley*. Northampton, Mass., 1863.

Langdon, George D., Jr. *Pilgrim Colony: A History of New Plymouth, 1620–1691*. New Haven, 1966.

Lockridge, Kenneth A. "Land, Population and the Evolution of New England Society, 1630–1790." *Past and Present*, no. 39 (April 1968), pp. 62–80.

——. *A New England Town: The First Hundred Years*. New York, 1970.

——. "The Population of Dedham, Massachusetts, 1636–1736." *Economic History Review*, 2d ser., XIX (1966), 318–44.

Lynes, Russell. *The Domesticated Americans*. New York, 1963.

MacLear, Anne B. *Early New England Towns: A Comparative Study of Their Development*. New York, 1908.

Main, Jackson Turner. *The Social Structure of Revolutionary America*. Princeton, N.J., 1965.

Merrill, Louis Taylor. "The Puritan Policeman." *American Sociological Review*, X (1945), 766–76.

Miner, Horace. *St. Denis: A French Canadian Parish*. Chicago, 1939.

Miner, Ward L. *William Goddard, Newspaperman*. Durham, N.C., 1962.

Morison, Samuel E. *Builders of the Bay Colony*. Rev. ed. Boston, 1964.

Morgan, Edmund S. *The Gentle Puritan: A Life of Ezra Stiles, 1727–1795*. Chapel Hill, N.C., 1962.

——. *The Puritan Dilemma: The Story of John Winthrop*. Boston, 1958.

——. *The Puritan Family: Essays on Religion and Domestic Relations in Seventeenth-Century New England*. Boston, 1944. Rev. paperback ed. New York, 1966.

—— (ed.). "The Colonial Scene, 1602–1800." American Antiquarian Society, *Proceedings*, LX (1950), 53–160.

Morris, Richard B. *Government and Labor in Early America*. New York, 1946.

Parkes, Henry Bamford. "New England in the Seventeen-Thirties." *New England Quarterly*, III (1930), 397–419.

Powell, Sumner Chilton. *Puritan Village: The Formation of a New England Town*. Middletown, Conn., 1963.

Rich, Wesley Everett. *The History of the United States Post Office to the Year 1829*. Cambridge, Mass., 1924.

Rutman, Darrett B. *Husbandmen of Plymouth: Farms and Villages in the Old Colony, 1620–1692*. Boston, 1967.

——. *Winthrop's Boston: Portrait of a Puritan Town, 1630–1649*. Chapel Hill, N.C., 1965.

Shipton, Clifford K. *New England Life in the Eighteenth Century; Representative Biographies from Sibley's Harvard Graduates*. Cambridge, Mass., 1963.

——. *Sibley's Harvard Graduates: Biographical Sketches of Those Who Attended Harvard College. . . .* 15 vols. to date. Boston, 1873–.

Sly, John Fairfield. *Town Government in Massachusetts, 1620–1930*. Cambridge, Mass., 1930.

Smith, Abbot E. *Colonists in Bondage: White Servitude and Convict Labor in America, 1607–1776*. Chapel Hill, N.C., 1947.

Smith, Bradford. *Bradford of Plymouth*. Philadelphia, 1951.

Select Bibliography

269

LEGAL HISTORY

Billias, George A. (ed.). *Law and Authority in Colonial America*. Barre, Mass., 1965.

Bloustein, Edward J. "Privacy as an Aspect of Human Dignity: An Answer to Dean Prosser." *New York University Law Review*, XXXIX (1964), 962–1007.

Breckenridge, Adam Carlyle. *The Right to Privacy*. Lincoln, Nebr., 1970.

Farrell, John Thomas. "The Administration of Justice in Connecticut about the Middle of the 18th Century." Ph.D. diss. Yale University, 1937.

Frese, Joseph R. "Writs of Assistance in the American Colonies, 1660–1776." Ph.D. diss. Harvard University, 1951.

Flaherty, David H. "Law and the Enforcement of Morals in Early America." In *Perspectives in American History*. Ed. Donald Fleming and Bernard Bailyn. Vol. V. Cambridge, Mass., 1971. Pp. 201–53.

———. (ed.). *Essays in the History of Early American Law*. Chapel Hill, N.C., 1969.

Haskins, George Lee. *Law and Authority in Early Massachusetts*. New York, 1960.

———. "Precedents in English Ecclesiastical Practices for Criminal Punishments in Early Massachusetts." In *Essays in Legal History in Honor of Felix Frankfurter*. Ed. Morris D. Forkosch. Indianapolis, 1966. Pp. 321–36.

Hoebel, E. Adamson. *The Law of Primitive Man: A Study in Comparative Legal Dynamics*. Cambridge, Mass., 1954.

Hofstadter, Samuel H. and George Horowitz. *The Right of Privacy*. New York, 1964.

Holdsworth, William S. *A History of English Law*. Vol. IX. London, 1926.

Jardine, David. *A Reading on the Use of Torture in the Criminal Law of England, Previously to the Commonwealth*. London, 1837.

Lasson, Nelson B. *The History and Development of the Fourth Amendment to the United States Constitution*. Baltimore, 1937.

Lea, Henry Charles. *Superstition and Force: Essays on The Wager of Law, The Wager of Battle, The Ordeal, Torture*. 4th ed. rev., Philadelphia, 1892.

Levy, Leonard W. *Origins of the Fifth Amendment: The Right against Self-Incrimination*. New York, 1968.

———, and Lawrence H. Leder. " 'Exotic Fruit': The Right against Compulsory Self-Incrimination in Colonial New York." *William and Mary Quarterly*, 3d. ser., XX (1963), 3–32.

Morgan, E. M. "The Privilege against Self-Incrimination." *Minnesota Law Review*, XXXIV (1949–50), 1–45.

Morris, Richard Brandon. *Studies in the History of American Law.* New York, 1930. 2d. ed., New York, 1964.

Page, Elwin L. *Judicial Beginnings in New Hampshire, 1640–1700.* Concord, N. H., 1959.

Parkes, Henry Bamford. "Morals and Law Enforcement in Colonial New England." *New England Quarterly,* V (1932), 431–52.

Pittman, R. Carter. "The Colonial and Constitutional Privilege against Self-Incrimination in America." *Virginia Law Review,* XXI (1935), 763–89.

Powers, Edwin. *Crime and Punishment in Early Massachusetts, 1620–1692: A Documentary History.* Boston, 1966.

Riesenfeld, Stefan A. "Law Making and Legislative Precedent in American Legal History." *Minnesota Law Review,* XXXIII (1949), 103–44.

Thompson, Faith. *Magna Carta: Its Role in the Making of the English Constitution, 1300–1629.* Minneapolis, 1948.

Warren, Samuel D., and Louis D. Brandeis. "The Right to Privacy." *Harvard Law Review,* IV (1890), 191–220.

Westin, Alan F. *Privacy and Freedom.* New York, 1967.

Wigmore, John Henry. *A Treatise on the Anglo-American System of Evidence in Trials at Common Law.* 10 vols. 3d ed., Boston, 1940.

Wolkins, George G. "Malcom and Writs of Assistance." Massachusetts Historical Society, *Proceedings.* 5th ser., LVIII (1924–25), 5–84.

Younger, Richard D. *The People's Panel: The Grand Jury in the United States, 1634–1941.* Providence, 1963.

RELIGIOUS HISTORY

Akers, Charles W. *Called unto Liberty: A Life of Jonathan Mayhew, 1720–1766.* Cambridge, Mass., 1964.

Boas, Ralph P., and Louise Boas. *Cotton Mather, Keeper of the Puritan Conscience.* New York, 1928.

Cross, Wilford Oakland. "The Role and Status of the Unregenerate in the Massachusetts Bay Colony, 1629–1729." Ph.D. diss. Columbia University, 1957.

Fulcher, J. Rodney. "Puritan Piety in Early New England: A Study in Spiritual Regeneration from the Antinomian Controversy to the Cambridge Synod of 1648 in the Massachusetts Bay Colony." Ph.D. diss. Princeton University, 1963.

Middlekauf, Robert. *The Mathers: Three Generations of Puritan Intellectuals, 1596–1728.* New York, 1971.

Miller, Perry. "The Half-Way Covenant." *New England Quarterly,* VI (1933), 676–715.

———. *Jonathan Edwards.* New York, 1949.

———. *The New England Mind: From Colony to Province.* New York, 1953.

———. *The New England Mind: The Seventeenth Century.* New York, 1939.

———. *Orthodoxy in Massachusetts, 1630–1650.* Boston, 1933.

———. "Preparation for Salvation in Seventeenth-Century New England." *Journal of the History of Ideas,* IV (1943), 253–86.

Morgan, Edmund S. *Roger Williams: The Church and the State.* New York, 1967.

———. *Visible Saints: The History of a Puritan Idea.* New York, 1963.

Murdock, Kenneth Ballard. *Increase Mather: The Foremost American Puritan.* Cambridge, Mass., 1925.

Nuttall, Geoffrey. *Visible Saints: The Congregational Way, 1640–1660.* Oxford, 1957.

Oberholzer, Emil, Jr. *Delinquent Saints: Disciplinary Action in the Early Congregational Churches of Massachusetts.* New York, 1956.

Pettit, Norman. *The Heart Prepared: Grace and Conversion in Puritan Spiritual Life.* New Haven, 1966.

Pope, Robert G. *The Half-Way Covenant.* Princeton, N.J., 1969.

Robinson, Lewis M. "A History of the Half-Way Covenant." Ph.D. diss. University of Illinois, 1963.

Rutman, Darrett B. *American Puritanism: Faith and Practice.* Philadelphia, 1970.

Seidman, Aaron. "Church and State in the Early Years of the Massachusetts Bay Colony." *New England Quarterly,* XVIII (1945), 211–33.

Shipton, Clifford K. "The New England Clergy of the 'Glacial Age.'" Colonial Society of Massachusetts, *Publications,* XXXII (1937), 24–54.

Stearns, Raymond R., and David H. Brawner. "New England Church 'Relations' and Continuity in Early Congregational History." American Antiquarian Society, *Proceedings,* LXXV (1965), 13–46.

Winslow, Ola Elizabeth. *Meetinghouse Hill, 1630–1783.* New York, 1952.

Ziff, Larzer. *The Career of John Cotton: Puritanism and the American Experience.* Princeton, N.J., 1962.

ENGLISH HISTORY

Bahlman, Dudley W. R. *The Moral Revolution of 1688.* New Haven, 1957.

Baldwin, Frances E. *Sumptuary Legislation and Personal Regulation in England.* Baltimore, 1926.

Barley, Maurice W. *The English Farmhouse and Cottage.* London, 1961.

——. "Farmhouses and Cottages, 1550–1725." *Economic History Review*, 2d ser., VII (1955), 291–306.

——. "Rural Housing in England." In *The Agrarian History of England and Wales*. Vol. IV. *1500–1640*. Ed. Joan Thirsk. Cambridge, 1967. Pp. 696–766.

Barnes, Thomas Garden. *Somerset, 1625–1640: A County's Government during the "Personal Rule."* Cambridge, Mass., 1961.

Bridenbaugh, Carl. *Vexed and Troubled Englishmen, 1590–1642*. New York, 1968.

Chalklin, C. W. *Seventeenth-Century Kent: A Social and Economic History*. London, 1965.

Coleman, D. C. "Labour in the English Economy of the Seventeenth Century." *Economic History Review*. 2d ser., VIII (1956), 280–95.

Davies, Margaret G. *The Enforcement of English Apprenticeship: A Study in Applied Mercantilism, 1563–1642*. Cambridge, Mass., 1956.

Dunham, William H., Jr. and Stanley Pargellis (eds.). *Complaint and Reform in England, 1436–1714*. New York, 1938.

Ellis, Kenneth. *The Post Office in the Eighteenth Century*. Oxford, 1958.

Everitt, Alan. "Farm Labourers." In *The Agrarian History of England and Wales*. Vol. IV. *1500–1640*. Ed. Joan Thirsk. Cambridge, 1967. Pp. 396–465.

George, Charles H., and Katherine George. *The Protestant Mind of the English Reformation, 1570–1640*. Princeton, N.J., 1961.

Hecht, J. Jean. *The Domestic Servant Class in Eighteenth Century England*. London, 1956.

Hill, Christopher. *Society and Puritanism in Pre-Revolutionary England*. London, 1964.

Hill, James W. F. *Tudor and Stuart Lincoln*. Cambridge, 1956.

Hoskins, W. G. *Leicestershire: the History of the Landscape*. London, 1957.

——. *The Making of the English Landscape*. London, 1955.

——. "The Rebuilding of Rural England, 1570–1640." *Past and Present*, no. 4 (Nov. 1953), pp. 44–59. Rpt. in Hoskins. *Provincial England*. London, 1963.

Laslett, Peter. "Clayworth and Cogenhoe." In *Historical Essays, 1600–1750, Presented to David Ogg*. Ed. H. E. Bell and R. L. Ollard. London, 1963. Pp. 157–84.

——. *The World We Have Lost*. New York, 1965.

Leconfield, Lord Hugh A. W. *Petworth Manor in the Seventeenth Century*. Oxford, 1954.

Lennard, Reginald (ed.). *Englishmen at Rest and Play: Some Phases of English Leisure, 1558–1714*. Oxford, 1931.

MacCaffrey, Wallace T. *Exeter, 1540–1640: The Growth of an English County Town.* Cambridge, Mass., 1958.

Marchant, Ronald A. *The Puritans and the Church Courts in the Diocese of York, 1560–1642.* London, 1960.

Nuttall, Geoffrey F. *The Holy Spirit in Puritan Faith and Experience.* Oxford, 1946.

Price, F. Douglas. "The Abuses of Excommunication and the Decline of Ecclesiastical Discipline under Queen Elizabeth." *English Historical Review,* LVII (1942), 106–15.

Schlatter, Richard Bulger. *The Social Ideas of Religious Leaders, 1660–1688.* Oxford, 1940.

Stephens, W. B. *Seventeenth-Century Exeter: a Study of Industrial and Commercial Development, 1625–1688.* Exeter, 1958.

Stern, Julius L. "His Brother's Keeper: The Buckinghamshire Justice of the Peace, 1678–1689." Ph.D. diss. Princeton University, 1960.

Stone, Lawrence. *The Crisis of the Aristocracy, 1558–1641.* Oxford, 1965.

Tate, W. E. *The Parish Chest: A Study of the Records of Parochial Administration in England.* Cambridge, 1946.

Thirsk, Joan (ed.). *The Agrarian History of England and Wales.* Vol. IV. *1500–1640.* Cambridge, 1967.

Trotter, Eleanor. *Seventeenth Century Life in the Country Parish with Special Reference to Local Government.* Cambridge, 1919.

Walzer, Michael. *The Revolution of the Saints: A Study in the Origins of Radical Politics.* Cambridge, Mass., 1965.

Webb, Sidney, and Beatrice Webb. *English Local Government: The Parish and the County.* London, 1906.

Whitaker, W. B. *Sunday in Tudor and Stuart Times.* London, 1933.

Willcox, William B. *Gloucestershire, 1590–1640: A Study in Local Government.* New Haven, 1940.

Index

Index

Acquaintanceship, range of, 98–103

Adams, John: on church membership, 152–53; discusses bundling, 78–79; on the functions of privacy, 4; on the home as a castle, 88; on inquisitiveness, 108–9; on limiting communications, 5; on privacy of letters, 123; on sleeping accommodations, 79; on solitude, 1, 74; on taverns, 72; on value of privacy, 12–13; visits a poor family, 39–40

Adams, Samuel, 127

Admission to church membership. *See* Church membership

Adultery, 92, 93, 207

Ames, William, 104*n*, 154, 208–9

Andover, Mass., 27, 192; family size in, 46–47; geographical mobility in, 102*n*, 103; home lots in, 29; parental authority in, 58; sharing homes in, 52*n*

Andrews, Joan, 203

Andrews, John, 90, 91

Anglican church, 152, 162

Anonymity, 2, 31, 98–103, 106, 110, 245

Antinomian controversy, 224

Apparitors, 152

Apprentices. *See* Servants

Architecture, 33–44

Ariès, Philippe, 79, 105

Artisans, 182

Ashcraft, Jedidiah, 230

Association of the Bar of New York City, 6*n*

Atwater, Moses, 68

Authoritarianism, 164–65, 180, 188, 190

Bal, Samuel, 197

Barber, Thomas, 54

Barley, Maurice, 34, 35*n*

Barnard, John, 64, 65

Barns, 81, 134–35, 194

Barnum, Richard, 218

Barrell, William, 108

Barrett, John, 59

Beaney, William M., 248–49

Beds. *See* Sleeping accommodations

Belfast, Maine, 132

Bell, Tom, 123

Bellingham, Richard, 116, 225, 234

Benedict, Ruth, 6*n*, 9

Bennett, Joseph, 131*n*–32*n*

Berkshire County, 51

Bernard, Richard, 222

Beverley, Mass., 148, 160

Bickerstaffe, John, 207

Biglow, Jonathan, 226

Bill of Rights, 248–49

Bishop, Bridget, 221

Bishop, Rebecca, 204

Black, Hugo, 249

Blackman, Jane, 231

Blancher, Nicholas, 43, 94

Blumenthal, Albert, 100, 109

Board of Trade, 210

Body of Liberties of 1641, 220–21, 232

Bonner, John, 42*n*

Bonner map, 31

Boone, Nicholas, 190, 191

Boston: crowding in, 31–32; disorderly houses in, 180; experience with tythingmen, 197–98; First Church of, 145; gossip in, 104–5; law enforcement in, 212–13; modesty in, 82–83; moral legislation in, 184; nightwatch in, 193–95, 217; opposition to tythingmen in, 199–201; postal service in, 115, 116; public houses in, 71; regulates

Endicott, John, 224
Engerson, Elisha, 43
England, architecture in, 34–35; authoritarianism in, 164–65; church discipline in, 152; constables in, 191; family government in, 56; folklore of, 96, 218; house lots in, 29–30; informing in, 207–8; interception of mail in, 125–26; judicial examination in, 227n, 228–29; moral legislation in, 180, 181; moral reform in, 164–65, 208; privacy in, 6–7; privilege against self-incrimination in, 232, 234, 237, 239; regulation of swearing in, 183; regulation of tobacco in, 183n; residency requirements in, 170; Sabbath observance in, 128n, 129n, 130; servants in, 60, 61n, 64n; solitary living in, 175; sumptuary laws in, 184–85; use of oaths in, 223–24; use of torture in, 220, 222, 235
Essex County, 38, 51, 93, 117; law enforcement in, 186, 197, 202–3
Exeter, England, 164, 170, 195

Fairfield, Conn., 220
Falmouth, Maine, 71, 79, 109
Families: daily life of, 70–76; lodgers in, 66–70; relations of parents and children in, 55–59; servants in, 59–66; sexual privacy in, 79–82; size of, 46–50, 55; sleeping accommodations in, 76–79
Fane, Francis, 210
Farms, 27, 28, 31n, 38, 57, 60
Farrell, John, 206
Fines, 206
Finlay, Hugh, 121, 211
Fireplaces, 52, 70, 73
Fires, 31, 183
Fiske, John, 144–45, 150
Fletcher, Joshua, 158
Fletcher, Thomas, 210
Floors, construction of, 42–43
Flynt, Henry, 90
Fornication, 62, 156, 158, 160, 202n, 207, 216, 228
Frank, Jerome, 167
Franklin, Benjamin, 108, 121–22

Frost, Stephen, 76

Gaming, 183n
Gardiner, Christopher, 125
Garvan, Anthony, 35n
Gatchell family, 218
Glass, window, 41–42
Gloucester, Mass., 74, 152
Goddard, William, 122, 127
Gold, Nathan, 220
Goodman, Mistress, of New Haven, 43
Gossip, 65, 104–6, 109–10
Gould, George, 91
Grafton, Mass., 104n, 157
Grand Jurors Duty Considered, 204, 205
Grand jury, 179, 186, 192; burden of office of, 214–15; duties and activities of, 89, 201–5; privacy of, 11
Gray, Hana, 91
Green, Joseph, 134
Greenland, Henry, 204
Greven, Philip J., Jr., 46–47, 52n, 102n
Griswold v. *Connecticut*, 248–49
Guilford, Conn., 68n
Guilt cultures, 9–10

Hadley, Mass., 29
Half-Way Covenant, 142–43, 153
Hallways, 40
Hamilton, Dr. Alexander, 33, 44n, 104–5, 108
Hampshire County, 102, 219, 238; grand jurors in, 201n, 203; law enforcement in, 186, 215; Sabbath observance in, 129; tythingmen in, 196–97
Hampton, Mass., 176, 187
Hansen, Chadwick, 223n
Hardy, Goody, 92
Harris, Nathaniel, 201
Harris, Samuel, 202
Harrison, Peter, 187
Hartford, 59, 106, 107, 179, 194, 215, 226
Harvard, Mass., 148
Harvard College, 90, 96, 109, 123
Harvest season, 73, 74, 132
Haskell, Nathaniel, 94
Haskell, William, 94

Haskins, George Lee, 225*n*
Haverhill, Mass., 176
Havighurst, Clark C., 248
Hayward, John, 116
Hempstead, Joshua, 228
Higginson, John, 143
Hill, Christopher, 57, 180*n*, 228
Hingham, Mass., 102
Hirst, Sam, 67–68
Hoar, Goody, 70
Hoebel, E. Adamson, 159*n*
Holdsworth, William, 228
Holland, Thomas, 81
Holman, Edward, 91
Holmes, Debora, 175
Homans, George, 176
Hooker, Thomas: on church discipline, 151, 152, 154, 155; on church membership, 141, 141*n*; on duties of elders, 139; on duties of a Puritan, 166; on the duty to inform, 208; on Relations by women, 143–44
Hoskins, W. G., 34, 35
Hospitality, 89–91
Houghton, Ralph, 173
Household inventories, 38–39, 41
Households, size of, 50–55
Houses: conceived of as castles, 85–88; internal divisions of, 52–53; lighting within, 74; locking of, 91; multiple occupancy of, 47, 50–55; partitioning of, 36–39; size of lots of, 28–31; storage of goods in, 70–71; used for commercial purposes, 71
How, Elizabeth, 68–69
Hubbard, Mr., of Salem, 95
Hull, Blanche, 207
Hull, John, 33
Hull, Mass., 148
Humfrey children, 221, 225, 233
Hunter, William, 121–22
Husbands and wives, 45, 49, 58–59, 93, 209
Hutchinson, Anne, 48*n*, 110, 205, 224; examination of, 12, 14, 231
Hutchinson, Thomas, 33

Idleness, 130, 178, 180–81
Illiteracy, 117–18

Immigration, 174
Indentured servants, 60. *See also* Servants
Indians, 26, 27, 63, 88–89, 193, 226, 230
Individualism, 20–21, 57–58, 244
Industrialization, 84, 246
Infancy, 9
Informers, 199, 200, 205–11
Ingersoll, B., 80
Ingersoll, Lydia, 80
Inns. *See* Taverns
Inquisitiveness, 107–9, 109–10
Intimacy: in community life, 103, 111–12; in country life, 217; and the duty of informing, 202, 209; as a facet of privacy, 2; within the family, 45, 70, 75–76, 83; in kinship networks, 100–102, 103; among neighbors, 96–97; on the Sabbath, 131; of servants with a family, 69–70; in taverns, 105–6
Ipswich, Mass., 36, 71, 93, 95, 141, 142*n*, 192, 204; described, 109; regulates drinking, 182
Isolation, 28, 33, 106, 216. *See also* Loneliness; Solitude

Jacobs, Margaret, 222, 230
James I, 130
James, Ann, 77
James, Phinehas, 77
Jardine, David, 220
Jay, John, 123
Jefferson, Thomas, 79*n*
Jeffries, David, 91
Johnson, Edward, 139, 172
Josselyn, John, 181
Judges, 219–20, 221, 230–31
Judicial examinations, 225–26, 227–31, 234–36, 240
Justices of the peace, 201, 228

Kane, Alexander, 68–69
Kent, Conn., 102
Kent, England, 34
King Phillip's War, 177, 178, 195
Kingston, Mass., 184
Kinship networks, 100–102, 103
Kitchen, John, 119
Kittery, Maine, 216–17